Renewable Energy Auctions

Renewable Energy Auctions

Lessons from the Global South

Edited by

Anton Eberhard
and
Wikus Kruger

OXFORD
UNIVERSITY PRESS

OXFORD
UNIVERSITY PRESS

Great Clarendon Street, Oxford, OX2 6DP,
United Kingdom

Oxford University Press is a department of the University of Oxford.
It furthers the University's objective of excellence in research, scholarship,
and education by publishing worldwide. Oxford is a registered trade mark of
Oxford University Press in the UK and in certain other countries

© Oxford University Press 2023

The moral rights of the authors have been asserted

Published in the United States of America by Oxford University Press
198 Madison Avenue, New York, NY 10016, United States of America

British Library Cataloguing in Publication Data

Data available

Library of Congress Control Number: 2023936679

ISBN 9780192871701

DOI: 10.1093/oso/9780192871701.001.0001

Printed and bound by
CPI Group (UK) Ltd, Croydon, CR0 4YY

Links to third party websites are provided by Oxford in good faith and
for information only. Oxford disclaims any responsibility for the materials
contained in any third party website referenced in this work.

Foreword

The urgency of fighting climate change is increasingly clear. Climate change is no longer a distant threat. Natural disasters are now occurring at a higher frequency and with stronger intensity than ever before, endangering natural environments and humans globally and threatening water and food security.

Moreover, achieving universal energy access, security, and reliability remains at the forefront of policy agenda as 733 million people remained without access to electricity and some 2.4 billion people still relied on traditional biomass for cooking in 2020. In many countries in the Global South, where there is access, electricity is unreliable, slowing down socio-economic development. In the Global North, economies are grappling with high energy prices and risks of shortages.

These developments show the need for immediate action towards an energy transition based on renewable energy to achieve the multiple objectives of climate goals, energy security, and affordability and to ensure universal basic rights such as access to energy, food, and water. Recent challenges related to supply-chain disruptions and the increasing cost of materials and equipment show that higher ambition is also needed when it comes to localizing supply chains.

Achieving an energy transition based on renewable energy as per the International Renewable Energy Agency's (IRENA's) World Energy Transitions Outlook (WETO) 1.5°C Scenario, which outlines a pathway for limiting global temperature rise to 1.5°C and bringing carbon dioxide (CO_2) emissions to net zero by 2050, will require annual investments in transition-related assets of around USD 4.7 trillion up until 2030 and USD 3.5 trillion per year from 2031 to 2050. Attracting investment at this scale requires a comprehensive set of enabling, deployment, and integrating policies. In addition, policies for structural change, as well as international collaboration in the form of financing, technology, and knowledge exchange, will be needed to ensure that the energy transition is just and inclusive and brings socio-economic benefits to all.

In the power sector, auctions are among the deployment policies needed to bring additional installed capacity to the scale required of 264 GW per year until 2050 in IRENA's 1.5°C Scenario. Auctions are increasingly adopted in countries with varying contexts (e.g. macroeconomic conditions, investment risks, level of development of the renewable energy sector, power market organizational structure) as the flexibility in their design enables their adaptation to the specific context to allow price discovery. The flexibility in their design also means that they can be applied to achieve context-specific objectives beyond price, such as timely completion of projects, system integration, and socio-economic development.

This book showcases a great variety of application of auctions, in terms of design and implementation, and presents lessons learned that are very valuable to countries that are either in the process of selecting the policy to deploy renewables or in the process of designing or implementing an auction. The case studies presented show how the success of an auction, like any other policy instrument, hinges on the long-term stability of the policy to provide an enabling environment for the sector to strive and serve the crucial objectives of greenhouse gas emissions and pollution reduction, energy access, security, reliability and affordability, and socio-economic development goals.

Dr Rabia Ferroukhi
Director, Knowledge, Policy and Finance Centre at IRENA
Diala Hawila
Programme Officer, Renewable Energy Markets at IRENA

Contents

List of Figures

List of Tables

List of Abbreviations

ABSA	Amalgamated Banks of South Africa
AC	alternating current
ACL	Ambiente de Contratação Livre (Brazil)
ACR	Ambiente de Contratação Regulada (Brazil)
ADIA	Abu Dhabi Investment Authority
AFD	Agence Française de Développement
AfDB	African Development Bank
AMUVIE	Asociación Mexicana de Unidades de Verificación de Instalaciones Eléctricas (Mexico)
ANEEL	Agência Nacional de Energia Elétrica (Brazilian National Electricity Agency)
AOP	adjusted offered price
APTEL	Appellate Tribunal for Electricity (India)
ATI	Africa Trade Insurance
AURES	Auctions for Renewable Energy Support
AZEL	Atlas Nacional de Zonas co Alto Potencial de Energías Limpias (National Atlas) (Mexico)
BAR	basic assessment report
B-BBEE	broad-based black economic empowerment
BCRA	Central Bank of Argentina
BEIS	Department for Business, Energy and Industrial Strategy
BG	biogas
BG–SL	biogas–sanitary landfill
BICE	Banco de Inversión y Comercio Exterior
BM	biomass
BNDES	Banco Nacional de Desenvolvimento Econômico e Social (Brazilian Development Bank)
BNIS	Big North Interconnected System (Chile)
BOO	build–own–operate
BOT	build, operate, and transfer
BSW–Solar	German Solar Association
BTU	British thermal unit
BW	bid window
CA	connection agreement
CAMMESA	Compañia Administradora del Mercado Mayorista Elétrico (Argentina)
CAPEX	capital expenditure
CAPM	capital asset pricing method
CBG	competitive bidding guidelines
CCC	fuel consumption account (Brazil)

CCEE	Câmara de Comercializaçäo de Energía Elétrica (Brazilian Market Authority)
CCGT	combined-cycle gas turbine
CCT TDA	City of Cape Town Transport and Urban Development Authority (South Africa)
CDC	Commonwealth Development Corporation
CDE	energy development account (Brazil)
CEA	Central Electricity Authority (India)
CEC	Copperbelt Energy Corporation (Zambia)
CEF	Central Energy Fund (South Africa)
CEL	clean energy certificate/cost estimate letter
Celg	Companhia Energética de Goiás (Brazil)
Cemig	Compania Energética de Minas Gerais (Brazil)
CENACE	Centro Nacional de Control de Energía (National Center for Energy Control) (Mexico)
CENFA	Centre for Financial Accountability (India)
CENORED	Central North Regional Electricity Distributor (Namibia)
CEO	chief executive officer
CER	Centre for Environmental Rights (South Africa)
CERC	Central Electricity Regulatory Commission (India)
Cesp	Companhia Energética de São Paulo (Brazil)
CFE	Consejo Federal de la Energía (Federal Commission of Electricity) (Mexico)
CFEE	Consejo Federal de la Energía Eléctrica (Federal Electricity Council) (Argentina)
CFURH	financial compensation for the use of hydro resources (Brazil)
CIA	Central Intelligence Agency
CIGRE	International Council on Large Electric Systems
CIS	Central Interconnected System (Chile)
CMSE	Electricity Sector Monitoring Committee (Brazil)
CNPE	National Council for Energy Policy (Brazil)
COD	commercial operation date
CONAMA	Conselho Nacionla do Meio Ambiente (Brazil)
COP 15	Fifteenth UN Climate Change Conference
Copel	Companhia Paranaense de Energia (Brazil)
COSATU	Congress of South African Trade Unions
CP	conditions precedent
CPI	capacity price index/consumer price index
CRE	Energy Regulatory Commission
CSIR	Council for Scientific and Industrial Research
CSL	contributor status level
CSP	concentrated solar power
CTU	central transmission utility
CUF	capacity utilization factor
DA	direct agreement
DBSA	Development Bank of South Africa

DBN	Development Bank of Namibia
DC	direct current
DEA	Department of Environmental Affairs (South Africa)
DECC	Department of Energy and Climate Change
DEFF	Department of Environment, Forestry and Fisheries (South Africa)
DFI	development finance institution
DfID	Department for International Development
DME	Department of Minerals and Energy (South Africa)
DMRE	Department of Mineral Resources and Energy (South Africa)
DN	directly negotiated
DoE	Department of the Environment (India), Department of Energy (South Africa)
DPE	Department of Public Enterprises (South Africa)
DPLG	Department of Provincial and Local Government (South Africa)
DPTS	development pole transmission system
discoms	distribution companies (India)
DSM	deviation settlement mechanism
DTS	dedicated transmission system
DWA	Department of Water Affairs (South Africa)
E&S	environmental and social
EAF	energy availability factor
EBITDA	earnings before interest, taxes, depreciation, and amortization
ECB	Electricity Control Board (Namibia)
ED	economic development
EER	energy reserve charge (Brazil)
EIA	environmental impact assessment
EIAR	environmental impact assessment report
EIB	European Investment Bank
EIGU	Energy Intensive Users Group South Africa
ELI	electricity distribution industry
EMBI	Emerging Market Bond Index
EMD	earnest money deposit
ENARSA	Energía Argentina Sociedad Anónima
ENRE	National Electricity Regulatory Entity (Argentina)
EPC	engineering, procurement, and construction
EPE	Empresa de Pesquisa Energética (Brazilian Energy Research Office)
ERA	Electricity Regulation Act (South Africa), Electricity Regulatory Authority (Uganda)
ERB	Energy Regulation Board (Zambia)
ERN	Environmental Resources Management
ERNC	Energías Renovables No Convencionales (Chile)
Erongo RED	Erongo Regional Electricity Distributor Company (Namibia)
ESS	system services charge (Brazil)
EvIS	Evaluación de Impacto Social (social impact evaluation) (Mexico)
FAP	proportional assignation factor
FC	financial close

FDI	foreign direct investment
FinnFund	Finnish Fund for Industrial Cooperation
FIRST	Facility for Investment in Renewable Small Transactions
FIT	feed-in tariff
FOB	free on board
FODER	Fondo Fiduciario para el Desarrollo de Energías Renovables (Fund for the Development of Renewable Energy)
GDP	gross domestic product
GEEREF	Global Energy Efficiency and Renewable Energy Fund
GEF	Global Environment Facility
GETFiT	Global Energy Transfer Feed-In Tariff
GHG	greenhouse gas
GIPF	Government Institutions Pension Fund
GoA	government of Argentina
GST	goods and services tax
GW	gigawatt
HFO	heavy fuel oil
IA	implementation agreement
IAEE	International Association for Energy Economics
IBAMA	Brazilian National Environmental Agency
ICB	internationally competitive bidding
IDC	Industrial Development Corporation
IEA	International Energy Agency
IEASA	Energia Argentina Sociedad Anónima
IEC	International Electrotechnical Commission
IEEE	Institute of Electrical and Electronics Engineers
IEP	Integrated Energy Plan
IFC	International Finance Corporation
IMF	International Monetary Fund
INDEC	Instituto Nacional de Estadistica y Censos de la República Argentina (Argentina National Statistics Institute)
INEGI	Instituto Nacional de Estadística, Geografia e Informática (Mexico)
INEP	Integrated National Electrification Programme (India)
IPP	independent power producer/project
IPPO	Independent Power Producers Office (South Africa)
IPPPP	Independent Power Producer Procurement Programme (South Africa)
IPSA	Índice de Precios Selectivo de Acciones (Selective Stock Price Index on the Santiago Stock Exchange)
IRENA	International Renewable Energy Agency
IRGA	interim rapid grid impact assessment
IRP	integrated resource plan
ISO	International Organization for Standardization
ISTS	interstate transmission system
JEMSE	Jujuy Energía y Minería Sociedad del Estado
JV	joint venture
KCM	Konkola Copper Mines

KUSUM	Kisan Urja Suraksha evem Utthan Mahabhiyan (Farmer's Energy Security and Upliftment Project)
kWh	kilowatt hour
LCOE	levelized cost of electricity
LIBOR	London interbank offered rate
LIE	Electrical Industry Law (Mexico)
LNG	liquified natural gas
LSMFEZ	Lusaka South Multi-Facility Economic Zone
LTE	Energy Transmission Law (Mexico)
LYOC	last year of the contract
MAE	Mercado Atacadista de Energia (Wholesale Energy Market Authority) (Brazil)
MASEN	Moroccan Agency for Solar Energy
MCO	marginal cost of operation
MD	managing director
MEM	Mercado Eléctrico Mayorista (Wholesale Electricity Market) (Argentina)
MEWD	Ministry of Energy and Water Development
MH	mini hydro
MIGA	Multilateral Investment Guarantee Agency
MINEM	Ministry of Mines and Energy (Argentina)
MISTRA	Mapunguwe Institute for Strategic Reflection
MMA	Ministério de Meio Ambiente (Brazilian Ministry of Environment)
MME	Ministry of Mines and Energy (Brazil, Namibia)
MNRE	Ministry of New and Renewable Energy (India)
MOA	memorandum of agreement
MoE	Ministry of Energy (Zambia)
MoF	Ministry of Finance
MOP	Ministry of Power (India)
MoU	memorandum of understanding
MVar	mega volt amp
MW	megawatt
MWh	megawatt hours
NAMCOR	National Petroleum Corporation of Namibia
NBFC	non-banking financing company
NCRE	non-convertible renewable energy
NDC	national determined contribution
NDP	National Development Plan
NEC	National Energy Council (Chile, Namibia)
Nedlac	National Economic Development and Labour Council
NEF	National Energy Fund (Namibia)
NEEEP	Nampower Equity Economic Empowerment Policy
NEEPCO	North Eastern Electric Power Corporation (India)
NEMA	National Environmental Management Act (South Africa)
NERSA	National Energy Regulator of South Africa
NES	National Electricity System (Chile)

NGO	non-governmental organization
NHHC	National Health Research Authority (Zambia)
NIRP	National Integrated Resource Plan (Namibia)
NLDC	National Load Dispatch Centre (India)
NOA	NorOeste Argentino
NORED	Northern Region Electricity Distributor (Namibia)
NPC	National Planning Commission (South Africa, Namibia)
NREL	National Renewable Energy Laboratory
NT	National Treasury (South Africa) (Namibia)
NTPH	National Thermal Power Corporation (India)
NTS	national transmission system
O&M	operations and maintenance
OCGT	open-cycle gas turbines
OECD	Organisation for Economic Co-operation and Development
ONS	Independent System Operator (Brazil)
OPIC	Overseas Private Investment Corporation
OPPPI	Office for Promoting Private Power Investment (Zambia)
PBG	performance bank guarantee
PDE	Plano Decenal de Expansão de Energia (Brazil)
PDN	previously disadvantaged Namibian
PIC	Public Investment Corporation
PMG	Parliamentary Monitoring Group (South Africa)
POI	payment-on-order instrument
PPA	power purchase agreement
PPIAF	Public–Private Infrastructure Advisory Facility
PPP	public–private partnership
PRODESEN	Programa de Desarrollo del Sistema Eléctrico Nacional (National Electric System Development Programme) (Mexico)
PROEOLICA	Progarma Emergiencial de Energia Eólico (Wind Power Plant Programme) (Brazil)
PROINFA	Programa de Incentivos às Fontes Alternativas de Energía Elétrica (Alternative Electricity Sources Incentive Programme) (Brazil)
PSA	power sales agreement
PSU	public-sector undertaking
PTI	Press Trust for India
PV	photovoltaic
R&D	research and development
RBI	Reserve Bank of India
RE	renewable energy
REA	Rural Electrification Agency (Zambia)
REDs	regional electricity distributors
REDZ	renewable energy development zone (South Africa)
REFiT	renewable energy feed-in tariff
REI4P	Renewable Energy Independent Power Producer Procurement Programme

REIPPPP	Renewable Energy Independent Power Producer Procurement Programme
REMP	Rural Electrification Master Plan (Zambia)
RenovAr	Programa de abastecimiento de energía eléctrica a partir de fuentes renovables
REPO	renewable energy power obligation
RES	renewable energy sources
RfP	request for proposals
RfQ	request for quotation
RfS	request for selection
RLDC	Regional Load Dispatch Centre (India)
RLSF	regional liquidity support facility
RMB	Rand Merchant Bank
RPO	renewable purchase obligation
RSA	Republic of South Africa
SABS	South African Bureau of Standards
SACU	South African Customs Union
SADC	Southern African Development Community
SAIPPA	South African Independent Power Producers Association
SALGA	South African Local Government Association
SANS	South African National Standards
SAPP	South African Power Pool
SAPVIA	South African Photovoltaic Industry Association
SAWEA	South African Wind Energy Association
SEA	Sustainable Energy Africa/strategic environmental assessment
SECI	Solar Energy Corporation of India
SED	socio-economic development
SEF	Strategic Fuel Fund
SELIC	Sistema Especial de Liquidacão e de Custódia (Special System for Settlement and Custody)
SENER	Secretaría de Energía (Energy Secretariat) (Mexico)
SEPC	Shanghai Electric Power Construction
SERC	State Electricity Regulatory Commission (India)
SHCP	Finance and Public Credit Secretariat
SIFEM	Swiss Investment Fund for Emerging Markets
SLC	stated local content
SLDC	State Load Dispatch Centre (India)
SMEs	small and medium enterprises
SOE	state-owned enterprise
SPCB	State Pollution Control Board (India)
SP–I4P	Small Projects Independent Power Producer Procurement Programme
SPV	special-purpose vehicle
SSA	sub-Saharan Africa
SSC	Qualified Services Provider
SSEG	small-scale embedded generation
STEM	short-term energy market

STU	state transmission utility
SWAPO	South-West Africa People's Organization
SWAWEK	South West Africa Water and Electricity Corporation
TCA	transmission connection agreement
Tcf	trillion cubic feet
TFSEE	electricity services inspection fee (Brazil)
TPL	total potential liabilities
TWh	terawatt
UDI	investment unit (Mexico)
UEA	United Arab Emirates
UETCL	Uganda Electricity Transmission Company Limited
UF	unidad de Fomento (unit of account, Chile)
UN DESA	United Nations Department of Economic and Social Affairs
UNPAF	United Nations Partnership Framework
US CPI	United States Consumer Price Index
USAID	United States Agency for International Development
UTM	Chilean peso
VRE	variable renewable energy
WACC	weighted average cost of capital
WARMA	Water Resources Management Authority (Zambia)
WBG	World Bank Group
WETO	World Energy Transitions Outlook
WPE	Wind Power Energia
WTO	World Trade Organization
ZDA	Zambian Development Authority
ZEMA	Zambia Environmental Management Agency
ZESA	Zimbabwe Electricity Supply Authority
ZESCO	Zambia Electricity Supply Corporation
ZPPA	Zambia Public Procurement Authority

List of Contributors

Rogelio Avendaño, Tetra Tech

Tiago de Barros Correia, Federal University of Rio de Janiero

Mridul Chadha, Bridge to India Energy (Pvt.) Ltd

Anton Eberhard, Power Futures Lab, Graduate School of Business, University of Cape Town

Anna V. Filipova, ES-3 Ltd, Bulgaria

Wikus Kruger, Power Futures Lab, Graduate School of Business, University of Cape Town

Raine Naude, Allan Gray

Natália Addas Porto, Federal University of Rio de Janiero

Vinay Rustagi, Bridge to India Energy (Pvt.) Ltd

Ignatio Rodríguez, Tetra Tech

Martín A. Rodríguez Pardina, AdHoc Consulting

Julieta Schiro, AdHoc Consulting

Pablo Serra, Department of Economics, University of Chile

Mauricio T. Tolmasquim, Energy Planning Program, Federal University of Rio de Janiero

1
Introduction

Wikus Kruger and Anton Eberhard

1.1 The trailblazing impact of renewable energy auctions in the Global South

Renewable energy auctions, also called competitive bidding or tendering pro-grammes, have become the subject of growing academic and practitioner interest. The renewable energy auction is now the most widely used policy tool for procuring utility-scale renewable energy projects across the globe, driven, in large part, by its ability to reveal prices and reduce costs through the power of competition. Auctions are consequently seen as an efficient mechanism for increasing affordable renewable energy investments at scale.

Furthermore, what is remarkable about auctions is that they have largely been pioneered, and have had the greatest impact, in the Global South. Brazil and Chile pioneered the use of auctions in the electricity sector in the early 2000s as part of a second wave of sector reforms meant to address energy security concerns. They have since been joined by the likes of South Africa and India, which have adapted the tool to achieve local objectives—to great effect. Auctions have been particularly effective not only at reducing energy costs in the global South—a key imperative in these emerging economies— but also in improving energy security and substantially increasing the share of renewables in the systems.

The impact of auctions is most apparent in sub-Saharan Africa: the region is chronically short of power, with the entire region's installed generation capacity being less than that of a single Organisation for Economic Co-operation and Development (OECD) country like Spain or South Korea. This impacts not only energy security but also energy costs as small utilities strug-gle to realize the benefits associated with economies of scale. Despite the desperate need for more power, Africa has been unable to attract sufficient investment into new power generation. It is only since 2012, driven largely by the growth in renewables procured through structured procurement pro-grammes such as auctions, that investment volumes have really started to pick

Wikus Kruger and Anton Eberhard, *Introduction*. In: *Renewable Energy Auctions: Lessons from the Global South*.
Edited by: Anton Eberhard and Wikus Kruger, Oxford University Press. © Oxford University Press (2023).
DOI: 10.1093/oso/9780192871701.003.0001

up significantly. For the energy-starved region, this represents an important glimmer of hope for increased energy security and reduced costs.

Of course, auctions are not the only, or necessarily the most effective, tool to increase renewable energy investment. Feed-in tariffs have been particularly successful at rapidly increasing investment in renewables, particularly in Europe but also in late adopters such as Vietnam. And while a global shift towards a more competitive investment system for renewables seems to be underway, it is important to note that the world's biggest renewable energy producer and consumer—China—has not done this primarily through auctions. Instead, China's experience affirms that auctions are but one of a number of tools available to policymakers to increase investment in renewables. Nevertheless, it appears that, for the moment at least, auctions are emerging as a leading instrument and, as such, warrant deeper analysis.

This book seeks to unpack the experiences of eight important cases from the Global South, each contributing a different perspective on how auctions can be usefully designed and implemented in various contexts. It does this at the hand of a unified analytical framework that seeks to situate auctions within the various investment contexts and understand how auction programmes have been adapted to suit various local needs and limitations.

This chapter provides a brief introduction on procurement methods, followed by an overview of the analytical framework and a short summary of the case study chapters. It starts by foregrounding the need for private investment into renewables (mainly through independent power projects) as well as the factors that determine both project price and investment outcomes.

1.2 The need for independent power projects

Public investment levels in renewable energy technologies, especially in the Global South, are insufficient to ensure a timely energy transition or address energy security concerns. Accordingly, a substantial level of private investment is needed. Independent power projects (IPPs)—utility-scale (> 5MW) power projects that are built, owned, and operated by the private sector—are the main source of private investment in power. Research into the factors influencing or determining both the investment size and realization of IPPs has identified contributing elements at two levels: project and country (Eberhard and Gratwick, 2011, 2013b; Eberhard et al., 2016, 2017; Gratwick and Eberhard, 2008b).

1.2.1 Project-level contributing elements to IPP success

At the project level, a secure revenue stream is essential for project success—that is, timely project realization and competitive prices. Most IPPs are project financed, meaning that they are highly leveraged (using 70–90% debt) and that debtors only have recourse to the revenue stream—and not to the assets of the project sponsors (equity investors)—for servicing the debt (Eberhard et al., 2016). A secure revenue stream, captured in a contract—called a power purchase agreement (PPA)—between the off-taker of power (usually a utility company) and the power project is thus critical. The PPA stipulates the price per unit of energy (kWh) (or sometimes also for capacity, MW) to be paid over a fixed period (usually 15–25 years) and also allocates risks for a range of events and issues, including payment default, transmission delays, *force majeure*, and so on. For a PPA to be considered 'bankable' (i.e. meeting the requirements of debt providers), it needs to allocate risks to those best able to control and/or influence them (Gratwick and Eberhard, 2011). A reasonable risk profile means that the cost of debt and equity (cost of capital) is also more likely to be reasonable and allows projects to charge more affordable tariffs (Eberhard et al., 2016).

However, it is not merely the cost of capital but also the providers thereof that determines project success. Experienced, committed, and development-orientated investors (both equity and debt providers) take a longer view and are more likely to help projects weather external and internal pressures, including through multi- and bilateral pressures on governments not to renege on contracts, with potential consequences for other country support programmes. This is one of the reasons why development finance institutions (DFIs)—such as the International Finance Corporation (IFC), the Nederlandse Financierings-Maatschappij voor Ontwikkelingslanden N.V. (Dutch Entrepreneurial Development Bank, FMO), the Kreditanstalt für Wiederaufbau (Green Climate Fund, KfW), Proparco, and others—are such prominent investors in, and lenders to, IPPs in emerging economies.

1.2.2 Country-level contributing elements to IPP success

At the country level, IPP success is influenced or determined by a handful of variables which include a stable investment environment encompassing factors such as political stability, economic growth prospects, sound macroeconomic policies, low levels of corruption and ease of doing business; clear (energy) policy that allows for private power investment accompanied by regulatory certainty on market access and electricity tariffs; and, importantly (because it is a factor that is often overlooked), a dynamic, least-cost power expansion planning framework based on realistic electricity demand scenario projections and up-to-date power-generation costs translated into competitive procurement processes in a timely manner (Eberhard et al., 2016).

Where these country- and project-level elements are in place, one should see projects reaching financial close (FC) and commercial operation dates (COD) in relatively short time frames at competitive prices.

1.2.3 IPP procurement methods

Given the recent emphasis of the planning-procurement nexus in the IPP literature (Eberhard and Gratwick, 2008; Eberhard et al., 2016), it is worth exploring the topic of the design and implementation of procurement programmes in greater detail. There are three main ways in which private power projects can be procured.

1.2.3.1 Direct negotiation
The first is direct negotiation (sometimes also called an unsolicited bid) between a project developer and the host government. This method suffers from limited transparency and long realization timelines and generally results in comparatively high project prices (tariffs), increasing the risk of contract renegotiations.

1.2.3.2 Feed-in tariffs
The second procurement method is the feed-in tariff (FIT), sometimes also called a renewable energy feed-in tariff (REFiT). This method emerged in Europe to support the rollout of renewable energy in a context where these technologies were initially not cost-competitive. A FIT's main feature is that the price at which projects will be selling electricity is set by a public administrative agency instead of by the market and where the process for concluding contracts is relatively simple, low cost, and fast, provided these documents are bankable. Projects are thus not competing on price but are contracted on the basis of technical and financial qualifying criteria, usually on a first-come, first-concluded basis. The FIT has proven to be superior to direct negotiation in that it is a structured process that provides price certainty, more transparency, and generally shorter project realization timelines (if implemented correctly).

1.2.3.3 Auctions/bidding

The third procurement method is an auction—also called competitive procurement, internationally competitive bidding (ICB), or tendering. It is a structured procurement programme (in contrast to direct negotiation) where contracts are awarded to projects with the lowest tariff.[1] An auction is distinct from a FIT in that it is the market, and not an administrative agency, that sets project prices through a competitive process. The level of competition is determined by the number of bidders (more bidders mean more competition) and also by the kinds of bidders (technically and financially stronger bidders mean more competition).

More competition should translate into lower project prices through three mechanisms.

The first is that bidders reveal more information about their real costs as they compete with each other, reducing information asymmetry between the private sector (developers/bidders) and the public sector (procurers) (Hubbard and Paarsch, 2015). This makes it the most transparent of the three procurement methods.

Second, competition not only reveals costs but also forces bidders to lower costs by squeezing margins or inducing innovation in an attempt to improve their odds of winning through offering the lowest price (Eberhard and Naude, 2017; Haufe and Gephart, 2018).

Third, even if a procurer might have full transparency on a developer's costs in a direct negotiation (an unlikely but not impossible scenario), the procurer does not know whether there might be someone better able to develop the project at a lower cost. A competitive procurement process provides the procurer with more certainty that they are getting the best price that the market—and not just a single entity—has to offer (del Río, 2017).

Auctions have become the dominant global method for procuring renewable energy, with 96 out of 195 countries having launched a renewable energy auction by early 2020. This growth in competitive procurement has largely been driven by continued record-breaking renewable energy prices announced in markets as diverse as Brazil, the United Arab Emirates (UAE), Zambia, Mexico, Morocco, Chile, Peru, the United States, Saudi Arabia, and Germany.

This book combines different bodies of literature to develop a comprehensive analytical framework (Figure 1.1) that integrates procurement design and implementation of programme-level factors in the analysis.

---

[1] Projects can also be scored on factors besides price, including project quality or socio-economic contributions, but in almost all cases, the general weighting is in favour of price.

Figure 1.1   Renewable energy auction analytical framework
Source: Authors' compilation.

1.3 The analytical framework

Auctions have been used to sell a variety of goods and services for centuries. One of the earliest written accounts of an auction mechanism being used was when the Roman Empire was sold by the Praetorian Guard in 193 AD. Since then, auctions have become widespread. Analysis of the auction mechanism has led to new theoretical insights—informing our understanding of pricing theory, competitive markets, and game theory. As a public-sector procurement mechanism, (reverse) auctions are particularly popular (Hubbard and Paarsch, 2016; Klemperer, 2004).

Auctions are essentially games of asymmetric information (Hubbard and Paarsch, 2016) that rely on the power of competition to close the information gap between the auctioneer and bidders. The level of competition is effectively increased by adding more bidders and/or replacing weaker bidders with stronger ones. To function effectively, auctions rely on rules that should be understood by everyone, not be subject to arbitrary change, and define how information will be gathered. A well-functioning legal system that ensures everyone sticks to the rules of the game is therefore important to support an effective auction (Kreiss et al., 2016).

In the electricity sector, auctions have been used to procure power for more than two decades. The first auctions took place in Brazil, Canada, Chile, China, Ireland, Portugal, and the United Kingdom in the 1990s and early 2000s (Lucas et al., 2013). After the initial power-sector reforms in the 1990s, a second wave of power-sector reforms—in the 2000s—was introduced (mostly in Latin America) in a context where many low-to middle-income countries were struggling to increase new electricity supply—and needed a new way of attracting generation capacity. Investors were more interested in bidding for long-term contracts than in constructing merchant plants that had to compete to sell power in power exchanges. Auctioning off these long-term agreements to the cheapest bidder proved to be effective at increasing power generation capacity at low cost (Elizondo-Azuela and Barroso, 2014; Maurer and Barroso, 2011).

Auctions have several benefits: they offer flexibility in terms of design, allow for 'real price discovery', offer greater certainty on procured quantities and prices, and provide binding commitments and increased transparency (Ferroukhi et al., 2015). Auctions have been criticized for imposing high transaction costs on bidders as well as on the auction organizer, for example, the host government (Eberhard et al., 2014). They also face the possibility of underbuilding and delays in construction, chiefly as a consequence of overly aggressive bidding by competitors that could result in prices being unrealistically low and projects being financially non-viable and unfinanceable (del Río and Linares, 2014; Ferroukhi et al., 2015; Maurer and Barroso, 2011).

Most authors—whether drawing on auction theory, or on empirical cases, or both—agree that good renewable energy auction design is aimed at stimulating as much competition as possible without sacrificing project quality and realization rates. This requires a fine balancing act since the push for, and dynamics of, competition can undermine both. The inverse is, of course, also true since excessive measures aimed at ensuring project realization can deter bidder entry, resulting in less competition and more costly projects (del Río, 2017; Haufe and Gephart, 2018; Kriess et al., 2016). The discussion of auction design choices in the following pages will accordingly be guided by, and regularly refer to, their impact on competition levels (and resulting prices) and project realization.

The programme level of analysis focuses on how procurement programmes are designed (auction design) and implemented (auction implementation). Auction design factors deal mainly with three choices: how the procurement volume (amount of energy or power) is determined and divided (auction volume), how auction winners are selected (winner selection), and how an auction ensures the timely execution (realization) of procured projects (auction effectiveness).

How the auction volume is determined and divided between technologies, projects, and bidders and, over time (rounds), is crucial for fully realizing the benefits of competition. The auction volume needs to be informed by a dynamic, least-cost planning framework that determines how much power is needed, by when, and from which sources. Finding the right balance in terms of setting auction volumes at levels large enough to attract sufficient competition but not so large that there is little competitive pressure is a crucial but difficult exercise, especially in small power systems such as those found in most sub-Saharan African countries.

Project sizes need also to be large enough to be able to benefit from economies of scale, with some technologies such as solar photovoltaic (PV) scaling down easier than, for example, wind. Furthermore, dividing the auction volume over time (as regular auction rounds based on a predictable schedule) stimulates market development and enables a country to benefit from industry learning rates, resulting in lower project costs and a pipeline of good-quality projects.

Winner selection is concerned with how bidders and/or projects are evaluated, ranked, and selected for awarding, and it is here that the need for transparent auction rules and their consistent application is most keenly felt. For the benefit of both the auctioning authority and the bidders, it is recommended that winner selection be as clear and simple as possible—especially in new markets and at least in the first rounds of bidding. Both bidders and the auctioning authorities need to understand, and be comfortable with, the rules, and as such, it is recommended that familiar sealed-bid, pay-as-bid auction formats be adopted.

It is furthermore recommended that bid scoring be based on price only, as far as possible, to allow for straightforward, transparent evaluation. Additional scoring criteria—where used—should ideally be limited to non-technical factors, such as social (including local ownership and content) and environmental performance—with the understanding that incentivizing such performance through the scoring process (instead of, or in addition to, qualification criteria) entails a trade-off in auction objectives, for example, price versus local content. It is also recommended that a ceiling price (also called a reserve price) be established based on a least-cost planning framework, regional benchmarking, or previous auction round result and that its existence—although not necessarily its actual level—be made known to the market to stimulate competition.

Auction effectiveness is concerned with whether awarded projects get built at all and/or on time and to what standard of quality. Ensuring auction effectiveness is best served by limiting participation in the bidding programme to strong, experienced bidders/sponsors through setting rigorous access requirements (primarily financial and technical track record); good projects, by setting late-stage, physical pre-qualification criteria (project preparation activities); and ensuring bidder commitment to project realization by requiring substantial financial pre-qualification commitments, that is, bid bonds/securities. It is also recommended to include any social and environmental performance requirements as part of the physical pre-qualification criteria. If staged bidding is used (normally with the aim of limiting transaction costs for both bidders and the auctioning authorities), the initial pre-qualification stage should screen bids based only on access requirements.

Clearly, these auction design choices interact with, and influence, each other, often implying trade-offs and careful balancing to achieve the ultimate auction objectives (Gephart et al., 2017). For example, setting very rigorous qualification criteria meant to ensure auction effectiveness for small auction volumes will likely depress competition levels, resulting in high project costs. In general, the greater the interest and competition in the programme, the less severe these trade-offs become. Ensuring sufficient competition is, however, not only influenced by how the procurement programme is designed but also by how it is implemented.

Auction implementation factors are essentially about establishing and maintaining the trust of potential bidders, necessary for ensuring sufficient competition, and about bringing procured projects to a financial close and commercial operation through the effective coordination of various (primarily public-sector) agencies and processes. Both of these goals—building trust, and supporting project realization—rely on the auction being implemented by a capable, well-resourced auctioning authority in a way that is seen as transparent and fair.

The implementing agency should ideally be results-driven and have a high level of skills, sufficient financial and human resources, and effective governance and leadership structures in place. The auction process needs also to be perceived as being just, not merely in terms of outcomes but also in how information is shared, how the process is run, and how bidders are treated.

Effective auction design and implementation is also about taking the various country- and project-level IPP-contributing elements of success on board. For example, auctions that are implemented in contexts where the off-taker of power is a sub-investment-grade, state-owned utility need to incorporate risk-mitigation and credit-enhancement measures to protect the project's revenue stream, including, for example, sovereign guarantees and letters of credit or escrow accounts as part of the request-for-proposals package.

Similarly, auctions that are, for example, implemented in jurisdictions with poor rule of law and/or powerful industry incumbents will need to demonstrate a high level of commitment to independence and transparency, both in terms of who is implementing the programme and how the security and integrity of the procurement process is ensured. Not incorporating these country- and project-level elements will depress competition levels and will likely result in high project costs and/or poor investment outcomes.

The following chapters of this book will see this expanded analytical framework (Table 1.1) being applied in case study countries to deepen our understanding of the factors underpinning renewable energy IPP outcomes. The case studies will go beyond the established country- and project-contributing elements of success to build a robust conception of the influence of programme-level factors, in particular, auction design choices and implementation factors.

1.4 Key terms and concepts

Before going further, it is important to clearly define some of the key concepts and terms used throughout this book.

Success is defined from the perspective of the host country government and includes two issues of importance for them: a low, contracted price of electricity delivered by the IPP and the contracted project being built and reaching commercial operation in a timely manner (project realization) (del Río, 2017; Eberhard and Naude, 2017). Throughout this book, the term 'success' will refer to both these aspects—unless it is expressly specified that we are only looking at one of these elements (for further detail on each, please see below).

Price outcomes refers to the contracted price of the electricity that will be delivered by the IPP as captured in the PPA, expressed in USD/kWh. This price is often also referred to as the *bid price* (Eberhard and Naude, 2016; Ferroukhi et al., 2015) or—in the case of more than one project—the *auction's (static) efficiency* (del Río, 2017). A 'competitive price' is an average price for an auction round that is close to or below the global levelized cost of electricity (LCOE) for that technology (as measured and reported by the International Energy Agency, IRENA) (IRENA, 2020).

Investment outcomes—again, defined from the perspective of the host country government—refers to awarded IPPs being realized—in other words, reaching financial close and commercial operation (Eberhard and Naude, 2016). *Project realization* is also the measure of what del Río (2017) terms auction *effectiveness*. These terms—*investment outcomes, project realization, auction effectiveness*—are used interchangeably throughout the text to refer to the same phenomenon—namely, projects reaching financial close and commercial operation in a timely manner.

Table 1.1 Analytical framework with expected price and realization impacts

Factors	Detail	Impact on price	Impact on realization
Country level			
Stability of economic and legal context	Stability of macroeconomic policies Legal system allows contracts to be enforced, laws to be upheld, and arbitration to be fair Repayment record and investment rating Experience with private investment	(+) Stable investment context lowers investment context risks, reducing cost of capital and leading to lower prices	(+) Stability of investment context—incl. judicial quality—improves realization
Energy policy framework	Framework enshrined in legislation Framework clearly specifies market structure and roles and terms for private- and public-sector investments	(+) Stable, clear policy framework lowers investment risks, reducing cost of capital and leading to lower prices	(+) Clear energy policy that allows for private investment improves project realization
Regulatory transparency, consistency, and fairness	Transparent and predictable licensing and tariff framework Cost-reflective tariffs	(+) Good regulatory quality lowers investment risks, reducing cost of capital and leading to lower prices	(+) Good regulatory quality, especially on licensing and tariff approval, improves project realization
Coherent sectoral planning	Power-planning roles and functions clear and allocated Planners skilled, resourced, and empowered Fair allocation of new-build opportunities between utilities and IPPs	(+) Coherent sectoral planning reduces investment risks, reducing cost of capital, leading to lower prices	(+) Coherent sectoral planning improves project pipeline development, improving project realization
Competitive bidding practices	Planning linked to timely initiation of adequately resourced, fair, and transparent competitive tenders/auctions	(+) Competitive bidding practices lower project prices	(=) No theoretical expectation around impact on realization

Continued

Table 1.1 *Continued*

Factors	Detail	Impact on price	Impact on realization
Programme level			
Auction design			
Competition-inducing, scale-friendly auction volume	Auction volume based on dynamic, least-cost power expansion plans. Auction volumes large enough to attract bidders but small enough to ensure competitive pressure	(+) Auction volume that is large enough to attract bidders but smaller than offered volume induces competition, leading to lower prices	(=) No theoretical expectation around impact on realization
Scale-friendly project size limits	Project size limits enable economies of scale	(−) Project size caps limit economies of scale, increasing prices	(+) Smaller projects are more easily realized, improving realization
Technology choice: neutral vs specific	Technology choices based on least-cost planning framework. Auction volume division between technologies balance price and energy security concerns	(−) Technology bands limit competition, increasing prices	(=) No theoretical expectation around impact on realization
Bid award limits	Bid award limits used to counter market domination or energy security concerns	(−) Bid award caps limit economies of scale, increasing prices	(+) Bid award limits spread realization risk, increasing overall realization
Bidding rounds	Regular, scheduled bidding rounds	(+) Bidding rounds increase competition and induce market learning, lowering prices	(+) Bidding rounds increase project pipeline development and market learning, improving realization
Winner selection	Winner selection criteria transparent and rational. Price remains key determinant	(−) Multiple bid scoring criteria dilute the importance of price and add additional cost drivers, increasing prices	(+) Multiple criteria (esp. technical) improve project preparation, improving realization
Price caps	Price caps (ceiling prices) set but preferable undisclosed	(+) Price caps induce competition, lowering prices	(=) No theoretical impact expectation, although price caps being set too low can result in no project being awarded

Physical (project/bid preparation) qualification criteria	Physical (project/bid preparation) qualification criteria set at high enough level to ensure cost certainty and realization probability	(−) High physical qualification criteria increase bidding costs, lowering competition and increasing prices	(+) High physical qualification criteria improve project preparation and cost certainty, improving realization
Financial (bid bond) qualification criteria	Bid bonds set to ensure commitment of qualified bidders	(−) Bid bonds increase bidding costs, lowering competition and increasing prices	(+) Bid bonds increase bidder commitment and cost certainty, improving realization
Auction access requirements	Auction access requirements—technical experience and financial status—limit participation to experienced, capable bidders	(−) High auction access requirements lower competition, increasing prices	(+) High auction access requirements increase likelihood of capable bidders being awarded, increasing realization
Penalty regime	Reasonable penalties (PPA reduction, liquidated damages, performance bonds) incentivize project performance	(−) Penalties increase project risks, lowering competition and increasing the cost of capital, increasing prices	(+) Penalty regime incentivizes project preparation and cost certainty, improving realization
Staged bidding process	Choice of one- vs two-stage bidding process balances transaction costs with time concerns	(−) Staged bidding reduces competition, increasing prices	(+) Staged bidding increases likelihood of capable bidder being awarded, improving realization
Pricing rule, auction format	Simple sealed bid, pay-as-bid auction format to reduce bidder risks	(+) Simple bidding format and pricing rule increases competition, leading to lower prices	(+) Simple bidding format reduces winner's curse risk, improving realization
Auction implementation			
Procurer	Procuring entity perceived as capable, benevolent, and acting with integrity	(+) Trust in the procuring authority increases competition, lowering prices	(=) No theoretical expectation around impact on realization

Continued

Table 1.1 *Continued*

Factors	Detail	Impact on price	Impact on realization
Procurement process	Bidding process is perceived as fair, transparent, and secure	(+) Trust in bidding process increases competition, lowering prices	(=) No theoretical expectation around impact on realization
Support to awarded projects	Auctioneer assists awarded projects to reach financial close and commercial operation	(=) No theoretical expectation around impact on price	(+) Auctioneer support to awarded projects to financial close and COD improves realization
Project level			
Favourable equity partners	Local capital/partner contributions are encouraged Partners have experience with, and an appetite for, project risk A DFI partner (and/or host country government) is involved Firms are development-minded and returns on investment are fair and reasonable	(+) Favourable equity partners require lower returns, lowering prices	(+) Favourable equity partners are experienced and capable (with potential halo effect), improving realization
Favourable debt arrangements	Competitive financing Local capital/markets mitigate foreign exchange risk Risk premium demanded by financiers or capped by off-taker matches country/project risk Some flexibility in terms and conditions (possible refinancing)	(+) Favourable debt arrangements lowers the cost of capital, lowering prices	(+) Debt from DFIs come with a halo effect, improving realization
Creditworthy off-taker	Utility is investment-grade rated, with full cost recovery through cost-reflective tariffs and high billing collection rates	(+) Credit-worthy off-taker reduces project risks and thereby the cost of capital, lowering prices	(+) Credit-worthy off-taker enables project to secure funding, improving realization

Secure and adequate revenue stream	Robust PPA (stipulates capacity and payment as well as dispatch, fuel metering, interconnection, insurance, *force majeure*, transfer, termination, change-of-law provisions, refinancing arrangements, dispute resolution, and so on) Security arrangements are in place, where necessary (including escrow accounts, letters of credit, standby debt facilities, hedging and other derivative instruments, committed public budget and/or taxes/levies, targeted subsidies and output-based aid, hard currency contracts, indexation in contracts)	(+) Secure revenue stream reduces project risks and thereby the cost of capital, lowering prices	(+) Secure revenue stream enables project to secure funding, improving realization
Credit enhancements and other risk-management and mitigation measures Strategic management and relationship building	Sovereign guarantees Political risk insurance Partial risk guarantees International arbitration Sponsors work to create a good image in the country through political relationships, development funds, effective communications, and strategic management of contracts, particularly in the face of exogenous shocks and other stresses	(+) Credit-enhancement and risk-mitigation measures reduce project risks to reduce cost of capital, lowering prices (−) Strategic socio-economic development commitments increase project costs, increasing prices	(+) Credit-enhancement and risk-mitigation measures enable projects to secure funding, improving realization (+) Strategic socio-economic development commitments improve project realization

Note: + denotes a positive impact on the outcome; − denotes a negative impact; = denotes no clear impact.
Source: Authors' compilation.

Independent power project (IPP) refers to a greenfield, utility-scale (5MW+), power-generation project where majority ownership (51+%) resides with the private sector and where the off-taker of power is most often a (state-owned) utility (Eberhard et al., 2016).

Implementation refers to the actions of the host country government—primarily represented by the auctioning authority (auctioneer)—to execute or administer the auction programme. In the context of this study, it refers to the characteristics of the auction implementing authority (Eberhard et al., 2014), the way that the auction process is rolled out and administered (Chiu et al, 2010; Zitron, 2006), and the support provided by the auctioning authority to awarded projects to help them reach financial close and commercial operation (Eberhard et al., 2014).

Contributing elements to success is a term used throughout the literature on IPPs (Eberhard and Gratwick, 2011; Eberhard et al., 2017) to refer to enabling factors (also called determinants or conditions) at both country and project levels that influence or determine the volume of IPP investments and the ongoing operation of IPPs. In the context of this study, the concept of 'contributing elements' is used in the same way, but the emphasis in the definition of success has shifted slightly (see above) to capture both price and realization outcomes.

1.5 Research focus

The empirical work is focused on the Global South, given the leading role played by countries in this region in the use of renewable energy auctions. We start by analysing auctions in Latin America, given the region's pioneering role in the use of auctions, before moving to India and finally to sub-Saharan Africa. The following section provides brief overviews of the case-study country chapters.

1.5.1 Brazil (Chapter 2)

Brazil pioneered the use of electricity auctions in the early 2000s, introduced as part of the country's second wave of power-sector reforms. The country has since developed a sophisticated auction process and institutional set-up that has secured large volumes of new generation capacity, including renewables, at competitive prices. The authors show how the auction programme design and implementation evolved over time to address changes in the market and provides important details on the risk-mitigation structures employed to secure investment and maintain competition.

1.5.2 Chile (Chapter 3)

Chile was the first country to liberalize its power sector in the early 1980s, yielding a complex power market structure. In recent years, several technology-neutral auctions have been run, awarding the majority of new capacity to renewable energy projects. The authors show how the auction design enabled renewable energy technologies to compete against more traditional sources. The chapter also analyses the interaction between the renewable energy auctions and the country's complex power-market structures.

1.5.3 Argentina (Chapter 4)

The Argentinian case analyses auction design and implementation decisions in a challenging investment context. Argentina's auctions benefited from a range of national and multilateral risk-mitigation structures and provisions, which resulted in competitive price outcomes. Nevertheless, project realization rates remain low as awarded projects struggled to secure financing, illustrating the necessity of incorporating investor requirements and commitment in auction design decisions.

1.5.4 Mexico (Chapter 5)

Recent power-sector reforms in Mexico led to the introduction of sophisticated auctions that incorporate spatial distribution and system integration challenges as well as a clean energy certificate mechanism. To maximize economies of scale, auctions were run through a centralized procurement process for both regulated and free consumers. Prices were record-breaking at the time, but the case also highlights the significance of political economy issues that reversed many power-sector reforms and resulted in low project realization rates.

1.5.5 India (Chapter 6)

India provides a fascinating case of the world's most ambitious auction programme under the banner of the country's National Solar Mission. Due to the federal governance system in India, parallel state and federal government renewable energy programmes have been run, securing good prices. India has also experimented with the use of solar parks to address land availability and other site-related risks and costs. A breakdown in the planning and procurement processes between the federal and state governments has, however, seen India struggle to maintain project realization rates. This is compounded by the poor financial standing of many state-level utilities, which necessitated a multipronged risk-mitigation approach.

1.5.6 South Africa (Chapter 7)

As a regional and global trailblazer, and the sub-Saharan African country with the most experience of the auction procurement framework, South Africa forms the first case study. In 2011, South Africa was the first country in sub-Saharan Africa to launch a dedicated renewable energy auction programme called the Renewable Energy Independent Power Producer Procurement Programme (REI4P). The programme procured 112 projects, representing 6,327 MW across multiple renewable energy technologies. The country has also witnessed the dramatic fall in project prices over four procurement rounds (2011–2015), representing a 50% price reduction in the case of onshore wind and close to 80% in the case of solar PV. REI4P, furthermore, features a high project realization rate, with 95% of procured projects in the first three rounds reaching commercial operation on time. South Africa's auction programme is renowned for the way that it incorporates a range of detailed socio-economic and economic development criteria and requirements in the auction process. It is regarded as an influential auction programme, not only in the region but also internationally. The last round of procurement was in 2015, but new procurement rounds were initiated in 2021.

1.5.7 Zambia (Chapter 8)

Zambia was the second country to run an auction in sub-Saharan Africa, through the IFC's Scaling Solar programme in 2015/2016. This was the first instance of this World Bank group-packaged approach being used and included a range of risk-mitigation and credit-enhancement measures. The resulting bid prices were globally competitive at the time of announcement and quite controversial in the sub-Saharan region. Despite delays in

Gratwick, K., Eberhard, A., 2008. An analysis of Independent Power Projects in Africa: Understanding development and investment outcomes. *Dev. Policy Rev.* 26, 309–338. https://doi.org/10.1111/j.1467-7679.2008.00412.x

Haufe, M.-C., Ehrhart, K., 2018. Auctions for renewable energy support – Suitability, design, and first lessons learned. *Energy Policy* 121, 217–224. https://doi.org/10.1016/j.enpol.2018.06.027

Hubbard, T.P., Paarsch, H.J., 2016. Auctions. MIT Press, Massachusets.

Klemperer, P., 2004. Auctions: Theory and practice. Princeton University Press. https://doi.org/10.1016/j.tig.2011.11.001

Kreiss, J., Ehrhart, K.-M., Haufe, M.-C., 2016. Appropriate design of auctions for renewable energy support: Prequalifications and penalties. *Energy Policy* 101, 512–520. https://doi.org/10.1016/j.enpol.2016.11.007

Lucas, H., Ferroukhi, R., Hawila, D., 2013. Renewable energy auctions in developing countries. International Renewable Energy Agency (IRENA), Abu Dhabi.

Maurer, L., & Barroso, L. (2011). *Electricity auctions: An overview of efficient practices.* World Bank Group. https://doi.org/10.1162/105864001316907973

Zitron, J., 2006. Public-private partnership projects: Towards a model of contractor bidding decision-making. *J. Purch. Supply Manag.* 12, 53–62. https://doi.org/10.1016/j.pursup.2006.04.002

2

Brazil

A Global Auctions Pioneer

*Maurício T. Tolmasquim, Tiago de Barros Correia,
and Natália Addas Porto*

2.1 Introduction: Brazil's power-sector reforms

The development of renewable energy sources (RES) in Brazil was the out-come of public policies and regulatory reforms implemented during the 1990s and 2000s. The Brazilian government launched the first institutional reform in 1995 to restore investment capacity and attract private capital to the power sector after severe hyperinflation and fiscal crises in the 1980s.

The institutional model designed in 1995, however, was not able to guarantee security of supply, and Brazilian consumers had to endure rationing of energy in 2001. Consequently, on 15 March 2004, the federal government approved Act 10.848, which started the second institutional reform of the Brazilian energy system, with four explicit aims (Tolmasquim, 2014): guarantee security of energy supply and resource adequacy in investment, ensure fair and cost-reflective tariffs, reintroduce central planning to cope with demand growth (indicative for generation expansion and determinative for transmission expansion), and build a stable regulatory framework. The second reform consequently promoted the use of energy auctions as the primary mechanism to procure energy and capacity with a long-term focus.

The first auction concluded under the framework of the second institutional reform in December 2004 procured energy from existing power plants. The auction acquired 1,192.7 terawatt hours (TWh) at an average price of US$ 23.12/megawatt hours (MWh). The total amount transacted, considering the eight-year duration of the contracts, surpassed US$ 27.5 billion. The first auction for greenfield projects was implemented on 16 December 2005, with 30-year contracts for hydropower plants and 15-year contracts for thermal power plants, including biomass. The outcome was the acquisition of 564 TWh at an average price of US$ 53.16/MWh. The total amount transacted,

Maurício T. Tolmasquim, Tiago de Barros Correia and Natália Addas Porto, *Brazil*. In: *Renewable Energy Auctions: Lessons from the Global South*. Edited by: Anton Eberhard and Wikus Kruger, Oxford University Press.
© Oxford University Press (2023). DOI: 10.1093/oso/9780192871701.003.0002

considering the duration of the contracts, surpassed US$ 29.9 billion. These two auctions laid the foundation for the design and implementation of the Brazilian auction programme.

Between December 2004 and October 2019, Brazil implemented 82 auction rounds and contracted 9.571 TWh of energy. More than 8.180 TWh was from new power plants, adding 105.2 gigawatts (GW) to the system—76.8 GW of which were from renewable energy. The success of the Brazilian auction programme depended, to a large extent, on the continuous attention paid by the public authorities to the design of the auctions, including the regulatory framework and the implementation process. The auctions have been implemented using the same rules and structure since 2004, with only minor adjustments in contractual clauses and in the bidding mechanism to mitigate the risk of connection delays.

Brazil's experience highlights the importance of considering three main goals when designing auctions: first, auctions must be attractive enough to investors to generate competition and to achieve optimal prices; second, the auction design must ensure the commitment and reliability of the bidders and their technical and financial capability to build projects on schedule and deliver the promised energy; third, the auction design should ensure the acquisition of the right mix of energy sources to safeguard the security of the electric system (Viscidi and Yépez, 2020).

To improve the attractiveness of the auctions, the public authorities provided comprehensive information about the auction programme, schedule, and technologies through a 10-year power-system expansion plan, including generation and transmission.

The bidding stage of the auction was preceded by a qualifying phase to ensure the commitment and reliability of the bidders. Developers had to provide land use rights and preliminary environmental permits as well as demonstrating their technical and financial capability to build projects on schedule to qualify. Bidders also had to provide a bid bond before joining the bidding stage of the auction, and winners had to provide surety and performance bonds before contract signing.

To ensure energy security and the optimal mix of sources, Brazil uses both technology-neutral and technology-specific auctions. Reserve capacity is also procured by public auctions, using the same scheme and methodology developed for energy procurement.

The following sections provide an introduction to Brazil and its power sector, a description and analysis of the Brazilian auction design, a reflection on the key lessons learned, and some conclusions.

2.2 Overview of Brazil's economy and power sector

Brazil is South America's largest country and the fifth largest in the world, covering over 8 million km^2. With a gross domestic product (GDP) of US\$ 2.020 billion in 2019 (Table 2.1 and Figure 2.1) and 210.15 million inhabitants, Brazil was the ninth largest economy in the world before the COVID-19 pandemic. However, the Brazilian economy had been struggling with a lack of dynamism since 2014: GDP grew by 0.5% in 2014; contracted by 3.55% and 3.28%, respectively, in 2015 and 2016 and grew by 1.32% in 2017 and 2018 and by 1.14% in 2019. The unemployment rate rose from 6.4% in January 2014 to 13.7% in March 2017.

Interest rates (Sistema Especial de Liquidação e de Custódia (Special System for Settlement and Custody) or SELIC[1]) and inflation have been on a downward trajectory since 2016. In April 2020, the annual consumer price index was 2.4%, below the target of 2.5–5.5% and considerably lower than the 10.67% recorded in December 2015 (Table 2.1). The SELIC dropped from 14.25% in December 2015 to 3% in May 2020.

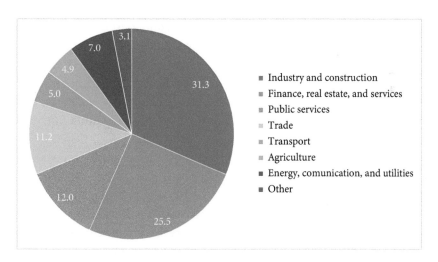

Figure 2.1 Contributors to the Brazilian gross domestic product (GDP), December 2019 (%)

Source: Brazilian Central Bank, www.bcb.gov.br (accessed June 2020).

---

[1] The central bank/interbank lending rate.

Table 2.1 Brazilian key economic indicators

	December 2015	December 2019	April 2020
Population	203.48 million	210.15 million	–
GDP	US$ 1.802 billion	US$ 2.020 billion	–
GDP annual variation	−3.55%	1.14%	–
GDP per capita	US$ 8.856	US$ 9.612	–
Unemployment rate (%)	8.9	11	12.6
Consumer price index (%)	10.67	4.31	2.4
Basic interest rate (%)	14.25	4.5	3.75
Corporate tax rate (%)	34	34	34
Sale tax rate (%)	17	17	17
Social security rate for companies (%)	28	28	28
Social security rate for employees (%)	11	11	11

Source: Brazilian Central Bank, www.bcb.gov.br (accessed June 2020).

2.2.1 Brazilian power sector

The Brazilian power sector was initially dominated by state-owned companies. The distribution service was provided by monopolist companies owned
by local state or municipal governments. Generation and transmission were
mainly supplied by the subsidiaries of the federal company Eletrobras[2] and
by companies owned by the state-level governments of São Paulo, Minas
Gerais, Goiás, and Paraná (Companhia Energética de São Paulo or Cesp;
Companhia Energética de Minas Gerais or Cemig; Companhia Energética
de Goiás or Celg; and Companhia Paranaense de Energia, or Copel, respectively). Eletrobras was responsible for planning the expansion of transmission
and power generation and the dispatch of power plants. The federal government retained the exclusive authority to enact electricity sector legislation
and was responsible for calculating end-user tariffs.

The state-led model worked well until the second oil price shock in 1979
and the deepening of the Brazilian fiscal and hyperinflation crisis during the
1980s. The power companies lost their financial health and investment capability due to the tariff control imposed by the federal government to reduce
the impact of inflation.

To restore the investment capacity and attract private capital to the power
sector, the Brazilian government launched the first institutional reform in

[2] Furnas, Chesf, Eletronorte, Eletrosul, Eletronuclear, and Itaipu.

1995, with the following goals (World Bank Group: Energy and Extractives, 2012):

- electricity generation, transmission, distribution, and trading/ marketing should be unbundled into separate segments;
- electricity generation should become a competitive activity at the risk of the independent power producers (IPPs), with prices set by the market;
- large consumers should be allowed to buy energy freely in the market;
- the transmission utilities should remain as a natural monopoly, with reg- ulation ensuring open access to generators, distribution companies, free consumers, and other transmission utilities;
- the distribution companies should also be treated as a natural monopoly and should remain responsible for providing distribution services with open access to free consumers and for buying energy from IPPs to supply their regulated customers;
- an independent regulator should serve as a watchdog for the market, interpreter of specific legislation, and guarantor of the stability of rules;
- boosting supply as an investment opportunity must be left to the market agents.

The institutional reform was only completed in 1997 when Congress approved the legal framework[3] that created the National Electricity Agency (*Agência Nacional de Energia Elétrica* or ANEEL), the Independent Sys- tem Operator (ONS) and the Wholesale Energy Market Authority (Mercado Atacadista de Energia or MAE) (Table 2.2).

According to the initial model, large consumers could sign power purchase agreements (PPAs) directly with IPPs or energy traders. Smaller consumers remained supplied by the local distribution company under a regulated tar- iff determined by ANEEL. The signed contracts, both by free consumers and distribution companies, had to be registered with the MAE. Any deficit between what was contracted through PPAs and what was consumed needed to be bought by free consumers and distribution companies on the spot mar- ket at the marginal cost of operation (MCO) calculated by the ONS. The ONS was also responsible for the dispatch of power plants (considering the MCO in a tight pool[4] approach), planning for the expansion of the transmission grid and granting grid access to consumers and producers.

---

[3] Acts 9.074, 9.427, and 9.648.
[4] In the tight pool model, the dispatch is centralized and based on predetermined variable costs. For comparison, in the loose pool model, the dispatch is centralized, but the generators are free to offer any price they like; such an approach is also referred to as price-based pools. Finally, the dispatch can be decentralized and entirely based on price.

Table 2.2 Key institutions in the Brazilian electricity sector

National Council for Energy Policy (CNPE)	The CNPE is the council of ministries (Mines and Energy, Foreign Affairs, Economy, Infrastructure, Agriculture, Science and Technology, Environment, Regional Development, Security Office and president of the EPE) and representatives of states, civil society and university that advise the president of the Republic in the formulation of energy policies.
Electricity Sector Monitoring Committee (CMSE)	The CMSE is formed by representatives of the MME, ANEEL, ONS, and CCEE and is responsible for monitoring energy security.
Brazilian Ministry of Mines and Energy (MME)	The MME is responsible for designing policies and ensuring the adequacy of energy supply, setting goals for universal electricity access and greenhouse gas emissions, and long- and medium-term central planning.
Brazilian National Electricity Agency (ANEEL)	ANEEL is responsible for regulating the entire value chain of the electricity sector, including tariff and rate setting for distribution and transmission services and the approval of the ONS annual budget. ANEEL is also responsible for generation and transmission auctioning. The board of ANEEL is composed of five directors, all appointed by the Brazilian president and confirmed by the Senate.
Brazilian Independent System Operator (ONS)	The ONS is responsible for granting grid access for producers and users, for short-term planning, for determining reinforcements and improvements in transmission assets (subject to ANEEL's approval), and for dispatching power plants according to the merit of cost and transmission constraints. Five directors compose the board of the ONS, three indicated by the MME and two elected by the IPPs and transmission agents.
Brazilian Market Authority (CCEE)	The CCEE is responsible for measuring the generation and consumption of each agent in the market, including the losses in the grid, for identifying contractual imbalances, and for clearing the market at the spot price. The CCEE is also responsible for the management of sectorial charges and funds used for fostering renewable sources and for subsidising low-income and rural customers supplied by distribution companies in the regulated market. The board of the CCEE is composed of five directors, the chairman indicated by the MME and four elected by the IPPs, the distribution companies, the free consumers, and the energy traders.
Brazilian Energy Research Office (EPE)	The primary role of the EPE is to support the MME with studies and research on long- and medium-term energy and transmission planning. The ONS retains responsibility for short-term transmission planning.
Brazilian National Environmental Agency (IBAMA)	IBAMA is responsible for the social and environmental licensing of generation and transmission projects with national impact. State-level agencies license projects with local impact.

Continued

Independent power producers (IPPs)	As a general rule, the IPPs are subject only to technical regulation regarding standards for operation and dispatch and the social and environmental conditions for licensing. Large hydropower plants, however, need a concession grant to exploit the generation potential of the rivers.
Transmission SPVs	The transmission SPVs are responsible for building, operating, and—at the end of the concession contract—transferring the transmission assets auctioned by ANEEL, as well as providing the investment in the reinforcements and improvements requested by the ONS and approved by ANEEL.
Distribution companies	The distribution companies are responsible for building, operating, and—at the end of the concession contract—transferring distribution assets in their service area and for contracting energy through the auctions of the ACR to supply their regulated customers.
Energy traders	The energy traders are agents that buy energy from IPPs to resell to free consumers.
Free consumers	The free consumers are large users of electricity that choose to procure their energy in the ACL, contracting with energy traders or IPPs. Once the choice for the ACL is made, free consumers must remain in the open market for at least five years.

Source: Authors' compilation.

The Ministry of Mines and Energy (MME) remained responsible for providing general guidance on sector regulation and granting concession contracts to large hydropower plants, transmission lines, and privatized distribution companies. New transmission utilities were auctioned as public–private partnership concessions based on a 'build, operate, and transfer' (BOT) model, and every new concession of a transmission utility was established as a special-purpose vehicle (SPV).

The institutional model designed in 1995 was not able to guarantee security of supply. In April 2001, the central hydropower plants' reservoir levels had dropped to around 32% of their maximum capacities, with energy deficit risks topping 15%, 10 percentage points higher than the acceptable threshold of 5%. On 1 June 2001, the government was forced to decree electricity rationing in Southeast, Centre-West, North, and Northeast Brazil. The government established consumption quotas as the main rationing mechanism. In parallel, the government also surcharged consumers for excess consumption, introduced bonuses for residential consumers whose energy use fell below their targets, and scheduled power cuts for residential consumers exceeding their quotas. The rationing resulted in total electricity consumption shrinking by 25%. Residential consumption fell by 13% and remained at this level during the following years, while self-production increased from 7.5% to 10.5% of consumption in six months (Hermes de Araújo et al., 2008).

In the same year, the government set up a commission to identify the structural and contextual causes of the imbalance between energy supply and demand. As the commission noted, the power-sector institutions could have addressed the vulnerability of the Brazilian power system earlier as this system had been teetering on the verge of collapse since 1999. Adverse hydrology merely precipitated the energy crisis, which was entirely foreseeable under the circumstances in place at that time. The main factor behind Brazil's electricity crisis was the delay in the start-up of operations of power-generation and transmission projects, together with the absence of new generation companies.

Indeed, the main reasons for the rationing were that the installed capacity did not follow the energy demand growth. The economic signal provided by the spot market in a hydro system with big reservoirs was too risky for investors who depend only on the spot market revenue. Most of Brazil's electricity is supplied by large hydroelectric plants. Unlike coal, oil, or gas plants, their cost of operation is practically zero. Thermal plants play an essential role in complementing the water system but not in competing with it. While the market would happily accept and pay a reasonable price for the production of new natural gas plants in the dry season, a 'wet' year would see little demand for gas generation, and the price paid for electricity would remain at a low level.

In short, building gas plants would be like making a climate-based bet for the next decade. Three rainy years in a row and the project would be bankrupt. Considering this, the lack of investment in Brazil is not a mystery. State-owned companies had their investments restricted due to a federal budget deficit and private companies considered the risks too high and the profits too low.

The power-rationing crisis of 2001 underscored the need to modify the market design of the Brazilian power sector. The absence of long-term PPAs was too risky for private capital. Consequently, on 15 March 2004, the federal government approved Act 10.848, which started the second institutional reform of the Brazilian energy system, with four explicit aims (Tolmasquim, 2014): guarantee security of energy supply and resource adequacy in investment, ensure fair and cost-reflective tariffs, reintroduce central planning to cope with demand growth, and build a stable regulatory framework.

Regarding security of supply and the fairness of tariffs, the second reform of the Brazilian energy system promoted (Correia et al., 2006):

- the separation of the regulated market (Ambiente de Contratação Regulada or ACR) into one where distribution companies procure energy contracts to supply captive consumers and a free market (Ambiente de Contratação Livre or ACL) where IPPs, energy traders, and free consumers can transact energy;
- the use of an auction scheme to procure energy for the ACR;
- the use of long-term contracts in the ACR to reduce price volatility and enable the use of accounts receivable arrangements as collateral for project financing;
- the obligation of contractual coverage by distributors and free consumers, leaving the spot market only for imbalances;
- the obligation to back all contracts with firm energy (physical coverage[5]) certified by the Brazilian MME from each power plant. In practice, the contracts must indicate which power plants will produce the energy and be limited to the firm energy certified by the MME for each plant. This avoids the situation in which a plant sells more energy through bilateral contracts than it can produce, given a certain risk level established by governmental regulation.

The second reform also restored central planning and the role of the MME in the oversight of the sector, with the creation, in 2004, of the Electrical Sector Monitoring Committee and of the Energy Research Office EPE to support MME with energy planning. The ONS retained the responsibility for short-term planning in transmission. Finally, to improve the regulatory framework, the reform replaced the MAE with a new market operator (Câmara de Comercialização de Energia Elétrica or CCEE) with more robust and more transparent governance and under the direct oversight of ANEEL. See Table 2.2 for more details on these institutions.

2.2.1.1 Power-sector structure

The second sectorial reform created a buoyant market with an increasing number of agents, especially IPPs, energy traders, and free consumers (Table 2.3).

---

[5] In Portuguese, *garantia física*. It refers to the expected generation of energy that the power plant will be able to provide under critical conditions, especially regarding the seasonality and variability of renewable energy (RE) sources.

The energy supply mix had also evolved from a system strongly dependent on large hydropower plants with a relatively small nuclear and fossil complement, to a system with deep penetration of wind, biomass, and solar (Table 2.4 and Figure 2.2).

The capital structure remained mixed, with state-owned and private companies competing in all activities and the private sector focused on new capacity investment rather than on the privatization of state-owned companies (Figure 2.3).

Table 2.3 Number of agents in the Brazilian electricity market, various years

Year	2000	2005	2010	2019
Independent power producers	17	87	290	1,488
Energy traders	5	47	93	341
Free consumers	0	470	940	7,057
Self-producers	0	14	34	76

Source: CCEE, www.ccee.org.br (accessed June 2020).

Table 2.4 The Brazilian electricity sector, December 2019

	GW	%
Total capacity	174.02	100.0
Large hydro	102.99	59.2
Wind	15.59	9.0
Gas	15.56	8.9
Biomass and waste	15.15	8.7
Oil	8.59	4.9
Small hydro	6.10	3.5
Coal	3.20	1.8
Solar photovoltaic (PV)	2.89	1.7
Nuclear	1.99	1.2
Others	1.96	1.1
Urban electricity access rates		**99.96%**
Rural electricity access rates		**98.20%**[a]
Peak demand	**85.97**	**GWh/h**

Note: [a] This value includes both on-grid and off-grid supply solutions.
Source: ANEEL, www.aneel.gov.br and EPE, www.epe.gov.br (both accessed June 2020).

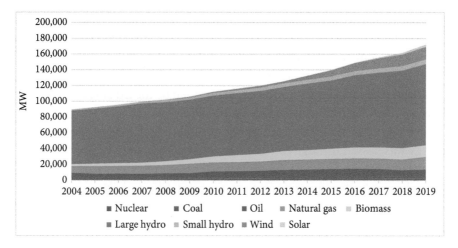

Figure 2.2 Installed electricity generation capacity, 2004–2019

Source: EPE, www.epe.gov.br (accessed June 2020).

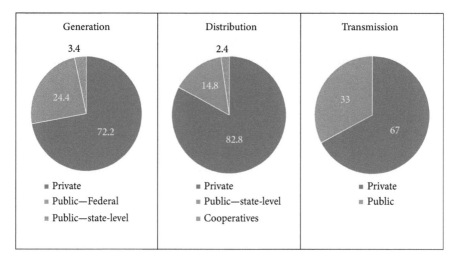

Figure 2.3 Brazilian power sector capital structure, 2019 (%)

Source: ANEEL, www.aneel.gov.br (accessed June 2020).

2.2.1.2 Tariff setting and financial sustainability

During the 1980s, in an effort to control hyperinflation, distribution tariffs were kept at artificially low levels. Still, since the state-level government owned most distribution companies, the Federal Treasury covered the deficit and financial losses of the companies. The burden of supporting inefficiently operating companies was thus borne by the Brazilian taxpayers (World Bank Group: Energy and Extractives, 2012). In 1993, the regulation was revised to improve the financial health of the transmission and distribution companies. Under the new regulatory framework, the transmission and distribution tariffs were defined in the concession contracts and became cost-reflective.

The transmission tariff was set by the winning bid in the transmission auction, while the distribution tariff was determined by the Brazilian Regulatory Agency considering a benchmark methodology to identify efficient levels of operational expenditure and capital expenditure (CAPEX). The price of energy was passed through to end users, according to the winning bid in the regulated energy auction or the contractual price in the free market.

Furthermore, the contracts also stipulate periodic and extraordinary tariff review mechanisms. Tariffs are indexed to Brazilian inflation and may be reviewed in the case that the ONS and ANEEL request investment in reinforcement and improvement of the assets. ANEEL must approve the value of the investment and the weighted average cost of capital (WACC)[6] that will be applied to remunerate the transmission and distribution companies' CAPEX. The WACC rate set in 2020 was 7.32% per year.

Electricity distribution is currently performed by 53 concessionaires, including public and private companies. Electricity distribution concessionaires cannot develop any activity relating to power generation, transmission, or energy trading. In addition, they can only acquire energy through auctions based on the lowest price and sell energy to captive power consumers under the tariff set by ANEEL.

The distribution tariff has two parts: Components A and B (Figure 2.4). Component A encompasses the costs of transmission, the energy contracts, and sectorial charges[7] and is entirely passed through to consumers since their costs, under the Brazilian regulation framework, are not manageable by the distribution companies. Component B embodies the distribution operation

---

[6] The WACC is the rate that a company is expected to pay, on average, to all its security holders to finance its assets. It is calculated as a weighted average cost of debt and equity. In general, WACC is used in financial modelling as the discount rate to calculate the net present value of a business/asset. In 2020, the WACC applied to the distribution and transmission sectors, respectively, was 7.32% per year and 6.96% per year after tax.

[7] The sectoral charges are meant to subsidize RE and low-income customers and to finance public policies:

- energy development account (CDE) to (i) subsidize energy generated from wind, small hydropower, biomass, and coal; (ii) ensure universal access to electricity; and (iii) subsidize low-income and rural customers;
- fuel consumption account (CCC): covers fuel costs of thermal power generation in stand-alone systems;
- electricity services inspection fee (TFSEE): to fund the operation of ANEEL;
- Alternative Electricity Sources Incentive Program (PROINFA): a feed-in-tariff programme that contracted RE sources in 2004, before the introduction of the auctions;
- financial compensation for the use of hydro resources (CFURH): to compensate the federal government, the states and the municipalities affected by water use and the loss of productive land caused by flooding areas required to form the reservoirs needed by hydropower plants;

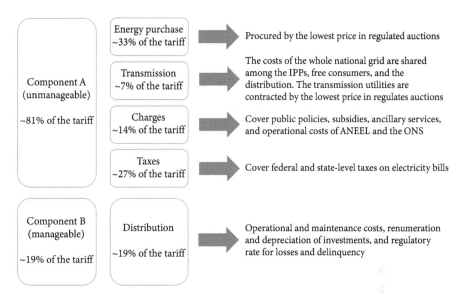

Component A (unmanageable)	Energy purchase ~33% of the tariff	→ Procured by the lowest price in regulated auctions
	Transmission ~7% of the tariff	→ The costs of the whole national grid are shared among the IPPs, free consumers, and the distribution. The transmission utilities are contracted by the lowest price in regulates auctions
~81% of the tariff	Charges ~14% of the tariff	→ Cover public policies, subsidies, ancillary services, and operational costs of ANEEL and the ONS
	Taxes ~27% of the tariff	→ Cover federal and state-level taxes on electricity bills
Component B (manageable) ~19% of the tariff	Distribution ~19% of the tariff	→ Operational and maintenance costs, renumeration and depreciation of investments, and regulatory rate for losses and delinquency

Figure 2.4 Brazilian distribution tariff-setting mechanism

Source: ANEEL, www.aneel.gov.br (accessed June 2020).

and maintenance costs, the remuneration and depreciation of investments, and the regulatory rate for losses and delinquency. ANEEL determines Component B according to a price-cap model that considers annual inflation, the expected efficiency savings (factor X), and benchmarks for efficiency for each kind of cost.

This approach ensured the financial health of the sector agents, especially the distribution companies that are the main off-takers of energy. According to ANEEL, in March 2019, 39 distribution companies (74%) had good and acceptable levels of economic and financial sustainability and 14 had negative earnings before interest, taxes, depreciation, and amortization (EBITDA).

2.2.1.3 Regulatory and policy framework

2.2.1.3.1 Regulatory framework

The power-sector regulatory framework is provided by a set of laws, decrees, and resolutions issued by the National Congress, the Presidency, the MME,

- research and development (R&D) and energy efficiency: encourages scientific and technological research related to the power sector. Concessionaires and permit holders engaged in public electricity distribution services must allocate a percentage of their net operating revenues each year to R&D of power-sector and energy-efficiency programmes for both supply and demand.
- energy reserve charge (EER): covers the costs of contracting reserve energy;
- system services charge (ESS): covers the costs incurred due to: (i) operating constraints, (ii) rendering ancillary services, and (iii) energy security.

In addition to the sectorial charges, the distributor also pays to cover the costs of the ONS and the CCEE.

and ANEEL. Over the past few years, the Brazilian electricity sector has undergone structural changes in its regulation. The objective has been the establishment of a model that would promote economic efficiency through the competitive environment, especially in the generation sector, which would make investments in the expansion of installed capacity feasible and guarantee service to the consumer market. Figure 2.5 illustrates the organization and institutions of the Brazilian power sector.

EPE deserves special mention as one of the most important institutional innovations of the new regulatory framework. Brazil's government determined that it was necessary to have an institution based on knowledge and technical excellence with permanent, high-level professional staff, tools, and a database suitable for the formulation of energy policies and decision support. EPE is a federal body, created by Act 10.847 on March 2004, mainly responsible for energy planning.

EPE develops 10-year plans (Plano Decenal de Expansão de Energia, or PDE), periodic bulletins, reviews, reports, and specific studies based on government guidelines. The PDE indicates the government's expectation about energy expansion according to an integrated view for all relevant energy sources and synergies with other economic sectors. The PDE also prioritizes transmission facilities to be considered by the MME to participate in transmission auctions.

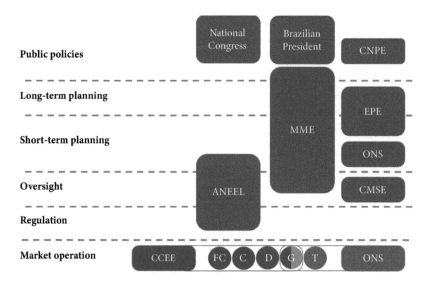

Figure 2.5 Brazilian regulatory framework
Source: Authors' compilation.

The EPE further provides a range of analyses and reports on energy statistics, energy efficiency, and socio-environmental studies, including environmental feasibility and sustainability of electricity and gas production and transmission sources, energy resource inventory, and prospects for preliminary environmental licensing processes of strategic hydropower and transmission projects.

2.2.1.3.2 Policy framework

The first incentive for renewable energy dates back to 1996 and is still in force for projects that requested grant untill March 2022. Act 9.427 established a 50% discount in transmission and distribution system tariffs for renewable energy. All other energy sources and consumers offset this cross-subsidy.

The first attempt to implement public policies with explicit targets for renewable energy was the wind power plant programme (Programa Emergencial de Energia Eólico or PROEOLICA). It was designed in 2001 to hire 1,050 MW of wind power plants until December 2003 using a feed-in-tariff approach. However, the PROEOLICA was never implemented.

In 2002, Congress approved the alternative energy programme PROINFA (Programa de Incentivos às Fontes Alternativas de Energia Elétrica)—also a feed-in tariff policy, aimed to acquire, in its first phase, 3,300 MW of renewable energy (RE) (1,100 MW each from wind, biomass, and small hydropower plants) under 20-year PPAs. The first phase was implemented in May 2004 and a total of 6,600 MW responded to the government call for projects (3,681 MW from wind, 995 MW from biomass, and 1,924 MW from small hydropower plants). The projects were selected according to the age of their environmental licences, and the unmet power of biomass was redistributed among the other sources (Costa, 2006). Table 2.5 illustrates the outcome of PROINFA's first phase.

PROINFA also provided for a second phase, where alternative renewable energy sources should serve 15% of the annual increase in electricity

Table 2.5 PROINFA's first-phase outcome

Source	Capacity (MW)	Price (US$/MWh)
Wind	1,422.92	65.94
Small hydro	1,191.24	37.76
Biomass	685.24	30.25
Total	3,299.40	

Source: Costa (2006).

consumption. Over a 20-year horizon, these sources would represent 10% of the total electricity consumption. However, because of the power-sector reform, the government decided not to implement the second phase. Instead, it decided to replace the feed-in-tariff policy with regulated auctions (presented in detail in section 2.3).

In 2016, the Brazilian government committed to increasing the share of non-hydro renewable sources in its power supply mix from 9% in 2014 to 24% in 2030. As shown in Table 2.4 and Figure 2.2, the installed capacity of wind, solar photovoltaic (PV), and biomass was already around 19% in 2019, and the 10-year energy expansion plan indicates that, including distributed PV, Brazil will achieve 34% in 2029.

2.3 The design of Brazil's renewable energy auctions

The Brazilian auction programme was created by Act 10.848 with the objective to provide an efficient, transparent, and competitive instrument for the awarding of long-term PPAs for captive consumers supplied by the distribution companies. Since 2005, all the energy contracts[8] in the ACR have been secured through an auction scheme prioritizing the procurement of greenfield projects to meet demand growth.[9] The auctions have been designed to provide long-term contracts to new power plants and facilitate their financing through project finance, where lenders provide loans based on the projected cash flows of the project rather than on the balance sheets of its sponsors.

There are five types of energy auctions: greenfield auctions, reserve auctions, renewable source auctions, existing power plant auctions, and adjustment auctions (Figure 2.6).

2.3.1 Greenfield auctions

The greenfield project auction aims to meet the increase in distributors' power demand by contracting energy from plants that have yet to be built.

---

[8] The electricity commercialization contract in the regulated market is a bilateral contract for the purchase and sale of electric energy and its associated capacity, signed between the selling company and the distribution company within the scope of the regulated market, as a result of auctions of electricity from existing generation plants and greenfield plants. In other words, there are no separate tenders to contract energy and capacity in Brazil. This situation can be explained by the large number of hydropower plants within the power system. With the increase of run-of-river hydropower plants and variable renewable sources, capacity is becoming an issue and the government has started to discuss the possibility of running capacity-only auctions.

[9] Originally, the auctions for new projects had a lead time of 3 or 5 years and lasted between 15 and 30 years.

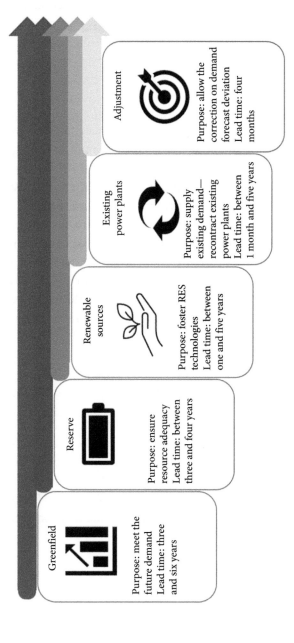

Figure 2.6 Brazilian auction scheme
Source: Authors' compilation.

Greenfield

Purpose: meet the
future demand
Lead time: three
and six years

Reserve

Purpose: ensure
resource adequacy
Lead time: between
three and four years

Renewable
sources

Purpose: foster RES
technologies
Lead time: between
one and five years

Existing
power plants

Purpose: supply
existing demand—
recontract existing
power plants
Lead time: between
1 month and five years

Adjustment

Purpose: allow the
correction on demand
forecast deviation
Lead time: four
months

This auction can be of two types: A-6 (plants that go into commercial operation in up to six years' time) and A-4 (in four years). The winners of the auction sign contracts with the distribution companies that are procuring energy. Only the consumers from the regulated market pay for this energy. The Brazilian government has implemented 31 rounds of greenfield project auctions with 30 rounds specifically for RE.[10]

2.3.2 Reserve auctions

The contracting of reserve energy was originally created to improve energy security in the National Interconnected System, with power from greenfield or existing plants specially contracted for this purpose. So far, reserve auctions have only contracted greenfield plants. The CCCE acts as a single buyer and signs contracts with all the winners of the auction. Reserve energy is accounted for and settled on the short-term market operated by the CCEE. This type of 'insurance' in the energy supply generated the reserve energy charge intended to cover these costs—including administrative, financial, and tax costs. As the reserve auction works as an insurance for all of the power system, the energy charges apply to all consumers from the regulated and free market. The Brazilian government has implemented nine rounds of reserve auctions, the last in 2017.

2.3.3 Renewable source auctions

The auction of renewable sources was instituted to meet the growth of the market in the regulated environment and increase the share of renewable sources—wind, solar, biomass, and energy from small hydroelectric plants—in the Brazilian energy system. In recent years, the government has been using only greenfield auctions to procure new RE plants. The Brazilian government has implemented three rounds of special auctions for RES, the first in 2007 and the last in 2015.

2.3.4 Existing power plant auctions

This auction was created to contract energy generated by plants already built and in operation whose investments have been partially or fully amortized

---

[10] RE includes all renewable energy sources, including large hydropower plants.

and, therefore, have a lower cost. The separation of the existing and greenfield energy auctions allowed the average price in the regulated market (ACR) to be calculated apart from the marginal expansion cost, thus contributing to fair electricity rates. Moreover, this offered distribution companies the possibility of signing agreements with the existing generation companies for shorter lead times and durations as a risk management tool designed to offset uncertainties in demand and the loss of free consumers. Finally, this separation prevented the existing plants from squeezing new plants out of the picture in the regulated market, thus helping to ensure energy security. In total, 21 rounds of existing power plant auctions have been implemented, 19 with specific products for renewable energy sources.

2.3.5 Adjustment auctions

This type of auction aims to adjust the distributors' energy contracting, addressing any deviations arising from the difference between forecasts made by distributors in previous auctions and the actual demand growth. As a result of this auction, the distribution companies sign short-term contracts (from three months to two years) with the auction winner. Seventeen rounds have been implemented since 2005, none with specific products for RES.

Auctions to procure greenfield power plants, reserve energy, and RES usually have a lead time to commercial operation of between three and six years. Project developers are awarded 15–30-year fixed tariff contracts (Figure 2.7).

In short, the new regulatory framework was designed to stimulate vast amounts of investment in the expansion of generation capacity necessary to

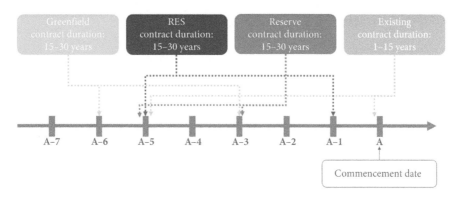

Figure 2.7 Lead time to commercial operation of the auctioned projects

Source: Authors' compilation.

Table 2.6 Key auction information

Design	Year of introduction	2005
	Frequency of auctions/rounds	82 rounds (61 rounds with specific products for RES)
		• 40 rounds for existing power plants, 21 with specific products for RES[a])
		• 30 rounds for greenfield projects, including the special rounds for the hydropower plants of Santo Antonio, Jirau and Belo Monte (28 rounds with specific products for RES)
		• 3 rounds for only RES power plants
		• 9 rounds for reserve energy (all with specific products for RES)
	Currency	Brazilian Reais (indexed to local inflation)
Implementation	Policy and regulation guidelines	Ministry of Mines and Energy
	Regulator	ANEEL
	Procurer	CCEE delegated by ANEEL
	Off-taker	Distribution companies and the CCEE (in the case of reserve energy)
Outcomes	New MW procured[b]	105.228 MW (76.862 MW from RES)
	Technology procured	Oil, coal, natural gas, wind, solar, biomass, small hydro, and large hydro

Note: [a] Only large and small hydropower plants; [b] Greenfield, RES, and reserve auctions.
Source: Authors' compilation.

meet fast-growing demand at the lowest cost possible (Tolmasquim, 2014). Table 2.6 presents the key auction information.

2.3.6 Auction design

The energy auctions in Brazil are conducted annually according to a schedule released by the MME. The auction process is led by ANEEL based on guidelines of the MME. An auction committee undertakes the main auction tasks, which are distributed among different institutions (EPE, CCEE, ANEEL, MME). Once an auction is concluded, the winning generator companies sign contracts directly with distribution companies or with the CCEE in the case of a reserve auction (Figure 2.8).

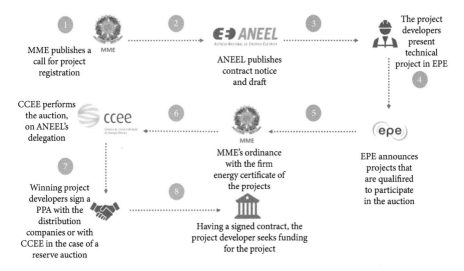

Figure 2.8 Auction process overview

Source: Authors' compilation.

The auctions have three stages (Figure 2.9): the first for registration and technical pre-qualification, the second for bid submission and the winners' selection, and a final stage for the legal and financial qualification of the preferred bidders, performed by the regulatory agency.

The first and third stages aim to reduce the risk of project failure. The assessment of the required documents in stage 1 is proactive to ensure the participation of the largest possible number of projects in the bidding phase (second stage). However, considering the large number of registered projects, the qualification process was split, and the legal and economic documents of preferred bidders were evaluated in stage 3 (see section 2.3.6.2). The second stage encompasses the bidding and the winner selection processes (see section 2.3.6.3).

Since energy auctions have been conducted regularly, investors already have a pipeline of projects planned, and there is no need for a long notice period to respond to the first-stage request for registration. Developers thus normally have a 30-day period during which they must respond to the call for registration. The EPE has 80 days to evaluate the projects and documents presented and to calculate the firm energy of each project.

In parallel, ANEEL opens a public consultation process for stakeholders to analyse the rules of the auction[11] and the draft contracts. Bidders have access to complete information about the auction, including the final version of the

---

[11] Including the detailed auction process, the price rule, and the winners' selection criteria.

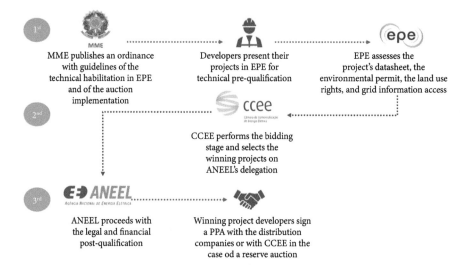

Figure 2.9 Auction stages
Source: Authors' compilation.

rules and contracts, the price cap, and the certified firm energy requirement (physical guarantee). The information about the total demand for the auction is not disclosed in advance in order to mitigate the risk of collusion.

Winners must secure all permits and licences, reach financial closure, complete the construction of the power plant, and connect it to the grid within the A–X period stipulated in the rules (see Figure 2.7). During the construction period, the investor can change some of the technical characteristics of their project. According to the rules of Brazil's A-6[12] auction of 2019, for example, it was possible to change the installed capacity, the turbine type and quantity of generating units, and the connection point of the power plant. Technical changes must conform to environmental permits, cannot modify the energy source initially indicated, and may not compromise the fulfilment of contractual obligations assumed in the auction, such as the amount of energy and capacity negotiated, the date of commencement, and the duration of the contract. Bidders in the 2019 auction were also allowed to complete the power plant construction early and sell energy in the Brazilian wholesale market. The auction rules made it clear that all risks and costs associated with changes in the technical characteristics and the plant's commercial operations date were the exclusive responsibility of the seller and could not be passed on to the buyers.

Energy auctions and contracts have evolved over the years. In the contracts for different sources and products, different delivery obligations are

[12] A-6 refers to the lead time of six years.

designed, such as the determination of wind or PV energy generation on an annual and four-year basis. Risk allocations are also distinct between auctions. In reserve energy auctions, the risk of generation insufficiency is allocated to all consumers while in new energy auctions (greenfield, RES) the risk is allocated to generators. Table 2.7 shows the Brazilian auction basic design in 2019.

2.3.6.1 Auction demand

Electricity demand in Brazil is usually constrained by the availability of energy (MWh) and not installed capacity (MW). The installed capacity is more than double the peak demand (Table 2.4) due to the seasonality and the stochasticity of the large hydro resources that dominate the Brazilian supply mix. Therefore, auction volumes are defined in terms of energy.

In the greenfield and RES auctions, each distribution company has to project, on an annual basis, the total amount of energy needed to supply

Table 2.7 The Brazilian auction basic design

Periodicity	Annually—usually two rounds per year
Project preparation	Bidders must secure social and environmental permits, land use rights, and interconnection agreements to be allowed to register for bidding
Stages	
Registration and qualification	Evaluation of the required permits and documents Verification of physical coverage
Bidding	Hybrid price rule—pay-as-bid with uniform pricing (highest accepted bid)
Auction demand	
Greenfield projects	Decentralized—distribution companies
RES	Decentralized—distribution companies
Reserve	Centralized—MME
Energy source	Technology-specific or group of technologies
Winner selection	Only price
Lead time	Between three and six years
Risks	
Seller	Construction, operation, equipment performance risks, and exposure to the spot market (in the case of the contract for energy—'quantity contract')
Buyer	Inflation and exposure to the spot market, in the case of the contract for availability
Liabilities	
Seller	Bid bonds and surety and performance bonds
Buyer	Payment financial warranties

Source: Authors' compilation.

their captive consumers for the next three to six years (Figure 2.10). The MME prepares the auction schedule based on this information. The Brazilian government has, on average, performed at least two auctions for greenfield projects per year.

The reserve energy auctions are meant to ensure the resource adequacy and energy security of the entire market and are conducted less frequently. The MME determines the demand for the reserve auction considering the contracting level of the distribution companies and free consumers, the balance among the different energy sources, and the evaluation of possible deviations between the physical coverage granted to the power plants and the real firm energy available to the system. The auction demand for all auctions (greenfield, existing power plants, RES, and reserve) is not disclosed to the bidders.

The auction demand is not sensitive to the price. Still, it can be reduced at the start of the auction by the use of an endogenous rationing mechanism, according to the following equation:

$$Final\ demand\ =\ min\left(Initial\ demand;\ \frac{Initial\ offer}{Adjustment\ parameter}\right)\quad (1)$$

where:
final demand = the demand that will be procured in the auction;
initial demand = the summation of the demand requested by the distribution companies or by the MME, in the case of the reserve auction;

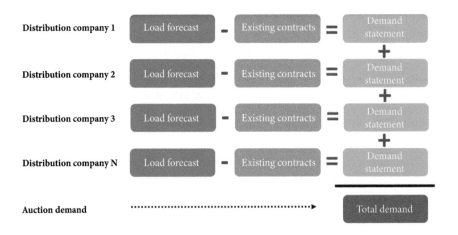

Figure 2.10 Auction demand: Centralized procurement
Source: Authors' compilation.

initial offer = the summation of the amount of energy offered by the bidders; adjustment parameter = an integer number, equal to or higher than 1, set by the MME before knowing the total offer to ensure a minimum level of competition in the auction.

Endogenous rationing, as described above, is reported to produce suboptimal results (both theoretically and in practice) if used to artificially increase competition or reduce final prices (Hanke and Tiedemann, 2020). This is not the case in the Brazilian approach since the mechanism aims to increase demand uncertainty to limit potential collusion among generators. Therefore, the adjustment parameter is discretionarily chosen by the MME before the second stage (the bidding process) begins and is usually equal or near to 1. On the other hand, considering the large number of initial offers in the Brazilian auctions, the mechanism has rarely been triggered. Moreover, the MME has the power to split the demand in the beginning of the auction among technologies and energy sources based on other criteria, such as political targets for renewable sources and energy security.

2.3.6.2 Qualification criteria and process

The qualification process aims to ensure that only committed and highly capacitated bidders are selected and that projects have a high likelihood of being built on time. Only bidders who meet the technical, environmental, social, legal, and economic criteria of the qualification process can sign the contracts awarded in the auctions. Unfortunately, the evaluation of all requirements may be time-consuming and costly for both bidders and auctioneers.

To reduce its transaction cost, the Brazilian auctioneer divided the tender into three stages (Table 2.8). The first is a pre-qualification stage focused on the technical, social, and environmental criteria of the projects. In the second stage, bidders must provide bid bonds and price bids.

During the pre-qualification process, the EPE also calculates the firm energy certificate of the submitted project. This is the foreseeable generation that, once approved by the MME, represents the maximum amount of energy that the project can commit to with energy contracts. The firm energy of wind and PV projects corresponds to the annual value of energy that could be generated with a probability of occurrence equal to or greater than 90% (p90) and 50% (p50), respectively.[13] The generation data used must be certified by independent entities.

---

[13] The use of a less stringent criterion for solar PV can be understood as a form of incentive.

Table 2.8 (Pre-)qualification criteria

Evaluation criteria	Stage 1 Pre-qualification	Stage 2 Bidding	Stage 3 Qualification
Land (acquisition and use rights)	✓	×	×
Social and environmental permits	✓	×	×
Grid connection assessment	✓	×	×
Technical criteria and evaluation	✓	×	×
Bid bond	×	✓	×
Price	×	✓	×
Legal criteria and evaluation	×	×	✓
Financial criteria and evaluation	×	×	

Source: Authors' compilation.

The last step is focused on the legal, economic, and financial qualifications for the investors and is therefore performed only after the selection of preferred bidders. This approach is used in auctions and tenders of all sectors in Brazil. It is based on the fact that legal and financial requirements are more subjective and more likely to be disputed by bidders. Unbundling the qualification process thus avoids the risk of dealing with many appeals and challenges of qualification documents from developers with no competitive bid.

The EPE usually concludes the pre-qualification process in 80 days, while ANEEL completes stage 3 in 10 days. There is no qualitative assessment of the information provided and the process in the first and last stages is not intended to rank the projects or to contribute to the winner selection process since this is based only on price. However, a project that does not comply with the qualification criteria will not be allowed to join the bidding process of the second stage or to sign the contract, depending on the case.

Once the last qualification phase has been completed, the winning bidders must reach the financial close of their projects within 6–12 months. The commercial operation date depends on the auction type and the investor's strategy. Some PV and wind plants that win the A-6 auction start commercial operation before the date established in the contract and sell the energy in the free market.

The following unpacks the qualification criteria outlined in Table 2.8.

2.3.6.2.1 Site selection and land use rights

Bidders are responsible for project site selection and preparation, which includes the acquisition of land use rights. Bidders are required to provide the coordinates of the proposed project site and proof of land acquisition or land use rights, such as a notarial lease or title deeds for the project site; an unconditional land option, sale, or lease-of-land agreement; or a conveyancer's certificate.

However, the MME and ANEEL engage with developers to define the sites of hydropower to secure the optimum use of hydraulic potential of the entire river, and for strategic large hydropower plants, the EPE may prepare studies and reports for site selection and may apply for the preliminary environmental permit.

2.3.6.2.2 Social and environmental permits

Bidders need to provide an environmental permit and a social and environmental impact assessment detailing the change in land and water use and the impacts of the generation process on local communities, wildlife, scenic view, and other relevant factors.

The Brazilian process for environmental permitting is decentralized and multidisciplinary. According to the type of activity involved and the extent of the expected environmental impacts, the administrative process can be performed by environmental agencies and public authorities (accountable for public policies on health, jobs, and historical and archaeological protection) at municipal, state, or federal level. The network of environmental agencies and public authorities form the Brazilian National Environmental System, which is coordinated by the Ministry of Environment (Ministério do Meio Ambiente or MMA) and has a deliberative body (Conselho Nacional do Meio Ambiente or CONAMA) to establish the directives of the permitting process according to Resolution CONAMA 237/1997.

Environmental permitting starts with the investor registering the project with the environmental agency of jurisdiction over the location and the kind of economic activity of the project,[14] with the presentation of an activity description sheet and an environmental impact declaration. After receiving and processing the information registered by the investor, the environmental agency prepares the Term of Reference for the permitting process, which establishes whether the project will follow a normal or a simplified course and defines the scope of the environmental studies and report that must be presented by the investor to obtain the permits.

In a standard process, investors must secure three sequential permits: the preliminary permit (Licença Prévia), the construction permit (Licença de Instalação) and the operational permit (Licença de Operação).

---

[14] As a general rule, most RE projects will be under state jurisdiction.

The preliminary permit approves the environmental feasibility of the project and establishes the conditions (additional studies or countermeasures to mitigate the environmental impact) for the construction permit. It is the most complex and time-consuming permit. Before securing the preliminary permit, the investor must prepare a full environmental impact assessment and its respective report and conduct public hearings with the local communities that may be affected by the project.

In the simplified process, the investor has to prepare only a simplified environmental report to obtain the construction permit. In both cases, the investor must comply with the construction permit conditions to receive the operation permit and conclude environmental licensing.

2.3.6.2.3 Grid connection assessment

Bidders must also provide a grid connection assessment indicating the need for 'shallow connection works' (works for the bidder's project connection to the system) and the approval of the ONS, indicating the feasibility of the intended connection. Once awarded preferred bidder status, developers must sign connection contracts with the transmission company and contracts for the use of the transmission grid with the ONS. The transmission tariffs charged by the ONS include a fixed and a locational component that developers need to consider in their bid. The preferred bidder is also responsible for covering the costs of the shallow connection works. In contrast, the transmission company covers the costs of the deep connection works that will be incorporated into the tariffs and divided among all users of the transmission system.

In the case of connection delays, the winning bidder is obliged to procure energy in the market to cover its contractual obligations, except in the case of *force majeure*.

2.3.6.2.4 Technical criteria and evaluation

For the technical evaluation, bidders must provide:

- small and large hydropower plants: a basic engineering project[15] approved by ANEEL containing all the necessary technical specifications for the estimation of cost and construction time, information on investment, and debt to the project;

---

[15] The basic engineering project, also called the basic project or preliminary project, is the set of documents that define the project and its most favourable cost in a given context.

- wind farms: the certification of anemometric measurements and the estimate of the electric energy production associated with the park, issued by an independent certifier; and
- PV plants: the certification of solarimetric data, and the forecast for electricity production, issued by an independent certifier.

For wind and PV plants, the bidders must also provide the project description memorial. The memorial presents the primary information of the project. For example, in the case of wind energy, the project description should include, among others, the following topics: general characteristics of the project (location and access, available infrastructure, wind potential and climatic conditions, and broad characterization of the land); connection system characteristics (attributes of the elevating electrical substation, description of the project connection); and project drawings.

2.3.6.2.5 Legal criteria and evaluation
After the bidding process, the winning bidders must still pass through a final legal and financial qualification process.

As part of the legal qualification process, bidders must provide the project ownership structure and proof of shareholders' fiscal good standing and compliance with labour regulations. In the case of projects with foreign companies or pension and investment fund shareholders, it is also required to commit to establish an SPV ahead of receiving the authorization to be an IPP. No term sheets from lenders are necessary.

2.3.6.2.6 Financial criteria and evaluation
For financial qualification, a bidder must demonstrate its investment capacity by providing the company (or shareholder, in the case of an SPV) audited balance sheet, statements, and other accounting and fiscal records of the past year.

2.3.6.2.7 Price cap
The Brazilian auctions make use of price caps both as an instrument to protect consumers from abuse of market power and collusion and as a signal to developers that want to prepare projects to join future auctions. The price cap is calculated by the EPE and approved by the MME, considering the fixed and variable costs of each energy source, the duration of the contracts, the taxes, and the regulatory WACC for generation via a cash flow assessment. The price cap is public, specific for each procured product or energy source,

and disclosed at least 30 days before the bidding stage. Table 2.9 presents the price caps used in 2018 and 2019.

2.3.6.2.8 Bankability

The MME designed the first draft of the PPAs for greenfield projects (in 2004) in close collaboration with the Brazilian Development Bank (Banco Nacional de Desenvolvimento Econômico e Social or BNDES), the main funder for investment in infrastructure in Brazil, with the purpose of having a contract suitable to back the loan needed to develop the project with its expected incomes (project finance model). Therefore, the PPAs are standardized and have explicit clauses setting out the conditions and procedures for a change in the control of the project and for the exercise of lenders' step-in rights (in which the lender intervenes in the execution and administration of the project to ensure its completion).

2.3.6.3 Bidder ranking and winner selection

The regular auction procedure is a hybrid model that occurs in two phases. The first phase is a descending-clock auction, or Dutch auction, of uniform price, that starts with a ceiling price defined by the MME (Figure 2.11). Bidders indicate how much they are willing to supply at this price. The auctioneer then lowers the price until the desired supply level is met, plus a certain margin. The auction uses an inflated demand level to stimulate competition in the second phase.

Phase 2 operates as a final pay-as-bid round for the winners of phase 1. Remaining bidders offer a final sealed price, which cannot be higher than the price disclosed in phase 1. The clearing price is determined when supply equals demand, and the winning bids are those lower than the clearing one (Figure 2.12).

Table 2.9 Brazilian price caps in 2018 and 2019

	Auction A-6, 18 October 2019 (US$/MWh)	Auction A-4, 28 June 2019 (US$/MWh)	Auction A-6, 31 August 2018 (US$/MWh)	Auction A-4, 4 April 2018 US$/MWh
Large hydro	69.68	71.64	73.79	85.34
Small hydro	69.68	71.64	73.79	85.34
Wind	46.21	51.74	57.76	74.78
PV	51.10	68.66	–	91.50
Biomass	71.39	77.36	78.37	96.48

Source: ANEEL, www.aneel.gov.br (accessed June 2020).

For simplicity, winner selection under the Brazilian auction scheme is based exclusively on price.

Starting in 2013, auctions with a lead time shorter than five years have been performed with a different approach due to the increase in construction timelines of transmission lines and the uncertainty about the auction's winners' location. This new design includes a preliminary phase to select the projects with connection feasibility through competition among projects with the same connection point. In the preliminary phase, bidders thus submit a single bid with price and quantity for each project. The auctioneer classifies bids according to their price at each connection point following the discriminatory price methodology (Figure 2.13). Projects that exceed the 'transmission margin', calculated by the EPE and ONS for each connection point indicated by the registered projects are excluded from the first and second phases of the auction. The winners then engage in the general auction process following the methodology described above (Figures 2.11 and 2.12).

From 2017, Brazil again changed the bidding process for transmission access. The new methodology is called a continuous trade reverse auction. The new design also has two phases, but in this first phase, bidders submit sealed bids with a price and quantity. Bids are evaluated by price, and the auctioneer classifies the 'temporary winners' as the lowest bids up to the market-clearing quantity (demand) while all other bidders are considered temporarily disqualified. The second phase is a descending clock iteration of three or five minutes (depending on specific auction rules), in which any

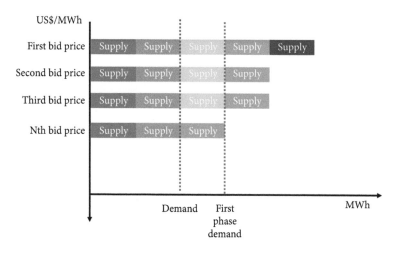

Figure 2.11 First phase: Uniform-price auction
Source: Authors' compilation.

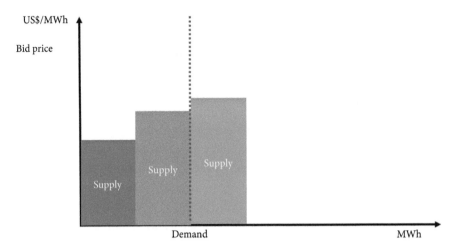

Figure 2.12 Second phase: Pay-as-bid auction
Source: Authors' compilation.

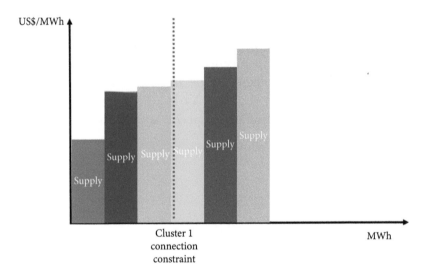

Figure 2.13 Preliminary phase for transmission dispute: Pay-as-bid auction
Source: Authors' compilation.

temporarily disqualified bidder can replace a temporary winner by submitting a bid lower than the marginal price minus a decrement. The decrement (the minimum difference between the marginal price of temporary winning bids and the new bids) is set by the auctioneer prior to the auction (Hochberg and Poudinet, 2018).

The price presented in the first phase (during the transmission point competition) cannot be increased in the second phase, and the bidders remain limited to their prior bid (price and quantity) until the current bidding price of the second phase reaches their price. At that moment, the bidders may submit a new bid with a lower price or remove their offer from the auction. The auction closes when the total supply has met the auction's demand, and the outcome can be a mix of uniform and discriminatory price, depending on how fierce the competition for the first phase was (Figure 2.14).

2.3.6.4 Buyer and seller liabilities

2.3.6.4.1 Financial pre-qualification and penalties

Bid, surety, and performance bonds. The bidders with projects pre-qualified in stage 1 must provide a bid bond of 1%[16] of the estimated investment. The purpose of the bid bond is to cover the risk that the submitting bidder might not abide by its offer. The bond will be executed if the awarded bidder does not sign the contract or does not present a surety and performance bond. The bid bond is also returned if the project does not win the auction.

Bidders must also provide a surety and performance bond covering the construction risks. The surety and performance bond is retained throughout the construction of the power plant. Its initial value must cover 5% of the investment. The reduction in the surety and performance bond has varied over time, depending on the energy source and on the year. For instance, in the A-6 auction performed in 2018, wind was allowed to reduce the bond as follows: beginning of concreting the bases of the generating units—10% reduction in the financial guarantee, start of the assembly of the towers of the generating units—40% reduction, start of operation and testing of the first generating unit—60% reduction. However, in the last A-4 auction performed in 2019, only small and large hydro were allowed to reduce the bond by 25% once the construction work starts, while all the other energy sources must retain the entire bond until commercial operation. The motivation for this change is not clear.

2.3.6.4.2 Risk allocation and penalties

The Brazilian auctions can procure for two categories of contract, depending on the allocation of the generation risk. The first category is the contract for 'energy quantity', in which the IPP bears the entire generation risk, including the imbalances caused by centralized dispatch orders. The 'energy quantity'

---

[16] The value corresponds to the highest amount allowed by Act 8.666.

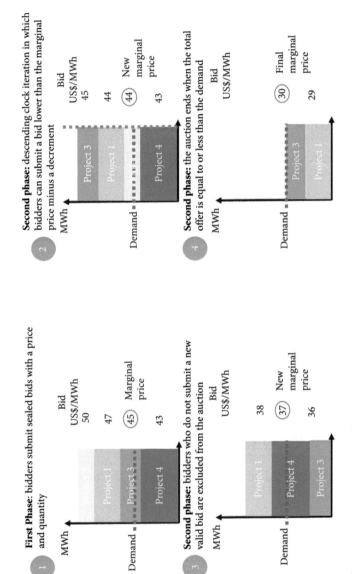

Figure 2.14 Continuous trade reverse auction (since 2017)

Source: Authors' compilation, based on Câmara de Comercialização de Energia Elétrica (CCEE).

contract is a standard financial forward contract in which generation companies receive a fixed amount from their distribution counterparts and the difference between the contracted amount and the amount produced or consumed is settled on the spot market. Like any term contract, these hedge agreements protect sellers against low prices on the short-term market (more frequent) and purchasers from high prices (less frequent but very steep).

The second type of contract is for energy availability, and the IPPs bear the ordinary risks of equipment reliability and performance but are not obliged to procure energy in the market when they are not dispatched. The 'availability contract' was initially designed to complement thermal power plants. It transfers the 'systemic' risks (hydrology), which cannot be managed by individual investors, to consumers. In the case of thermal power plants, it avoids the situation in which the investor hedges against infrequent dispatch due to long periods of good hydrology by overpricing energy in the auction. It resembles the capacity mechanism known as a 'reliability option' or the financial concept of 'call options' since the IPPs receive a fixed payment in exchange for the obligation that their generation capacity will be available when some given strike price is reached or when the system needs to dispatch the power plant out of merit order due to transmission congestion, system reliability, or other reasons. In other words, the distributor pays a fixed revenue for exercising the option and the variable cost is the strike price. Whenever the spot market price exceeds the strike price, the option buyer (distributor) exercises the option right (generation).

Since 2018, the MME has changed wind power plant contracts from availability to quantity. It did the same with the solar energy contracts in 2019. Since then, wind and solar plants have to buy electricity in the spot market if their production is lower than the amount sold in the auction.

ANEEL also modified contracts in 2019 to take wind and solar energy seasonality into account. Up until that point, a project's total annual energy generated was adjusted monthly according to the generation profile. For instance, in the Northeast region, the winds blow more between May and November; the power plants could choose to generate more in this period and less in the other months as long as the total annual generation meets the contract amount. After 2019, energy production must follow the distribution load seasonality. So generation seasonality risk has passed from the consumers to the generator.

Considering that the auctions procure greenfield projects, several construction and operational risks need to be considered and contractually allocated. If a project fails to comply with the contractual timetable and performance standards, it has to procure an equivalent amount of energy with a price rebate. The price rebate is set according to the lowest value among (i) the contractual price reduced by 15%; (ii) the average of the spot price in the month; and (iii) cost of the energy procured by the sellers in the energy market to fulfil their contractual obligation. Non-compliance may also result in the issuing of penalties such as fines, the early termination of the contract,[17] and the temporary impediment to participate in further auctions and to contract with the government for up to two years. Most of the environmental and social, technical, and business risks are allocated to the developer, and all exceptions are expressly defined in the contracts.

Developers are protected against political and regulatory risks, including change in taxation, inflation, and in the case of fossil power plants, exchange rates and variation in international fuel prices. The price of the energy is indexed to the consumer price index. Brazil has persistent and volatile inflation rates, and in this context, indexing seeks to maintain the real value of the seller revenues along with the cash flow. Thus, the feasibility and risk analysis of the project, especially for obtaining funding, can be accomplished without the need for forecasts about expected inflation. The allocation of the inflation risk to consumers reduces the value of bids and the final price of the auction.

Undue delays in the environmental permitting processes are compensated for by extensions in contractual duration.

Finally, until 2015, if the sellers proved that the power plant had been completed and was prevented from generating because of delays in deep connection works, their contractual obligations were suspended. However, since then, the grid connection risk has been allocated to the sellers. The shift in the transmission risk allocation followed changes to the approach for transmission planning and expansion. Until 2015, the EPE used the outcome of the energy auction to evaluate the transmission solution with minimum global cost and to consolidate the transmission expansion plan that will be used by the MME and ANEEL as the reference for the transmission auctions. However, over time, power plants began to be built further and further away from the load, making transmission lines longer and environmental licensing more complex and time-demanding. As a result, there started to be more power plants completed before the necessary transmission works.

The MME and EPE consequently started planning transmission expansion in advance, contracting transport corridors for the development of sites with energy potential before the energy auctions. In such a context, once the generator can evaluate but not manage the risk of connection delay, the change in

---

[17] In case of long delay in completion. The early termination can be asked for by the developer, the off-taker, or be a discretionary decision of ANEEL, respecting the right of all sides to be heard.

the allocation of the transmission delay risk aims to incentivize developers to bid projects that will be connected to existing transmission points or, at least, to points already under construction. The introduction of a 'transmission margin' competition before the auction (see section 2.3.6.3) further reduces the transmission delay risk.

2.3.6.5 Securing the revenue stream and addressing off-taker risk

Investor confidence can be significantly improved through the provision of payment guarantees by off-takers, resulting in more competitive offers and higher realization rates.

In the Brazilian scheme, the energy may be contracted by distribution companies or procured directly by the MME, in the case of reserve energy. In the first case, total demand is aggregated, and each preferred project signs off-take contracts with each distribution company, thereby reducing payment risks through a portfolio effect. Moreover, the distribution companies include the energy cost in Component A (Figure 2.4) of the distribution tariffs and transfer it to the regulated consumers. In the second case, reserve energy is funded by an energy levy that is collected among free and regulated consumers.

To secure the revenue stream and to limit off-taker risk, the distribution companies must provide an accounts receivable assignment to the IPP, meaning that revenue collected from end users will be deposited into a specific bank account, under the supervision of a managing bank, which will ensure that energy purchase contracts will be paid before the funds are made available to the distribution companies (Figure 2.15).

Finally, considering the complexity of the contracts and the market uncertainties, the Brazilian contracts establish arbitration as the primary mechanism for dispute settlement. The arbitration instrument is usually faster than the judicial and administrative courts and ensures that the arbitrators will be experts.

2.3.7 Auction implementation

Auction success, in general, is as much dependent on good auction design as on bidder trust in the auction process. The presence of a mandated, credible, well capacitated and well resourced agency responsible for managing and implementing the auction process is a critical success factor. Coordination among government entities is also essential to the success of the auction. The inputs of various government departments and agencies impact

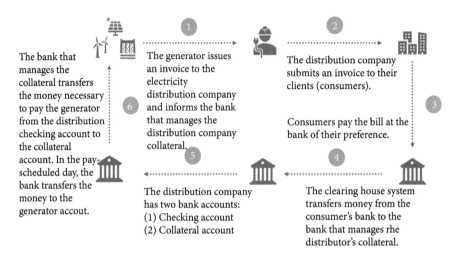

Figure 2.15 Accounts receivable scheme
Source: Authors' compilation.

the process of project pre-qualification, mainly because developers need to secure preliminary environmental permits and land use rights, which means a long and difficult process of engagement with federal, local, and state-level authorities (Figure 2.16).

In the Brazilian scheme, the auction programme is implemented by four institutions. The MME is responsible for setting the guidelines, the schedule, and the design of the auction, including bidding rules and winning selection criteria, and for issuing the call for projects registration.

The EPE is responsible for the pre-qualification stage, assessing the registered projects' datasheet and the documentation for land use rights and environmental permits. The information collected by the EPE during the pre-qualification process is used to prepare a technical note on the price cap of the auction and the maximum amount of energy each project will be allowed to sell. The EPE technical notes support the MME decision about those issues.

ANEEL prepares the draft contracts, performs the auction with the technical support of the CCEE, conducts the technical and financial qualification of the preferred bidders, and oversees the signature of the contracts and the completion of the projects in due time. The energy contracts are signed by the distribution companies and the reserve contracts by the CCEE.

The role of each institution is determined by Decree 5.163 but reflects the division of responsibilities established by the Brazilian regulatory framework, especially by Acts 9.427 and 10.848, that creates ANEEL and regulates the production and procurement of energy to the regulated consumers.

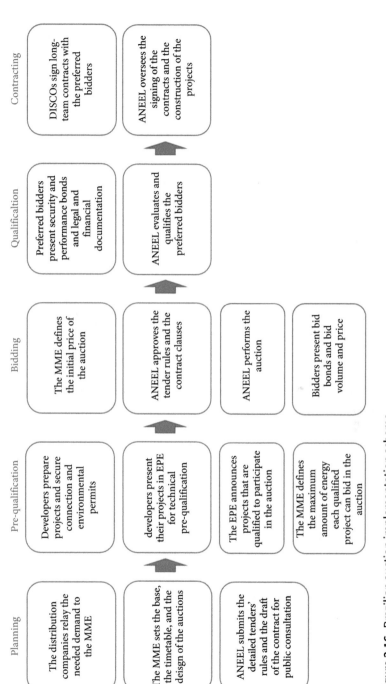

Figure 2.16 Brazilian auction implementation scheme

Source: Authors' compilation.

The designed process is complex and time-demanding but has been performed with a high level of transparency (every auction is preceded by a public consultation) and predictability, contributing to an increase in bidder confidence in the process and in political support.

The auction programme is funded by the buyers and sellers proportionally to the contracted energy. If the auction is cancelled or performed without the sale of energy, the auction costs will be paid entirely by the buyers in proportion to their announced demand. The cost of each auction is, however, low and covers only the expenditures of the CCEE since the MME, ANEEL, and the EPE are funded by public budget. The total cost of the thirtieth greenfield auction, performed on 18 October 2019, was, for example, US$ 13,000.

Finally, the auctions are performed electronically using a platform developed by the CCEE. The integrity of the process, the outcomes, and the security of the information exchanged during the auction are audited by an independent third party.

2.4 Results from Brazil's renewable energy auctions: An established track record of success

Brazil's regulated auctions contracted 9.571 TWh of energy between December 2004 and October 2019, of which 8.180 TWh was from new (greenfield) power projects, adding 105.2 GW (76.8 GW of RE) to the grid (Figures 2.17 and 2.18).

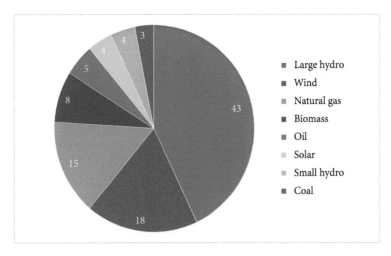

Figure 2.17 Brazilian auction outcomes: Contracted capacity (%)
Source: CCEE, www.ccee.org.br (accessed June 2020).

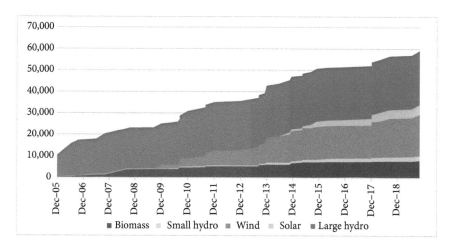

Figure 2.18 Brazilian auction outcomes: New capacity of renewable energy services (RES)

Source: CCEE, www.ccee.org.br (accessed June 2020).

The auction scheme also fosters the growth of non-conventional renewable sources in Brazil. This process was accompanied by an initial increase in the price of biomass and small hydro until December 2009, when the competition of wind power plants reversed the trend. The competitiveness of wind technology is partly explained by the worldwide reduction of the equipment costs due to technological advances and economies of scale but also reflects the development of local investment capacity. Additionally, the period was characterized by a gradual reduction in the cost of capital in Brazil.

In 2013, however, the wind price trends reversed again, and wind energy prices returned to the initial US$ 55/MWh level in November 2015, while the biomass price reached a peak of US$ 89/MWh in April 2015 (Figure 2.19). Two effects contributed to the price hike: first, the growth in the number of projects facing construction delays and the bankruptcy of a large local equipment provider increased investors' risk perception; second, the return of inflation acceleration in Brazil also reversed the downward trend in the basic interest rate (SELIC), making financing scarcer and costly.

Finally, the entry of solar PV energy into the market and the return of the interest rate reductions from 2015 gave new impetus to the reduction of energy prices in Brazil (Figure 2.19).

On the other hand, the emphasis of the Brazilian scheme on procuring new power plants implies a residual risk of delay or bankruptcy. Figures 2.20, 2.21, and 2.22 present the situation of 374 power plants in construction in October 2019 and show the capacity (in MW) deployment to comply with the contracted timetable. About 7% of solar PV, 30% of wind, and 50% of biomass

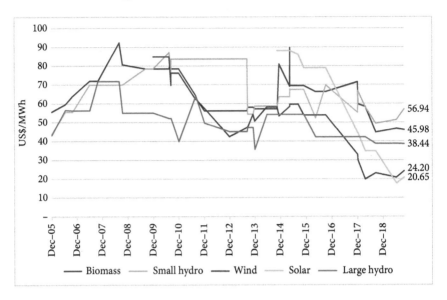

Figure 2.19 Brazilian auction outcomes: Prices

Source: CCEE, www.ccee.org.br (accessed June 2020).

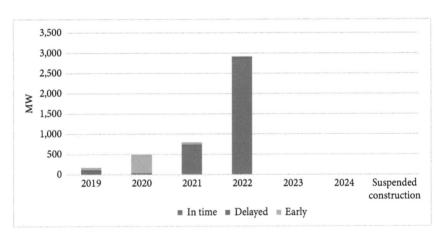

Figure 2.20 Photovoltaic (PV) power plants: Compliance with construction timetable

Source: ANEEL, www.aneel.gov.br (accessed June 2020).

power plants are delayed. More relevant, 14% of wind and 12% of biomass power plants do not even have a probable date of completion, indicating a strong likelihood that the contracts will be terminated.

The leading causes of delays are construction cost overruns (18%); the unanticipated difficulty of obtaining financing (26%); the difficulty obtaining construction, operation, and environmental permits (18%); delays in

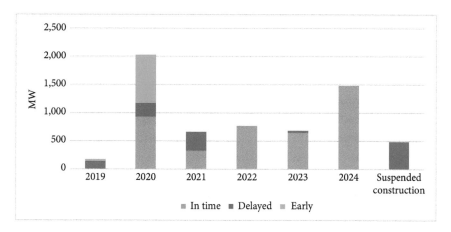

Figure 2.21 Wind power plants: Compliance with construction timetable
Source: ANEEL, www.aneel.gov.br (accessed June 2020).

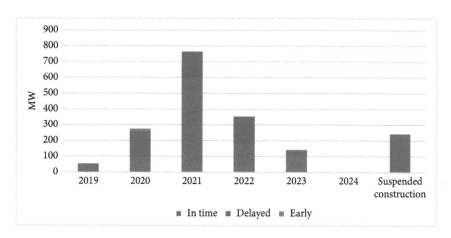

Figure 2.22 Biomass power plants: Compliance with construction timetable
Source: ANEEL, www.aneel.gov.br (accessed June 2020).

connecting to the transmission system (20%); and problems with equipment suppliers (12%).

As previously discussed, project realization delays and contract termination have plagued the Brazilian auctions in recent years (see section 2.3.6.3 and 2.3.6.4.2).

To reduce the environmental risk, the Brazilian auction scheme has a pre-qualification phase where the investors must present, at least, a preliminary environmental permit. However, some features of the Brazilian environmental licensing process make it very long, complex, and uncertain, and securing the preliminary permit does not guarantee that the construction and operation permits will be issued. Indeed, a report by the legislative consultancy of the Brazilian Federal Senate pointed out the main flaws of the environmental licensing process (Hofmann, 2015):

- the environment impact assessments and reports' extensive focus on the negative impact of the project, ignoring the positive externalities;
- the excessive imposition of conditioning factors and mitigating actions by the public authorities;
- the multiplicity of actors with discretionary power;
- the frequent judicial control;
- the absence of a strategic environmental policy;
- the scarcity of systematized environmental data and public information; and
- the excess of bureaucracy and the use of vague terms such as 'low environmental impact' and 'directly or indirectly affected area' in the resolutions and guidelines provided by CONAMA and the MMA.

Finally, despite following all the rules, the environmental, construction, and operation permits are not bonded. Thus, any public authority involved in the licensing process may request further studies and revise its previous understanding regarding the permits at any time, especially if an environmental or archaeological finding is identified. Thus, environmental risk in Brazil is very relevant and difficult to mitigate.

Transmission connection challenges were the result of the previously discussed approach to transmission system expansion planning and tendering, which initially would only commence after energy auctions were finalized. It is hoped that the new approach outlined in sections 2.3.6.3 and 2.3.6.4.2 will help to address this bottleneck.

Finally, the company IMPSA founded Wind Power Energia (WPE) in December 2006 to produce wind and hydroelectric equipment in Pernambuco. At the end of the first semester of 2014, the economic and financial situation of WPE began to deteriorate. After delays in the payment of international debts, on 5 December 2014, WPE requested judicial reorganization to avoid bankruptcy. The immediate outcome was the interruption of the delivery of all contracted equipment, amounting to an installed capacity of 1,580 MW, which resulted in the construction delay of 26 projects totalling 579.2 MW (ANEEL, 2016).

2.5 Lessons learned from Brazil's renewable energy auctions

The Brazilian auctions have been successful in scaling up private investment and the deployment of RE at fair prices, confirming that auctions are effective and efficient at revealing prices under uncertainty. Nevertheless, contracting power plants in the project phase involves risks related to cost overruns, construction delays, and price volatility that cannot be completely mitigated. Brazil's experience highlights important lessons on how these risks can be dealt with, both in terms of how auctions are implemented and designed.

2.5.1 Auction implementation

Effective and efficient auctions start with a comprehensive regulatory framework. The responsibility of each institution that takes part in the auction programme must be clearly defined and understood by all stakeholders. The institutions must act in cooperation and under the coordination of a single organization that clearly defines the role and the boundaries for each institution. Second, institutions must be adequately funded and provided with human resources.

Participating in auctions has significant transaction costs, including the cost of preparing and developing the project, obtaining permits, and providing bid bonds and other financial warranties. If auctions are not part of a periodic and predictable process, the risk of potential bidders is amplified, reducing their participation and, therefore, competition in the auction, so increasing the final price. Therefore, auctions should be as recurrent, transparent, and predictable as possible. The preparation and disclosure of a medium- and long-term expansion plan further assists greatly in this regard. Additionally, the high frequency and predictability of the auctions, combined with financing support from BNDES, reduced the investment risk for equipment manufacturers and construction service providers, increasing local content in the power plants without the need for specific requirements stipulated in the auction rules.

Developers and investors also need enough time to engage with the auction programme. Lead times must correspond with the longest time necessary to develop the project, secure the necessary permits and licences, and deploy a new power plant. The contract duration should also be long enough to provide investors with some cash-flow stability and predictability during the time required for loan maturity. Consequently, the contract duration should reflect the capital intensity of the technology, the principles of project financing, and the discount rate involved. The use of a portfolio of off-takers (aggregated demand of distribution companies) backed by an accounts receivable mechanism significantly mitigates payment risk and improves the developers' ability to access finance.

Auctioned contracts must be as straightforward and concise as possible, in order to avoid the ambiguity that may result in future litigation, but must also allocate the liability for the most common risks, limit exposure of each party involved, and clearly outline the procedures to be followed in the event of a claim.

The Brazilian experience also demonstrates that the auction programme can be used to address multiple goals with the use of complementary auctions with differences in the lead time, contract duration, and contractual obligations. The auction may demand specific renewable sources or multiples sources (mix of technologies or even technology neutral), but each energy source has an individual contract, specially designed to conciliate the need of the power system and the features of different energy sources.

2.5.2 Auction design

The design of energy auctions must consider three main goals. First, auctions must be attractive enough to investors to generate competition and to achieve optimal prices. Second, the auction design must ensure that the preferred bidders are reliable and have the technical and financial capability to build the projects on schedule and deliver the promised energy and capacity. Third, the auction design should ensure that the right mix of products is contracted to achieve the resource adequacy of the electric system (Viscidi and Yépez, 2020).

To improve competition, secure the bidder's commitment, and reduce the time needed to analyse more subjective aspects of legal and financial qualification, the Brazilian auctions are performed following three stages: the technical pre-qualification phase, the bidding phase, and the legal and financial qualification phase (only for the winning bids of the second stage).

Another challenge to auction design is to mitigate the winner's curse risk, understood as the failure of the investor to measure all project risks and costs (Krishna, 2002). The winner's curse cannot be entirely avoided, but there are some approaches to the design of the auction and the contracts that can mitigate its effects (Correia et al., n.d.). First, the auction rules, the draft contracts, and all the information necessary for the investor to elaborate on their bidding strategy must be made available well in advance. Second, a qualification phase mitigates part of the risk, given that the bidders must prove the feasibility of the project by presenting environmental permits and financial guarantees. Third, the auction's design may help to reduce the winner's curse risk. The time and money spent to prepare the projects and participate in the auction are a sunk cost and may influence bidders' strategy. The higher the sunk cost, the greater the risk aversion of losing the auction and the greater the aggressiveness of the bidder. Aggressive bidders think that it is more important not to lose the auction than seize a small gain of slightly increasing the bid. Consequently, the auctioneer may expect lower prices under a pay-as-bid sealed auction than under a pay-as-clear auction, but the trade-off might be a higher risk of the winner's curse in this scenario. On the other hand, a pay-as-clear process might extract less surplus from the seller and result in slightly higher prices but reduce the risk of the winner's curse.

The remaining risk must be addressed by the contracts. Contracts have multiple purposes. Primarily, they are both a legal and financial tool that protects both buyer and seller from spot price volatility. Additionally, contracts provide a predictable revenue stream that can be used as collateral for long-term financing of new projects and give commercial feasibility to existing power plants in markets with significant participation of variable RE or of energy sources with low marginal cost. Finally, contracts allocate risks, define liabilities, and offer guidance to act in cases of unanticipated contingencies. Therefore, to fulfil its objectives, the contract must be designed following certain principles (Correia et al., n.d.):

- simplicity: the contract must be as simple as possible to facilitate the understanding and enforcement of its clauses;
- coherence and comprehensiveness: the contractual clauses must be coherent with each other and with the regulatory framework and market development. The set of terms must be adequate, effective, and credible and ensure capacity to respond to a changing environment;
- clarity: the contract must clearly stipulate obligations, rights, and responsibilities;
- proportionality: the contract must provide a fair allocation of risk and liability;
- compliance promotion: the contract needs to be self-enforceable, and the potential conflict of interest must be mitigated by positive economic incentives and the reduction of administrative costs;

- reality check: the policymaker or regulator accountable for the contract design must systematically assess the contract fulfilment and the sectorial outcomes to ensure that the intended objectives have been efficiently and effectively achieved. Identified flaws should be solved in the new contract;
- funding: the contract must provide predictability and stability to the IPP cash flow.

One relevant risk for the procurement of power plants still in the project stage is the conciliation of the construction time of the power plant connection works and the deep connection works needed in the transmission grid. The combination of pre-emptive transmission corridor expansion, preliminary project elimination by connection point, and a reallocation of risk to generators for transmission delays is hoped to have sufficiently decreased the likelihood of this risk being realized.

2.6 Conclusion: A pioneering programme that is still world leading

Brazil is one of the pioneers in the systematic use of energy auctions as an instrument to support public policies. The Brazilian government structured its current auction programme in 2004 with the objectives of achieving energy security, improving the efficiency of electricity contracting for captive consumers, and promoting diversification of energy supply (especially for RE).

The auction programme achieved all initial objectives and was successful in unlocking private investment in new capacity. More significantly, the auction programme fostered the growth of non-conventional renewable sources in Brazil at increasingly competitive prices. The competitiveness of wind and solar technologies is partly explained by the worldwide reduction in the equipment costs, due to technological advances and economies of scale, but also reflects the development of local investment capacity and the design of the auction programme.

Regarding the implementation process, the responsibility of each institution that takes part in the auction programme is clearly defined under a comprehensive regulatory framework and understood by all stakeholders. Additionally, the Brazilian programme has benefited from the performance of adequately funded institutions provided with qualified technical personnel. In fact, since 2004, the auctions have performed following the same rules and structure, with only minor adjustments in contractual clauses and in the bidding mechanism (mostly to deal with transmission connection delays).

In terms of auction design, the simplicity of winner selection criteria and the use of different stages for the qualification of projects and pre-ferred bidders reduces the time consumed in the tender and mitigates the risk of litigation during the process. Moreover, because they are central-ized mechanisms, the design of the auction can help to reduce some risks related to the contracting and implementation of infrastructure projects. In the case of the Brazilian experience, special attention was given to reduc-ing the risk of off-taker payment and to the risk of delay in the construction of projects.

The off-taker of the energy auctions is the pool of all distribution compa-nies. Therefore, each preferred project signs a different contract with each distribution company in the pool, and only a fraction of the energy is com-mitted in each contract, mitigating the risk of payment. On the other hand, the amount of energy acquired by each distribution company is divided among several projects and the risk of delay is thus also mitigated. The auction also seeks to mitigate construction risk by using a pre-qualification process and by requiring surety and performance bonds.

Nevertheless, auctions are not able to overcome competitive market struc-ture problems or mitigate all risks associated with the implementation of infrastructure projects. Still, it is important that contracts establish the obli-gations and liabilities of generators and buyers. In the Brazilian approach, the majority of the risks related to the environmental licensing, site selection, and connection with the grid are allocated to generators, assuming that even when they are not able to manage the risk, they are better able to evaluate and price the risk.

Although there is not a one-size-fits-all auction model, other countries may use some of Brazil's lessons to implement energy auctions.

The existence of a stable institutional framework, where the role and responsibility of each institution in the electricity sector is clear and respected, is fundamental to the design and implementation of auctions. It is up to the sectoral Ministry to define a policy for renewable sources, clari-fying the expansion goals and the mechanisms to achieve them. For this, the existence of permanent technical staff, trained and with access to databases and mathematical optimization models, are essential for the elaboration of expansion plans. Staff can act exclusively at the Ministry or, as in Brazil, they can be part of an institution created to prepare the system expansion studies and assist the Ministry and other stakeholders in decision-making.

Equally, it is crucial to ensure that the regulatory agency has the technical and legal conditions to autonomously implement auction policies and guidelines, once they are defined, without interference from other government spheres.

Investors have high costs to participate in the auctions. They must locate and rent the appropriate land, contract anemometric or solarimetric data certification, prepare the project and the studies of connection to the power grid, conduct detailed studies of environmental and socio-economic impacts, and obtain the prior licence, deposit the bid bond, and so on. Therefore, it is essential to guarantee holding at least one annual auction to provide investors with security that, if they lose the auction, they will have new opportunities in the following years.

The greater the number of investors interested in the auction, the greater the auction competition and potential for success. The challenge for countries that are just initiating their auction programme is to attract a sufficient number of bidders. Thus, wide broadcasting of the auction is important. For example, Brazil discloses auctions at national and international events.

A frequent problem in encouraging local investors to participate in auctions is accessing finance. In Brazil, the National Bank for Economic and Social Development played a crucial role in financing auction winners. As shown, the auctions for guaranteeing long-term contracts have been an efficient mechanism for Brazil to attract investments from national and multinational private companies.

2.7 References

ANEEL (Brazil National Electricity Agency) (2016). 'Nota Técnica No. 309/2016-SCG/ANEEL'.

Correia, T. B., Melo, E., Costa, A. M., and Silva, A. J. (2006). 'Trajetoria das Reformas Institucionais da Industria Eletrica Brasileira e Novas Perspectivas de Mercado'. *Economia, 7*(3), 607–627.

Correia, T. B., Tolmasquim, M. T., and Hallack, M. (2020). *Guide for Designing Contracts for Renewable Energy Procured by Auctions.* Inter-American Development Bank: https://publications.iadb.org/publications/english/viewer/Guide-for-Designing-Contracts-for-Renewable-Energy-Procured-by-Auctions.pdf

Costa, C. do V. (2006). 'Políticas de Promoção de Fontes Novas e Renováveis para Geração de Energia Elétrica: Lições da Experiência Européia para o Caso Brasileiro'. Rio de Janeira. http://www.ppe.ufrj.br/images/publica%C3%A7%C3%B5es/doutorado/Claudia_do_Valle_Costa.pdf

Hanke, A.-K., and Tiedemann, S. (2020). *How (Not) to Respond to Low Competition in Renewable Energy Auctions Endogenous Rationing in Renewable Energy Auctions. 817619* (Brussels: AURES II project). http://aures2project.eu/wp-content/uploads/2020/06/AURES_II_Policy_Brief_End_Rationing.pdf

Hermes de Araújo, J. L. R., de Aragão da Costa, A. M., Correia, T., and Melo, E. (2008). 'Energy Contracting in Brazil and Electricity Prices'. *International Journal of Energy Sector Management, 2*(1), 36–51. https://doi.org/10.1108/17506220810859088.

Hochberg, M., and Poudineh, R. (2018). 'Renewable Auction Design in Theory and Practice: Lessons from the Experiences of Brazil and Mexico'. Oxford Institute for Energy Studies, https://www.oxfordenergy.org/publications/renewable-auction-design-theory-practice-lessons-experiences-brazil-mexico (accessed 18 April 2023).

Hofmann, R. M. (2015). *Gargalos do Licenciamento Ambiental Federal no Basil* (Rio de Janeira: Consultoria Legislativa).

Krishna, V. (2002). *Auction Theory* (Burlington, MA: Elsevier).

Tolmasquim, M. T. (2014). *Novo Modelo do Setor Elétrico Brasileiro* (2nd edn) (Rio de Janeiro: SYNERGIA EDITORA).

Viscidi, L., and Yépez, A. (2020). 'Clean Energy Auctions in Latin America'. Inter-American Development Bank, https://www.thedialogue.org/wp-content/uploads/2020/01/Clean_Energy_Auctions_in_Latin_America.pdf (accessed 18 April 2023).

World Bank Group: Energy and Extractives (2012). 'International Experience with Private Sector Participation in Power Grids: Peru Case Study', in *Energy Sector Management Assistance Program.* (Washington DC: World Bank). pp. 1–35. https://openknowledge.worldbank.org/server/api/core/bitstreams/13fbff81-3205-54c6-afe3-1eabc0cbbab1/content

3
Chile

Fostering Competitive Renewable Energy in a Complex Market

Pablo Serra

3.1 Introduction: Locating Chile's auctions in its complex market structure

The Chilean Electricity Act of 1982 created an electricity market where power generation companies and large customers negotiate energy supply contracts. The Act provides the interconnection of all electricity companies in the same area and open access to the transmission facilities. The Act further provides the coordination of electricity companies through an independent body—the Coordinator—to maintain the security of supply and operate the system at minimum cost[1]. Accordingly, the Coordinator dispatches the plants available for generation in ascending order of operating cost until demand is covered. Plant dispatch is thus independent of existing supply contracts. Hence, power-generation companies need to transfer energy between themselves to reconcile their contractual obligations with dispatch orders. The Coordinator computes these reconciliations on an hourly basis.

This chapter focuses on the energy supply contracts that distribution companies, as mandated by law, auction on behalf of their regulated customers. The auctioneer—the pool of distribution companies—auctions long-term contracts (up to 20 years) at least 5 years before the start of supply. It selects the bids that meet the total energy requirements at the lowest cost. A contract awardee also receives a capacity payment, which equals the energy withdrawn by the distribution companies attributed to that contract during the system's peak demand hours, valued at the contractual capacity price.

[1] These rules created a marketplace for generators and large consumers, including distributors, to trade energy supply contracts.

Pablo Serra, *Chile*. In: *Renewable Energy Auctions: Lessons from the Global South*. Edited by: Anton Eberhard and Wikus Kruger, Oxford University Press. © Oxford University Press (2023). DOI: 10.1093/oso/9780192871701.003.0003

The Act required bidders to back up their bids with installed or planned power plants, which could be of any technology, including fossil-fuel power plants. In early auctions, the capacity-backing requirement played the role of guaranteeing contract performance. Since the 2017 auction, the rules require bidders to show that they will have the capacity to supply the electricity offered during the first five years of the contract.

Awardees are contractually obliged to deliver energy according to the needs of the distribution companies' clients. They can purchase power on the spot market to cover any shortfall in supply. This arrangement allows generators backed by non-dispatchable renewable energy (RE) technologies to participate in the auctions. On the other hand, the exposure to the spot price is a risk for them. They may have energy shortfalls in hours when the spot price is high and, conversely, energy surpluses when the spot price is low.

In 2015, to reduce the risk of exposure to the spot price for variable RE, Chile's government introduced the auctioning of power supply contracts restricted to time blocks reflecting the generation profile of wind and solar photovoltaic (PV) plants. The available results point to a limited benefit for RE bidders.

In the tenders held between 2015 and 2017, the auctioneer awarded contracts totalling 323,400 megawatt hours (MWh) (16,170 MWh per year for 20 years). The number of bidders grew dramatically compared to previous years, and the prices offered fell sharply. The sharp drop in RE generation costs, especially PV and wind power, explains this change. All new projects backing bids during this period were RE plants, and the trend of awarded prices closely followed those in successful auctions for RE energy in the rest of the world.

This outcome is striking given bidders' exposition to spot prices, which is not necessarily true in other countries. The auctions have also been performance-effective. All the awardees have fulfilled their financial obligations arising from their participation in the system's mechanism to settle imbalances, except for an awardee in the 2010 auction.

In this chapter, we analyse the Chilean auction design, implementation, and results against the backdrop of the power market design. Section 3.2 provides some essential background about Chile's economy. In Section 3.3, we describe the power sector. In Section 3.4, we focus on energy auctions. In Section 3.5, we present the programme's results. Section 3.6 outlines the lessons learned and makes some recommendations, and Section 3.7 contains our conclusions.

3.2 Overview of Chile's economy

Chile is located in the south of South America and borders the Pacific Ocean to the West and the Andes Mountains to the East. The country shares borders with Argentina, Bolivia, and Peru and has approximately 19.1 million inhabitants, of whom 7.9 million live in the 'Metropolitan Region', that includes the capital, Santiago.

Politically, the country is a democracy with a presidential regime and a bicameral legislature. Since the return to democracy in 1990, following the end of the military dictatorship of Augusto Pinochet, the country enjoyed remarkable political stability. However, social unrest has increased recently due to discontent with the country's unequal wealth distribution.

The country experienced high economic growth from 1990 to 2015, reaching one of the highest gross domestic product (GDP) per capita in Latin America in current and purchasing-power-adjusted terms (Figure 3.1). As a result, Chile is classified as a 'high-income' country by the World Bank and is a member of the Organisation for Economic Co-operation and Development (OECD). Chile ranks 59 out of 190 countries in the World Bank's Doing Business ranking and has deep, competitive financial markets.

Recently, the country's economic fortunes have declined due to the wave of protests that started in October 2019, the deterioration of its terms of trade due to conflicts between China and the United States, and the crisis caused by the COVID-19 pandemic.

Social unrest has caused uncertainty in the business environment, especially after the referendum on 25 October 2020, in which almost 80% of

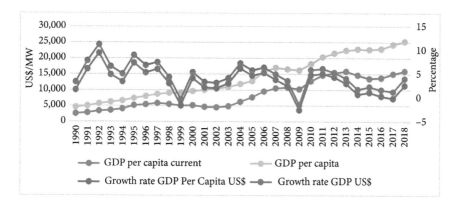

Figure 3.1 Chile's GDP per capita and growth rate, 1990–2018
Source: World Bank.

voters approved changing the constitution. These events led to a significant depreciation of the Chilean peso, which dropped 19.9% against the US dollar between 18 October 2019, when protests began, and 18 March 2020, when the government declared a state of emergency due to the coronavirus pandemic. The local Selective Stock Price Index, which measures the performance of the 40 most traded stocks on the Santiago stock exchange, fell 44.4% in the same period.[2]

3.3 Chile's power sector

3.3.1 National Electric System

Chile's National Electricity System (NES) links the city of Arica with the Chiloé Islands through a transmission network that extends for about 3,000 km and covers a long and narrow territory where 797% of Chileans live. The NES resulted from the interconnection on 21 November 2017 of two systems: the Big North Interconnected System (BNIS), with 5,288 MW, and the Central Interconnected System (CIS), with 17,081 MW. By 2019, the NES had an installed generation capacity of over 25 gigawatts (GW) and supplied a maximum demand of 11 GW (Table 3.1).[3]

Figure 3.2 shows strong growth in installed capacity from 2010 to 2019. It also reflects a highly concentrated market, although decreasing over time. In 2019, four companies (AES Gener, Enel, Engie, and Colbún), of which local investors control only one (Colbún), accounted for 78% of the total generation.

Figure 3.3 shows the evolution of installed capacity by technology. Until the mid-1990s, hydropower was the dominant source. In the CIS, it accounted for 86% of total power generation in 1995. From the 1990s, the growing opposition from environmental and indigenous groups slowed the construction of new hydropower plants. Since then, only two hydroelectric power plants have started operation: Ralco in 2004 and Angostura in 2014. The rapid expansion of combined-cycle gas turbines (CCGTs) fuelled by Argentine natural gas brought by pipelines offset the decline in hydroelectricity investment.

---

[2] Since that date, the Chilean peso has appreciated, and the stock market index has partially recovered due to decreased unrest and terms of trade improvement.

[3] Three reasons explain the low usage of the system's installed capacity: (i) the high (50%) participation of RE technologies with an average capacity factor of 31%, (ii) the low dispatch of gas-fired plants due to the high cost of generating power with liquefied natural gas (LNG), and (iii) over-investment in backup capacity caused by a regulatory failure (see section 3.6.1).

Table 3.1 Key information on Chile's electricity sector, 2019

Technology	Installed capacity (MW)	Installed capacity (%)	Generation (GWh)	Generation (%)
Coal	4,825	19	28,372	36.8
Natural gas	4,840	19	14,127	18,3
Diesel	3,140	13	552	0,7
Hydro reservoir	3,355	13	9,230	12
Hydro run-of-river (> 20 MW)	2,820	11	9,729	12,6
Mini hydro run-of-river (< 20 MW)	516	2	1,834	2,4
Biomass	514	2	1,819	2,4
Cogeneration	18	0	130	0,2
Geothermal	40	0	202	0,3
Solar	2,886	12	6,300	8,2
Wind	2,136	9	4,799	6,2
Total	25,090	100	77,094	100
Electricity access rates (%)				
Urban	100			
Rural	96.5			
Peak demand (MW)	10,900			

Source: Commission, 2020, http://energiaabierta.cl/blockchain; https://www.cne.cl/en/estadisticas/electricidad (both accessed 16 April 2023).

From 2005, due to Argentina's restrictions and taxes on gas exports, diesel plants were built to substitute CCGTs. Also, some CCGTs became dual-fuel plants. After the construction of gas terminals, gas-fired generation recovered somewhat, but coal-fired power plants covered the demand growth due to lower costs. In recent years, due to strong citizen opposition to the construction of fossil-fuel power plants and the sharp drop in solar and wind costs, these non-conventional renewable energies (NCREs) expanded rapidly (Figures 3.3 and 3.4)[4].

3.3.2 Power-sector structure

Creating the institution for designing and implementing the energy markets was the first milestone in Chile's electric reform (Figure 3.5 and Table 3.2).

---

[4] The NCRE legal definition excludes hydroelectric plants > 20 MW.

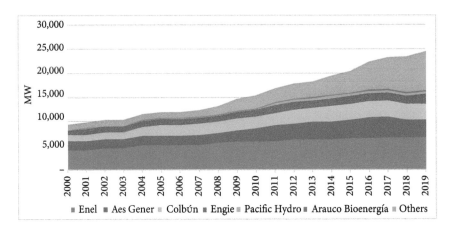

Figure 3.2 Installed capacity by owner, national electrical system (NES)

Source: Authors' compilation based on Commission (2020), http://energiaabierta.cl/blockchain (accessed 13 April 2023).

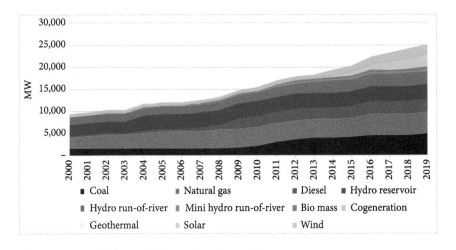

Figure 3.3 Installed capacity by technology, NES

Source: Authors' compilation based on Commission (2020), http://energiaabierta.cl/blockchain (accessed 13 April 2023).

The National Energy Commission (Commission), instituted in 1978, was made responsible for, among other functions, proposing sectoral policies and calculating regulated tariffs.[5] The Commission's primary task was the elaboration of the Electricity Act of 1982, which laid the foundations for the

---

[5] Previously, the sectoral policy had been mainly in the hands of Endesa, the largest state-owned electric company in charge of the country's electrification plan.

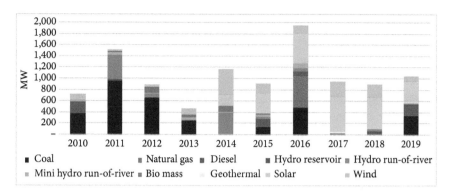

Figure 3.4 New installed capacity, NES

Source: Authors' compilation based on Commission (2020), http://energiaabierta.cl/blockchain (accessed 13 April 2023).

current regulation. The law distinguished three activities—generating, transmitting, and distributing electricity—although it did not initially prohibit vertical integration.

The government, as well as enacting the new Act, restructured the electricity sector, creating new companies from the old, state-owned companies. The government separated the two largest electricity companies (Endesa and Chilectra) into seven generation companies and eight distribution companies and privatized most of them between 1986 and 1989.[6]

Since its inception, the Electricity Law has undergone numerous changes. The following summarizes the latest version, incorporating some historical footnotes.

3.3.2.1 Generation

Following the cost minimization mandate, the Coordinator dispatches plants in ascending order of operating cost until demand is met (merit-order dispatch). Generators need to cover their contractual supply obligations by generating sufficient power (and being dispatched) or buying power on the spot market. In each hour, a generator's energy surplus (deficit) equals the difference between its injections into the system, following the Coordinator's dispatch orders, and its energy withdrawals to fulfil its contractual supply obligations. In turn, its surplus (deficit) of capacity equals the difference between its availability to supply energy reliably at times of peak demand, the so-called sufficiency power, and the peak energy demand of its customers.[7]

---

[6] The subdivision also created two small, vertically integrated companies in the country's south.
[7] A generator's sufficiency power is the sum of the sufficiency power of its plants. The sufficiency power of a plant considers the available statistical information from the last five years and, thus, is unrelated to

The Act stipulates valuing these reconciliation transfers using peak-load pricing[8] consisting of energy and capacity charges. The former equals the system's short-term marginal cost of generation, while the latter is the marginal cost of capacity. The Coordinator approximates[9] the energy charge by using the operating cost of the last unit dispatched and the capacity charge by using the annuity that pays for the cheapest possible generating units capable of supplying additional power at peak hours.

The mechanism for adjusting hourly energy imbalances is not a market in itself. However, the administratively computed energy price matches the equilibrium price if the market were perfectly competitive (see, for instance, Arellano and Serra, 2010). Thus, using an almost universal denomination, we refer to it as the spot market and the system's short-term marginal energy cost as the spot price.

3.3.2.2 Transmission

The Act provides that the Commission is responsible for developing annual transmission expansion plans to identify the projects required by the system. The Coordinator publicly auctions the expansion projects based on the annual payments requested to build and operate the project for 20 years.

The Commission computes the remuneration of facilities exceeding 20 years and non-auctioned old ones. Generators pay each transmission segment remuneration through a two-part tariff. It consists of a variable-usage charge equal to the marginal congestion cost and a fixed component that covers the difference between the transmission remuneration and the congestion revenue. Generators finance the fixed charge in proportion to their energy sales, irrespective of the segments they use. Most contracts to supply unregulated customers provide for the pass-through of the fixed cost to customers.

Those facilities built primarily to supply energy to unregulated users or evacuate it from generating plants, which are known as dedicated

---

its past, present, or future generation. It includes forced outage rates, maintenance, fuel availability for thermal units, water availability in hydroelectric plants, and plant factors in solar and wind plants. The sufficiency power for a solar or wind power plant equals the minimum between its lowest annual capacity factor and the simple average of its capacity factor for each of the 52 hours with the highest demand. The plants' sufficiency powers are scaled down so that their sum equals maximum demand plus a reserve margin.

[8] It corresponds to the pricing at the marginal cost of a non-storable product (Boiteux, 1960).

[9] This definition of instant marginal cost ignores constraints, such as plant ramp-up times, that affect system dispatch and is, therefore, an approximation of the actual marginal cost of the system (Muñoz et al., 2021). It has become less accurate with the expansion of PV and wind plants.

transmission systems (DTSs), are paid for by their users.[10] The Act distinguishes a particular type of dedicated system: the development pole transmission system (DPTS). The DPTSs evacuate energy from areas the Ministry of Energy classified as generation development poles. The latter is a territorially identifiable area with renewable energy resources whose exploitation using a single transmission system is in the public interest.

Finally, the Act also limits the ownership stakes of generators or distributors in transmission companies to 8% individually and 40% when combined and excludes owners of transmission facilities from participating in generation or distribution.

3.3.2.3 Distribution

The Act considers electricity distribution companies to be natural monopolies and thus regulates them. Regulated customers—those with a maximum demand below 0.5 MW or with a maximum demand between 0.5 and 5 MW who choose to be regulated—purchase electricity from distribution companies.[11] They pay a tariff composed of the average price at which distribution companies purchase electricity from generators, the transmission cost, and the distribution cost.[12] The latter is set through a regulated process so that an efficient company achieves a given rate of return on its assets. The Commission calculates this rate using the capital asset pricing model (CAPM)[13] but is limited to a range between 6% and 8%.[14] Distribution companies purchase energy (and power) on behalf of their regulated customers by auctioning long-term procurement contracts.

3.3.3 Tariff levels and financial sustainability

The risk profile of the largest electricity companies in Chile is moderate (Table 3.3). The sector's financial health is better measured under conditions of systemic stress, situations for which risk classifications are less reliable.

---

[10] Initially, transmission service providers and generators directly negotiated the transmission tolls. In 1990, a legal amendment set up a mandatory binding arbitration process if parties did not reach an agreement. The actual regulation dates from 2016.

[11] Until 2004, regulated customers were those with a maximum demand of less than, or equal to, 2 MW.

[12] It also includes a charge for financing the Coordinator and the Energy Expert Panel.

[13] The CAPM expresses the relationship between systemic risk and expected returns on assets. The formula for calculating the expected return of an asset given its risk is as follows:

$$ER_i = R_f + \beta_i(ER_m - R_f),$$

where ER_i = expected return on investment, R_f = risk-free rate, β_i = systemic risk of the investment, and $(ER_m - R_f)$ = market risk premium.

[14] Before 2019, the discount rate was fixed at 10%.

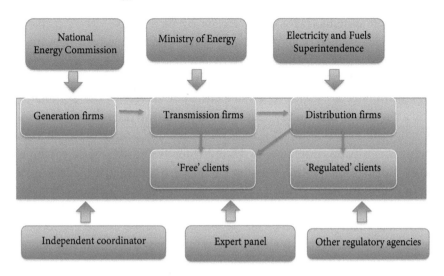

Figure 3.5 Chilean power sector institutional set-up

Source: Authors' compilation.

The Chilean system has experienced and survived a few of these situations, including severe droughts.

The risk of non-payment for generators holding contracts to supply regulated customers is low. The contract off-takers—the distribution companies—have a low insolvency risk. The tariffs of these companies are set through processes that offer guarantees to the parties. The independent Expert Panel resolves discrepancies, and the risk of regulatory expropriation is therefore remote.

3.3.4 Policy framework

The country's electricity policy aims to ensure a safe and efficient supply with a low environmental impact. The current focus is reducing emissions and increasing competition in the auctions to supply regulated customers. The first policy objective is reducing pollution in the so-called sacrifice zones and contributing to the global reduction of greenhouse gas emissions in response to social demands and international commitments.[15]

The primary tool to reduce greenhouse gas emissions is promoting NCRE. In 2005, a legal amendment exempted RE plants smaller than 9 MW from

---

[15] Chile's 'National Contribution to the Paris Climate Agreement 2015' commits the country to a 30% reduction in greenhouse gas emissions per unit of GDP by 2030 compared to 2007.

Table 3.2 Key institutions in Chile's electricity sector[a]

The Ministry of Energy	Created in 2010, it is responsible for preparing and coordinating plans, policies, and regulations for the proper functioning and development of the sector (including compliance assurance). It carries out a prospective study of the electricity sector every five years called the energy planning process. When needed, the Ministry implements up to two public auctions a year to cover the unmet part of the obligation for 20% of the energy withdrawn by the generators to be non-conventional renewable energy (NCRE).
National Energy Commission	This agency, created in 1978, is linked to the President of the Republic through the Ministry of Energy. It is responsible for determining prices, tariffs, and technical standards that electricity companies must follow. The Commission develops annual expansion plans for the transmission system, taking into account the five-year prospective plan developed by the Ministry. It designs, coordinates, and directs the implementation of the auctions that distribution companies must carry out to contract the electricity supply for their regulated customers.
Electricity and Fuels Superintendence	Created in 1985, it is linked to the President of the Republic through the Ministry of Energy. It ensures that companies comply with the sector's regulations and that the Coordinator fulfils its functions and legal obligations. It receives and resolves user complaints and determines whether firms must compensate users in case of a service outage.
National Independent Coordinator	Headed by a five-member board, the Coordinator is responsible for, among other tasks, (i) formulating the system's operation and maintenance programmes, (ii) dispatching power plants, (iii) calculating the hourly marginal costs of the system, (iv) computing the economic transfers between companies, and (v) implementing international auctions for the construction and operation of the new transmission projects and the expansion of existing ones. A committee composed of the head of the National Energy Commission, a System of Senior Public Officials Council councillor, an Energy Expert Panel member, and a Competition Tribunal judge elect the Coordinator's board members.
Energy Expert Panel	Created in 1994, the Energy Expert Panel members are appointed by the Competition Tribunal. It rules on discrepancies about (i) matters expressly indicated in the laws and (ii) those arising between the Coordinator and the companies subject to its coordination concerning internal procedures, instructions, and any other act of coordination of the system's operation and the electricity market. The rulings are binding on all participating in the process, and no ordinary or extraordinary appeals are admissible.

Note: [a] The Environmental Evaluation Service approves the Environmental Qualification Resolutions required for developing new projects, and the Superintendence of the Environment monitors compliance with environmental regulations. Their decisions may be appealed before the environmental courts.
Source: Authors' compilation.

Table 3.3 Fitch ratings of Chilean electricity companies

Company	Date	Distri- bution (%)	Trans- mission (%)	Gene- ration (%)	Ratings	
					Local	Inter- national
Chilquinta Energía S.A.	November 2020	85	15	–	AA	–
Compañía General de Electricidad S.A.	April 2019	66	34	–	A+	–
Transelec S.A.	January 2020	–	100	–	AA–	BBB
Engie Energía Chile S.A.	June 2020	–	–	100	AA	BBB+
AES Gener S.A.	July 2020	–	–	100	A+	BBB–
ENEL Chile S.A.	January 2011	20	–	80	AA+	A–
Colbún S.A.	December 2020	–	–	100	AA	BBB+

Source: https://www.fitchratings.com (accessed 16 April 2023).

paying transmission tolls, and benefited plants between 9 and 20 MW proportionally. It also gave NCRE generators the right to supply up to 5% of regulated customers' demand at the average price of standing contracts.

No NCRE generator used this right to supply because the price was not attractive for them, and in 2008, a new amendment replaced it with a renewable energy power obligation (REPO). The REPO stipulates that at least 10% of the energy that generators with an installed capacity of more than 200 MW supply their customers has to come from their own or contracted NCRE facilities. The non-compliance fee was set at 0.4 "unidades tributarias mensuales" (UTM) ($\approx$ US\$ 25, using the 31 December 2020 exchange rate) for each MWh of NCRE deficit.

In 2013, the government increased the REPO to 20%. It also established that the Ministry of Energy would conduct up to two public auctions per year for the uncovered portion of the REPO.[16] So far, it has not been necessary to hold these auctions, and it is unlikely that this will happen in the future since NCRE has been so competitive in the 'normal' auctions.

Finally, the 2016 legal amendment introduced the DPTSs to favour NCRE expansion. It allows constructing a single transmission system to evacuate the energy for all the plants in the area, taking advantage of scale economies.

---

[16] Since the amendment has transitional articles that lower the requirement for existing energy supply contracts, the 20% requirement will only come into full force in 2025.

Generators would only pay for the capacity they use. So far, the Ministry has not identified any development pole.[17]

3.3.4.1 Planning

The Ministry of Energy conducts a 30-year prospective study of the electricity sector called the energy planning process every five years. This study is the basis for developing plans, policies, and regulations for the proper functioning and development of the sector. It includes electricity supply-and-demand projections. The Commission must consider the prospective study in the annual transmission planning process mentioned earlier.

The government does not undertake distribution planning, although the tariff-setting process considers non-binding expansion plans. Nevertheless, distribution companies are obliged to provide service to anyone who requests it, and failure to comply with this requirement could lead to the cancellation of the concession.

Regarding generation, there is no formal planning process beyond the Ministry's prospective study, but authorities have various tools to ensure energy security. First, the yearly power sufficiency balance that measures the system's ability to supply peak demand alerts authorities about potential capacity gaps. Second, the Commission prepares an annual report with projections of the expected availability of electricity in the following years (see section 3.4.2.1).

3.4 The design of Chile's energy auctions

This section analyses the legal framework introduced in 2005 that has governed the energy auctions held since then (see Table 3.4[18]). It obliges distribution companies—individually or collectively—to auction five years in advance long-term contracts (up to 20 years) to cover the energy needs of their regulated customers. Auctioneers must choose the combination of bids that minimizes the supply costs. The award prices are the contract awardees' bid prices (pay-as-bid). The off-takers are the distribution companies, which pass on the awarded prices to their customers.

---

[17] These pole areas resemble the South African Renewable Energy Development Zones (REDZs), defined as geographical areas most suitable for the rollout of wind and solar energy projects and the supporting electricity grid network (McEwan, 2017).

[18] Until 1998, distribution companies bought energy for their regulated customers at a price set by the regulator. From that year onwards, distributors had to auction supply contracts at a price that could not exceed a ceiling set by the regulator.

Table 3.4 Key auction information

Design	Year of introduction	2005
	Frequency of auctions/rounds	15 rounds to date
	Volume requested per auction (maximums)	2015: 1,200 GWh/year 2016: 12,430 GWh/year 2017: 2,200 GWh/year Demand is divided into hourly or quarterly blocks. Commission determines volume based on demand estimations by the distribution companies.
	Technology requested (supply specification)	Technology neutral (includes fossil fuels)
	Power purchase agreement length	Up to 20 years (before 2015: up to 15 years)
	Currency	US$. Energy price is indexed to the weighted average of five international price indexes with weights chosen by bidders. Capacity price is indexed to the US consumer price index (CPI).
Implementation	Policy and regulation guidelines	Energy Ministry
	Regulatory authority	National Energy Commission
	Procurer	National Energy Commission
	Off-taker	Distribution companies
Outcomes	MWh procured 2015–2017	Volume requested
	Capacity of projects backing successful bids 2015-2017	Wind 3,919 MW, solar 1,822 MW, mini hydro 18
	Prices (2017, US ¢/kWh)	Energy: average: 3,25 Daytime block (8am–6pm), average: 3,16, lowest bid: 2,15 (solar PV) Capacity (power): 7.9980 US$/kW/month (set in auction rules)

Source: Authors' compilation based on the database provided in https://www.licitacioneselectricas.cl (accessed 16 April 2023).

While the auctions are for electricity supply, the rules require bidders to specify the capacity that supports their bids. This pre-qualification condition is technology-neutral and can include uncontracted standing installed capacity or new projects.

In 2015, authorities dissatisfied with the auctions' outcomes amended the Act to expand the role of the Commission and increase competition, especially by reducing the risks to new entrants. The main changes were

(i) entrusting the Commission to convene, design, coordinate, and direct the execution of the auctions; (ii) keeping price ceilings reserved until the opening of bids; (iii) increasing the time to start supply from 3 to 5 years; and (iv) extending the maximum duration of contracts from 15 to 20 years.

The reform also allows awardees who supported their bids with projects to request their postponement for up to two years or terminate the contract if the projects are delayed or prove unfeasible for reasons beyond their control. The auction rules had established rates of 10 Unidad de Fomento (unit of account, UF) (US$ 409) per month of delay and 360 UF (US$ 14,730) for the termination of the contract per GWh contracted for the last year of the contract (LYOC). Awardees can make these requests up to three years after signing the contract. The new regulation also permits awardees to request a contract change in the event of permanent modifications in regulations or taxes that significantly increase costs.[19]

As explained below, the 2015 amendment to the Electricity Act also provides that auctioneers should minimize the cost of supply, taking into account supply security and diversification objectives. The diversification objective led to the decision to tender supply contracts for time blocks that fit the generation profile of variable RE technologies. Time blocks purport to reduce the risk of spot price exposure for variable RE and thus encourage their installation.

3.4.1 Awardees' power payments

Successful bidders receive capacity payments in addition to the energy payment. Distributors pay suppliers for the energy delivered at the peak hour, valued at the capacity price set out in the auction rules. In each billing period, distribution companies allocate the energy they withdrew during the system's peak demand hour among its suppliers based on the energy each generator supplied during the time block that contains the maximum hourly demand recorded. Distributors inform the Coordinator of the allocation among suppliers of their energy withdrawal at the system's peak demand hour needed to calculate the reconciliation power transfers.

---

[19] The 2017 and 2019 auction terms consider a cost increase of 2% or more significant, while in 2015, the figure was 10%. The Commission has to authorize any contractual amendment, and interested parties, including consumer associations, may appeal against the decision to the Expert Panel.

3.4.2 Auction design

The information below considers the rules for the three auctions held after the 2015 legal amendments. They are broadly similar except for the significant increase in guarantee requirements from 2017. Changes include the provision performance bond, doubling the bid bond per unit, and requiring bidders to show that their projected capacity is enough to supply their contracts. This change may respond to concerns about the economic viability of contracts awarded in previous years at prices that some analysts considered surprisingly low (Cruzate, 2017; del Río, 2017). However, bid prices fell sharply again in the 2017 auction.

The auction process begins with an international request for proposals and the publication of the auction terms. Potential bidders have three months to consult the auctioneers about the auction rules. The auctioneer, in turn, has approximately one month to provide public responses. The deadline for submitting proposals is about six months after the beginning of the process (Table 3.5).

Bidders submit administrative and financial proposals in separate sealed envelopes. The auctioneer first opens the administrative envelope, and those bidders passing this stage go on to the next. Then the ceiling prices are revealed, and the bidders whose price bids exceed them can modify their bids according to directions set in the auction rules (see section 3.4.2.3), after which comes the public opening of the financial proposals. Finally, the auctioneer chooses the winning bids.

3.4.2.1 Auction demand

Annually, the Commission prepares a report projecting the electricity available capacity and demand for the following years. After drawing up the report, the Commission initiates an auction process if necessary, considering the distributors' obligation to contract the energy to supply their regulated customers five years in advance.[20] It prepares and publicizes the auction rules. The rules must specify, at least, the energy that distributors must auction, the supply time blocks (see below), the years covered by the contract, and the criteria and algorithms for the economic evaluation of the bids.

Supply blocks are a relatively unique feature of Chilean auctions. The 2017 auction, for instance, offered three hourly time blocks: block A: between 11:00pm and 07:59am the next day; block B: between 08:00am and 5:59pm;

---

[20] This report is subject to the same regime of observations submitted to the Commission and dispute adjudication by the Panel as any other regulatory action of the Commission.

Table 3.5 Schedule of the three last auctions

2015–02	2015–01	2017–01	Stage
19 June 2015	29 May 2015	30 January 2017	International call for tenders. The consultation period and the sale of the auction terms start
7 August 2015	30 December 2015	26 April 2017	End of the consultation period
26 August 2015	29 January 2016	31 May 2017	Last date for answering queries
28 August 2015	11 July 2016	11 August 2017	Last date to modify auction bases
14 October 2015	27 July 2016	11 October 2017	Deadline for submission of proposals
14 October 2015	4 August 2016	19 October 2017	Publication of evaluation of administrative proposals
21 October 2015	9 August 2016	24 October 2017	Submission of rectified administrative proposals and opening of the envelope with the ceiling price
19 October 2015	12 August 2016	26 October 2017	Day for submitting rectified economic proposals
23 October 2015	16 August 2016	30 October 2017	Public release of economic offers
26 October 2015	17 August 2016	3 November 2017	Announcement of the first-round awardees or call for the second round of bids
4 November 2015	25 August 2016	9 November 2017	Second-round bid submission (if needed)
4 November 2015	25 August 2016	10 November 2017	Declaration of second-round awardees (if needed)
10 November 2015	31 August 2016	15 November 2017	Deadline to report the auction's results to the Commission
4 March 2016	30 September 2016	15 December 2017	Contract signing
4 March 2016	30 October 2016	15 January 2018	Contract registration in the Electricity and Fuels Superintendence

Source: Authors' compilation based on the database provided in https://www.licitacioneselectricas.cl (accessed 16 April 2023).

and block C: between 6:00pm and 10:59pm. Block A resembles the PV generation profile, and block B is in line with the profile of wind generation. A generator that wins a contract in block A must deliver energy to the contracting distribution company only during that hours.

The 2017 auction also tendered quarterly (seasonal) blocks, having in mind run-of-river hydropower plants. These plants have greater water availability in the third and fourth quarters of the year because of winter rains and the later melting of mountain snow (James, 2017). Two bidders with run-of-river hydropower projects submitted bids for the third and fourth, but neither won. The terms for the cancelled 2019 auction did not repeat the quarterly blocks.

The auction rules also divide the time blocks into sub-blocks to facilitate small firms' participation. The sub-blocks are simply a fraction of the total block, usually of equal size. For example, a 5,000 MW time block subdivided into 100 sub-blocks of 50 MW each. Bidders can submit a bid price for each sub-block or sub-block package. They can also condition a bid submitted for a sub-block package on winning a minimum number of them. For example, a bidder submitting a bid for 80 sub-blocks in block A may condition it on winning at least 60.[21] Bidders may also link bundles of different blocks into a conditioned bid. A generator could submit offers to supply 50 and 40 sub-blocks in blocks A and B, respectively, but conditioned on winning both bundles or neither.[22] These conditioned bids are referred to as linked bids.

3.4.2.2 Qualification criteria and process

The law establishes that a by-law will determine the requirements and conditions bidders must satisfy. The by-law further expands on these obligations but relegates the details to the auction rules. Parties interested in participating in an auction must first acquire the auction rules. To bid, they need to provide specified legal and financial company documents, detail the generation sources that support their bids, and provide a bid bond. There are no additional requirements.

3.4.2.2.1 Legal and financial pre-qualification

Chilean or foreign legal entities may participate in the auctions under the same conditions, individually or in a consortium or association. Bidders who are not a corporation or a joint-stock company incorporated in Chile with power generation as their only line of business are obliged to constitute one if they win a contract. To this end, they must provide a guarantee of 100 UF (US\$ 4,090) for each GWh offered for the LYOC.

---

[21] The need to secure bidders a minimum amount of energy to build a project justifies this option.
[22] A potential bidder with a dispatchable generation technology can improve its bid by ensuring the sale of energy throughout the day at attractive prices, not just at certain hours of the day.

Bidders must also submit audited financial statements for the previous three years and be rated no less than BB+ (Chilean classification) by a risk-rating company listed in the auction rules.[23] For bidders that back their bids with generation projects, a risk classification report prepared by one of these risk-rating companies must evaluate the projects, including the experience in the field of the developer or sponsor of the projects.

3.4.2.2.2 Bid bonds

In the 2017 auction, bidders had to provide bid bonds of 200 UF (US$ 8,180) for each GWh offered for the LYOC. The auctioneers must collect the bid bond when a bidder withdraws or fails to comply with the auction rules. The auctioneer returns bonds to unsuccessful bidders. Awardees receive their bid bonds back once they have signed the respective supply contract and delivered the guarantees provided in the contract (see section 3.4.2.4.1).

3.4.2.2.3 Generation sources that back up the bid

Bidders must identify existing and projected power-generation sources backing up their offers, specifying the technology; installed capacity; current or planned location; start-up date, when appropriate; primary fuel (and its provider), when applicable; existing or expected point of connection to the system; and the predicted capacity factors. There are no caps on project sizes.

Bidders must also indicate their current contracts with free and regulated customers and their expected generation capacities based on design capacity and the projected capacity factors for the first 5 years of the supply period. Moreover, from 2017 onwards, the auction terms restrict bidders to offering an amount of energy not exceeding their expected capacity minus the amount currently contracted for that period. The 2019 cancelled auction terms further applied this condition to each time block.

Bidders proposing new projects must submit a Gantt chart with the construction milestones, including obtaining the environmental permit and electrical concessions; ordering major equipment; commencing construction; achieving 25, 50, 75, and 100%, respectively, of work progress; testing interconnection; and entry into operation. A technical auditor selected by the awardee from the public registry of consultants evaluates the fulfilment of the milestones. Non-compliance with the construction schedule results in the sanctions detailed in section 3.4.2.4.1. The 2019 auction terms established

---

[23] Risk rating companies must be established in Chile, although some are local branches of international companies such as Moody's, Standard and Poor's, and Fitch Ratings.

that in duly justified cases,[24] awardees might request the replacement of a project by another, paying a penalty of 50 UF per GWh (approximately US$ 2,046) of energy awarded for the LYOC.

Awardees are responsible for connecting their plants to the nearest transmission system. They pay transmission tolls to their owners if they feed their energy into the national grid through dedicated systems. The Act provides guidelines for calculating the tolls, and generators can appeal to the Panel if they disagree with the dedicated systems owners' calculations.

Information on the availability of transmission capacity is available to generators through the annual transmission system expansion plans. The auction terms establish that delays in the entry into operation of the transmission lines included in the expansion plan in force on the date of submission of bids, and to the extent that such delays prevent compliance with the contract, constitute *force majeure*[25] to determine the contractual responsibilities of the successful bidders described in section 3.4.2.4.1.

On the other hand, since the contracts are awarded five years before the start of supply, this information is available for the annual transmission planning processes. Likewise, the auction rules provide that distributors must inform the Commission annually of the increases in power demand for the following years per withdrawal point in the system.

Bidders that back up their submissions with new projects procure their sites. They can purchase or rent land from private owners or bid for a 40-year public land concession in the Ministry of National Properties' auctions.[26] In the case of geothermal projects, potential bidders have to request exploration and exploitation concessions from the Ministry of Energy. The Commission website provides information on solar and wind generation resources throughout the territory.[27]

The north of Chile, mainly the Atacama and Antofagasta regions, has the highest concentration of PV farms due to the appropriate climatic conditions. Wind resources for installing wind farms distribute throughout the coastal zones and the Andean foothills. However, wind farms also tend to be located

[24] No details on what would constitute duly justified cases are available. Since it has never been applied, there is no case law.
[25] Article 45 of the Civil Code defines *force majeure* as an unforeseen event that cannot be resisted, such as a shipwreck, an earthquake, the capture of enemies, and acts of authority by a public official.
[26] The bidding variables are the annual lease offered, the percentage of the yearly income from injected energy offered, and the installed capacity per hectare.
[27] The Solar Resource and Meteorological Data Scan offers information on radiation (global horizontal, global inclined, direct normal, and diffuse horizontal) and meteorological conditions (cloud frequency, temperature, and wind speed) (Molina et al., 2017). In turn, the Wind Energy Explorer is a tool for analysing wind resources, which provides the results of a numerical simulation of wind and air density conditions and a wind generation calculator for each point in the country.

in the northern zone, where they have a lower environmental impact and encounter less social rejection due to lower population density.

The Atacama and Antofagasta have large areas of desert, a significant part of which is public property, with limited occupation by mining operations. Therefore, finding sites for NCRE projects should not be hard. However, given that generators pay the costs of interconnecting to the transmission system, there is competition for land close to electrical substations, especially those in the national grid, to avoid incurring high connection costs and paying charges to the owners of DTSs.

Antofagasta, the capital of the region of the same name, is 418 km north of Copiapó, the capital of the Atacama region, which, in turn, is 678 km north of Santiago, the main demand centre. Despite the substantial energy demand from local mining activities, the northern regions should produce RE surpluses, which the interconnection between the BNIS and the CIS in 2017, and its subsequent strengthening, was able to evacuate. Further PV and wind generation expansion will require a new transmission line connecting both zones.

The regulations establish 'early' qualification criteria in the sense that they do not require bidders to have environmental permits, land rights, interconnection agreements, or a commitment from the lender before bidding. The construction milestones to be met by successful bidders include these requirements explicitly or implicitly.

However, bidders will likely have all these documents ready or at a very advanced stage before bidding. Getting environmental permits approved is a long, uncertain process that adds significant realization risk. Also, a bidder already winning a contract has less bargaining power concerning land rights and interconnection agreements. Further, delays in commercial operation result in heavy penalties and financial liabilities (discussed in section 3.4.2.4.1), a risk that bidders try to avert.

3.4.2.3 Winner selection

The award criterion is solely financial. It does not include social aspects such as the percentage of domestic ownership or local labour. Neither does it limit the energy that auctioneers can allocate to a single bidder. The Commission defines the formulas for indexing the award prices or the framework within which the bidders can set them and decides whether the evaluation of bids takes account of the indexation formulas.

The most recent auctions required bidders to indicate the following for each of their bids: (i) the bid price in US$/MWh, (ii) the minimum number of sub-blocks to win, (iii) possible links between bids submitted to different blocks, and (iv) the parameters of a price indexation formula that is a weighted average of five price indices (four fuel price indices and the US capital price index, CPI), where the sum of the fuel index weights cannot exceed 0.7.[28] The auctioneers must choose a combination of bids that minimizes the total cost of supplying all of the energy requirements using the present value of projected bid prices, the so-called levelized bid prices (see box 3.1 for an example).[29]

Box 3.1 Example of bid prices

Consider an auction supplying two annual blocks of 60,000 MWh and 40,000 MWh divided into 100 sub-blocks each. Two bidders submit bids. Bidder 1 offers (a levelized price of) US$50/MWh for 100 sub-blocks in both blocks and bidder 2 offers US$30/MWh for 80 sub-blocks in the second block. All three bids are unconditional. In this case, bidder 1 is awarded the entire block 1 and 20 sub-blocks in block 2, and bidder 2 is awarded 80 sub-blocks in block 2.

Next, imagine that bidder 1's submission to block 2 is conditional on being awarded all the sub-blocks. In this case, bidder 1 wins both complete blocks. By adding a third bidder who bids US$60/MWh for 30 sub-blocks in block 2, the combination that allows the supply of all demand at minimum cost would award the entire block 1 to bidder 1, 80 sub-blocks in block 2 to bidder 2, and the remaining 20 sub-blocks in block 2 to the third bidder. Finally, if bidder 1 conditions its bids on winning both or neither of the two blocks, it wins both.

As mentioned, the auction rules allow bidders whose bids exceed the ceiling price to submit a new bid. For example, in 2017, a bidder whose bid price was higher than the ceiling price but lower than the ceiling price +2.5% could match the ceiling price. A bidder with an original exceeding the ceiling price +2.5% could submit the ceiling price minus 5%.

---

[28] The fuel prices are the monthly diesel oil parity price; the monthly average of Brent crude oil, based on Argusen's reports; the monthly coal parity price, calculated by the Commission based on the Platts International Coal Report for free-on-board (FOB) prices and the Shipping Intelligence Weekly for ocean freight; and the Henry Hub natural gas monthly average price.

[29] The levelized price is the average for the first 10 years of supply of the present values of the bid prices projected according to the indexation formula proposed by the bidder, discounted at a 10% rate. Denoting P_{bid} = the bid price, PPI = the price index projection, EB = the energy offered, Start = the number of years between the bid submission and the beginning of the supply (six), N = the number of years considered in the projection (10), and r = the annual discount rate (10%), the expression for levelized prices is

$$P_{levelized} = \frac{\sum_{i=0}^{N-1} \left(\frac{P_{bid} \cdot PPI_{Start+i} \cdot EB_{Start+i}}{(1+r)^{Start+i}} \right)}{\sum_{i=0}^{N-1} \left(\frac{EB_{Start+i}}{(1+r)^{Start+i}} \right)}$$

3.4.2.4 Buyer and seller liabilities

3.4.2.4.1 Guarantee requirements and penalties

The auction terms require bids to include a liability insurance policy covering damage caused to personnel, third-party property, or the environment and a disaster insurance policy to rebuild or repair facilities damaged during construction, where appropriate, and their operation. The minimum coverage under these guarantees is CH$ 3,000,000 (US$ 4,200). The 2017 auction rules also required awardees to provide a performance bond for 600 UF (US$ 24,549) per GWh in the LYOC, valid for up to 15 months after the start date of supply.

Non-compliance penalties range from the loss of the contract to the forfeiture of the performance bond. Auctioneers must execute the performance bond of an awardee for the benefit of regulated customers when, inter alia, (i) the awardee fails to fulfil its supply commitment during the first 12 months, (ii) the contract is terminated early for reasons attributable to the supplier, or (iii) the project that supports the bid is not put into operation at least 2 months before the expiration of the performance bond, if applicable. Auctioneers may claim compensation for damages not covered by the performance bond in case of contract non-compliance.

For an awardee backing its bid with a new project, a delay of more than 60 days in fulfilling two construction milestones (as per the Gantt chart) results in a fine of 30 UF (US$ 1,228) for each GWh in the LYOC. Failure to pay this penalty within 30 days results in the collection of the performance bond.

The distributors are obliged to terminate a contract in advance, with the prior approval of the Commission and without any compensation to the awardee, if (i) the awardee fails to comply with the obligations arising from its participation in the balance of injections and withdrawals of energy and power during two consecutive months, (ii) a court issues a resolution liquidating the supplier, and (iii) the supplier incurs severe and repeated breaches of the contractual obligations and does not remedy them within 30 days.

Furthermore, the distributor may terminate the contract early if the supplier is in serious breach of its contractual obligations not remedied within 90 days, obtains a risk rating lower than BB+ during the term of the contract and does not improve it within 12 months, and if the performance bond is executed.

3.4.2.4.2 Risk allocation

The auction design seeks to reduce bidders' risks to obtain competitive bid prices. The choices regarding contract lengths, price indexation, and currency

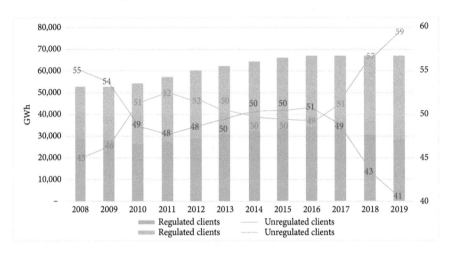

Figure 3.6 Evolution of energy withdrawals

Source: Yearbook NEC (2019).

selection expressed in the bidding terms reflect this purpose.[30] The clauses that allow awardees to request modification or termination of the contract also reduce their risk.

Successful bidders, however, face a demand risk with their contracts as they only invoice for the actual demand of the distribution companies. In recent years, many regulated consumers have chosen to deregulate (Figure 3.6). This migration is due to the rise in the regulated price resulting from high auction award prices up to 2014, parallel with a sharp fall in the spot price in recent years. As a result, successful bidders will sell less energy at contracted prices and more at spot prices.

This situation will significantly impact small, undiversified, variable RE generators since their exposure to the spot price represents a greater risk. Moreover, their contract sales will receive the most competitive prices recorded from 2015 onwards, when they started to bid, unlike large companies awarded contracts auctioned before 2015 at high prices (see section 3.5).

3.4.2.5 Securing the revenue stream and addressing off-taker risk

The contracts' off-takers—distribution companies—are investment grade. They are authorized to cut off service to their customers who have unpaid bills, so they have a rate of non-collection in the order of 1%, which the

---

[30] If the auction rule had the same capacity price indexation as the one set by the Commission for capacity exchanges between generators, successful bidders' capacity payment would equal their sufficiency power times the capacity price. In addition, how distributors allocate their peak energy consumption among their suppliers would be irrelevant.

calculation of tariffs considers a cost. The Commission approves the supply contracts signed by public deed with the distribution companies. As a result, the possibility of distributors not paying generators for power withdrawn has been remote.[31]

3.4.3 Auction implementation

Auctions have generally enjoyed wide-ranging support. Congress had a broad consensus when it approved the new auction design in 2005. Also, industry analysts mostly expressed a favourable opinion of the changes introduced, except for some specific criticisms (Moreno et al., 2012; Bustos-Savagno, 2019). Lately, however, there have been voices questioning the outcomes of auctions between 2010 and 2014, which resulted in the awarding of contracts at very high prices.[32]

The social unrest that started in October 2019 forced the government to postpone the price increase for regulated consumers that should have taken effect in November 2019. The more recent auctions were highly competitive, with distributors being able to award contracts at significantly lower prices than in 2010–2014. Thus, no political or social rejection is expected in the future.

The institutions in charge of implementing the auctions are the Commission and the distribution companies. The former is responsible for convening, designing, coordinating, and directing their implementation, which includes writing the auction rules and preparing the standard supply contract to be signed by auctioneers and awardees.[33] The Commission formalizes the contracts through an administrative act, after being informed by the auctioneers on the evaluation and award of the contracts.

The distribution companies, for their part, carry out the auction processes subject to the rules and other requirements set by the Commission. In that sense, they are responsible for managing the auctions. Between 2006 and 2011, the distribution companies held simultaneous auctions with a coordinated award mechanism that allocated all contracts. The contracts differed between companies in terms of duration and price. Since 2012, they have

---

[31] Due to the COVID-19 pandemic, Congress enacted a law allowing regulated consumers to defer payment for service.

[32] See https://www.emol.com/noticias/Economia/2017/11/16/883537/Cuentas-de-luz-subirian-12-al-2020-por-altos-precios-en-licitaciones-con-modelo-antiguo.html (accessed 20 April 2023).

[33] Until the 2015 legal change, the Act provided that the Commission approved the auction rules and that auctioneers informed it of the results. The disappointing auction outcomes in early 2010 and the expertise acquired by the Commission over 10 years of monitoring the auctions explain these changes.

carried out centralized auctions for the sum of their demands. To do so, they appoint a person to run each auction on their behalf.

These institutions are the natural choice to implement the auction processes. The distributors are the contract off-takers and manage the auctions. For instance, they inform the system Coordinator about the allocation among the various suppliers of their energy withdrawals and power requirements. For its part, the Commission, as a regulatory body, has a direct interest in the auctions to supply energy to regulated customers.

The distributors have the capacity and experience to carry out complex auctions in different areas as they recurrently tender the construction of new facilities. Also, between 1998 and 2005, they carried out energy auctions to supply their regulated customers, although in a different legal framework. The Commission is recognized for its technical expertise and considerable experience supervising auctions.

The distribution companies bear the expenses incurred in implementing the auction processes. In return, the Act establishes that the auction terms may regulate the use of the resources obtained from the sale of auction terms (request for proposal (RfP) documentation and contracts), which must be limited to financing activities related to the auction processes. In the 2019 auction, the cost of auction rules was CH$ 2 million (US$ 2,815) plus VAT.

Two regulatory features strengthen the integrity of the process: the obligation of transparency and the supervision by the Commission. First, the Act provides that auctions shall be public, non-discriminatory, and transparent. It also provides electronic publication (the official webpage of the auctions, Commission, Electricity and Fuels Superintendence, and the Coordinator) and a daily newspaper with a national circulation of the precise timetable with the process milestones. Some of these correspond to public activities, including the reception of administrative and financial proposals and their subsequent opening, of which notarized minutes are taken. Likewise, the auctioneers must draw up notarized minutes of the evaluation process of the administrative proposal and the award of the financial bids. Auctioneers must also publish the submissions in full and the software for awarding the contracts.

The person responsible for the auction process signs the clarification circulars with consultations and responses about auction rules after approval by the Commission. The clarification circulars, as well as the notarized acts, are sent both in writing and via email to the interested parties. The websites mentioned above also publish them.

A second element in ensuring the integrity of the auction process is the supervisory role played by the Commission. Firstly, the Commission establishes many of the auction regulations and requirements. Secondly, auction rules require that auctioneers report to the Commission on fulfilment of the calendar milestones, particularly the evaluation of the bids and the subsequent awarding of the contracts.

3.5 Results from Chile's energy auctions: The ascendancy of renewables

Table 3.6 summarizes the 21 auctions held in the CIS since 2006.[34] The first column lists the administrative name of each auction, which, until 2011, when distributors auctioned their supply needs separately, includes the abbreviated name of the distributor. In what follows, we group the independent but simultaneous auctions held until 2011, reducing their number to 15, and label each with its submission deadline. In cases where it was necessary to carry out further auction rounds to award the total amount of energy offered, these are treated as separate auctions since they had different submission dates and were open to new bidders.

Below, the groups of related bidders count as one. Figure 3.7 shows that the number of bidders was low and trending downwards until August 2014. In subsequent auctions, bidders increased substantially. In the last 6 tenders, out of 130 offers, only 8 did not pass the administrative stage: one in the December 2014 auction and 7 in the October 2015 auction.

As of December 2014, most new bidders supported their bids with projects only. In the 2017 auction, there was a partial trend reversal, explained by the low amount of energy tendered compared with the previous auction and the steep increase in the guarantees required, which mainly affected small participants with less financial backing.

Two periods can also be distinguished concerning prices. From 2006 to 2013, the award prices reached or approached the ceiling prices, except in 2009, when the number of bidders showed a circumstantial increase. From 2014, the bid prices started to move away from their ceilings and descend, reaching US$ 32.5/MWh in the October 2017 auction, a substantial fall from a maximum of US$ 138.9/MWh attained in the December 2012 auction.

Figure 3.8 shows that in the auctions held between March 2011 and August 2014, the energy submitted by bidders was either less than or slightly above

---

[34] Excludes tenders declared unsuccessful, of which five were between 2012 and 2013.

Table 3.6 Summary of successful auctions since 2006

Auction	Call date	Bids reception date	Award date	GWh tendered	GWh bid	GWh awarded	Bidders	Reserve price	Mean bid price	Mean award price	Support period
2006-1-CHL	18 April 2006	31 October 2006	13 November 2006	4,500	7,300	4,500	2[a]	62.7	56.5	53.6	1 January 2010–31 December 2022
2006-1-CHQ	6 March 2006	31 October 2006	13 November 2006	910	2,044	807	3	62.7	54.5	52.2	1 January 2009–30 April 2015, 1 May 2010–30 April 2015
2006-1-SAESA	6 March 2006	31 October 2006	13 November 2006	3,582	10,582	3,582	3[a]	62.7	54.8	49.9	1 January 2010–31 December 2019
2006-1-Emel	6 March 2006	31 October 2006	13 November 2006	2,010	2,630	868	2	62.7	56.9	55.6	1 January 2010–31 December 2019
2006-1-CGE	22 March 2006	31 October 2006	13 November 2006	2,310	7,010	2,310	3[a]	62.7	56.2	54.4	1 January 2010–31 December 2021, 1 January 2010–31 December 2013
2006-1-2-Emel	11 December 2006	31 January 2007	8 February 2007	1,130	2,080	1,130	2	62.7	55.8	54.6	1 January 2010–31 December 2024

2006-2-CHL	20 September 2006	7 July 2007	23 July 2007	6,600	5,700	4,200	2	61.7	60.3	59.3	1 January 2011–31 December 2021, 1 January 2011–31 December 2023, 1 January 2011–31 December 2025
2006-2-2-CHL	11 December 2007	11 March 2008	31 March 2008	1,800	1,800	1,800	1	71.1	65.8	65.8	1 January 2011–31 December 2023
2008-1-CHQ	14 July 2008	30 January 2009	5 February 2009	1,936	6,050	1,936	4	125.2	100.9	93.6	1 December 2010–31 December 2023
2008-1-SAESA	14 July 2008	30 January 2009	5 February 2009	935	4,787	935	5	125.2	100.5	96.1	1 January 2010–31 December 2021
2008-1-CGE	17 June 2008	30 January 2009	5 February 2009	5,940	18,300	4,950	5	125.2	105.6	110.1	1 January 2010–31 December 2024

Continued

Table 3.6 *Continued*

Auction	Call date	Bids reception date	Award date	GWh tendered	GWh bid	GWh awarded	Bidders	Reserve price	Mean bid price	Mean award price	Support period
2008-1-2-CGE	7 April 2009	7 July 2009	10 July 2009	935	2,118	935	6	125.2	108.9	99.5	1 January 2010–31 December 2021
2010-1-CHQ	27 October 2010	16 March 2011	24 March 2011	715	1,265	715	3	92.0	89.4	89.0	1 January 2013–31 December 2026, 1 January 2014–31 December 2026, 1 January 2015–31 December 2026
2010-1-CHL	27 October 2010	16 March 2011	24 March 2011	1,980	2,228	1,485	1	92.0	91.1	91.0	1 January 2014–31 December 2027
2012-1	15 March 12	10 April 12	16 April 12	924	924	924	1	129.5	129.5	129.5	1 May 2012–31 December 2014
2012-3-2	14 November 2012	6 December 2012	7 December 2012	1,650	247.5	247.5	1	140.0	138.9	138.9	1 January 2013–31 December 2014
2013-1	20 June 13	20 November 13	29 November 13	5,000	3,900	3,900	2	129.0	128.9	128.9	1 December 2013–31 December 2024
2013-3	30 December 1013	5 August 2014	14 August 2014	5,000	750	750	1	120.2	112.0	112.0	1 December 2014–31 December 2025

2013-3-2	17 September 2014	1 December 2014	12 December 2014	14,300	32,130	12,705	15	120.2	110.7	107.3	1 January 2016–31 December 2030, 1 January 2017–31 December 2031, 1 January 2018–31 December 2032, 1 January 2019–31 December 2033
2015-2	15 June 2015	14 October 2015	26 October 2015	1,200	9,427	1,200	29	108.1	84.5	79.3	1 January 2017–31 December 2036
2015-1	29 May 2015	27 July 2016	17 August 2016	12,430	98,485	12,430	61	94.0	60.3	47.6	1/1/2021–12/31/2040, 1 January 2022–31 December 2041
2017-1	30 January 2017	11 October 2017	2 November 2017	2,200	13,412	2,200	22	81.5	42.7	32.5	1 January 2023–31 December 2042

Note: [a] Gener and Guacolda count as one company.

Source: Authors' compilation based on the database provided at https://www.licitacioneselectricas.cl (accessed 16 April 2023).

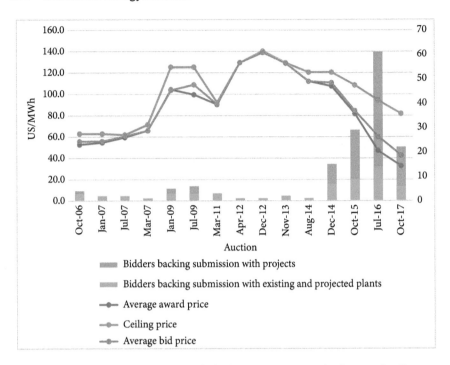

Figure 3.7 Energy auctions: Average bid prices, average award prices, and ceiling prices

Source: Authors' compilation based on the database provided in https://www.
licitacioneselectricas.cl (accessed 13 April 2023).

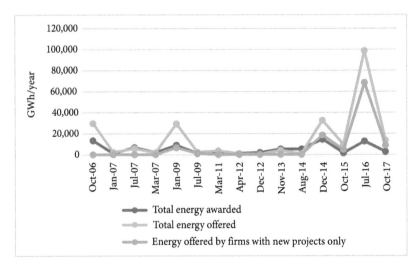

Figure 3.8 Energy auctioned, energy offered, and energy offered by bidders with new projects

Source: Authors' compilation based on the database provided in https://www.
licitacioneselectricas.cl (accessed 13 April 2023).

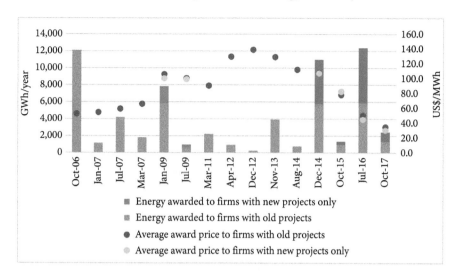

Figure 3.9 Energy awarded to bidders with and without old plants: Amounts and average prices

Source: Authors' compilation based on the database provided in https://www. licitacioneselectricas.cl (accessed 13 April 2023).

the amount auctioned. From December 2014 onwards, the energy bid far exceeded the auctioned amount, indicating vivid competition. Also, the energy offered by bidders backed by new projects was significant from that date onwards and enough to cover all demand.

Figure 3.9 shows the energy awarded to bidders who partially or fully supported their bids with existing plants and those that backed their tenders only with new projects. As from the December 2014 auction, the latter group won a significant part of the auctioned energy, generally at slightly lower prices.

Table 3.7 shows the number and capacity of projects that have supported bids since November 2013: 92 projects with a total capacity of 10,447 MW. Most are either solar PV plants or wind farms. In the August 2014 auction, only one generator backed with existing projects submitted a bid.

In what follows, we analyse the probable causes of the change in the auctions' outcomes at the end of 2014. The mentioned slowing in the construction of hydroelectric plants with dams in the 1990s, the principal source of power generation until then in the CIS, initially had a limited impact. From 1997, the commissioning of gas pipelines interconnecting with Argentina allowed for meeting power demand increases with gas-fired plants at reasonable prices. With the Argentinean restrictions on gas exports starting in 2005, spot prices jumped (Figure 3.10).

Table 3.7 Projects that backed winning bids by type of technology, November 2013–October 2017

Auction reception date	Wind		Solar		Mini hydro		Thermoelectric	
	Number projects	Capacity (MW)	Number projects	Capacity (MW)	Number project	Capacity (MW)	Number project	Capacity (MW)
November 2013	1	61	2	100	0	0	0	0
December 2014	4	465	18	1,848	5	41	2	975
October 2015	5	485	9	713	0	0	0	0
July 2016	23	3,194	12	1,263	3	18	0	0
October 2017	5	725	3	559	0	0	0	0
Total	38	4,830	44	4,483	8	59	2	975

Source: Authors' compilation based on the database provided in https://www.licitacioneselectricas.cl (accessed 16 April 2023).

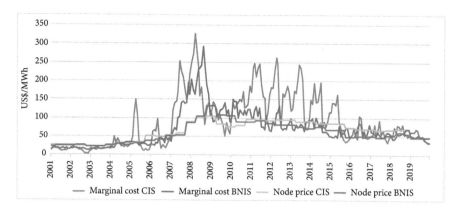

Figure 3.10 Monthly average spot price and node prices for NES

Source: Authors' compilation based on Coordinator (2020), https://www.coordinador.cl/operacion/graficos/operacion-real/costo-marginal-real and Commission (2020), http://energiaabierta.cl/blockchain (accessed 13 April 2023).

Later, coal-fired plants replaced gas-fired plants in supplying demand growth. However, citizen opposition made it very difficult to obtain environmental permits for their construction in the CIS, and the environmental authorities last approved a plant in 2009. As a result, the possibility of building new gas- or coal-fired power plants was virtually closed.

This situation led to a sharp increase in the spot price in the CIS in early 2010, with annual average prices reaching US$ 183 per MWh in 2011 and US$ 178 in 2013, far exceeding the auction ceiling prices (Figure 3.10). This situation may have made it more attractive for generators to skip auctions and to reserve energy for future sale in the spot market, assuming that they did not anticipate the subsequent fall in both auction award prices and spot prices. An alternative or complementary explanation is that the few companies that owned the existing baseload plants exerted their market power as the generation costs of the oil-fired plants exceeded the auctions' ceiling prices.

Within this context, the main driver of the change in the auctions' outcomes from December 2014 was the reduction in the levelized cost of electricity (LCOE) of RE technologies. IRENA (2015) reports that the global weighted average LCOE of solar PV halved between 2010 and 2014, a cost reduction process that continues. IRENA (2018, 2020) states that the global weighted average LCOE of utility-scale PV fell 73% from 2010 for projects commissioned in 2017. In turn, the LCOEs reported by the US Energy Information Administration in the Annual Energy Outlook for projects in this country show a similar drop (Table 3.8).

Table 3.8 Levelized cost of new generation resources in the US (current US$ per KWh)

	2012	2013	2014	2015	2016	2017	2018	2019
Commercial operation date	2017	2018	2018	2020	2022	2022	2022	2023
Onshore wind	96	86.6	80.3	73.6	58.5	55.8	48	42.8
PV	152.7	144.3	130	125.3	74.2	73.7	59.1	48.8

Source: Annual Energy Outlook, US Energy Information Administration, 2012–2019. Yearly outlooks are released in December of the previous year.

This drop in RE generation costs has been particularly beneficial for Chile. Few countries have as much NCRE potential, and as much need for RE, as Chile (del Río, 2017)[35]. The learning resulting from the incipient local investments in RE generation in the early 2010s must also have helped reduce costs, initially driven by demand from large unregulated customers wanting to reduce their carbon footprint and the attractiveness of selling energy at high spot prices.

Other changes that helped increase RE's competitiveness relate to the transmission system. First, the interconnection of the two major systems in November 2017 allowed RE plants in the north to operate in a more flexible system that includes hydro plants with reservoirs. Second, the reinforcement of the transmission system linking the Atacama region, which hosts most of the recent PV projects, with the main demand centres allowed for the evacuation of energy previously curtailed due to transmission congestion.[36]

The trend in award prices in Chilean auctions is in line with those reported in IRENA's reports and the Annual Energy Outlook of the US Energy Information Administration, as shown in Figure 3.11.[37] This similarity is another indication that the primary cause of the fall in the bid prices is the substantial drop in LCOEs of RE technologies, which allowed for the entry of new firms with competitive prices. In that sense, changes in legislation that reduce entry barriers also contributed to lower prices, but to a lesser extent, an issue discussed in section 3.6.

---

[35] According to Ascencio-Vásquez et al. (2019), the world's best location for PV is the Atacama Desert in Chile because of the very high irradiation and a stable number of sun hours due to the relative proximity to the Equator, resulting in capacity factors of 35% (Cruzate, 2017). Similarly, there are strong wind, geothermal, and hydropower resources nationwide.

[36] The delayed entry into operation of the Cardones-Polpaico line curtailed approximately 6% of NCRE generation and decoupled node prices in 2018. Projects without contracts sold their energy at low prices and even zero (Cruzate, 2017). NCRE curtailment fell with this line's commissioning in May 2019.

[37] The comparisons are not direct. In Chile, the awardees face price risk, but, on the other hand, they receive a capacity payment.

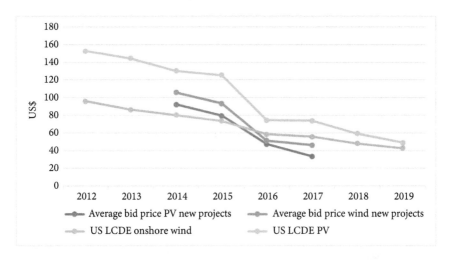

Figure 3.11 Average bid prices in Chilean actions by firms backing their bids with non-convertible renewable energy (NCRE) projects and US levelized cost of energy (LCOE)

Source: Table 3.8 and authors' compilation based on the database provided in https://www.licitacioneselectricas.cl (accessed 13 April 2023).

Next, we argue that the auctions have been successful by considering two measures of success distinguished in the literature: cost-effectiveness and investment-effectiveness (Gephart et al., 2017). The available evidence suggests that, at least since the end of 2014, auctions have been cost-effective, with prices in line with global trends.

As mentioned, the Act obliges bidders to back up their bids with installed or projected plants. In the auctions held between December 2012 and October 2015, the projects with an entry date until January 2019 backing winning bids totalled 4,650 MW. Of this total, 2.087 MW are operating, and 600 MW are under construction. The abandonment of 1,963 MW corresponds to the dropping of some projects by successful bidders who won less energy than they bid for and authorizations to replace projects with existing plants. Also, Commission approved bidders' requests to delay the commissioning of their projects due to the COVID-19 pandemic but without altering their contractual supply obligations to their customers.

The information about abandonments and delays is not readily available. Nevertheless, it is unlikely that awardees could hide project delays as independent consultants audit the construction milestones. Moreover, off-takers are legally obliged to follow up on such milestones and have no reason not to report delays or apply sanctions. The only known case of an awardee not building a project is that of Generadora Metropolitana, which won a contract in the December 2014 auction. The company backed its bid with a CCGT project, which it abandoned in 2019 due to the inability to obtain a favourable environmental resolution.[38]

The standard definition of auction investment efficiency (i.e., the ability to ensure that projects reach commercial operation successfully) does not apply directly here. Chile auctions supply contracts instead of capacity contracts. Thus, the measure of success is that awardees meet their obligations to pay for the energy and power withdrawn from the system by their contract counterparties. So far, only one awardee, Central Campanario, has failed to comply, despite reaching its commercial operation date (COD) on time.[39]

3.6 Lessons learned from Chile's energy auctions

3.6.1 Auction design

Chile has considerable experience in electricity supply contract auctioning. Over time, successive governments have introduced numerous changes in the design and execution of the auctions. This section draws lessons from this experience.

Kruger and Eberhard (2018) caution that overly aggressive bidding may result in such low prices that some successful bidders' proposals are unfeasible. The Chilean experience provides some clues on balancing cost-effectiveness and investment-effectiveness. Good auction design should therefore seek to achieve a balance between these two objectives.

Higher qualification requirements for bidders and lower risks for awardees increase the likelihood that projects will succeed. The downside of higher qualification conditions is that they may reduce cost-effectiveness by decreasing the number of potential participants and raising their costs. In turn, lowering risks for bidders should increase competition but at the expense of transferring risk to consumers.

---

[38] In December 2017, because of the lack of progress with the environmental permits, the company bought four existing plants that added up to 750 MW and claimed it had enough capacity to back up its contract. The Commission threatened to go to arbitration to invalidate the contract for a severe breach. However, the parties finally reached an agreement whereby the company committed to installing two solar plants of 300 MW each between 2022 and 2023.

[39] In 2018, it won a contract for an amount of energy that meant its plant had to operate at an unattainable capacity factor. Also, it indexed the price bid to the US CPI, although its project was a CCGT plant. By January 2010, it had reached COD. However, a tsunami in February 2010 left some power plants inoperable, raising the system's spot price above the Campanario contract price, which, in turn, was below its variable cost. The company continued withdrawing energy from the system to supply its clients, coming insolvent in a couple of months, leaving other generators with an uncollectible claim.

In this sense, the designs in which auctioneers first determine which bidders pass the financial and technical solvency prerequisites and then award contracts based exclusively on price bids have two advantages. First, price-only competition contributes to a more cost-effective outcome. Second, it does not require combining in one indicator aspects as different as the bid prices and parameters of financial soundness and know-how. The administrative requirements should ensure that those that comply with them have a good chance of successfully carrying out their projects.

Notwithstanding the above, Chilean regulations provide measures to deal with situations where a project is delayed or outright cancelled. The 2015 Act reform introduced the possibility of calling for short-term tenders to cover the energy needs that may arise from unexpected events, including project cancelation. Moreover, the auction rules, for example, contain provisions allowing an awardee facing financial problems to transfer the contract to another company with the Commission's approval, provided that the transferee takes over all the contractual obligations. Likewise, in the event of the insolvency of the awardee, the project financiers may auction the supply contract on a similar condition.

The Commission has recently tightened the qualification conditions, probably in response to a rapid increase in bidders. It seems prudent to increase the prerequisites as, with more competition, the possibility of project failure increases due to a higher winner' curse.

An alternative to attract competitors to the auctions and have them bid competitive prices is to reduce their risks. Chile's auction design, introduced in 2005, aims to do precisely this by offering long-term contracts and award prices in US dollars adjusted according to costs. Regulated consumers absorb these risks as they are exposed to cost changes and exchange rate fluctuations over several years. However, consumers are generally in a better position to absorb these risks as the electricity bill usually accounts for a minor part of their expenses.[40]

The 2015 legal reform introduced several changes that further reduced the awardees' risks. As mentioned, the changes allow for (i) postponing COD or outright cancelling the contract, (ii) modifying contracts in the event of permanent changes in regulation or taxes that significantly increase awardees' costs, and (iii) replacing a project with another (2019 auction).

On the other hand, the Chilean auction design subjects bidders to two relevant risks: exposure to spot price and demand risk. The former affects

---

[40] Electricity accounts for 2.3% of spending on the basket of goods and services representative of consumption in Chile's urban households. See https://www.ine.cl/estadisticas/economia/indices-de-precio-e-inflacion/indice-de-precios-al-consumidor (accessed 20 April 2023).

generators with non-dispatchable technologies, while it may benefit other generators.[41] The 2015 legal change intends to mitigate the spot price exposure risk by allowing the auctioning of energy in time blocks adjusted to the generation profiles of RE technologies.

Table 3.9 summarizes the results of all auctions that incorporated time blocks. In the auctions held from 2014 to 2016, a few bidders that submitted unlinked bids won contracts, and the average award prices differed between time blocks. However, in the 2017 auction, no unlinked bids won contracts, and neither did average award prices vary between time blocks.

These results follow from the award mechanism that selects the combination of offers that meets the demand at the lowest cost. Although auction rules divide the day into time blocks, they allow bidders to link their bids submitted to different time blocks by conditioning them to be awarded all or none. Thus, bidders with unlinked offers can only win a contract if there are enough unlinked offers in the other time blocks at competitive prices or if the linked offers leave room in that time block. The auction results show that these conditions are rarely met since unlinked bids that have won contracts are rare, with none in the last one.

Eliminating linked offers would avoid leaving out very competitive block-specific bids. This solution would be imperfect at best. Bidders that used to submit linked bids in the previous auctions would probably make more aggressive price bids in the blocks where they expect to find more competition and compensate them with higher price bids in the others, probably without significantly altering the average auction price results.

A more effective policy to reduce the risk of spot price exposure would have been to correct that design error in the electricity market that encourages the over-installation of inefficient backup plants, which, in Chile, are oil-fired units (see Table 3.1). The plants' capacity payment depends on their sufficiency power, irrespective of their efficiency. Table 3.10 shows the enormous variety in performance and, consequently, in operating costs of oil-fired power plants, with some consuming per unit up to 150% more than the most efficient ones.

In 2012, the twenty-fifth lowest percentile diesel plant had operating costs of US$265/MWh. Thus, the plant in the least efficient quartile determined the spot price at around 1,300 hours in the year, with its value sometimes exceeding US$ 300/MWh (Figure 3.12). Moreover, exposure to high spot prices entails a financial risk for all bidders supporting their bid submissions

---

[41] The 2005 auction design did not consider this risk because, in those years, no bidder backed its submissions with NCRE projects.

Table 3.9 Time block results by auction

Block type	Auction denomination bids reception date	Blocks	GWh auctioned	GWh awarded	Bidders with non-linked bids[a]	Successful bidders		Mean bid price	Minimum bid price	Mean award price
						Total	Non-linked bids			
Quarterly block	2017/01, October 2017	1 January–31 March	125	125	0	5	0	48.2	35.3	35.3
		1 April–30 June	125	125	0	5	0	48.2	35.3	35.3
		1 July–30 September	125	125	2	5	0	49.7	35.3	35.3
		1 October–31 December	125	125	2	5	0	49.7	35.3	35.3
Time block	2017/01, October 2017	23:00–07:59 (next day)	528	528	3	3	0	46.0	25.4	31.8
		08:00–17:59	778	778	2	3	0	38.1	21.5	31.6
		18:00–22:59	394	394	1	3	0	46.1	25.4	31.8
	2015/01, July 2016	23:00–07:59 (next day)	680	680	6 (11)	7	0	67.3	43.1	50.5
		08:00–17:59	1 000	1 000	23 (25)	6	1	42.3	29.1	41.9
		18:00–22:59	520	520	4 (8)	10	3	61.4	43.1	52.6
		24-hour block	10 164	10 164	-	13	-	61.9	31.8	47.6

Continued

Table 3.9 *Continued*

Block type	Auction denomination bids reception date	Blocks	GWh auctioned	GWh awarded	Bidders with non-linked bids[a]	Successful bidders		Mean bid price	Minimum bid price	Mean award price
						Total	Non-linked bids			
	2015/02, October 2015	23:00–07:59 (next day)	370	370	3	3	0	88.2	78.9	82.1
		08:00–17:59	550	550	14	3	2	81.1	64.8	74.6
		18:00–22:59	280	280	3	3	0	92.8	78.9	85.1
	2013/03-2, December 2014	23:00–07:59 (next day)	250	50	1	2	0	110.2	110.0	110.2
		08:00–17:59	500	270	4	5	3	95.7	89.0	95.7
		18:00–22:59	250	15	1	2	0	117.0	111.1	117.0
		23:00–07:59 (next day)	250	75	2	1	0	102.2	100.6	100.6
		08:00–17:59	500	470	5	2	2	90.8	79.9	83.7
		18:00–22:59	250	45	2	1	0	102.0	100.6	100.6
		24-hour block	11 000	10 049	–	6	–	111.5	90.0	109.1

Note: [a] Independent firms. The total firms that submitted bids are in brackets.
Source: Compiled by authors based on the database provided in https://www.licitacioneselectricas.cladd (accessed 16 April 2023).

with new projects. In fact, in case of a COD delay, they must buy the energy on the spot market to supply their contracts.

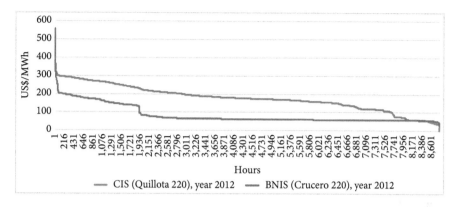

Figure 3.12 Hourly marginal cost of electricity duration curve, 2012

Source: Authors' compilation based on Coordinator (2020), https://www.coordinador.cl/operacion/ graficos/operacion-real/costo-marginal-real (accessed 13 April 2023).

In recent years, the value and the variability of the spot price have fallen and, thereby, the risk associated with spot price exposure. Figure 3.12 shows the annual averages of the spot price for each hour of the day in the two systems in 2012. In the CIS, the hourly marginal cost decreased to less than one-third between 2012 and 2017. At the BNIS, the drop was somewhat less. Annual averages may hide significant differences between days, but, on average, the effects of exposure to the spot price should be less relevant, especially in 2017, when marginal costs were significantly lower.

Table 3.10 Variable cost of oil-fired power plants

	CIS August 2012		CIS October 2015		NES January 2020	
	Specific consumption	Variable cost	Specific consumption	Variable cost	Specific consumption	Variable cost
	Ton/ MWh	US$/ MWh	Ton/ MWh	US$/ MWh	Ton/ MWh	US$/ MWh
Median value	0.26	282.61	0.26	162.4	0.25	189.5
Maximum	0.43	455.43	0.43	396.5	0.39	269.1
Minimum	0.17	169.24	0.17	83.5	0.16	98.2
Max./Min.	2.5	2.7	2.5	4.7	2.4	2.7

Source: NEC, Fijación de precios de nudo de corto plazo, Informe Técnicos Definitivos.

3.6.2 Auction implementation

In Chile's auctions, the law obliges the off-takers, the distribution companies acting on behalf of their regulated clients, to make all their actions in
the bidding process transparent and non-discriminatory, giving the Commission a broad supervisory role. These conditions tend to guarantee the fairness
of the procedures, which is an attractive feature for potential bidders. Also,
successive legal changes have created an institutional framework to provide
impartiality guarantees in applying electricity market rules to awardees. The
system Coordinator is fully independent, and its decisions can be appealed
to the Panel of Experts, reducing the risks of discriminatory treatment by the
authorities, especially for new entrants.

3.6.3 Site availability

In Chile, as in South Africa, awardees of auctions are responsible for selecting, preparing, and securing project sites, which is probably the right policy.[42]
However, governments should ensure the availability of a wide choice of sites,
even if they are not responsible for selecting them.

The Commission website provides information on solar and wind
resources throughout the territory. The state, which owns a significant percentage of the land suitable for solar and wind power plants in the Atacama
Desert (Insunza, 2015), has also been auctioning site concessions for RE
generation. On the other hand, there are unresolved issues related to site
access. The mining statute takes precedence over any other economic activity in the country, which could hinder financing RE projects (Insunza,
2015).

The availability of sites also relates to expanding the transmission grid
to the areas with the best RE resources. These zones generally differ
from those of conventional power plants. Chile suffered delays in building local transmission lines to evacuate RE to the national transmission
system (NTS) and strengthening the NTS installations that transport RE
to the consumption centres. The unanticipated rapid deployment of RE
projects and the prolonged processes of obtaining electrical easements
delayed the commissioning of new transmission lines. This setback likely
affected the participation of RE generators in the auctions. Introducing the
transmission system development poles in 2016 attempted to tackle this
problem.

[42] Available experience in the sub-Saharan region indicates that developer-led site selection in auctions
of RE projects has been more successful than government-led approaches (Kruger et al., 2019).

3.7 Conclusion: Auction innovation in a complex market

Since 2015, bid prices in Chilean auctions have fallen considerably, in line with international RE cost trends and driven by fierce competition. A favourable business climate and a low country risk also helped this outcome. Off-takers (distribution companies) benefit from a low non-payment rate and a regulatory system that guarantees their rights, ensuring a secure project revenue stream to suppliers. A well-developed financial system guarantees to fund projects for incumbents and new entrants.

Despite the successful integration of NCRE into the country's generation mix, authorities should anticipate that the system's costs will rise with the increasing penetration of variable RE generation. Indeed, there will be a higher need for ancillary services, mainly frequency control (primary, secondary, and tertiary). The Chilean regulatory changes from 2020 socialize these costs instead of charging those causing them. This criterion could lead to a drastic upsurge in these costs. The need for ancillary services could fall if the energy storage cost reduces enough to become cost-effective in providing the system with flexibility. However, it will still be necessary to assign the costs appropriately.

3.8 References

Arellano, M. S., and Serra, P. (2010). 'Long-Term Contract Auctions and Market Power in Regulated Power Industries'. *Energy Policy*, *38*, 1759–1763.

Ascencio-Vásquez, J., Brecl, K., and Topič, M. (2019). 'Methodology of Köppen-Geiger Photovoltaic Climate Classification and Implications to World Wide Mapping of PV System Performance'. *Solar Energy*, *191*, 672–685.

Boiteux, M. (1960). 'Peak-Load Pricing'. *Journal of Business*, *33*(2), 157–179.

Bustos-Salvagno, J. (2019). 'Chilean Experience on Long-Term Electricity Auctions'. International Association for Energy Economics (IAEE) Energy Forum/Third Quarter 2019.

Cruzate, J. (2017). 'El mercado de Energías Renovables No Convencionales (ERNC) en Chile: Un sector de éxito, incertidumbres y futuros'. *Cuadernos de Energía*, *52*, 5–8.

del Río, P. (2017). 'Designing Auctions for Renewable Electricity Support: Best Practices from around the World'. *Energy for Sustainable Development*, *41*, 1–13. doi: 10.1016/j.esd.2017.05.006.

Gephart, M., Klessmann, C., and Wigand, F. (2017). 'Renewable Energy Auctions: When Are They (Cost) Effective?'. *Energy & Environment*, *28*, 145–165.

Insunza, X. (2015). *Análisis crítico del estatuto jurídico de la minería como barrera para el desarrollo de la energía solar en chile*, Tesis para optar al grado de magíster en políticas pública (Santiago: Universidad de Chile).

IRENA (International Renewable Energy Agency) (2015). *Renewable Power Generation Costs in 2014* (Abu Dhabi: International Renewable Energy Agency).

IRENA (2018). *Renewable Power Generation Costs in 2017* (Abu Dhabi: International Renewable Energy Agency).

IRENA (2020). *Renewable Power Generation Costs in 2019* (Abu Dhabi: International Renewable Energy Agency).

James, C. S. (2017). 'Chile's Creativity Comes to the Fore in Its 2017 Energy Auctions'. *Clean Energy Review* (September). https://www.linkedin.com/pulse/chiles-creativity-comes-fore-its-2017-energy-auctions-st-james/

Kruger, W., and Eberhard, A. (2018). 'Renewable Energy Auctions in Sub-Saharan Africa: Comparing the South African, Ugandan, and Zambian Programs'. *Wiley Interdisciplinary Reviews: Energy and Environment, February*, 1–13. https://doi.org./10.1002/wene.295.

Kruger, W., Stritzke, S., and Trotter, P. (2019). 'De-risking Solar Auctions in Sub-Saharan Africa—A Comparison of Site Selection Strategies in South Africa and Zambia'. *Renewable and Sustainable Energy Reviews, 104*(January), 429–438.

McEwan, C. (2017). 'Spatial Processes and Politics of Renewable Energy Transition: Land, Zones and Frictions in South Africa'. *Political Geography, 56*, 1–12.

Molina, A., Falvey, M., and Rondanelli, R. (2017). 'A Solar Radiation Database for Chile'. *Scientific Reports, 7*, 14823. https://doi.org/10.1038/s41598-017-13761-x.

Moreno, J., Moreno, R., Rudnick, H., and Mocarquer, S. (2012). 'Licitaciones para el abastecimiento eléctrico de clientes regulados en Chile dificultades y oportunidades'. *Estudios Públicos, 125*, 139–168.

Muñoz, F. D., Suazo-Martínez, C., Pereira, E., and Moreno, R. (2021). 'Electricity Market Design for Low-Carbon and Flexible Systems: Room for Improvement in Chile'. *Energy Policy, 148*, Part B.

4

Argentina

Auctions in a Challenging Investment Context

Martín A. Rodríguez Pardina and Julieta Schiro

4.1 Introduction: Capitalizing on abundant renewable energy resources despite economic instability

In May 2016, the Argentinian government launched its Programa de abastecimiento de energia eléctrica a partir de fuenter renovables (RenovAr) programme to manage the auction of renewable energy (RE) generation projects. In the four auction rounds run between 2016 and 2019, the programme attracted bids amounting to 18,573 megawatts (MW), of which 4,654 MW[1] were awarded at an average price of US$55.4/megawatt hour (MWh). Of the awarded projects, 31% (1,411 MW) began operations on schedule. This meant that the share of RE in Argentina increased from 1.9% of total generation in 2015 to 6.5% by December 2019.

The RenovAr programme differed from previous ones in two basic respects. The first was the use of competitive auctions to assign 20-year power purchase agreements (PPAs). The second was the establishment of a trust fund—the Fondo Fiduciario para el Desarrollo de Energías Renovables (Fund for the Development of Renewable Energy) (FODER)—to provide loan guarantees and investment financing in an attempt to mitigate the macroeconomic and sectoral risks linked to RE investment in Argentina.[2]

The auctions have been highly competitive, particularly with regard to solar and wind energy, with bids repeatedly exceeding the auctioned volumes. This has, in turn, given rise to highly competitive and downwardly trending

---

[1] In fact, 4,726 MW was awarded, but five contracts for 73 MW were subsequently cancelled.
[2] FODER is a fiduciary fund, with a publicly owned bank (Banco de Inversión y Comercio Exterior) as trustee, through which the state initially guaranteed energy payments as per the PPAs, and made it possible that projects could exercise a 'put option' if the state failed to meet certain contracted obligations.

Martín A. Rodríguez Pardina and Julieta Schiro, *Argentina*. In: *Renewable Energy Auctions: Lessons from the Global South.*
Edited by: Anton Eberhard and Wikus Kruger, Oxford University Press. © Oxford University Press (2023).
DOI: 10.1093/oso/9780192871701.003.0004

prices, comparable to those achieved by other countries in the region that are exposed to substantially lower financial risks.

When analysing the growth of RE usage in Argentina, certain distinctive elements of its economy and its energy sector are worth highlighting. Going from the general to the particular, these are:

- chronic macroeconomic instability;
- competitive primary energy sources;
- the institutional fragility of the electricity sector;
- the lack of a comprehensive sectoral investment plan;
- limitations of the transmission system.

Macroeconomic instability has characterized the country since the late 1990s. This is reflected in a high country-risk premium; meaning that the cost of capital is high.[3] This has had a direct impact on RE installations in Argentina in three ways. First, the RE sector is capital-intensive—with capital costs representing 80–90% of total costs. Second, it requires foreign investment. Third, RE is politically sensitive because its adoption has the potential to affect end-user electricity prices. As for many countries, finding mechanisms to mitigate and control the financial risks has therefore been fundamental to the design and implementation of Argentina's RE development policy.

Argentina's wind and solar resources are among the most abundant in the world . In the northwest region, solar radiation ranges from about 1.8 MWh/m^2 to 2.2 MWh/m^2 per year (Righini and Gallegos, 2011). In Patagonia, in the extreme south of the country, wind resources allow utilization factors greater than 50% (Jimeno et al., 2017). On the other hand, Argentina also has the third-largest reservoir of shale gas and shale oil, with estimated reserves of over 802 trillion cubic feet (Tcf) of natural gas in Northern Patagonia's Vaca Muerta formation (RunRún Energético, 2018). The abundance and diversity of primary energy sources means that no single technology dominates the country's energy sector. It therefore makes sense for the country to try to adopt strategies that optimize the contribution of different sectors by balancing minimum cost and ensuring the security of supply, the diversification of primary sources, and the minimization of emissions, etc.

In the early 1990s, Argentina's electricity sector was organized as a highly competitive market. After a massive macroeconomic crisis struck in 2002, the sector slowly mutated into a single-buyer system in which the government

---

[3] See Garrison (2020). Between 2009 and 2019, the interest rate on Argentina's sovereign bonds averaged more than 755 basis points over US bonds, with values exceeding 1,000 basis points over more than 20% of this period.

plays a central role in investment. However, the system has neither a well-defined institutional framework nor a clear allocation of responsibilities. For several years, the government has delegated the functions of procurement agent and sole buyer to the wholesale electricity market administrator, Compañía Administradora del Mercado Mayorista Eléctrico (CAMMESA).[4] As shown in this chapter, the absence of a clearly defined institutional energy system and well-coordinated governance mechanisms has placed some limits and conditionalities on the design and implementation of RE policies. In addition, the lack of an agency or mechanism that is responsible for medium- and long-term planning for the energy sector as a whole has proven a significant obstacle to the development of RE.

In 2015, Argentina adopted a renewable portfolio standard, with a target of 20% RE in the country's total generation mix by 2025. Based on this legal mandate, the RenovAr programme began a series of auctions for the incorporation of RE installations. At the same time, the government ran other auctions in the electricity sector (for thermal power, cogeneration, gas power plant closure, transmission expansion, etc.) and implemented other non-regulatory policies (such as subsidies for the development of shale gas) with no coordination across the energy sector as a whole. Furthermore, the elements of these programmes—volumes, locations, price differentiation by technology, etc.—do not respond to an optimized expansion plan and are, in some cases, clearly inconsistent. This increased the financial risks related to the RenovAr programme.

A specific issue related to the lack of long-term planning is the expansion of the electricity transmission network. The primary energy sources in Argentina are located at great distances from the main load centres. For example, wind resources in the south and solar resources in the west and northwest, are thousands of kilometres from the greater Buenos Aires metropolitan area, which uses approximately 35% of the electricity generated in the country (CAMMESA, 2019: 21). Naturally, transmission capacity has limited the volumes and sites available for RE installations. Thus, mechanisms for planning and allocating transmission capacity and expanding the network have to be closely coordinated with new generation projects (both RE and conventional).

The RenovAr programme has been influenced—both in its design and implementation—by these factors. The success of the first rounds—in terms of attracting offers at highly competitive prices—decelerated strongly as a

---

[4] CAMMESA was originally established to manage dispatch and act as a clearing house for financial transactions in the energy sector.

result of Argentina's 2018 macroeconomic crisis. Not surprisingly, fewer bidders took part, and bid prices were higher in the fourth round, which was held in 2018 and 2019. Similarly, with the change of administration after the 2019 presidential election, and the COVID-19 crisis that began in early 2020, the construction of awarded projects has slowed considerably.

In this chapter, we analyse the design, implementation, and results of the first four rounds of the RenovAr programme that took place between May 2016 and mid-2019. Sections 4.2 and 4.3 provide some basic background about Argentina and its energy sector. In section 4.4, we focus on the energy auctions. In section 4.5, we present the programme's results. In section 4.6, we outline the main lessons learned and make some recommendations. Our conclusions are contained in Section 4.7.

4.2 Overview of Argentina's economy

Located in the southern cone of Latin America, Argentina is large, geographically diverse, and sparsely populated. With a total area of 2.78 million km², the country is the second largest in the region (behind Brazil) and the eighth largest in the world. As of December 2019, the human population was 45 million, yielding a population density of 16 inhabitants per square kilometre.[5] The country stretches about 3,800 km, north to south, and is about 1,400 km at its widest point, east to west. It contains a great diversity of climates (with historical minimum and maximum and temperatures of −35°C and 49.1°C) and terrain that varies from rainforest in the northeast to large, fertile plains in the centre, mountain ranges in the west and semi-arid desert regions in the south.

With a gross domestic product (GDP) of approximately US$ 450 billion, Argentina has one of Latin America's largest economies. With its extraordinarily fertile land, it is a leading food producer, and its natural resources in the form of gas and lithium reserves offer great potential for RE. However, historical volatility, linked to an accumulation of institutional obstacles, has impeded development so that approximately 35.4% of the urban population live in poverty.[6]

In 2018, a series of external and internal difficulties hit hard. These included severe drought, financial volatility following the US Federal Reserve's

---

[5] As estimated by Argentina's National Statistics Institute (INDEC, n.d.); according to World Bank data, this is 70% less than the overall population density in sub-Saharan Africa in 2018, which they estimated at 51 people per square kilometre (World Bank, 2018b).

[6] See https://www.worldbank.org/en/country/argentina/overview (accessed 20 April 2023).

adjustment of its interest rate,[7] and negative perceptions regarding the pace of fiscal reforms. The peso devalued significantly. At the time of writing, in mid 2020, the annual inflation rate was above 50%, with GDP having contracted by 2.5% in 2018 and 3% in 2019.

4.3 Argentina's power sector

4.3.1 Introduction

Argentina's electricity mix is dominated by thermal generation (mainly combined-cycle gas turbines) followed by large hydro. By December 2019, installed capacity in Argentina's national grid was almost 40 gigawatts (GW).

The evolution of installed capacity from 2009 to 2019 is shown in Figure 4.1. Although Argentina's energy mix is still dominated by thermal and large hydro generation (see Table 4.1), energy from RE sources has risen in importance since 2015 and now amounts to 6.5%.

Peak demand in the system reached 26.3 GW (on 8 February 2018). Adjusting installed capacity by average availability and load factors for each

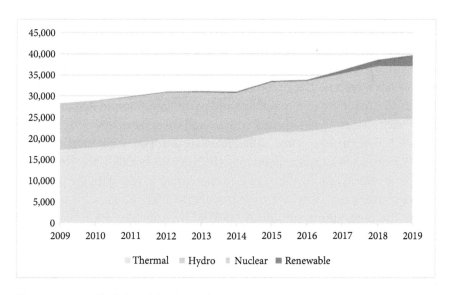

Figure 4.1 Installed electricity, Argentina, 2009–2019
Source: Compañia Administradora del Mercado Mayorista Eléctrico Sociedad Anónima (CAMMESA) (various); Secretaría de Energía (2019a).

---

[7] When the US Federal Reserve increases interest rates, the cost of debt in emerging economies tends to increase, and disinvestment often follows.

Table 4.1 Argentina's installed capacity, December 2019

Capacity	GW	%
Thermal		
Combined cycle	11.25	28.3
Gas turbine	7.4	18.6
Steam turbine[a]	4.25	10.7
Diesel	1.66	4.2
Total thermal	24.56	61.8
Renewable		
Wind	1.61	4.1
Hydro	0.50	1.3
Solar	0.44	1.1
Biogas	0.04	0.1
Biomass	0.002	0.01
Total renewable	2.592	6.61
Hydro	10.81	27.2
Nuclear	1.76	4.4
Total	39.722	100.01

Note: [a] Uses gas or heavy fuel oil for heating.
Source: CAMMESA (December 2019).

technology (hydro and renewables have particularly low load factors of around 40%), net installed capacity stands at 37 GW, which means that the country has a reserve margin of 40%. This is due partly to over-investment since 2015 (including in renewables) and partly to economic stagnation.

Electricity access is widespread, with overall coverage of over 95% reported in 2018.[8] Nevertheless, some differences are evident, with rural coverage at 85% and urban at more than 95% (IEA 2019). In 2000, the Renewable Energies in Rural Markets Project was established to facilitate the provision of energy access to dispersed rural populations far from distribution networks. The programme subsidizes 100% of the capital costs related to the installation of individual photovoltaic (PV) and/or wind systems; mini-grids (hydro/solar/wind/hybrid); solar systems for thermal purposes (cookers, ovens, and hot water tanks); and PV systems for pumping drinking water and other productive uses.

---

[8] International Energy Agency electricity access database, see: https://www.iea.org/reports/sdg7-data-and-projections/access-to-electricity (accessed 20 April 2023)

4.3.2 Power-sector structure

Starting in 1992, the restructuring of Argentina's power sector (through Act 24.065) was a textbook example of the reform paradigm that gripped the sector globally in the 1990s. The reforms included massive privatization, vertical and horizontal unbundling, the introduction of a competitive wholesale market, and the creation of an autonomous regulator. Figure 4.2 shows the outcome of this process as of 2019 and Table 4.2 provides a brief description of the main players.

As the main representative of the executive branch of the federal government, the Energy Secretariat is the central player and is in charge of several functions. First, it is responsible for defining and implementing policy through the promulgation of rules and regulations governing the wholesale electricity market. Second, the Secretariat chairs the CAMMESA Board and holds veto power. Third, it has indirect competence on regulatory matters, which makes it responsible for the appointment of three of Argentina's National Electricity Regulatory Entity (ENRE's) five directors and the administrative appellate body for all decisions made by ENRE. Fourth, it is involved in monitoring state-owned generation companies. Finally, it chairs the Federal Electricity Council (Consejo Federal de la Energía Eléctrica, CFEE),

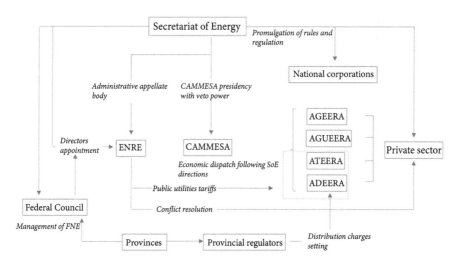

Figure 4.2 Overview of Argentina's energy sector, 2019
Source: Authors' compilation.

Table 4.2 Key institutions in Argentina's electricity sector, 2019

Energy Secretariat within the Ministry of Productive Development[a]	The Energy Secretariat is the main government body responsible for the design and implementation of energy sector policies. Its main functions include: defining wholesale market rules to be implemented by CAMMESA, chairing CAMMESA (with the power of veto), serving as an appeal body to ENRE decisions, appointing directors of SOEs in the energy sector, chairing Federal Energy Council, etc.
National Electricity Regulatory Entity (ENRE)	ENRE is an autonomous body responsible for regulating electrical activity and ensuring that companies in the sector (generators, transmitters, and distributors) comply with their obligations as established in the regulatory framework and in their concession contracts.
Wholesale electricity market administrator (private company) (CAMMESA)	CAMMESA plans the operation of the interconnected system, including the seasonal planning used by the Energy Secretariat to determine the seasonal price that is charged to distribution companies' customers. In addition, CAMMESA plans yearly, semi-annual, quarterly, monthly, weekly, and hourly electricity dispatch
Generation companies	Between them, 45 mostly private companies own 410 generation units, 27 self-generation units, and 8 cogeneration units.
Transmission companies	A total of eight companies are involved in transmission (one extra-high voltage and seven backbone/trunk network).
Distribution companies	Of the 29 distribution companies, 17 are 'concessioned' to the private sector and 12 are provincial SOEs. In addition, 584 cooperatives are also involved in distribution.
IEASA (formerly ENARSA)	IEASA is an SOE engaged in the exploitation of oil and natural gas and in the production, industrialization, transport, and commercialization of oil, natural gas, and electricity. It serves as the main gas provider to CAMMESA.
CFEE (Federal Electricity Council)	The Council advises on and coordinates energy policies developed by the federal government and the provinces. It also administers the Fondo Nacional de Energía Eléctrica (National Energy Fund).
Financial institutions	Banco de la Nación Argentina and Banco de Inversión y Comercio Exterior (BICE), a trustee of FODER.

Note: [a] The Ministry of Productive Development is a relatively new structure; before 2019, there was a Ministry of Energy and between 2015 and 2018, a Ministry of Mines and Energy (MINEM).
Source: CAMMESA (December 2019).

which is responsible for the management of the National Energy Fund (Fondo Nacional de la Energía).[9]

[9] The National Energy Fund was established to help finance further electrification. The fund derives its income from a surcharge on the rates paid by distribution companies and large users in the wholesale market as well as from interest on loans it provides.

As, the sector regulator, ENRE's main role is to protect users' rights. This includes establishing and enforcing transmission and distribution tariffs as well as quality standards and service rules and regulations. It is also the first stop for all sector stakeholders when dispute resolution is required.

Argentina's 23 provinces hold power over electricity distribution through concession contracts or, in some cases, as direct owners of electricity companies and are key stakeholders in the system. An important part of provincial responsibility is channelled through the provincial regulatory authorities (which fix distribution tariffs at provincial level) and the CFEE (which manages the Energy National Fund and nominates two of ENRE's five directors).

Private actors are the other key stakeholders in the electricity sector. As mentioned, almost all generation (with the exception of nuclear plants and two large binational hydro generators), transmission, and more than half of the distribution (in terms of number of users) is under private ownership (in the case of thermal generators) or private management (through concession contracts in the case of hydro generation, transmission, and distribution).

In the generation segment, all electricity is traded via a wholesale electricity market (Mercado Eléctrico Mayorista, MEM). As originally conceived, the MEM was a competitive space in which thermal generators bid for fuel prices and hydro generators bid for energy prices on a quarterly basis. The marginal cost of the marginal generator in each hour defined the system marginal price that was paid to every generator producing in that hour. In addition, a capacity payment was paid to all generators included in an unconstrained pre-dispatch.

As a result of the 1990s reforms, international competitive bidding was carried out to privatize all existing thermal generation, and 30-year concession contracts were awarded for the operation and maintenance of hydro generation plants. Two large international hydro generators—Yacyretá and Salto Grande—and the two existing nuclear plants remained under state control.[10] Further generation expansion was then left to market forces, with free entry to all new generation companies.

During the 1990s unbundling process, the transmission system was also split into a single extra-high-voltage (500/220 kV) company—Transener—and seven regional, high-voltage (220/132 kV) transmission companies. The operation and maintenance of these companies was concessioned for 95 years through an internationally competitive bidding process. Transmission services are regulated by ENRE through a revenue cap mechanism. Connection

---

[10] The hydro stations are 'international' in the sense that Yacyretá is on Argentina's border with Uruguay and Salto Grande is on the border with Panama.

and use-of-system charges are levied on generators, distributors, and large users to cover the annual revenue cap. Independent transmission companies are expected to bid for the construction as well as the operations and maintenance of new transmission lines when coalitions of beneficiaries (generators, distributors, and large users) request such expansion.

As noted, electricity distribution falls under provincial jurisdiction except for the greater Buenos Aires metropolitan area, which is under federal control. The federal government and 11 of the 23 provinces (representing approximately 60% of total users) have privatized distribution through long-term concession contracts. Distribution companies are able to sign long-term PPAs with any generator or buy from the wholesale market.[11] For most privatized companies, distribution tariffs are subject to a price cap, with pass through of transmission and wholesale electricity prices.

Large electricity users are allowed to buy directly from any generator or supplier while paying distributors and transmission companies a tolling (use-of-wires) fee. Initially, the threshold for large users was set at 1 MW but this has gradually been lowered to 30 kW. As of 2019, the system had 2,600 large users, with another 6,000 in distribution companies; their total demand amounted to 23,561 GWh (18% of system demand).[12]

In 2002, following a massive macroeconomic crisis, the government froze energy (electricity and gas) prices at the wholesale and retail level. This lasted, with minor adjustments, for over 13 years. As a result, the power sector evolved towards a de facto single-buyer system, in which the government provided most of the gas to thermal generators and paid them an energy conversion fee. During this period, the government undertook most new investment in generation through a newly created state-owned energy company Energía Argentina Sociedad Anónima (ENARSA).

By 2015, subsidies to the energy (electricity and gas) sector, which were almost nil in 2001, had climbed to nearly 3% of GDP (Secretaría de Energía, 2019a). In 2016, a new administration ended the price freeze but made no major changes to the wholesale electricity market, which still functions as a single-buyer model. Also in 2016, the government began auctioning PPAs with new and existing generation companies for additional capacity. CAMMESA acted as the off-taker for all contracts with an explicit warranty from the federal government.

---

[11] Distributors bought from MEM at a seasonal price defined by the Secretary of Energy as the average of the expected spot price for the following quarter.

[12] CAMMESA, *Informe Mensual*, December 2019.

4.3.3 Tariff levels and financial sustainability

The legal framework adopted in 1992 made economic and financial sustainability a clear objective for the energy sector. However, as noted, after the 2002 crisis, end-user rates and wholesale market prices were frozen within a high-inflation context, creating a large financial gap in the sector.

After an almost 13-year tariff freeze, the new administration that took office in December 2015 began a process of normalization. This included a review of transmission and federal distribution companies' tariffs and increasing the wholesale prices paid to generators. Thus, the electricity sector deficit decreased from US$ 11,812 million in 2015 (representing 1.8% of GDP) to US$ 3,737 million in 2019 (0.9% of GDP) (Secretaría de Energía, 2019a).

In December 2019, another new administration took office and immediately decreed a new six-month rate freeze. Given high inflation and the COVID-19 crisis, this freeze is likely to be extended for a longer period, thus deepening the deficit once again.

In the wholesale market, CAMMESA has assumed the role of sole buyer in all PPA contracts signed with both thermal and new renewable generators. As per the regulations, CAMMESA's collection and payment mechanism 'socializes' the collectability risks. If, in any month, the money collected by CAMMESA from distributors doesn't cover the cost of generation, the shortfall is meant to be covered by an interest-free loan from the treasury. If the treasury does not provide a loan (and, so far, it has not), CAMMESA reduces payments to all generators and transmission companies in proportion to the shortfall. This means that the collectability risk should be borne first by the state and then collectively by all creditor agents, that is, generator and transmission companies.

Some PPAs (including for RE projects) contain clauses giving them priority in this situation such that the rule of proportionality among all participants is limited by the existence of privileged creditors. By the end of 2019, distributors' debt to CAMMESA amounted to nearly US$ 650 million (approximately 11% of annual sales to distributors) (Secretaría de Energía, 2019b).

The precarious financial situation of the sector, combined with the chronic macroeconomic crisis, led to specific risk-mitigation mechanisms being established for PPAs involved in RE auctions; these are discussed in section 4. 4.1.8.

4.3.4 Regulatory and policy framework

As noted, the power sector's regulatory framework is set out in laws and regulations drafted by the Energy Secretariat. At the start of the 1990s reform process, Act 24.065 of 1991 established the following objectives for the sector: protecting users' rights; promoting competitiveness in the electricity market; encouraging investments to secure long-term supply; promoting operational reliability and efficiency; enhancing equity, freedom of access, and non-discrimination; encouraging widespread use of electricity transmission and distribution facilities; regulating transmission and distribution; ensuring fair and reasonable tariffs; and creating adequate tariff-setting structures.

Since 1998, specific laws have been promulgated to advance the development of RE. In that year, Act 25.019 declared electricity generation from RE to be of national interest and established various incentives (mainly tax exemptions) to ensure its prioritization. Act 26.190 of 2006 affirmed all tax incentives and created a renewable energy feed-in tariff programme. The values for the feed-in tariff were established and the Act indicated that these were to be funded through the National Energy Fund (see n 9 above). However, neither of these laws had much effect in terms of attracting RE investment. Part of the reason for this was that the laws set out tariffs payable in the local currency (pesos/kWh), with a quarterly adjustment mechanism based on the variation of the average cost of generation in the wholesale market. In the context of the country's high inflation rates (which have consistently been above 15% per annum since 2000) and the freezing of wholesale tariffs, payment in pesos was unattractive for investors.

At the end of 2015, Act 27.191 amended the 2006 legislation. The 2015 Act established a renewable energy portfolio standard with the short-term objective of ensuring that 8% of national electricity consumption would be supplied from RE sources by the end of 2017. The medium-term objective was stated as being to increase the contribution of RE to the energy mix to 20% by the end of 2025. The new law was a key element in international commitments made by Argentina to addressing climate change.[13]

Argentina's current legal framework provides a set of short- and medium-term objectives for RE in an attempt to provide predictability for

---

[13] Renewable energies are a major component of the national determined contribution (NDC) presented by the Argentinian government to the UN Framework Convention on Climate Change. The revised version of Argentina's NDC, published in November 2016, set the unconditional greenhouse gas (GHG) emission reductions target at 18% and the overall target (conditional plus unconditional) at 37% by 2030 (World Bank, 2017).

investments.[14] The regulatory framework has been adapted and improved to encourage the diversification of the national energy matrix, to increase the participation of RE, thus reducing dependence on fossil fuels. As mentioned in the introduction, one of the most significant aspects of the framework was the creation of a trust fund for renewable energy development, FODER, to mitigate macroeconomic risks and address the financing difficulties facing the sector. The legislation also includes provisions for fiscal incentives, such as exemption from import duties and certain other taxes; accelerated amortization; advance VAT refunds; and incentives for the incorporation of local components, equipment, and products in the generation business. The then Ministry of Energy and Mining was also instructed to establish the contracting mechanisms needed to meet the stated RE participation goals and to promote technological and geographical diversification.

However, as in so many countries, one of the major limitations of Argentina's electricity sector is the absence of a medium- and long-term planning mechanism. The sectoral reform of the 1990s was based on a concept that delegated all generation and transmission investment decisions to the market. Since 2002, the reform process has been rolled back, significantly increasing the role of the state in the sector but without introducing any formal planning mechanisms. For example, the RE tenders have been developed without coordination and consideration of other tenders being issued for the electricity and gas sectors.

4.4 The design of Argentina's RenovAr programme

Framed by Act 27.191, and hence shaped by its objectives and instruments, the RenovAr programme was launched in 2016, seeking to incorporate 10,000 MW of RE into the energy matrix by 2025. So far, the programme has been carried out through periodic auctions in which companies present investment projects and the price at which they are willing to sell electricity if they are awarded a 20-year PPA. Between 2016 and 2018, four auction 'rounds' occurred, (RenovAr1, RenovAr1.5, RenovAr2, and RenovAr3), with few variations in their main features (see Table 4.3).

The RenovAr programme is designed to achieve several objectives. These are: to allocate contracts transparently and competitively, to minimize the

---

[14] Act 27.191 has since been complemented by Decree 531.16 and other pieces of legislation, which sets out the policy objectives in more detail and indicates how these objectives could be achieved.

Table 4.3 Key features of RenovAr auctions, Argentina, 2016–2019

Round number	RenovAr1	RenovAr1.5	RenovAr2	RenovAr3
Date of RfP	May 2016	October 2016	September 2017	November 2018
Design				
Volume requested[a]	1 GW	600 MW	1,768 MW	400 MW
PPA length	20 years			
Currency	US$ (indexed)			
Regional capacity required	No		Yes	
Implementation				
Policy and regulation authority	Undersecretariat for Renewable Energies and Energy Efficiency			
Regulator	Ente Nacional Regulador de la Electricidad (ENRE)			
Procurer	CAMMESA			
Off-taker	CAMMESA			
Outcomes				
MW adjudicated	1,142 MW	1,282 MW	2,043 MW	259 MW
Prices weighted average (US¢/MWh)	Solar: 59.8 Wind: 59.4 Mini hydro: 105.0 Biomass: 110.0 Biogas: 154.0	Solar: 54.9 Wind: 53.3	Solar: 42.8 Wind: 40.9 Mini hydro: 98.9 Biomass: 117.2 Biogas: 160.6 Biogas–SL: 129.2	Solar: 57.5 Wind: 58.0 Mini hydro: 103.4 Biomass: 106.1 Biogas: 158.6 Biogas–SL: 129.5

Note: [a] The MW requested in Round 1.5 was small because it was aimed at bidders who had been unsuccessful in Round 1. Round 3 was dubbed 'Mini-RenovAr' because it aimed to attract companies that run small power plants.
Source: CAMMESA (December 2019).

long-term costs to consumers, to respect the legal mandate regarding the technological and geographical diversification of the energy sector, and to set incentives for the development of a national industry capable of manufacturing RE generation equipment.

The first round, RenovAr1, required 1,000 MW of RE, split between technologies (wind, solar PV, biomass, biogas, and small hydro). The bidding terms and conditions set out the maximum available tax benefits they could claim through accelerated depreciation, advance VAT returns, etc.) and the investment reference value (per MW and per technology) (see section 4.4.1.3).

For Round 1, a reserve (or ceiling) price was set per technology (in US$/MW), but the amount was not made public until after bids had been submitted, and projects exceeding this price were automatically disqualified.

The government did not explain why they withheld this information, and its impact is unclear. However, according to the International Finance Corporation, which played an advisory role in the process, this resulted in lower prices.

The International Finance Corporation (IFC) advised the government not to disclose its price cap until bids were opened. This was prescient as the average price for Round 1 ultimately was US$ 20–30/MWh below the envisaged price cap. In Round 1.5, the average price from Round 1 was announced as the new cap (IFC, 2018: 11).

On the other hand, Menzies et al. (2019) have argued that the secret reserve price might have discouraged some participants, particularly providers of biogas, biomass, and small hydro. Offers received for these technologies amounted to far less than the auctioned volumes. As Menzies et al, pointed out,

> The bid ceiling price was undisclosed, which created some uncertainty amongst potential bidders as regards pricing their bids and it is probable that at least some would-be bidders opted not to participate in round 1 due, to some extent, to this uncertainty.
>
> **(Menzies et al. 2019: 17)**

4.4.1 Auction design

RenovAr was designed as a two-envelope, single-round auction, with the process from the publication of the request for proposals (RfP) to contract signing lasting between six (RenovAr1) and 14 months (RenovAr3). All interested bidders were required to buy the RfP at a cost of around US$ 12 000, payable to CAMMESA.

For RenovAr1, however, a draft of the RfP was first made available to all interested parties (not just prospective bidders) via an open and non-binding public-consultation process that lasted about six weeks. In this phase, any interested party could make comments and suggestions on the draft. After this, the final RfP was subject to a consultation process that lasted about a month. Several modifications were made and eight circulars were issued to clarify different aspects of the process. A similar process was followed in subsequent rounds—seven circulars went out for RenovAr2 and RenovAr3.

For RenovAr1, interested bidders had from 25 July to 5 September 2016 (40 days) to prepare and submit proposals, although they had access to the draft RfP from late May of that year. The assessment process, from bid opening to award notification, lasted about a month. Rounds 2 and 3 followed a similar schedule, while RenovAr1.5 was shorter because it involved projects that had already been part of RenovAr1.

As regards the signing of the PPAs, RenovAr1 allocated a short period that was probably too optimistic. From RenovAr2 onwards, the time period varied between 167 and 179 days. Figure 4.3 shows the timeline of RenovAr 1, and Table 4.4 summarizes the time frame of each round, allowing for comparison between them.

RenovAr1.5 had no open non-binding consultation process linked to the RfP, only a binding one that was limited to those participating in the auction. This was because RenovAr1.5 was seen as an extension or a 'second phase' of RenovAr1, with participation limited to bidders that had been unsuccessful in the first round. In RenovAr2, the consultation period was extended by about two weeks. However, the evaluation period and the consequent awarding of bids was similar across these two rounds, although in RenovAr2, PPA signing was scheduled over five months after awards.

In the case of RenovAr3, the final RfP was published over three months after the release of the draft. Bidders had 10 weeks to prepare and present their offers. The evaluation period took over 40 days, which was longer than previous rounds, and the awarding of winning bids also took slightly more time (11 versus 5 or 6 days). PPA signing, on the other hand, began only a week later.

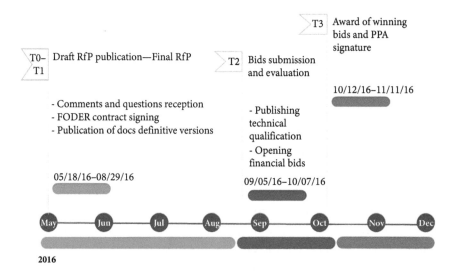

Figure 4.3 Timeline for Programa de abastecimiento de energia eléctrica a partir de fuentes renovables (RenovAr1)

Source: CAMMESA (various).

Table 4.4 Timetables for RenovAr's first four rounds

Milestones	RenovAr1	RenovAr1.5	RenovAr2	RenovAr3
Draft RfP issued (T0)	18 May 2016	28 October 2016	16 August 2017	14 November 2018
Public comment and questions	T0 + 96	–	T0 + 42	T0 + 119
Final RfP available for purchase (T1)	29 August 2016 T0 + 103	28 October 2016 T0	14 October 2017 T0 + 59	13 March 2019 T0 + 119
Bid submission (T2)	5 September 2016 T1 + 7	11 November 2016 T1 + 14	19 October 2017 T1 + 5	30 May 2019 T1 + 78
Technical qualification published	T2 + 28	T2 + 11	T2 + 32	T2 + 36
Financial bids open	T2 + 32	T2 + 12	T2 + 35	T2 + 42
Winning bids awarded (T3)	12 October 2016 T2 + 37	25 November 2016 T2 + 14	29 November 2017 T2 + 41	22 July 2019 T2 + 53
PPA signed	T3 + 30	T3 + 168	T3 + 167	T3 + 179

Source: CAMMESA (various).

4.4.1.1 The two-envelope process

Technical bids, submitted in envelope A, were first assessed by CAMMESA, which ensured that all legal and technical requirements were met, and then ranked bids based on stated local content (SLC).[15] These rankings were then sent to the Energy Secretariat as a non-binding recommendation. The Secretariat assessed the recommendations, approved a final ranking, and informed CAMMESA (for a more detailed explanation of the bid qualification process, see section 4.4.1.6).

At this point, CAMMESA opened the financial proposals, submitted in envelope B. The financial proposals had to state the offered price, whether a World Bank guarantee was required, the minimum capacity for partial allocation, the energy commitment, and the minimum energy commitment. When comparing bids, CAMMESA had to consider the information submitted in both envelopes and estimate the adjusted offered price (AOP, in Spanish Precio Ofrecido Ajustado)) per technology (see Table 4.10).

---

[15] The SLC was computed as the value of local content in electromechanical equipment as a proportion of total value, that is, the cost of imported electromechanical components, plus international insurance, plus international freight, all calculated at the destination in Argentina plus the sum of the national components incorporated.

CAMMESA sorted the B envelopes according to each technology and discarded bids in which the AOP exceeded the maximum award price established for each technology type. The bids were then ranked according to the merit order established per technology until the offered capacity equalled the required capacity (by technology) or the maximum capacity per interconnection point as set out in the RfP (for more on ranking, see section 4.4.1.5).

CAMMESA then submitted a non-binding report to the Energy Secretariat recommending the award of PPAs to the selected bidders. Shortly after this, the ministry instructed CAMMESA to confirm the awards and proceed with the signing of PPAs.

On signing a PPA, successful bidders received confirmation of the price per kWh as stated in their bids (pay-as-bid). Thus, their 'offered price' became the 'awarded price' with the addition of annual adjustments and incentives.

4.4.1.2 Auction demand

As noted, Argentina's electricity sector lacks a medium- and long-term planning mechanism that guides investment decisions. Without a coherent investment programme, the expansion of generation and transmission infrastructure tends to take place as a result of short-term decisions that often lack adequate economic justification. RE is no exception.

Alongside RenovAr's auctions, the government implemented auctions for thermal units (Res 021) and cogeneration units (Res 287). They also planned, but did not carry out, auctions related to the expansion of transmission capacity. Each of these processes were developed autonomously and without reference to any integrated plan for the electricity sector or for the energy sector as a whole.[16]

As noted, the main objective of the RenovAr auctions was to achieve the RE volumes established in Act 27.191. However, achieving the goals set out in the law required the installation of nearly 2.7 GW of renewable capacity by 2017 and an additional 750 MW each year from 2018 to 2025.[17] Table 4.5 shows the volumes auctioned in the first four rounds. Besides the lack of an integrated plan for the energy sector, the RenovAr programme itself lacks a mechanism for setting the frequency and volume of its own auctions. Each round has simply been announced by the government a few months before issuing the final RfP.

---

[16] In fact, while the RE auctions were taking place, the government was subsidizing the development of shale gas extraction in the Vaca Muerta field by paying guaranteed minimum prices for gas that were above international prices.

[17] This assumes energy growth of 4% per annum between 2017 and 2025 and an average utilization factor of 40% for RE.

The second round (RenovAr1.5) deserves to be highlighted because it responded directly to the 'excess supply' evident in the response to RenovAr1, when offers for 6.3 GW were received in answer to the call for 1 GW. On the one hand, this led to the awarding of 1.14 GW (14% more than stipulated). On the other hand, two weeks after awarding winning bids from the first round, the government announced RenovAr1.5 and called for an additional 400 MW to be supplied by those projects that had qualified in the first round but had not been offered an award.[18]

A similar process was followed in RenovAr2, but this time identified as two phases of a single round. In the first phase, 1,200 MW of capacity were auctioned and offers for over 9,300 MW were received. The excess offers were concentrated in solar (with a demand of 550 MW and bids received for 3,811 MW) and wind (with a demand of 450 MW and bids received for nearly 5,300 MW). In the face of this excess capacity (over 675% at the aggregated level), a second phase was opened in which projects not awarded during the first phase were offered the option of signing PPAs at a price given by the weighted average of bids awarded in the first phase (for each technology). For wind and solar bids, only projects in the most competitive regions were considered, that is, Buenos Aires, Patagonia, and Comahue regions for wind and Northwest

Table 4.5 Auctioned RE volumes, by MW, Argentina 2016–2019

RenovAr1	RenovAr1.5	RenovAr2	RenovAr3
Total demand			
1 000 MW	600 MW	1,200 MW (Phase 1) 567.5 MW (Phase 2)	400 MW
Requested technology			
600 MW wind	400 MW wind	Phase 1	350 MW wind and
300 MW solar	200 MW solar	550 MW wind	solar
80 MW biomass and		450 MW solar PV	25 MW biomass
biogas		100 MW biomass	10 MW biogas
20 MW small hydro		50 MW hydroelectric, 35 MW	5 MW biogas–SL
		biogas	10 MW small
		15 MW biogas–SL	hydro
		Phase 2	
		275 MW wind	
		225 MW solar PV	
		67.5 MW biomass and biogas	

Source: CAMMESA (various).

[18] In RenovAr 1.5, maximum prices applied (based on the weighted average of awarded projects in RenovAr1), and bidders had to resubmit all documentation. Technical aspects could be changed (so that they could lower bid prices) but bid capacity and project location had to stay the same.

and Cuyo regions for solar; see Appendix A for maps of Argentina's solar and wind resources. As a result of the second phase, an additional 568 MW of capacity was awarded.[19]

In all rounds, apart from RenovAr1, a regional requirement was set out in the respective RfPs. The country was divided into regions and maximum capacity additions, per technology, were set for each region (see Table 4.6). Similarly, restrictions regarding the distribution of RE projects were applied to the provinces within each region. No other site restrictions were applied.

The allocation of regional quotas responded, to some extent, to the limitations of the transmission system. However, by setting limits per province, the government could make progress with its political objective of ensuring balance in RE investments across regions.

4.4.1.3 General conditions set for the auctions

In addition to volume quotas, some general conditions were set for the different RenovAr rounds as summarized in Table 4.7. As noted, in Round 1, bidders were not informed of the reserve (ceiling) price that had been set for each technology. The first step in the economic assessments of the offers required CAMMESA to check that the offered price was below the reserve price. If it was not, the offer was automatically rejected.

Table 4.6 Regional MW quotas allocated for solar and wind in RE auctions, Argentina 2016–2019

RenovAr1	RenovAr1.5	RenovAr2	RenovAr3
None	Wind: Argentina divided into four regions (Comahue, Patagonia, Buenos Aires, and 'the rest') allocated 100 MW each. Solar: two regions (NOA, 'the rest') allocated 100 MW each.	Wind: four regions (Comahue, Patagonia, Buenos Aires, and 'the rest'): 200 MW each but 'rest' 100 MW and (Comahue + Patagonia + Buenos Aires) < 450 MW Solar: three regions (NOA, Cuyo, 'the rest'): 200 MW each but 'rest' 100 MW and (NOA + Cuyo) < 350 MW	Wind and solar: Region 1: 40 MW Regions 2, 3, and 7: 60 MW Regions 4 and 5: 30 MW Region 6: 70 MW + < 20 MW was allocated to each province (except Buenos Aires)

Source: CAMMESA (various).

[19] A cap was applied per technology as follows: 275 MW for wind, 225 MW for solar, and 67.5 MW for biomass and biogas combined.

In the next two rounds, the reserve price for each technology was established as the average of the offers awarded in the previous tenders and this was made public. For RenovAr3, the RenovAr2 figure became the reserve price—except for wind and solar, for which the combined reserve price was slightly increased.

Restrictions on the minimum and maximum size of each project were also specified. Minimum size restrictions generally related to ensuring certain economies of scale. Maximum size limits, on the other hand, were aimed at preventing too much concentration in the market. In the first three rounds,

Table 4.7 General conditions set for RE auctions, Argentina, 2016–2019

Parameter	RenovAr1	RenovAr1.5	RenovAr2	RenovAr3
Reserve price per technology (US$/MWh)	Kept secret (RfP Article 3.6) Wind: 82 Solar: 90 BM: 110 BG: 160 MH: 105	Made public (weighted average of awarded offers in Round 1) Wind: 59.39 Solar: 59.75	Made public (weighted average of awarded offers in Rounds 1 and 1.5)[a] Wind: 56.25 Solar: 57.04 BM: 110 BG: 160 BG–SL: 130 MH: 105	Made public: Wind and solar: 60 BM: 110 BG: 160 BG–SL: 130 MH: 105
Projects' required capacity (min., max. MW)	Wind and solar: 1–100 BM: 1–65 BG: 1–15 MH:0.5–20	Wind and solar: 1–100	Wind and solar: 1–100 BM and MH: 0.5–50 BG: 0.5–10	Wind, solar, BM, BG, BG–SL, and MH: 0.5–10
Investment reference value (million US$/MW)	Wind: 1.6 Solar: 1.3 BM: 2.5 BG: 5 MH: 3	Wind: 1.6 Solar: 1.3	Wind: 1.4 Solar: 0.9 BM: 3 BG: 5.5 BG–SL: 2.5 MH: 3	Wind: 1.4 Solar: 0.9 BM: 2.5 BG: 4.5 BG–SL: 1.3 MH: 2.8
Maximum execution period	All: 730 days (but solar in certain interconnection points, 900 days)	All: 900 days	Wind, solar, BG, BG–SL, and MH: 730 days (but solar at certain interconnection points, 900 days) BM: 1,065 days.	Wind and solar: 730 days BM, BG, BG–SL, and MH: 1,095 days.

Note: [a] For RenovAr2's second phase, the reserve prices in US$/MWh were wind: 40.27, Solar: 41.76, BM: 106.73, BG: 156.85 (Res 473, MINEM)
Source: CAMMESA (various).

the objective was to attract offers for large projects, that is, solar and wind power at up to 100 MW and biogas and biomass at up to 15 and 30 MW, respectively.

By contrast, RenovAr3 targeted small projects (known as MiniRen) with the aim of attracting capital from non-traditional sources into RE as well as to optimize the use of capacities available in medium-voltage networks and to promote regional development.[20]

In all rounds, the specifications included an investment reference value (in million US$/MW) for each technology. These values did not enter the bid analysis process or the determination of the merit order. However, they constituted a maximum value for eventual investor compensation in the event of default by any of the parties (see section 4.4.1.7). The values set remained unchanged for the first two rounds and were modified (with reductions for solar and wind power and increases for other technologies) from RenovAr2 onwards.

The maximum authorized tax benefits (such as accelerated amortization and advance VAT refunds) relevant for each technology were also specified in the auction design, as shown in Table 4.8.

For each technology, a maximum project execution time was also established. These periods were kept unchanged across rounds. However, in RenovAr 1.5, it was extended from 730 to 900 days, and in RenovAr 3, 1,095 days was allowed for biomass, biogas, and mini hydro. In all rounds except RenovAr3, extra points were awarded to bids in which commitments were made to shorter construction periods. The AOP resulted from multiplying

Table 4.8 Maximum fiscal benefits linked to RenovAr auction rounds in US$/MW, 2016–2019

Technology	RenovAr1 (US$/MW)	RenovAr1.5 (US$/MW)	RenovAr2 (US$/MW)	RenovAr3 (US$/MW)
Wind	960,000	960,000	700,000	630,000
Solar PV	720,000	720,000	425,000	382,500
Biomass	1,250,000	1,250,000	1,500,000	1,125,000
Biogas	2,500,000	2,500,000	2,750,000	2,025,000
Biogas–SL	–	–	1,250,000	585,000
Mini hydro	1,500,000	1,500,000	1,500,000	1,260,000

Source: CAMMESA (various).

[20] See the Energy Secretariat's Resolution 100/2018 (RESOL-2018-100-APN-SGE#MHA) of 14 November 2018, https://www.argentina.gob.ar/normativa/nacional/resoluci%C3%B3n-100-2018-316407/actualizacion (accessed 20 April 2023).

the offered price by a loss factor[21] and also by an amount (in US$/MWh) for the period of time between the offered execution term and the maximum execution term.[22] Projects could be fined if agreed deadlines were not met (see section 4.4.1.7).

The inclusion of an incentive for early installation of generation facilities responded, in part, to a perceived risk of a lack of generation capacity in the market. In practice, however, time differences between offers (with a maximum of 975 days in advance for a biomass project in RenovAr2 versus zero days in 60 offers made across the first 3 rounds) did not affect their ranking in the adjudication process.

4.4.1.4 Site selection and transmission access

Land availability is not a major problem for RE development in Argentina (see Menzies et al., 2019). According to Jimeno, et al. (2017), the rental price of land for wind farms, is US$ 5,000–10,000 MW/year. For land with potential for solar PV installations in Mendoza province, the purchase price is about US$ 2,000/ha. In other provinces with high solar potential, the price ranges from US$ 2,000 to US$ 5,000/ha. In provinces such as Jujuy and Salta, government land (terrenos fiscales) can be accessed very affordably.

Because Argentina's traditional primary energy sources (gas and large hydroelectric projects) are located at a great distance from the main centres of energy consumption, its high-voltage transmission grid is central to national energy provision. The greater Buenos Aires metropolitan area, for example, accounts for around 35% of the country's electricity demand. Similarly, for RE, the areas that have the greatest abundance of solar radiation (the northwest) and consistently high wind speeds (the south) are thousands of kilometres from the main centres of consumption (see Appendix A). Access to the national grid is therefore crucial to RenovAr's success.

The rules regarding access to the transmission network have varied slightly from round to round. In RenovAr1, the tender included an annex that specified the maximum capacity that could be connected at each point in the network. As the specifications were clarified, it became evident that the number specified did not necessarily correspond to a technical maximum but was, instead, the MW limit available to bidders. Although the total limit available for the 500 kV network was 1,700 MW (or 70% greater than the volume tendered), specific restrictions applied at each line, substation, and node point in

---

[21] In RenovAr3, the offered price was adjusted by the forced generation displacement (US$ 5/MWh).

[22] In RenovAr1, this was US$ 0.15/MWh for every 30 consecutive days between the offered and maximum execution term. In RenovAr1.5 and RenovAr2, the amount was US$ 0.005/MWh for each day between the offered and maximum execution term.

the network. These limits affected the final awards to the extent that more bids were received for certain connection points than the available capacity at that point would handle. RenovAr1.5 kept the same rules as well as the connection limits per connection point (net of the volumes awarded in RenovAr1).

In RenovAr2, transmission availability was based on an 'expanded transmission system', which included transmission investments due to be completed in the following 30 months. A take-or-pay clause was included to shield bidders from the risk of transmission works not reaching completion. This covered generators for demand risks linked to delays in grid expansion by guaranteeing payment for energy they couldn't deliver as a result of transmission restrictions. In RenovAr3, which focused on small projects, the delivery point was specified as a connection between 13.2 kV and 66 kV, and no predetermined limits were set.

Regarding costs, a 'shallow connection' approach has been adopted; that is, bidders have to cover the costs of all investments necessary to ensure the correct operation of connections at the delivery point but can exclude any adaptation costs that the system might need. In Argentina, electricity transmission concessionaires are obliged to operate and maintain *existing infrastructure only*. Expansion of the system is carried out by independent carriers and tends to be linked to specific tenders, with the costs being borne by the 'beneficiaries' of said expansions. Any deep connection costs arising from the incorporation of RenovAr projects have been subject to these rules. Accordingly, all project bids had to include the costs of installing transmission lines and transformer stations as well as the measurement and control equipment required to connect the generation plant to the delivery point.[23]

4.4.1.5 Qualification criteria and process

Participation in all four rounds was open to local and international individuals as well as private legal entities. Bids had to be submitted by means of a specific purpose entity constituted in the Argentine Republic. Both foreign and local individuals or legal entities that are legally disqualified from entering into contracts (for reasons such as bankruptcy, criminal records, etc.) were not permitted to bid.

As described in section 4.4.1, the auctions were run as single-stage, two-envelope sealed bids. Besides providing background information, such as statutory and legal data, bidders had to provide a bid bond and also provide evidence of minimum amount for each MW of offered bid capacity. This

---

[23] Following the general regulations of the electrical transmission system, and having built the transmission facilities, bidders could transfer these to a concessionaire for operations and maintenances.

helped reduce the risk of awarded projects not having sufficient financial or legal capacity to become operational.

4.4.1.5.1 Level of project preparation

The technical qualification criteria for all four rounds can be described as intermediate. In their bids, participants had to show evidence of only basic feasibility studies and preliminary commitments related to their chosen site, connections to the transmission network, and the availability of equipment. Apart from an environmental impact study, bidders were not required to submit detailed research on any technical or financial aspect.

The environmental study had to comply with established national standards and show that construction of the project could start on the stipulated date. Environmental impact assessments had to include a feasibility study and cover the construction phase as well as ensuring that surveillance programmes would be established to monitor environmental impact throughout the useful life of the project. According to interviews with actors involved in the preparation of the environmental studies, these were quite standard, took only a couple of weeks to prepare, and were reasonably affordable—costing about US$ 3,000–4,000 for a 20 MW wind project.[24]

Bidders were responsible for securing rights and permits for the use of the properties on which projects would be developed. As part of the technical description, they had to provide documentation proving the properties' availability for the full term of the supply contract. This could be through provision of a property title, a rental, or a usufruct contract and/or an irrevocable option to purchase, rent, or benefit from usufruct. In the case of real estate in the public domain, certified copies of the status of the land had to be accompanied by copies of the administrative acts that allow their use by such projects.

All sites involved had to be identified and located on maps and satellite charts, with plans and diagrams detailing the location of the generation plant as well as access and circulation routes. Bidders also had to show that they had obtained any necessary federal, provincial, and municipal permits related to the use of land.

---

[24] According to the IFC (2018: 11),

> Each province initially wanted its own Environmental and Social (E&S) rules to apply in the projects located in their jurisdictions. IFC recommended a universal approach whereby IFC Performance Standards would apply across provinces. This standardisation of E&S requirements provided comfort to bidders pursuing projects in multiple locations and to lenders accustomed to IFC's standards. The use of IFC performance standards was also critical to ensure project eligibility for the World Bank guarantee and increased preference for RenovAr over one-off tenders.

In addition, bidders' technical offers had to include a static and dynamic study of the transmission network, with the opinion of an independent consultant confirming the feasibility of injecting the projects' power at the relevant delivery points. This study also had to be approved by the carriers to which projects were to be connected. These studies cost from US$ 10,000–15,000 and take about a month to complete.

Information regarding the availability or feasibility of the RE resources also had to be included in the technical offer. Bidders had to guarantee that the resources were available and that no restrictions had been imposed on their use. This information had to be confirmed by an independent consultant in a report that contained details about the resource measured at, or close to, the site. If the measurement mechanism was located outside the site, the bidders had to prove that they were entitled to use the information.[25] Accordingly, the technical bids had to include expected energy production, assuming the proposed plant design and its respective typical curves according to the technology applied, as well as an estimate of associated losses and uncertainties informing energy production estimates at different probability levels.[26]

Data on the proposed technologies had to include studies and documentation certifying the performance of the equipment to be used, the capacity to be installed, and a technical description of all components and ancillary facilities. For each electromechanical component, the percentage of local content had to be stated.[27] Along with this, plant operation and maintenance plans had to be submitted.

No specific requirements were set out regarding the financial resources required for bids. Bidders just had to present a proposed date for financial close as part of the general performance term and schedule of works, including terms for financial close as well as dates for the start of construction, equipment delivery, and commercial operation authorisation.

In summary, technical requirements at the bidding stage were limited to reports on project feasibility by independent consultants and/or affidavits from bidders. No in-depth studies were required. Given the high rate of qualification, it seems that these requirements were not considered stringent. In practice, the majority of bids passed the technical assessment phase. On

---

[25] For wind, bidders had to present a minimum of a year of wind measurements and an EPR by an independent consultant. For solar, they had to submit an Extended Producer Responsibility (EPR) report by independent consultant. For biomass (BM), biogas (BG), and biogas–sanitary landfill (BG–SL), bidders had to state the source and sustainability of the BM/BG resource. For mini-hydro projects, they had to supply an affidavit confirming resource availability and energy production calculations.

[26] Expected production at P50–P90–P99 for wind, solar, and hydro projects and expected gross and net production for the rest of the technologies.

[27] The percentage of local content had to be computed as mandated by Joint Resolution No. 123 of the Ministry of Energy and Mining and No. 313 of the Ministry of Production, passed on 5 July 2016.

average, over the four rounds, only 13% of bids were rejected on technical grounds. Details regarding offers presented and accepted in each round are shown in Table 4.9.

Clearly, this approach maximized competition by facilitating bidder participation, but it ran the risk of a high number of projects not materializing. However, by including a bid bond and a performance guarantee with relatively high values once the contract had been awarded, the RenovAr programme attempted to minimize the risk of projects not reaching completion.

The fact that bidders did not have to show evidence that they had access to the financial resources committed to their projects has probably been the most risky aspect of the RenovAr bidding process. The risk is that awarded projects might not reach financial closure and must therefore face the loss of the guarantee bond. In practice, several projects have not reached financial close, particularly after the 2018 financial crisis (see section 4.5 for more on this).

4.4.1.6 Bidder ranking and winner selection

Once compliance with the formal and technical requirements (guarantees, permissions, etc.) had been verified, CAMMESA proceeded to rank accepted bidders for each technology. For this stage, CAMMESA calculated a score based on each bid's SLC and the maximum SLC set for each technology. The SLC score was computed based on the value of local content in electromechanics facilities as a proportion of total value.[28]

Table 4.9 Received, qualifying, and non-qualifying bids per RE auction, Argentina 2016–2019

| Round | Number received | Bids | | | |
| | | Qualifying | | Non-qualifying | |
		Number	%	Number	%
RenovAr1	123	105	85	18	15
RenovAr1.5	47	45	96	2	4
RenovAr2	228	192	84	35	16
RenovAr3	56	52	93	4	7
Total	454	394	Av. 87	59	Av. 13

Source: CAMMESA (various).

[28] The offer with the highest SLC obtained 100 points and the others were allocated a proportional percentage based on the 'Poner Formula', whereby the offer with the highest SLC obtained 100 points and

The SLC ranking was added to all the documentation contained in each bid's envelope A and sent to the Energy Secretariat. The Secretariat assessed the tax benefits requested by each bidder. Based on the bidders' requests and the maximum applicable benefits, they determined the benefits to be allocated to each project and provided a justification for each amount. From this, the Secretariat determined which bids qualified and instructed CAMMESA to inform the qualifying bidders.[29]

CAMMESA then opened the sealed financial proposals (envelope B) submitted by the qualifying bidders. Based on the parameters of the economic offer, CAMMESA defined a merit order for each technology; the specifics of which, for each round, are shown in Table 4.10.

To rank the bids, an AOP was computed according to the rules defined in the RfP as follows:

$$AOP = OP \times PDI_{LF} - (US\$\ 0.005/MWh \times D_{OPT-MPT}),$$

where AOP = adjusted offered price, OP = offered price, PDI_{LF} = loss factor related to the interconnection point, and $D_{OPT-MPT}$ = number of days by which the offered execution term is shorter than the maximum execution term.[30]

Given the large distances between the primary energy sources and the centres of energy consumption, the inclusion in the formula of a loss factor—a known parameter that was part of the RfP[31]—allowed the auction process to reflect the impact that different locations have on transmission costs.[32] The second adjustment ($D_{OPT}-_{MPT}$) incentivized early development of the generation facility.

For RenovAr 3, the formula was changed slightly. The loss factor was replaced by a factor that reflected liquid fuels savings associated with the reduction of network restrictions—that is, a differential for the forced generation displacement of US\$ 5/MWh.[33] The change was made because there are

the others a proportional percentage that was calculated as follows:

Score based on SLC = SLC × 100 / SLCMax,

where: 'SLC' means the SLC included in the bid, and 'SLCMax' means the maximum SLC of all bids submitted for each technology.

[29] Mostly a formal review of the process carried out by CAMMESA.

[30] For example, for RenovAr1, the maximum execution term was 730 days, so a project with an offered price of US\$ 95/MWh (and a PDI_{LF} of 1,049) to be completed in 550 days (180 days less than the maximum) would have an AOP of 98.72, that is, 95 x 1 049 – (0.005 x 180).

[31] The loss factor of RenovAr1 interconnection points, for example, varies between a minimum of 0.9578 and a maximum of 1.1193.

[32] This is consistent with the energy ministry's general rules, whereby the remuneration of all generators is computed using transmission-node factors.

[33] This refers to the displacement of thermal generation using fossil fuels other than natural gas.

no computed node factors for medium-voltage (13.2–66 kV) connections. In addition, the change reflects the programme's objective of locating RE generation facilities in areas where the use of available transmission capacity in medium-voltage networks can be optimized. In this instance, no incentives were offered for early installation.

Once the AOP for each bid was computed, CAMMESA sorted the financial proposals according to technology and discarded all bids in which the AOP exceeded the reserve price. Bids were then ranked by AOP, from lowest to highest by technology, and adjudicated until the offered capacity equalled the required capacity (by technology and region, where applicable)[34] or the maximum capacity at the interconnection point, both set in the RfP. As shown in Table 4.10, if prices between bids differed by less than 3%, the one with a greater proportion of SLC was ranked higher.

At the end of this process, CAMMESA submitted a non-binding report to the energy ministry recommending that PPAs be awarded to the selected bidders. After analysing the report, the ministry instructed CAMMESA to notify bidders of the awarding of the contracts and proceed with the signing of PPAs. If the Secretariat decided to modify or reject CAMMESA's analysis, in whole or in part, a well-founded report substantiating this had to be prepared and made public.

4.4.1.7 Buyer and seller liabilities

While requirements for participation in the auction were relatively low, stringent provisions were established if awarded developers failed to comply with PPAs, with different penalties linked to construction and production delays (see Table 4.11).

At the bidding stage, participants had to agree to all the obligations contained in the bidding terms and conditions. This included a bid bond in favour of CAMMESA for US$ 35,000 per MW of offered capacity. The guarantees were executed in the event that any bidders: withdrew their offer before the expiration of the original term; were found to have falsified information; refused to sign the supply contract in accordance with the provisions of the RfP, if awarded; or would not supply the contract performance guarantee.[35] This provision sought to discourage the submission of reckless offers.

Complementing this measure was the minimum capital requirement, which sought to ensure bidder solvency once awards had been allocated.

---

[34] Bids were pre-awarded according to the established POA merit order, verifying in each case that the bid capacity added to the capacity already pre-awarded did not exceed the required capacity by technology and region indicated or the maximum power in the interconnection point.

[35] The bid bond was returned to non-awarded bidders and to awarded bidders once they signed the PPA contract.

Table 4.10 Adjusted offered price calculations and ranking criteria, RenovAr 2016–2019

Aspect	RenovAr1	RenovAr1.5	RenovAr2	RenovAr3
Adjusted offered price (AOP) calculation	Offered price × relevant interconnection point (PDI) loss factor minus US$0.15/MWh for each 30 consecutive days between the offered and maximum execution term[a]	Offered price × relevant PDI loss factor minus US$0.005/MWh for each day in which the offered execution term is advanced with respect to the maximum execution term		Wind and solar: offered price Biomass, biogas, Biogas–SL, mini-hydro: offered price minus differential for forced generation displacement[b] (US$5/MWh)
Ranking criterion	AOP ranking, per technology. If tie (less than 3% difference), then according to SLC. If still tie, then draw.	AOP ranking, per technology. If tie (less than 3% difference), then according to SLC. If still tie, then by lower fiscal unitary benefits. If still tie, then draw.	AOP ranking, per technology. If tie (according to technology, with wind and solar less than US$ 1/MWh difference; MB and MH at US$2/MWh; BG and Biogas–SL US$ 3/MWh), then by SLC. If still tie, then by earliest commercial operation date. If still tie, then draw.	Wind and solar: based on offered price. If tie (less than US$1/MWh difference), then by SLC. If tie, then by lower fiscal benefits. If still tie, draw. Biomass, biogas, Biogas–SL, mini-hydro: based on AOP. If tie (MB, Biogas–SL and MH less than US$2/MWh difference, BG less than US$3/MWh difference), then by SLC. If tie, then by lower fiscal benefits. If still tie, then draw.

Note: [a] This means that the sooner a project came online, the lower its evaluated price was.
[b] The forced generation displacement difference was applied to projects that proved the replacement or displacement of fossil-fuel-based generation (other than natural gas) by means of corresponding electrical studies, and in accordance with the Letter of Agreement on Technical and Commercial Connection. CAMMESA analysed the effectiveness of the proposed displacement when analysing bids and, if relevant, used this to help calculate the AOP.
Source: CAMMESA (various).

Effectively, the successful bidders had to sign a PPA that replaced the bid bond with a contract-compliance guarantee (performance bond) of US$ 250,000 per MW of bid capacity. This guarantee remained in force until 180 days after the start of commercial operation. The high value of this compliance guarantee sought to ensure that the development of the investment project fulfilled the terms promised in the bid. The aim was to discourage aggressive offers while ensuring that the technical qualification requirements were kept relatively low.

Although no penalties were put in place for missing the partial milestones (such as financial close, start of construction, arrival of equipment, etc.), if the proposed schedule was delayed, bidders had to increase their contract compliance guarantee by 20%. Together with the guarantees, the bidding rules established sanctions for bidder breaches. These included fines for each day if the scheduled commercial start date was delayed and penalties for any generation deficit with respect to the minimum guaranteed volume.

As shown in Table 4.11, the PPA also granted the buyer an option to acquire the project in the event of certain breaches by the seller. The price of the call option was set at an amount equal to 75% of the net book value[36] plus any outstanding debts to the seller. These measures all sought to ensure contractual compliance. However, the amounts involved created substantial financial risks for bidders. Consequently, after the 2018 financial crisis saw Argentina losing access to capital markets and having to resort to an International Monetary Fund (IMF) bail out, many of the awarded projects were unable to obtain the necessary financing to carry out the investments. The Energy Secretariat then granted extensions to avoid the suspension of projects.[37]

4.4.1.8 Securing the revenue stream and addressing off-taker risk

The main challenge to RE development in Argentina is the risk facing private investors in the context of chronic macroeconomic instability. The costs of debt and equity capital are high and access to sources of long-term finance is limited.

The RenovAr programme seeks to shield investors from these risks in several ways. These include a standardized 20-year PPA, dollar-denominated energy pricing, protection against the possible non-transferability of the peso, the establishment of FODER to guarantee payments with sovereign

---

[36] Original value depreciated linearly over 20 years, that is, 5% per year.

[37] For example, Resolution No. 285/2018 (of June 2018) and Resolution No. 52/2019 (of February 2019) authorized successful bidders to request an extension to the dates agreed to in the PPAs, subject to certain conditions. In addition, on 9 September 2019, the Undersecretariat for Renewable Energies issued a note instructing CAMMESA to temporarily suspend all warning notices regarding non-compliance with dates committed to in the PPAs: a month later, on 7 October, the Undersecretariat withdrew the instruction.

Table 4.11 Guarantees and penalties, RenovAr

Guarantee	RenovAr1	RenovAr1.5	RenovAr2	RenovAr3
Bid bond	Guarantees of US$35 000/MW of offered capacity for at least 180 consecutive days, automatically renewable for 90 consecutive days,[a] had to accompany each bid submitted			Same logic but US$50k/MW of offered capacity
Supply contract compliance (performance bond)	US$250k/MW of contracted power, for not less than 1 year, and renewable for a period of 180 days following the scheduled operation date. Bidders had to submit a guarantee for every supply contract awarded.			
Contract compliance	In case of delays longer than 60 days, the seller had to increase the contract compliance guarantee by 20% of the amount in force at the time to reach: scheduled financial close, the scheduled construction start date, or the scheduled equipment arrival date[b]			
Commercial operation	A penalty of US$1 388/MW of contracted capacity was payable for each day of delay in reaching the scheduled commercial operation date			
Energy supply	US$160/MWh was payable for each MWh of energy supplied below the minimum committed for each year			
Sell option	The seller gives the buyer a call option to annex the project if: • the commercial operation does not begin on or before the scheduled date • the performance bond is not increased as required • a strategic partner is changed without the buyer's prior written consent • safety and quality standards are not met			

Notes: [a]The duration of the bond was tied to the expected duration of the awards process. The number of days is specified so that if the government doesn't make a decision or takes longer than anticipated, bidders are not required to keep to the terms of their bids. This is standard practice and reflects the fact that some government tenders are never awarded or formally cancelled. [b]The rationale was that any partial delay would increase the chances of the project not reaching commercial operation on time, thus requiring an increase in the guarantee.
Source: CAMMESA (various).

support, provision for international arbitration in case of disputes, an option for the investor to buy projects in cases of non-compliance by CAMMESA, and the option of access to a World Bank guarantee. In addition, both the PPA and the FODER contracts were standardized and non-negotiable, and both contracts were made public as part of the draft RfP during the consultation process held before each round.

For Argentina's RE market to be efficient and dynamic, foreign investment is crucial. To protect investors and lenders from exchange-rate risks, the RenovAr programme has, so far, offered investors 20-year PPAs with dollar-denominated prices (US\$/MWh).[38] As the market administrator and off-taker, CAMMESA acts on behalf of all wholesale market agents, and even though it is backed by a sovereign guarantee, it remains a private company. Consequently, the PPAs are governed by private law.

Projects' energy remuneration (US\$ per MWh) arises from the bid (now called the awarded) price) and subject to an *annual adjustment factor* (growing at 1.7% per year) plus an *incentive factor* (payable each year at a decreasing rate).

The *annual adjustment factor* was set to reflect the expected US inflation rate and was used instead of a price index based on actual inflation.[39] Complementing the dollar-denominated rates, FODER covers investors for the risk of the peso becoming difficult to convert into dollars or other currencies and the possibility of limits being placed on transferring money out of Argentina.

According to the RfP, the purpose of the *incentive factor* is 'to favour and encourage the prompt installation and commercial start-up of the generation plants by means of a nominal increase in the awarded price that improves the revenues and financial situation of the projects'. The factor values were presented in the RfP (see Table 4.12).[40] From a financial point of view, by increasing payments at the beginning of the project and decreasing them at the end, the incentive factor is equivalent to a reduction in the cost of capital. The specific impact is a function of the rate of return.[41]

The most innovative element in the regulatory framework was the establishment of FODER, a trust fund aimed at fostering investment in RE. In addition to PPAs, all RenovAr-awarded projects had to sign a standard agreement with FODER. FODER was set up to play two roles: one linked to finance and the other as a guarantor (see Figure 4.4).

---

[38] Although payments are made in pesos according to a 'reference exchange rate' published by the Central Bank (BCRA), various clauses give investors partial protection against the risk of non-convertibility and non-transferability.

[39] Some historical precedents exist for dollar-denominated contracts in Argentina; during unbundling and privatization of the energy sector in the 1990s, some end-user tariffs were set in dollars and indexed according to US inflation. However, as a result of the 2002 crisis, laws were passed 'pesifying' tariffs and prohibiting indexation. The inclusion of an adjustment factor, rather than an indexing rate, in the RenovAr PPAs is partly an attempt to avoid restrictions on indexation.

[40] Incentive factors were modified slightly in the following rounds. In RenovAr1.5, the factor started at 1.2 in 2017, reaching 0.80 by 2036. RenovAr2 had the same factor as RenovAr1.5 but moved on a year, starting at 1.2 in 2018 and reaching 0.80 by 2037.

[41] For example, an internal rate of return of 7% per year without an incentive factor produces an increase of 80 basis points; that is, it results in a return of 7.8%.

Table 4.12 RenovAr1
incentive factor values

Year	Incentive factor value
2016–2018	1.25
2019–2020	1.15
2021–2024	1.10
2025–2028	1.00
2029–2032	0.90
2033–	0.80

Source: RfP (2016: Annex 9).

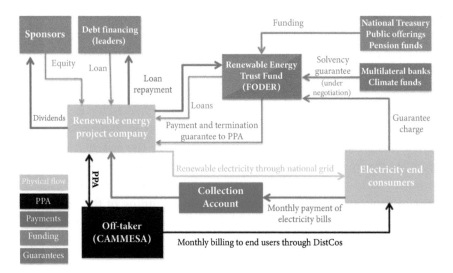

Figure 4.4 Role of the Fund for the Development of Renewable Energy (FODER)
Source: Energy Secretariat (various).

In its financing role, FODER was meant to supply long-term finance to RE projects through loans, equity, subsidized interest rates, and/or any other financial instrument that could facilitate the execution and financing of RE projects. In practice, the fund has not yet played this role. In the first RenovAr rounds, Argentina's financial situation was good, and access to international capital markets was fluid. In this context, there was little need to allocate public funds to FODER's financing account since the sector authorities expected all the projects to qualify for market finance.[42] When the financial situation

---

[42] A private initiative proposing a financing mechanism to FODER´s financing account through simultaneous financing and energy auctions was dismissed by government officials as unnecessary.

deteriorated in 2018, no public funds were available, and FODER had no access to external funding.

In its role as guarantor, the primary financial instruments developed by FODER are payment guarantees that are implemented through escrow accounts (the Cuenta de Garantía and its sub-accounts). These were designed to provide liquidity support for ongoing PPA payments and ensure any payment obligations emerging from the rights of independent power producers (IPPs) to sell their project to FODER if macroeconomic conditions or sector-specific risks materialize.[43] Often referred to as a 'put option', this kind of termination coverage is often sought by the private sector in emerging markets.

If CAMMESA failed to make a PPA payment, the seller could request that FODER make the payment, which, after confirming with CAMMESA, would proceed with the payment. Consequently, FODER's guarantee account had to have sufficient funds to cover all of CAMMESA's monthly energy-payment obligations for a given time period. In Rounds 1 and 1.5, the guarantee covered a 12-month period. From Round 2 onwards, this was reduced to 180 days. If funds in the guarantee account were insufficient, FODER would ask the Ministry of Energy to replenish its funds. If the ministry was unable to do so, the World Bank guarantee would kick in and/or the generators could exercise their 'put option', which allowed them to terminate the PPA early and/or sell the project.

The payment for the put option was established as 100% of the net (i.e. linearly amortized) assets, considering as initial value the lesser of the reference value by technology (as set out terms and conditions of the bid) and the audited value (according to commonly accepted international standards and approved by FODER's executive committee).

As part of their economic proposal, bidders could also choose to take a World Bank guarantee. In this case, the World Bank acts as guarantor for the state's obligation to send the necessary resources to the FODER so that it can meet the project selling price.[44] This further mitigates country-based risks such as payment failures, policy changes, and exchange-rate fluctuations.

The World Bank guarantee included up-front fees. These were payable once, on a date set, by FODER in accordance with the date on which the

---

[43] These risks include: non-payment by the buyer that goes unremedied by FODER for more than four consecutive months or six months in a year, currency non-convertibility or non-transferability that materially harms the buyer, and modifications to the World Bank guarantee or FODER that are detrimental to the buyer.

[44] The World Bank's International Bank for Reconstruction and Development guarantee an aggregate amount of US$ 480 million to backstop the government's failure to fund FODER when it has to pay a Put Price to eligible RE sub-projects as a result of IPPs exercising a put option. At the sub-project level, the guarantee is limited to a maximum of US$ 500,000 per MW (World Bank 2017).

World Bank Guarantee Agreement was signed. In addition, ongoing guarantee fees had to be paid up front and thereafter twice a year, depending on the guarantee term (see Table 4.13). These costs were defined and set by the World Bank's International Bank for Reconstruction and Development and were the same as those to which the FODER was subject, under the World Bank Guarantee Agreement.

In case of disputes, the PPA and the FODER agreements allow for arbitration in accordance with the Arbitration Rules of the United Nations Commission on International Trade Law.

All these measures sought to ensure, to the extent possible within the Argentine context, the revenue stream for RenovAr projects. Initially, the programme was successful in attracting a large number of investors, as shown in the success of the first RenovAr rounds.

However, after the 2018 crisis, the country's macroeconomic situation made it extremely difficult for projects in their initial stages to reach financial close. In practice, FODER has not been able to act as a hedge against sovereign risk beyond the World Bank guarantees. Accordingly, the deterioration of the country's financial situation has had a direct impact on the attractiveness of investing in RE.

4.4.2 Auction implementation

RenovAr was launched relatively quickly and initially enjoyed strong and widespread political support. In October 2015, congress approved Act 27.191.

Table 4.13   Fees associated with the World Bank guarantee

Cost item	Composition and value
Up-front fees	Front-end fee of 25 basis points of the guaranteed amount Initiation fee of 15 basis points of the guaranteed amount Processing fee of 50 basis points of the guaranteed amount Reimbursement of external legal counsel expenses incurred by the World Bank's International Bank for Reconstruction and Development (proportional to the guaranteed amount)
Guarantee fees	8 year-term and below: 50 basis points 8–10 years' term: 60 basis points 10—12 years' term: 70 basis points 12–15 years' term: 80 basis points 15–18 years' term: 90 basis points 18–20 years' term: 100 basis points

Source: CAMMESA information.

After the administration change in December 2015, the incoming authorities created a new Undersecretariat for Renewable Energy. Sebastian Kind, a former advisor to the (then-opposition) senator who had proposed the law, was appointed as undersecretary by President Mauricio Macri. By the end of March 2016, Decree 531/2016 was approved, specifying the rules governing the practical implementation of Act 27.191, and the first auction took place in May of the same year.

To help run the auction, Argentina sought technical support from multilateral credit organizations. Accordingly, the Ministry of Energy and Mining, with World Bank Group encouragement, conducted investor roadshows in the United States, Europe, and Argentina (see World Bank, 2018a). In the face of persistent investor reluctance, the World Bank launched its package of guarantees to backstop the guarantees that the government had put in place through FODER.

According to a World Bank report,

> The WBG [World Bank Group] supported GoA [government of Argentina] to size the program, based on estimated needs and financing available, and develop standardized legal documents for RenovAr auctions. The International Bank for Reconstruction and Development and teams from the IFC reviewed all key Program documents and provided feedback to GoA based on international experience in similar programs, with a particular focus on ensuring a fair and balanced project risk allocation between the private and public sector, with an objective of minimizing the public sector financing/support and to ensure a market success of the program. The Bank also supported GoA, as needed, to expand its reach to the global private sector investor base.
>
> (World Bank, 2017)

Discussions with the Argentine government, bidders, and lenders indicated that the World Bank's engagement played a critical catalytic role in attracting the large number of bids to the initial auctions rounds (World Bank, 2018a).

Although the role of the WBG was important as a catalyst for private investment, its participation in the auction design and implementation didn't involve significant resources as it was not part of a long-term programme. According to the IFC (2018),

> Scaling can be done with limited resources if the incentives are in place: IFC's engagement in RenovAr did not require a large, fully staffed, multi-year, funded programme. IFC's upstream engagement was carried out by a few people with a limited budget for external advisors. Within IFC, RenovAr was possible because

of driven individuals with keen knowledge of the market as well as supportive management that worked with the team to get funding and remove barriers. The team was driven by a direct request from a very committed government client that wanted to make things happen and that sought advice from both the Bank and IFC.

The energy ministry made CAMMESA responsible for the technical implementation of the auction programme. CAMMESA is in charge of the physical dispatch and also acts as a clearing house for all financial flows in the sector. Although not part of its original mandate, CAMMESA had proven experience in the implementation of auction processes. It had previously, at the request of the government, occasionally acted as a procurement agent in the purchase of gas for generators and the expansion of gas transportation capacity as well as in helping to manage capacity and cogeneration auctions.

In general, the process has been seen as highly transparent. Following local regulations, all envelope-opening events were carried out in public with the participation of bidders who wanted to attend and before a notary, who certified the procedure. The results of each evaluation—both technical and financial—were made public. As noted, CAMMESA also had to prepare a report evaluating the technical bids and submit this to the Energy Secretariat.

Under the Macri administration, from 2015 to 2019, RE development clearly had political support. Although no comprehensive plan was developed for the energy sector as a whole, RE seemed to be a priority. With the subsequent change of administration, in December 2019, political support for RE has decreased significantly. The fact that rates have been set in dollars has become controversial in the context of the strong devaluation of the peso.

4.5 Results from Argentina's renewable energy auctions

It can be argued that the RenovAr programme has been successful in its primary objectives. In the four rounds held so far, investments for over 4,726 MW were awarded, of which 1,411 MW were in operation by January 2020. Bid prices were competitive when compared to those in the wider region and particularly so given the macroeconomic context.

Figure 4.5 shows the shift in prices for awarded projects, per technology and round. When considering all technologies, the weighted average price fell 16% between RenovAr1 (US$ 61.33/MW) and RenovAr2 (US$ 51.48/MW) and increased by 30% in RenovAr3. The shifts at the aggregate level are also reflected in the individual technologies. In all cases, prices decreased from the first to the third rounds and increased in the fourth.

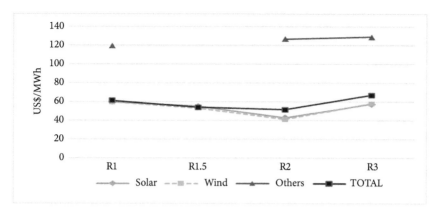

Figure 4.5 Evolution of prices for awarded projects per technology, RenovAr, 2016–2019

Source: CAMMESA (various).

The first two rounds are worth a closer look. RenovAr1 and RenovAr1.5 unfolded within a short period of time. In economic terms, RenovAr1.5 can be seen as a price-improving iteration of RenovAr1. The outcome was successful: an average price decrease of 12% was accomplished with 64% of accepted offers.[45] This price decrease challenges the wisdom of the programme having contracted 1,142 MW—14% more than the 1,000 MW volume originally set for RenovAr1. If the originally tendered volume had been awarded, it is likely that more bidders excluded from RenovAr1 would have submitted lower bids for RenovAr1.5. In effect, contracting above the set objective of 1,000 MW created a cost overrun for the system that can be estimated at over US$ 3.1 million/year.[46]

The average price in the third round (RenovAr2) was also affected by the mechanism adopted. In the first phase of this round, 1,200 MW were requested and 1,409 MW were awarded. Offers for over 9,400 MW were received, resulting in an average price of US$ 53.27/MW for awarded technologies. In the second phase, non-awarded bidders were invited to come on

---

[45] The most extreme case was that of Project EOL-32, which was the bid with the highest price in RenovAr1. The same project was submitted for RenovAr1.5 at the lowest price in the auction, having decreased its offer by over 50% (from US$ 114 to US$ 55/MWh).

[46] For example, EOL-46, a wind project above the required capacity of 600 MW, had a price of US$ 67.19/MW (and a capacity of 99.75 MW). Similarly, SFV-13, a solar project above the required capacity of 300 MW, bid a price of US$ 58.98/MW (and a capacity of 100 MW). Had these projects not been awarded in RenovAr1 and still participated in RenovAr1.5, they might have offered discounts similar to the average offered for their respective technologies. Their prices would then have come down to US$ 60.34/MW and US$ 54.23/MW, respectively. Assuming a utilization factor of 25% for SFV and 35% for wind, the average annual energy generated by these two projects would be around 525,000 MWh/year, and the monetary difference would be worth over US$ 3 million a year.

board with a price computed based on Phase 1 results. Per technology, these were US$ 40.27/MW for wind, US$ 41.76/MW for solar, US$ 106.73/MW for biomass, and US$ 156.85/MW for biogas.[47] In this phase, an additional 634 MW was awarded, giving rise to an average price for this phase of US$ 47.54/MW.

Three factors help to explain the higher prices evident in the fourth round. The first is related to the design of the auction: unlike in the previous rounds, neither incentives nor adjustment factors applied to the bid price, and with no adjustments over time, bid prices have to be higher to achieve the same financial results.[48] The second factor relates to the fact that RenovAr 3 (Mini RenovAr) was aimed at smaller developments: the average awarded project size in the first three rounds was 30 MW, while in RenovAr3 it was 6.8 MW. Economies of scale help to explain the higher prices. The third factor relates to conditions at the time of the auction: the impact of the country's macroeconomic crisis cannot be overstated.

Table 4.14 shows the estimated country risk for Argentina, as measured by J.P. Morgan's Emerging Market Bond Index Plus, at the time of each round.[49] In May 2019, when the RenovAr bids were submitted, the country risk was between 450 and 560 basis points above the average observed at the time of the previous rounds. The resulting higher cost of capital also helps to explain why bids were higher.[50]

Table 4.14 Country risk for Argentina according to JP Morgan, 2016–2018

Round	RenovAr1	RenovAr1.5	RenovAr2	RenovAr3
Bid submission	5 September 2016	28 October 2016	19 October 2017	30 May 2019
EMBI+	4.50	4.48	3.60	9.14

Source: CAMMESA (various).

[47] Specifically, prices for BM and BG technologies were computed as the weighted average price of the awarded contracts in Phase 1 and considering only 50% of the scale incentive. For wind and solar, on the other hand, the prices were computed as the weighted average price of the awarded contracts in Phase 1 but considering projects in certain regions (Buenos Aires, Patagonia, and Comahue for wind projects and NorOeste Argentino (NOA) and Cuyo for solar).

[48] As compared with auctions that include adjustment and incentive factors, supressing these factors requires, *ceteris paribus*, an increase in the bid price of around 11% to keep projects' internal rate of return constant at 10%.

[49] J.P. Morgan's Emerging Markets Bond Index Plus (EMBI+) tracks total returns for traded external debt instruments (external meaning foreign currency denominated fixed income) in the emerging markets. Values shown are the indicator's average over the 10 days before bids presentation.

[50] According to figures on investment, operational expenditure, and utilization factors supplied by Lazard Asset Management, a 500-basis-point difference in the cost of capital—going, for example, from 7% to 12%—provokes a 33% difference in the cost per MWh of a wind project (from US$ 28.34 to US$ 37.77) and of 38% in a solar project (from US$ 43.64 to US$ 60.22).

However, caution must be taken when analysing these figures. Even if competitive prices were undeniably obtained, the costs associated with the (free) guarantees given by FODER should be considered an economic subsidy. On the other hand, the variable nature of RE—particularly wind and solar—renders the comparison between renewable and energy sources that offer more stable levels of capacity and supply inaccurate.

The comparison of RE generation prices with the cost of other traditional technologies is particularly relevant in Argentina, where shale gas potential is vast.[51] Figure 4.6 shows RE penetration in a least-cost expansion programme at different gas prices, assuming a cost of capital equal to 7% in nominal terms.

With gas prices around US$ 2.28/million British thermal units (BTU), RE generation is not competitive and its optimal penetration will not reach even 10% of total system generation by 2030. In fact, the portfolio dictated by Act 27.191 will become a cost overrun for the system if the gas price goes below US$ 3/million BTU. However, if gas costs more than US$ 4.48/million BTU, RE technologies could become dominant, and their participation could reach almost 40% by 2030. Clearly, a higher cost of capital has a substantial effect on optimal RE penetration.

In terms of technologies, wind and solar have dominated both received bids and awarded capacity. With the exception of RenovAr1.5 (which was aimed

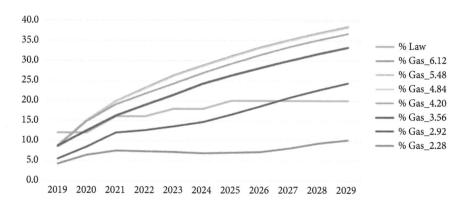

Figure 4.6 Projected renewable energy penetration at varying gas prices, Argentina, 2019–2030 (%)

Note: The green line displays the renewable energy (RE) share values established by Act 27.191. These values were obtained using an integrated gas and electricity dispatch model that simulates the Argentine market assuming a 5% real and expected inflation in the United States of around 2% per annum.
Source: CAMMESA.

---

[51] Argentina has some of the world's largest reserves of shale gas and shale oil in the Vaca Muerta formation, see https://www.argentina.gob.ar/energia/vaca-muerta/inversiones (accessed 20 April 2023).

only at wind and solar projects), all rounds established limits for awarded capacity for each technology. Substitution between technologies was not allowed, so each round can be seen as having constituted a set of between two and six simultaneous and independent auctions.[52]

In the first three rounds, bids of between five and ten times the required volumes were received for wind and solar generation, while, for the other technologies, the bids received were lower than the auctioned volumes. This situation reversed in the last round. The focus on small projects meant that the solar and wind bids were below the available volume (283 MW offered against 350 MW requested) and those of the other technologies exceeded the auctioned capacity. The aggregated results of the four rounds are shown in Figure 4.7.

Table 4.15 shows tendered, offered, and awarded capacity for each technology in each round.

In the first three rounds, bids of between five and ten times the required volumes were received for wind and solar generation, while, for the other technologies, the bids received were lower than the auctioned volumes. This situation reversed in the last round. The focus on small projects meant that the solar and wind bids were below the available volume (283 MW offered against 350 MW requested) and those of the other technologies exceeded the

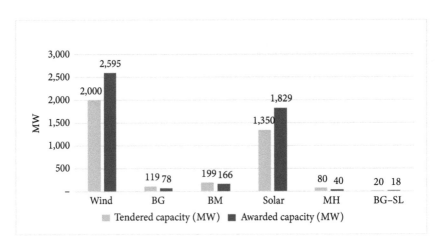

Figure 4.7 Total tendered and awarded capacity per technology, RenovAr, 2016–2019

Note: BG = biogas; BM = biomass; MH = mini hydro; BG–SL = biogas–sanitary landfill
Source: CAMMESA (various).

---

[52] Technology limits were sometimes aggregated so that the number of simultaneous auctions varies per round.

Table 4.15 MW tendered, offered, and awarded by round, RenovAr, 2016–2018

Round	MW status		Wind	Solar	Biogas	Biomass	Mini hydro	Biogas-SL	Total
RenovAr1	Required		00	300	15	65	20	–	1,000
	Received		3,468	2,811	9	45	11		6,344
	Awarded		707	400	9	15	11		1,142
RenovAr1.5	Required		400	200	–				600
	Received		1,561	925					2,486
	Awarded		765	516					1,281
	Required	Phase 1	550	450	35	100	50	15	1,200
		Phase 2	275	225	68		–		568
RenovAr2 Phases 1&2	Received	Ph 1	3,811	5,291	57	187	32	15	9,393
		Ph 2	666	557	35	117	21	13	1,409
	Awarded	Ph 1	328	260	21	26	–		635
		Ph 2							
RenovAr3[a]	Required		350		10	25	10	5	400
	Received		155	128	19	26	10	15	353
	Awarded		129	97	13	9	7	5	260

Note: [a] In this round, 12 projects (with a total capacity of 62.75 MW) qualified technically but were not awarded. They were then invited to enter into supply contracts and to sign an agreement with FODER based on the minimum price per technology awarded in the auction.
Source: CAMMESA (various).

auctioned capacity. The aggregated results of the four rounds are shown in Figure 4.7.

A similar pattern is evident in awarded projects. In the first three rounds, both wind and solar were over-contracted, while bids for the remaining technologies did not cover the available quota (with the exception of biomass in the second round, which was also over-contracted). In the third round, more biogas was awarded than the available quota (13 MW awarded against 10 MW required) and for biogas–SL, the quota was filled exactly (5 MW). For all other technologies, the awarded capacity was lower than the available quota. It should be noted that this round was the only one in which the awards bids amounted to substantially less than the quota offered (259 MW awarded out of 400 MW available). As noted, Argentina's macroeconomic situation in 2019 partly explains this difference.

The relatively low number of biogas, biomass, and small hydro bids that were submitted in Round 1 was partly due to the fact that the RenovAr programme was developed and launched quite fast. The developers of power generation projects based on these technologies were relatively unprepared for the development of auction bids (Menzies et al., 2019).

One of the objectives of Argentina's RE legislation was to foster the development of a local RE-related industry (with jobs and other benefits). Nevertheless, to maximize price competition, the IFC advised the government to remove local content as one of the components in the formula for evaluating bids (IFC, 2018). They argued that this was key to attracting financing from bilateral institutions. In the trade-off between the developmental objective set out in the law (developing local manufacturing capacity) and the objective of maximizing price competition by attracting as many bidders as possible, a compromise had to be reached. The solution was to make the SLC not a direct awarding criterion but to include it as tiebreaker criterion. Thus, if two projects bid at the same price, the SLC was used to determine fiscal benefits and to compute the cost of the World Bank guarantee.[53] See Table 4.16 for average SLC in qualifying and awarded projects in each round.

Some distinctive features arise from our analysis of this. First, in most cases, the subset of awarded projects shows a higher average SLC than the average across all qualifying projects.[54] Since the selection was based on bid price, regardless of local content, this suggests that incorporating more local content did not adversely affect project costs. Second, average local content

---

[53] The World Bank guarantee was discounted by one basis point per percentage point of SLC.
[54] This was not true for RenovAr1.5's weighted average, but RenovAr1.5 was a subset of RenovAr1 and was limited to wind and solar so its SLC is not strictly comparable to that of other rounds.

Table 4.16 Average stated local content per round, RenovAr, 2016–2019

Round	All qualifying bidders		Awarded bids	
	Weighted %	Simple %	Weighted %	Simple %
RenovAr1	12.5	20.1	13.8	27.0
RenovAr1.5	18.1	24.7	17.6	27.4
RenovAr2	23.6	26.9	29.6	26.7
RenovAr3	52.4	38.8	52.5	40.1
Average	20.0	26.4	23.8	29.6

Source: CAMMESA (various).

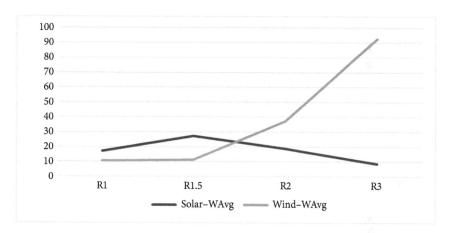

Figure 4.8 Weighted average capacity of wind and solar projects by stated local content, RenovAr, 2016–2019 (%)
Source: CAMMESA (various).

of projects seems to be gradually increasing over time. However, this funding should be treated with caution since the third round focused on smaller projects, and its values are not strictly comparable. Taking just the first three rounds into account, the simple average of SLC is larger than the weighted average in most cases, which indicates that local content decreased according to project size in these rounds too. In terms of technologies, SLC for wind projects increased over time but decreased for solar (Figure 4.8).

According to Walter Lanosa, (CEO of Genneia, one of Argentina's larger energy companies) and vice-president of the Cámara Eólica Argentina), the wind-energy value chain associated with the construction of turbines is similar to that of the automotive sector, and Argentina has a well-established track record for the assembly of auto parts (Lanosa, 2020). For this reason, wind projects in the RenovAr programme created good opportunities for local metal-working and mechanical engineering businesses.

Third. if the results are analysed by awarded companies, the concentration of awards is generally high—with a few companies winning several projects. Provincial companies were awarded 825.3 MW (17% of the total awarded capacity). Provincial participation is even higher when considering total capacity per technology, with provincial companies winning 22% of awarded capacity in mini hydro, 15% of total wind capacity, and 24% of solar capacity.

Table 4.17 shows the number of companies with projects awarded in each round and the percentage of the total MW won by the top three and the top five companies. Concentration decreased over the first three rounds and considerably increased in the fourth, where just one company (Elawan Energy Developments SL) accounts for 46% of total awarded capacity (with over 115 MW of wind capacity). The companies accounting for 50% of overall capacity contracted over the four rounds are presented in Table 4.18.

Interestingly, companies controlled by provincial governments (through total or partial ownership) feature prominently among award winners. As state-owned enterprises (SOEs), these companies are arguably less driven by market considerations and profit-maximization. They also have certain advantages, such as land ownership and access to direct finance from foreign governments. Table 4.19 shows the projects awarded to provincial companies per technology.

Provincial companies were awarded 825.3 MW (17% of the total awarded capacity). Provincial participation is even higher when considering total capacity per technology, with provincial companies winning 22% of awarded capacity in mini hydro, 15% of total wind capacity, and 24% of solar capacity.

Table 4.17 Number of awarded companies per round, RenovAr, 2016–2019

Round	1	1.5	2	3	Total
Number of projects	29	30	88	38	185
Number of companies	20	18	59	22	107
Capacity	1,142	1,282	2,043	259	4,726
Percentage won by the top three companies	50	41	33	61	19
Percentage won by the top five companies	68	56	44	69	29
Number of firms accounting for 50%	3	5	6	1 (46%)	11

Note: This is less than the sum of all companies in all rounds as some companies won projects in more than one round.
Source: CAMMESA (various).

Table 4.18 Capacity concentration across the four RenovAr rounds, 2016–2019

Company	Awarded capacity		No. of projects and technology
	MW	%	
Latinoamericana de Energía	311.9	7	6 (solar, wind, mini hydro)
JEMSE	300.0	6	3 (solar)
PE Arauco	294.8	6	3 (wind)
Isolux Ingenieria	277.7	6	3 (solar, wind)
Genneia	259.4	5	4 (wind, BM)
CP Renovables	233.6	5	3 (wind)
PCR	200.0	4	2 (wind)
Envision Energy	175.0	4	3 (wind)
Empresa Mendocina se Energía	148.1	3	11 (solar, wind, mini-hydro)
Energia Sustentable	126.8	3	5 (solar)

Source: CAMMESA (various).

Table 4.19 MW awarded to companies owned (or partly owned) by provincial governments, RenovAr, 2016–2019

Firm	Province	Solar	Wind	Mini hydro	Total
JEMSE	Jujuy	300.0	–	–	300.0
PE Arauco	La Rioja	–	294.8	–	294.8
EMESA	Mendoza	93.7	50.0	4.4	148.1
Centrales de la Costa	Buenos Aires	–	38.0	–	38.0
EPEC	Córdoba	40.0	–	4.5	44.5
Total		433.7	382.8	8.9	825.4
Percentage of total capacity		24	15	22	17

Source: CAMMESA (various).

To cite just a few examples:

- When Jujuy Energía y Minería Sociedad del Estado (JEMSE), the provincial energy and mining company in Jujuy Province was awarded a 300 MW solar plant, it won the largest project awarded in the RenovAr programme (see Box 4.1).
- La Rioja province owns Parque Eólico Arauco (Arauco Wind Farm). Originally developed under Resolution No. 108/2011, the wind farm started operations in 2011, with an installed capacity of 25 MW. Through the first three rounds of RenovAr, the company was awarded a further 294.8 MW.
- Mendoza province's energy company, EMESA, was awarded solar, wind, and mini hydro projects. In total, these represent 148.1 MW, making this

company the third highest awarded among the provinces and the ninth highest nationally.

Box 4.1 JEMSE's Cauchari Project

The Cauchari Solar Park, located in Jujuy Province, is one of the largest PV projects in Argentina, harvesting 300 MW over an area of 650 hectares. JEMSE (Jujuy Energía y Minería Sociedad del Estado), a company owned by the provincial authorities, was awarded the project in the first RenovAr auction, held in September 2016. The national authorities have since complemented this with the construction of a substation to transmit the generated energy.

The Exim Bank of China provided a loan of US$ 331.5 million to help finance the solar park, which (officially) cost US$ 541.5 million. The loan is backed up by a sovereign guarantee from the Argentinian government. In addition, the provincial authorities issued a 'green bond' in the US financial market for another US$ 210 million.

The construction and supply of materials is being carried out by two Chinese companies, Power China and Shanghai Electric Power Construction (SEPC).

JEMSE is negotiating with Chinese entrepreneurs to expand of the project by another 200 MW at an estimated cost of US$ 300 million. If successful, the solar project will end up costing more than US$ 900 million, with a 10-year repayment term on the principal debt.

Before the approval of the law, several provinces had started planning—generally with the support of development agencies in developed countries[55]—to boost investment in RE. For these provinces, the RenovAr programme helped projects that had been planned for years to materialize. To an extent, part of RenovAr's initial success can be explained by the fact that these provincial firms already had projects in the pipeline when the programme was launched.

4.5.1 Project status by early 2020

While the RenovAr programme has so far been successful in attracting bidders across its different rounds, project implementation is taking longer than

---

[55] For example, San Juan and San Luis provinces received support from the German Solar Association (BSW–Solar); Mendoza province also started its own projects several years before the RenovAr programme.

the stipulated time periods. Once a project is awarded, the first step is signing the PPA and the standard contract with FODER. The signing of the PPA is significant because this is when bidders have to replace the offer guarantee or bid bond (US$ 35k/MW in all rounds, except RenovAr3, where it was US$ 50k/MW) with a supply contract compliance guarantee (US$ 250k/MW). This clearly raises the financial risk if the project is not developed as per the contract.

Different rounds stipulated different time periods for the signing of the PPA, with RenovAr1 (at 30 days) being much shorter than the subsequent rounds (around 170 days) (see section 4.4.1). As shown in Table 4.20, all awarded projects from the first three rounds were signed (except for those cancelled).

After the financial crisis of 2018, Argentina lost access to capital markets and had to resort to an IMF bail out. Consequently, several of the awarded projects were unable to obtain the necessary financing. To avoid projects being suspended, the energy ministry granted extensions. For the fourth round, RenovAr3, only five PPAs have not been signed, but the deadline has been extended again because of the COVID-19 pandemic.

Five project contracts have been terminated (one from RenovAr1, one from RenovAr1.5, and three from RenovAr2), representing a total of 72.5 MW (1.5% of awarded capacity); see Table 4.21.[56] The projects that have signed PPAs can be categorized as in production, under construction, and not started (see Table 4.22).

While the status of projects not yet in operation is not officially tracked and updated, data from March 2019 indicates that construction had not started

Table 4.20 Status of RenovAr project PPAs by January 2020

| Round | Awarded | | Cancelled | | PPA not yet signed | |
Number	MW	Number	MW	Number	MW	% MW
RenovAr1	29	1,142	1	2	0	0	0
RenovAr1.5	30	1,282	1	35	0	0	0
RenovAr2	88	2,042	3	36	0	0	0
RenovAr3	38	260	0	–	5	56	22
Total	185	4,726	5	73	5	56	1.2

Source: CAMMESA (various).

[56] Little information is available on the causes of the cancellations; one was cancelled for breach of milestones, another was cancelled by CAMMESA, and the other three had not signed PPAs before the corresponding deadline. The capacity has not been reallocated.

Table 4.21 RE power projects awarded in RenovAr1, 1.5, and 2, and subsequently cancelled

Project name	Round	Technology	MW
Huinca Renancó	1	Biogas	1.6
P.S. Sarmiento	1.5	Solar	35.0
C.T. Generacion Virasoro	2	Biomass	3.0
C.T. Kuera Santo Tome	2	Biomass	12.9
P.S. SAUJIL II	2	Solar	20.0
Total			72.5

Source: CAMMESA (various).

Table 4.22 Number, size, and status of projects with signed PPAs from RenovAr1, 1.5, and 2

Round	PPA signed		In production			Under construction/not started		
	No. of projects	MW	No. of projects	MW	% MW	No. of projects	MW	% MW
R1	28	1,140	15	438	38	13	702	62
R1.5	29	1,247	18	638	51	11	608	49
R2	85	2,007	21	335	17	64	1,672	83
Total	142	4,394	54	1,411	Av. 32	88	2,983	Av. 68

Note: RenovAr3 projects are not shown because the deadline for signing the corresponding PPAs had not expired when this data was collated.
Source: CAMMESA (various).

on over one-third of the projects (3 from RenovAr1, six from RenovAr1.5, and 47 from RenovAr2). As noted. this large proportion can be explained by problems associated with securing financing after 2018.

According to Constantini and Di Paola (2019), a survey of firms that have been awarded with PPAs in the RenovAr programme identified the inexperience of local banks with project finance (not just linked to RE) as the major financial obstacle they have faced; they indicated that the macroeconomic situation was the second major issue (Figure 4.9).

While the two issues are clearly related, it is important to note the kinds of restrictions that can arise within the local financial sector when designing RE auctions.

On average, of the 4,394 MW linked to signed PPAs, 32% is operational. Distribution varies across rounds. As noted, the first two rounds occurred within a fairly short time period. From these rounds, the percentage of

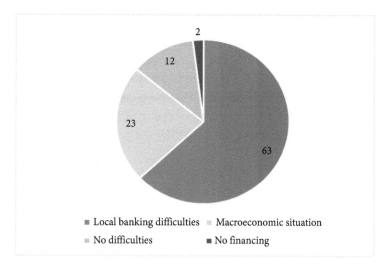

Figure 4.9 Sources of financial difficulties identified by awarded projects after signing power purchase agreements (PPAs) (%)
Source: Constantini and Di Paola (2019: 7).

capacity that is already operating is larger than that from RenovAr2 (38% and 51%, versus 17%).

Since mid-2018, the government has extended the deadlines several times. While extensions have been necessary in the deteriorating macroeconomic conditions, they have also prevented the execution of the corresponding guarantees and contributed to delays on contracted projects. This, in turn, casts doubt on the efficiency and appropriacy of the auction mechanism adopted, which was based on relatively low entry requirements (in terms of progress in the technical and financial aspects necessary to qualify in the tender) and high fines for non-compliance.

4.6 Lessons learned from Argentina's renewable energy auctions

4.6.1 Auction implementation

The adoption of a clear legal framework with well-defined objectives and mechanisms aimed at mitigating macroeconomic risks has been a determining factor in the development of RE in Argentina. Since the 1990s, several RE promotion programmes have been run in Argentina, but until the legal framework was adopted in 2016, none of these had much impact. The legal framework now includes RE portfolio standards, an auction mechanism for project selection, and a guarantee fund to mitigate economic risks.

By 2016, after 13 years of an electricity-tariff freeze, the government was taking various steps to improve the financial situation of the electricity sector. For example, apart from a social tariff that protects the poorest 1.5 million households, a three-year plan was announced to eliminate energy subsidies by 2019.[57] The latter step improved CAMMESA's credit standing and sent a positive signal to investors.

Political support for RE was a key factor. Fundamental to the success of the RenovAr programme was strong commitment from the government that took office in December 2015 and the presence of a sector champion in the office of the Undersecretary for Renewable Energy, who, as noted, had been involved in drafting new legislation to govern the auctions. The RenovAr programme also successfully secured political support countrywide. Regional quotas and restrictions on the distribution of projects within each region helped to secure the support of provincial authorities. While the quotas were partly based on the limitations of the country's transmission system, they also reflected an attempt to achieve a balance of RE investment across the various regions.

In addition, the Macri administration developed a clear strategy to ensure that the new law was implemented. The first element in this strategy was enlisting the help of international agencies—specifically the World Bank Group—to ensure that international best practices were adopted and that investors' concerns were well understood. As the IFC (2018: 7) put it, 'The IFC team was tasked with providing advice on the overall attractiveness of the program for private investors and developing bankable project documentation. The World Bank team started working on a guarantee program to support the financing of RenovAr projects.'

A second key element in the strategy was putting all the technical aspects of the process in the hands of CAMMESA. As manager of the dispatch and the clearing of all commercial transactions in the wholesale electricity market, and with extensive experience in managing tenders for gas and thermal power investments, CAMMESA had enough in-house know-how and credibility in the market.

A third element was the development of a highly participatory process. Consultation rounds held before the final RfP documents were issued and a responsive communication mechanism during the auction were essential in ensuring the transparency and integrity of the process.

---

[57] In 2015, these subsidies amounted to 4% of GDP.

Coordination with the transmission system was a fourth crucial element in the RenovAr programme. To ensure efficient use of existing capacity, the maximum power that could be connected at each point in the existing network was specified in the first two rounds. In the third round, transmission availability was based on an 'expanded transmission system' and included transmission investments that had to be completed over the following 30 months. To shield bidders from the risk of transmission works failing to reach completion, a take-or-pay clause was included in PPAs. Transmission charges for new RE projects follow a 'shallow connection costs' approach.

One of the main limitations of the programme is the lack of a predefined schedule for the auction rounds. This is exacerbated by the fact that no long-term investment plans for the energy sector or the renewables industry have been developed. The resulting uncertainty increases the risks related to the programme's sustainability in the medium and long term. As Viscidi and Yepez (2019: 11) have pointed out, 'Auctions held at regular intervals or scheduled well in advance can improve long-term confidence in a country and encourage bidders to invest the time and resources necessary to familiarise themselves with the market.'

4.6.2 Auction design

Perhaps the major factor in the success of the RenovAr programme so far has been its comprehensive approach to mitigating risks for investors and developers. Payment and termination guarantees—provided through FODER—substantially reduced off-taker risk. The fact that most of the risk was transferred away from the developers and onto the state helped to increase investor appetite in early rounds and played a considerable role in reducing bid prices (Menzies et al., 2019). Although government leaders were initially reluctant to carry these risks, they eventually acknowledged that this was necessary for attracting investors and creating the kind of track record that would encourage those investors to carry some of these risks in future (IFC, 2018).[58]

Setting relatively low technical requirements for participation in the auction and relatively high penalties for non-compliance is, in theory, an efficient way of ensuring a reasonable level of competitiveness between bidders. To

---

[58] According to the IFC (2018), the Argentinian government initially wanted investors to carry energy-balancing costs through market clearing, include local content in their bids, allow provinces to use their own environmental and social rules for projects in their jurisdictions, and set a public reserve price in the first auction.

present bids in a RenovAr auction, participants had to provide only basic technical feasibility studies. This kept the costs of participation relatively low. However, to discourage irresponsible offers and ensure that only serious bids were submitted, costly bid and performance guarantees were imposed. For bidders with serious intentions to develop the offered capacity, these guarantees involve few sunk costs and do not represent a significant financial risk because the amounts are reimbursed if bids are unsuccessful or when commercial operations begin (as long as this occurs according to the agreed schedules) (Menzies et al., 2019).

This mechanism successfully attracted a large number of bids to all rounds. However, not all accepted bids projects have reached financial close or met the dates stipulated for starting commercial operations. In part, the 2018 macroeconomic crisis is to blame for this. Although, as discussed, the RenovAr programme was designed to shield investors from certain sectoral and other economic risks, it was unable to protect them from macrosystemic failure. When the Argentinian government had to apply for an IMF bail out, it was cut off from international markets, and several investors were unable to finance their projects. In response, the government decided not to execute guarantees—that is, not to penalize investors for risk over which they had no control. In the short term, the decision can be considered a positive move—it is keeping projects alive in the event that the investment situation changes. However, not executing the guarantees has the potential to create a credibility problem for the programme that could have serious repercussions in the medium to long term.

4.7 Conclusion: The need to design for long-term auction success

The RenovAr programme has been successful in attracting developers, despite high levels of economic uncertainty. In our view, two elements of the programme have been key to its success. The first was the use of competitive auctions to assign 20-year energy contracts. The second was the establishment of FODER—a guarantee and investment fund that aimed to mitigate the sectoral and the macroeconomic risks facing investors.

When analysing the Argentine experience, the distinctive elements of its economy and its energy sector have to be factored in. These include chronic economic instability, the existence of competitive primary energy sources, institutional fragility within the electricity sector, the absence of comprehensive sectoral investment planning, and the country's limited transmission system.

Developing mechanisms to mitigate and minimize financial risk thus became a basic condition for the development of the RE sector. Accordingly, as shown, the RenovAr programme includes several elements aimed at securing the successful bidders' revenue streams and shielding them from financial risks, such as the lack of off-taker payments and currency devaluations as well as changes related to policy and exchange controls. These elements include standardized 20-year PPAs with a trust fund that guarantees payments with sovereign support plus the option of a World Bank guarantee, US-dollar-denominated energy pricing, provisions for international arbitration, and a sell-option in favour of the investor in case of non-compliance by CAMMESA.

Initially, the programme was successful in attracting a large number of investors. However, after Argentina's 2018 financial crisis, it became clear that the trust fund could not, in fact, protect investors against sovereign risk (beyond the World Bank guarantee). Consequently, some projects that were still in their initial stages have found it extremely difficult to reach financial close, and the ongoing deterioration of the country's financial situation has had a direct impact on RE investments. In addition, the lack of an agency or mechanism with responsibility for sector-wide medium and long-term planning has also limited the development and implementation of Argentina's RE policies.

The main objective of the RenovAr programme was to ensure enough investment to cover the RE generation share as set out in the legislation. Nevertheless, when the programme was launched, Argentina was facing the risk of generation shortages. For this reason, in the three first rounds, points were awarded in the bid evaluations to projects that made commitments to shorter construction periods, and penalties were levied if projects failed to meet the deadlines they proposed.

Developing a local RE industry was a further general objective even though local content was not included in the criteria for evaluating bids. Instead, SLC was used as a criterion when two projects bid at the same price. SLC was also considered to determine possible tax benefits for which projects could apply and to reduce the costs of the World Bank guarantee.

Overall, our assessment of the RenovAr programme is positive. However, some aspects of its design and implementation could be improved.

First, Argentina lacks a medium- and long-term planning mechanism for the electricity sector to guide investment decisions. The development of RE has been no exception. Prior to RenovAr, RE tenders were held without any consideration of other tenders for electricity or gas. Furthermore, the RenovAr programme itself lacked a public mechanism to set the frequency and volume of the auctions to be held. Thus, each round was announced by the government only a few months before the call.

Interestingly, tax benefits are not considered in determining merit order for the economic offers.[59] This means that, for some projects, total costs (price plus fiscal support) can be higher than projects that have a higher price but a lower total cost. Of course, the narrow sectoral interest is to minimize project price, but the total cost (including tax incentives) is ultimately the cost that electricity consumers pay. Thus, this oversight partly reflects the need for an overarching vision that is capable of utilizing RenovAr as a tool of national energy and economic policy and not as an isolated programme.

Second, the RE legislation makes provision for several tax incentives. Nevertheless, the incentives were not considered when ranking the financial merits of the bids. Disregarding the incentives can result in favouring bids whose total cost (price plus fiscal support) is higher than bids that have a higher price but a lower total cost. This oversight also reflects the lack of a wider vision within the RenovAr programme; that is, RE should be seen as one aspect of an overarching national energy and economic policy and not as an isolated issue.

Third, delays in project implementation reflect the problems associated with securing financing after the deterioration of Argentina's macroeconomic situation in 2018. In hindsight, the lack of any requirement for bidders to provide evidence of the financial resources they had available to commit to the project has probably created the greatest risks for both bidders and the RenovAr programme. Awarded projects that cannot reach financial close, in what has become a highly volatile economic context, risk losing their performance bond. Part of FODER's intended role was to supply long-term finance to RE projects through loans, equity, subsidies to interest rates, etc. In practice, however, the trust has not fulfilled this part of its mandate, and its failure in this regard is likely to be costly in terms of developing RE in Argentina in the medium term.

Finally, while the RenovAr programme has not specified different SLC preferences for the different technologies, a differentiated approach aimed at maximizing local impact might be worth exploring.

---

[59] Only in the case of a tie between two projects (i.e. a price difference of less than 3% and the same local content) was fiscal cost considered in the merit ranking.

4.8 References

CAMMESA (Compañía Administradora del Mercado Mayorista Eléctrico) (various). 'Informe Mensual'. Monthly reports, https://portalweb.cammesa.com/memnet1/Pages/descargas.aspx (accessed 20 April 2023).

CAMMESA (2019). 'Informe Anual 2019'. Annual report, https://portalweb.cammesa.com/MEMNet1/Documentos%20compartidos/Informe%20Anual%202019%20v%20larga%2006Jun.pdf (accessed 20 April 2023).

Constantini, P., and Di Paola, M. M. (2019). 'Programa renovar: ¿Éxito o fracaso?' Policy Brief, Fundación Ambiente y Recursos Naturales, https://farn.org.ar/wp-content/uploads/2020/06/FARN_Programa-RenovAr_Exito-o-fracaso.pdf (accessed 20 April 2023).

Garrison, C. (2020). 'S&P Joins Fitch, Moody's in Downgrading Argentina Amid Coronavirus Crisis'. *Reuters*, 7 April, https://www.reuters.com/article/us-argentina-ratings/sp-joins-fitch-moodys-in-downgrading-argentina-amid-coronavirus-crisis-idUSKBN21P365 (accessed 20 April 2023).

IEA (International Energy Agency) (2019). *World Energy Outlook 2019* (Paris: IEA).

IFC (International Finance Corporation) (2018). 'RenovAr (Argentina): Scaling (Express Edition)'. https://www.ifc.org/wps/wcm/connect/987eeec6-6259-4c00-8e21-fbf49813a47b/scaling-infra-argentina-08.pdf?MOD=AJPERES&CVID=mSCMXzz (accessed 20 April 2023).

INDEC (Instituto Nacional de Estadística y Censos de la República Argentina) (n.d.). 'Proyecciones nacionales'. https://www.indec.gob.ar/indec/web/Nivel4-Tema-2-24–84 (accessed 20 April 2023).

Jimeno, M., Grundner, C., Brückmann, R., and Hoeft, M. (2017). *Enabling PV & Wind in Argentina: A Framework Assessment* (Berlin: Eclareon).

Lanosa, W. (2020). 'Actualidad del sector eólico[. Webinar hosted by the Association of Large Users of Electrical Energy in Argentina, 14 July 2020.

Menzies, C., Marquardt, M., and Spieler, N. (2019). 'Auctions for the Support of Renewable Energy in Argentina: Main Results and Lessons Learned'. Report, D2.1-AR, Auctions for Renewable Energy Support II (AURES II), http://aures2project.eu/wp-content/uploads/2020/02/AURES_II_case_study_Argentina.pdf (accessed 20 April 2023).

Righini, P., and Gallegos, H. G. (2011). 'Mapa de Energía Solar Colectada Anualmente por un Plano Inclinado: Un Ángulo óptimo en La República Argentina'. Paper presented at the Ibero American Conference for Hydrogen and Renewable Energy, http://www.electroimpulso.com.ar/ENERGIASOLAR/

RADIACION%20SOLAR/carta%20radiacion%20solar%20argentina.pdf (accessed 20 April 2023).

RunRún Energético (2018). 'Ministro calcula que reserva de gas convencional llega a 132 TCF'. 27 July, https://www.runrunenergetico.com/ministro-calcula-que-reserva-de-gas-convencional-llega-a-132-tcf (accessed 20 April 2023).

Secretaría de Energía (2019a). 'Argentina: Evolución de subsidios, oferta y demanda de energía 2015–2019: Gas, electricidad y petróleo'. November, http://www.energia.gob.ar/contenidos/archivos/Reorganizacion/sintesis_balance/2019-11-20_SE_Subsidios_oferta_y_demanda_de_energia_Argentina_2015-2019_dist.pdf (accessed 20 April 2023).

Secretaría de Energía (2019b). 'Balance de gestión en energía 2016—2019: Emergencia, normalización y bases para la transformación'. December, http://www.energia.gob.ar/contenidos/archivos/Reorganizacion/sintesis_balance/2019-12-09_Balance_de_Gestion_en_Energia_2016-2019_final_y_anexo_pub_.pdf (accessed 20 April 2023).

Viscidi, L., and Yepez, A. (2019). 'Clean Energy Auctions in Latin America'. Inter-American Development Bank, https://publications.iadb.org/publications/english/document/Clean_Energy_Auctions_in_Latin_America.pdf (accessed 20 April 2023).

World Bank (2017). 'Combined Project Information Documents/Integrated Safeguards Data Sheet: Appraisal Stage. Report No. 112150'. http://documents1.worldbank.org/curated/en/651501484830399149/text/112150-PSDS-P159901-Box402872B-PUBLIC-Disclosed-1-17-2017.txt (accessed 20 April 2023).

World Bank (2018a). 'Argentina: Renewable Energy Auctions'. Financial solutions brief, http://pubdocs.worldbank.org/en/263381518200588533/Briefs-Guarantees-ArgentinaAuctions.pdf (accessed 20 April 2023).

World Bank (2018b). 'Population Density (People per Sq. Km of Land Area)'. https://data.worldbank.org/indicator/EN.POP.DNST (accessed 20 April 2023).

5
Mexico

The Promise and Politics of Auctions and Reforms

Ignacio Rodriguez and Rogelio Avendaño

5.1 Introduction: Mexico's reform-minded auction programme

Mexico embarked on a power-sector reform programme in 2013 to develop a new electricity market. The reform objectives included modernization of the industry, improving competitiveness, and fostering social and economic development. On 20 December 2013, the Mexican government published the Energy Sector Constitutional Reform, with the following main objectives: attract investments to modernize the energy sector, increase Mexico's competitiveness, increase energy exports and reduce dependency on imports, reduce energy costs, and increase national energy security.

The key aspects of the sector reform included the following (with the associated Articles in the modified Constitution):

- Article 25: establishes the Empresas Productivas del Estado for the vertical and horizontal unbundling and restructuring of the state-owned Consejo Federal de la Energía (Federal Commission of Electricity, CFE);
- Article 27: retains state ownership of the planning, power system control, and dispatch power market functions, as well as the transmission and distribution services, but allows contracts with private-sector providers;
- Article 28: CFE and private developers can carry out electricity generation activities in an open and fully competitive electricity market under a well-defined regulatory framework.

Ignacio Rodriguez and Rogelio Avendaño, *Mexico*. In: *Renewable Energy Auctions: Lessons from the Global South*. Edited by: Anton Eberhard and Wikus Kruger, Oxford University Press. © Oxford University Press (2023). DOI: 10.1093/oso/9780192871701.003.0005

The sector reform included the following institutional reorganization:

- Secretaría de Energía (Energy Secretariat, SENER): the Energy Secretariat remained the lead institution for energy sector policy, planning, and execution (including transmission projects);
- Energy Regulatory Commission (CRE): the establishment of the Energy Regulatory Commission as the independent regulator for the market participants;
- Centro Nacional de Control de Energía (National Center for Energy Control, CENACE): the market operator—covering the power system dispatch and control functions that used to be part of CFE—was transformed into a decentralized public entity;
- CFE: the state-owned utility was segmented into 14 independent entities, each in charge of various parts of the value chain, with some, such as generation and retail services, focused on competing with the private sector.

Mexico implemented three energy auctions in the post-reform period (2016 and 2017), which awarded 8 gigawatts (GW) of new generation capacity at some of the lowest renewable energy prices worldwide, resulting in investment commitments of more than US\$ 9 billion. The first auction awarded 6 wind and 12 solar contracts to 11 companies at an average price of US\$ 47.79/MWh. The second auction awarded 10 wind, 33 solar, 6 hydroelectric, 1 geothermal and 6 combined-cycle (gas) contracts to 22 companies with an average price of US\$ 33.47/MWh. The third auction awarded six wind, nine solar, and one turbogas (open-cycle gas turbine or OCGT) contracts to eight companies with an average price of US\$ 20.57/MWh.

The results from these first post-reform energy auctions were shaped by the newly established competitive legal and regulatory framework, the competitiveness of local wind and solar resources, a strong local private-sector response, and investors' expectations associated with the quickly evolving and growing electricity sector.

However, it was also expected that the reform would become the basis for strengthening the CFE, which was not achieved during that period. In 2018, Andrés Manuel López Obrador won the presidential election, leading to a major shift in Mexico's political landscape and government policies, shaped by a populist/socialist agenda. The government has, for example, paused some of the sector reform processes and cancelled further energy auctions. This has understandably caused great uncertainty in the energy sector.

The government's current focus is to strengthen and improve the financial viability of CFE and promote its hydroelectric and natural gas projects, while also addressing issues of power system intermittency, reliability, and transmission congestion. The current policy favours the dispatch of CFE baseload generation plants while limiting the economic dispatch from variable renewable energy sources. Investors and environmental groups are challenging the current policy and have been able to halt some of these modifications until a final decision is made by the courts.

Nevertheless, CENACE, the market operator, remains unbundled, and the independent regulator (CRE) remains mandated to fulfil its functions, providing the opportunity for a competitive market in generation. New auctions are expected to be revived in the near term by building upon the current legal and regulatory framework and the competitiveness of renewable energy sources.

The following sections provide an introduction to the country and power-sector context; a description and analysis of the auction design, including auction volumes, qualification criteria and processes, bidder ranking and winner selection, buyer and seller liabilities, and approaches to project and credit enhancement; an analysis of auction implementation arrangements, including key role-players/decision-makers and overall institutional context; and key lessons learned and implications for auction design and implementation.

5.2 Overview of Mexico's economy

Located in the southern portion of North America, Mexico covers 1,972,550 square kilometres (761,610 square miles) and is the thirteenth largest country in the world. With approximately 128,649,565 inhabitants (CIA (2020) estimate), it is the tenth most populous country.

The United Mexican States is a federation comprising 31 states whose government is representative, democratic and republican, based on a presidential system. The Constitution establishes three levels of government: the federal union, the state governments, and the municipal governments.

Mexico has the eleventh largest economy in the world but has underperformed since the 1990s in terms of growth, inclusion, and poverty reduction compared to similar countries. Mexico maintained average gross domestic product (GDP) growth rates of around 2% between 1980 and 2018, limiting progress in convergence relative to high-income economies. Total GDP came to US$1.22 trillion in 2018, with inflation at 4.28%. On a per-capita basis, economic growth has slowed, on average, to 1.6% over the past five years.

5.3 Mexico's power sector

As of December 2018, the total installed generation capacity was 73,206 megawatts (MW), including CFE and independent power producers (IPPs), reflecting an increase of 3.1% from 2017 (67,958 MW) (IEA, 2018). The electricity access rate was 99%, as shown in Table 5.1, which also includes the installed capacity by technology (SENER, 2019).

Electricity generation increased from 280,365 gigawatt hours (GWh) in 2014 to 317,278 GWh in 2018 (Table 5.2). A significant increase in wind and solar generation (Table 5.3) was derived from private actors' self-supply projects. There were also projects predating the clean energy auctions that deliver energy directly to CFE.

5.3.1 Power-sector structure

Before the reform, SENER was responsible for power-sector policy and system planning, while CFE was responsible for the growth and development of the electricity market. Private-sector participation was limited to

Table 5.1 Key information on Mexico's electricity sector

Total capacity (MW installed, 2018)	73,206
Combined cycle gas	25,569
Hydroelectric	12,610
Thermal conventional (fuel oil)	11,909
Coal	5,394
Wind	4,764
Bioenergy	3,503
Turbogas (OCGT)	3,222
Solar	1,821
Nuclear	1,611
Cogeneration	1,401
Internal combustion (diesel)	701
Geothermal	701
Electricity access rates	
Urban and rural	99%
Total energy production (GWh, 2018)	317,278 GWh

Source: Authors' compilation with information from SENER (2019).

Table 5.2 Evolution of the generation mix in GWh per year

Technology	2014	2015	2016	2017	2018
Thermal	215,566	225,977	235,698	243,265	243,740
Hydroelectric	38,875	30,858	30,847	31,903	32,436
Nuclear	9,677	11,577	10,567	10,883	13,555
Bioenergy and geothermal	6,341	6,693	6,558	6,628	5,974
Wind and solar	7,272	9,036	10,446	10,800	14,609
Total	277,731	284,141	294,116	303,479	310,314

Source: Authors' compilation with information from SENER (2019).

Table 5.3 Energy generated by source between 2014 and 2018

Technology	2014	2018	Difference (%)
Thermal	184,587	221,359	20
Hydroelectric	38,875	32,436	−17
Nuclear	9,677	13,555	40
Bioenergy and geothermal	6,341	5,974	−6
Wind and solar	7,272	14,609	101

Source: Authors' compilation with information from SENER (2019).

IPPs selling electricity to CFE under specific contracts. The system operator was embedded in CFE and the regulator (CRE) only oversaw private-sector projects.

The legal framework also allowed for the establishment of 'self-supply projects' where a private entity could build its own generation project. This led to the establishment of 'self-supply societies', where a private generation company owned by a group of partners could supply electricity to those partners and, in some cases, make use of CFE's transmission and distribution lines.

The reform opened up power generation and retail to the participation of the private sector to promote a more competitive model. It also expanded the scope of SENER and CRE's mandates and separated the market operator CENACE from CFE by creating a new independent entity.

CFE was divided into 14 subsidiaries and companies: CFE Corporate; six generation subsidiaries; one transmission subsidiary; one distribution subsidiary; one basic supply subsidiary (serving the regulated sector and subsidized customers); one subsidiary for legacy contracts (power purchase agreements [PPAs] signed prior to the reform); one subsidiary company for qualified supply (serving the non-regulated consumers); one subsidiary company for primary fuel purchase, CFE Energia; and one subsidiary company for international markets, CFE Internacional.

Based on this structure, CFE's income is obtained mainly from the sale of goods and services, in addition to various income streams derived from the company's activities, such as the sale of natural gas to third parties. CFE also receives tax revenue from subsidies and transfers from the federal government. Between 2012 and 2018, CFE's total revenue grew on average 2.1% per year.

The new electricity sector structure is shown in Figure 5.1. Generation includes the power plants from the state-owned CFE generation projects and the independent private generators. As of 2018, CFE owned 57% of the total generation capacity, while 18% was supplied by IPPs selling directly to CFE and 25% was owned by the private sector as self-supply. CENACE is the market operator responsible for the economic dispatch of generation assets and overall market operation oversight. Transmission and distribution are still controlled by the state-owned CFE subsidiaries, but private-sector participation is allowed under a strict legal and financial framework. Retailing includes the following:

- CFE Basic Services is the regulated retailer, representing customers with loads below 1 MW. The regulation allows for the establishment of other

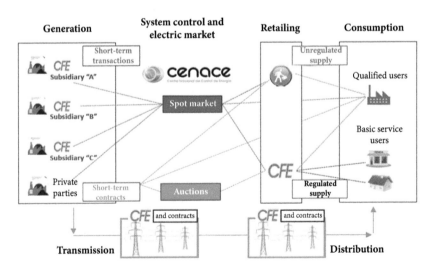

Figure 5.1 Structure of Mexico's electricity sector

Note: US$ 1 = 19.50 MXN.
Source: Authors' compilation.

regulated retailers, but to date there are none. The regulated tariffs are determined by the Treasury and CRE (with an associated subsidy). Since 2016, the regulated retailers must acquire their products and services through the energy auctions to ensure the lowest available prices.

- CFE Qualified Services subsidiary is one of the unregulated retailers in the market representing users with loads above 1 MW. The current framework also allows other retailers to participate. These retailers may acquire their products through PPAs, the spot market, or auctions. New customers with loads above 5 MW can acquire their electricity directly in the spot market or from power producers through PPAs.

Table 5.4 provides a brief description of the roles and legal mandates of the key institutions in the electricity sector.

5.3.2 Tariff levels and financial sustainability

CRE is officially responsible for tariff-setting and publishes the methodology for calculating and adjusting final tariffs. However, the Treasury is responsible for determining the subsidies to be allocated to specific tariffs, which CRE must apply. The tariff-setting methodology includes the charges associated with the CFE regulated rates of transmission, distribution, CENACE, and the regulated small-to-medium customers (Basic Supply) that are not included in the wholesale electricity market.

These tariffs are applied to consumers with loads below 1 MW, taking into account location/region, economic activity, and consumption levels, among other things. Subsidized tariffs are included for the residential sector and some agricultural and aquaculture customers.

In the case of residential customers, a seasonal, regionalized, and four-tiered consumption tariff-setting approach is used: (i) the four tiers (base, low, intermediate, high) are based on consumption ranges that also take household income into account—the first three tiers are partly cross-subsidized by the fourth; (ii) based on the associated climatic conditions, seven regions are considered—this also impacts the ranges of the various consumption levels of the four tiers; and (iii) two seasons are considered, 'summer' and 'out of summer'. The four-tier consumption levels increase in the summer season. This approach is based on the fact that electricity consumption is much higher during summer in certain regions of the country, and households with different incomes require different subsidy levels based on their consumption.

Table 5.4 Key institutions in Mexico's electricity sector

Energy Secretariat (SENER)	Develops country's energy policy within the current constitutional framework to guarantee a competitive, high-quality, economically viable and environmentally sustainable supply of energy that is required for national development.
Energy Regulatory Commission (CRE)	Autonomous regulatory agency, meant to ensure market transparency and efficiency in the service of greater competition and sustainability in the sector.
National Centre for Energy Control (CENACE)	Power system dispatch and control (formerly part of the CFE) is an independent entity whose purpose is to exercise operational control of the National Electric System, the wholesale electricity market operation, and guarantee impartiality in access to the national transmission network and the general distribution networks.
CFE Transmission	Provides power transmission as a public service, including the financing, installation, maintenance, management, operation, and expansion of the infrastructure.
CFE Distribution	Responsible for electricity distribution, including financing, constructing, maintaining, managing, operating, and expanding the system.
CFE Basic Services Provider (SSB retail services)	Retailer to deliver electricity to anyone who requests it in terms of the provisions of the law. It has legacy contracts (prior to the reform) and new contracts from users with loads below 1 MW. The law mandates that CFE Basic Services must purchase all the required products through long-term energy auctions.
Qualified Services Provider (SSC)	Entity which purchases electricity from the wholesale electricity market in order to supply qualified users (loads above 1 MW) within the electricity supply contract under CENACE guidelines.
Generators	A permit holder that has power plants with capacities above 0.5 MW. Generators participate directly in the competitive wholesale electricity market and can participate in auctions to enter into contracts with qualified users and qualified service providers to sell their electricity and associated products.
Finance and Public Credit Secretariat (SHCP, Treasury)	Proposes, directs, and controls the Federal Government's policy in financial, fiscal, spending, income, and public debt matters. It has a significant role in the yearly definition of subsidized tariffs.

Source: Authors' compilation with information from SENER and the CRE.

Table 5.5 provides an example of the tariff tiers grouping for Mexico City. Due to the region's climate, there are no seasonal tariff variations as for the rest of the country.

For the country as a whole, and as of 2020, it is estimated that 98% of residential customers are subsidized (more than 37.5 million customers) and only 2% are in the non-subsidized blocks (750,000 customers).

The subsidy works as a transfer of resources from the federal government to CFE. The average subsidy granted during the last government period (2012–2018) was US$ 640 per customer over the entire period. To reduce CFE's

Table 5.5 Example of subsidies applied in domestic tariffs

	Subsidized			Non-subsidized
	Base	Low	Intermediate	High
	1–75 kWh/month	76–125 kWh/month	126–249 kWh/month	>250 kWh/month
MXN	0.837	1.012	2.962	4.372
US$	0.033	0.040	0.118	0.175
Difference from non-subsidized (%)	81	77	33	–

Note: On 25 April 2020, US$ 1 = 24.98 MXN.
Source: Authors' compilation with information from the CRE and CFE.

financial deficit (and the consequent need for subsidies), CFE must purchase electricity through auctions at the lowest available prices. The bankability of the contracts is ensured through the financial strength of CFE Corporate as holding company.

During the third auction, buyers beyond CFE could purchase electricity through a market clearing house that centralized the transaction with the independent market operator CENACE. The market clearing house is a mechanism for addressing the complexity of an auction-based market with increasing numbers of buyers and sellers. It effectively binds all the future contracts for energy, capacity, and clean energy certificates (CELs), providing certainty to the market and, in a sense, acting as a financial guarantee mechanism by reducing the risk of contract failure. Further information on the clearing house and the pricing methodologies is presented in section 5.4.

5.3.3 Regulatory and policy framework

The electricity sector in Mexico has its regulatory and policy framework based on the Constitution, the Energy Transition Law (LTE), the Electricity Industry Law (LIE), and the associated regulations. These laws and regulations result in the development of a Programa de Incentivos às Fontes Alternativas de Energía Elétrica (National Electric System Development Programme, PRODESEN) on an annual basis with a horizon of 15 years (SENER, 2019). PRODESEN establishes 'the objectives, goals, strategies, and priorities that must be adopted to satisfy the demand in the National Electric System, while ensuring efficiency, quality, reliability, continuity, security and sustainability' (SENER, 2019). PRODESEN is effectively a combination of the national policy with the results of the long-term power system planning outputs (using PLEXOS software).

PRODESEN's framework for public policy covering the period 2019 to 2033 includes the following objectives:

- sovereignty, national energy security, and sustainability;
- SENER directs the activities of the National Electric System, including generation, transmission, distribution and commercialization, and coordination with other entities to issue policies and regulations to achieve rational and sustainable use of all energy resources;
- to guarantee the supply of electricity to all consumers, in compliance with the criteria of efficiency, quality, and reliability;
- the application of the same regulation, competitiveness, and transparency rules to all participants in the sector, including the establishment of tariffs in relation to costs;
- compliance with international commitments on clean energies to address climate change; and
- strengthening CFE as a state-owned company.

PRODESEN is an indicative instrument in terms of energy policy and potential generation projects, but it is a prescriptive instrument for transmission projects. Further information on the contents and objectives of PRODESEN is included in Appendix A.

According to the LIE, all electricity consumers are 'obligated entities' that need to comply with clean energy requirements. All retailers (representing their clients) and other market participants must fulfil this requirement. To ensure compliance with the clean energy goals in the power sector, Mexico has implemented a CEL system. According to the current regulation, generators will receive one CEL for each MWh of clean energy generated, which can be sold in the market.

According to the LIE, 'clean energies are those from sources of energy and processes for electricity generation where emissions or waste, if any, does not exceed the thresholds established in the issued administrative regulations' (Art. 3, frac. XXII). Among the clean energy sources considered are wind power, solar radiation, hydro, nuclear, ocean energy, geothermal, bioenergy, methane and biogas, hydrogen, gasification from waste, efficient cogeneration, energy from sugar mills, and energy from the sequestration of carbon dioxide. A more extensive and detailed list is included in Appendix B.

SENER defined a clean energy target of 25% by 2018 and 35% by 2024, following Mexico's international commitments (Figure 5.2).

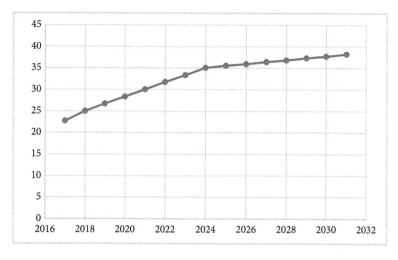

Figure 5.2 Clean energy trend, 2017–2031 (%)

Source: Authors' compilation with information from Programa para el Desarrollo del Sistema Eléctrico Nacional (PRODESEN) (SENER, 2018).

Table 5.6 CEL obligations up to 2022

Year	Requirement (%)
2018	5
2019	5.8
2020	7.4
2021	10.9
2022	13.9

Source: Authors' compilation with information from SENER (2018).

SENER sets the clean energy target for CFE during the first three months of each year for the following three years. Once established, the percentage cannot be reduced for a future year. The current requirements as a percentage of all the consumed electricity are shown in Table 5.6.

A penalty is allocated to the obligated entities that do not meet the requirement and their obligation to acquire CELs will remain in place. Other non-obligated entities—as voluntary participants—may also acquire CELs through the auctions or in the open market.

5.3.3.1 Current status of the energy reform in Mexico

All energy reforms are iterative, long-term processes, with governments normally issuing changes and recommendations and addressing flaws, gaps, or areas of opportunity. Such is the current case in Mexico, where some of the most prominent identified gaps relate to the competitiveness of CFE. The current government has indicated that it wants to build on the power-sector reform established under the previous administration to improve the conditions and stability of the National Electric System without negatively affecting the state-owned company or public finances.

Some of the main actions and reviews proposed by the current government to address the identified gaps and strengthen the position of the CFE are:

- reviewing and updating the current model of transmission fees and tariffs to reflect the real costs associated with the services;
- including any new PPA in the wholesale electricity market;
- reorganizing CFE to strengthen its generation divisions so that it can compete with the private sector;
- amending secondary regulation so the CFE basic supplier is not bound to buy energy only through auctioned long- and medium-term contracts but can also do so through taking advantage of commercial and market opportunities or to address emergency situations (such as the 2019 blackouts in the Yucatan Peninsula or the 2020 electricity supply deficit in the Baja California Sur Peninsula);
- replacing the governing body of CRE, including the appointment of new directors, to strengthen CFE in the market, including the review, modification, and update of the current mechanisms to determine regulated fees and tariffs for generation, transmission, and distribution to reflect the real costs associated with the services;
- halting mid- and long-term energy auctions and other initiatives, such as the first private transmission auction, to review the conditions that limit the competitiveness of CFE generation and transmission companies. An example is the fact that the first three auctions were limited to delivering energy and products in less than three years, the project portfolios were limited to solar and wind power technologies, and other technologies such as hydro and biomass were excluded; and
- reviewing the reorganization of CFE as the new administration considers this unbundling as inappropriate and argues that it weakened CFE by resulting in increased costs, hampered administrative specialization, and created inefficiencies.

On 25 March 2019, SENER issued an amendment to the regulations which initially ordered this unbundling, now allowing the CFE generation subsidiaries to reorganize and reunify, if required, and to allow CFE to increase cooperation and coordination between its various entities, share employees and their capacities between divisions under certain conditions, and allow the use of scale economies to improve operational efficiency and cost reduction in commercial activities.

5.4 The design of Mexico's renewable energy auctions

The long-term auctions in Mexico are considered one of the cornerstones of renewable energy expansion in the country. The main motivation is to increase clean energy generation and capacity at competitive prices by fostering competition. CELs are the associated mechanism to ensure greenhouse gas emission reductions and are auctioned as an integrated package along with energy and capacity.

The post-sector-reform auction process was initiated in 2016. Since then, three auctions have been performed: two in 2016 (31 March and 23 September) and one in 2017 (22 November). CENACE is the main auction-implementing entity due to its neutrality and technical capabilities to execute the process. During the transition period, SENER was in charge of leading the first three auctions, with CRE providing oversight and compliance monitoring. The fourth auction was supposed to see SENER passing on the responsibility to CRE but keeping CENACE as the implementing entity.

The prices obtained for energy were combined with the CELs as a package. Table 5.7 provides a summary of the products, volumes, technologies, and investments of the three auctions.

CENACE plans and executes the auction based on the information contained in PRODESEN, starting with the issuing of bidding rules and a detailed calendar of the process.

5.4.1 Auction design

The auctions' main features include multi-product—capacity, electricity generation, and CELs; regional and hourly adjustments of bid prices; and technology-neutral auctions. The auction design is a multi-stage process with four main milestones (Figure 5.3).

The auction process starts with the bid announcement, which invites the sector to participate in the auction and provides the process milestones that each participant must go through. The bid rules are then issued to the public so potential bidders can decide whether they are interested in participating. If

Table 5.7 Key auction information

Design	Frequency of auctions	Three auctions since 2016 One round per year Third round included market clearing house
	Products requested	Energy (MWh) Firm capacity (MW) CEL
	PPA length	15 years for energy, 20 years for CEL
	Currency	US$ (indexed)
Implementation	Policy and regulation guidelines	Energy Secretariat (SENER)
	Regulator	CRE
	Procurer	CENACE
	Off-taker	CFE (three auctions) Private sector (since the third auction)
Outcomes	MWh procured	20.16 TWh/y
	Technology procured	Wind, solar, hydro, turbogas (for firm capacity)
	Results' summary	**Auction 1 (31 March 2016):**

Auction 1 (31 March 2016):

5.4TWh/y of clean energy
5.4 million CEL
Average price of US$ 47.79 (MWh including CEL):

- Wind: US$ 55.39 (25% of energy including CEL)
- Solar: US$ 45.25 (75% of energy including CEL)

Lowest solar bid worldwide at US$ 35.50 MWh
18 contracts awarded to 11 companies
Estimated investment of US$ 2.6 billion
Estimated capacity of 2,585 MW

Auction 2 (23 September 2016):

9.27TWh/y of clean energy
8.9 million CEL
Average price of US$ 33.47 (MWh and CEL):

- Wind: US$ 35.29 (43% of energy and 41% CEL)
- Solar: US$ 31.56 (54% of energy and 53% CEL)
- Geothermal: US$ 37.31 (2% of energy and CEL)
- Hydro: No energy assigned but 3% of CEL

Solar bid: US$ 27.00 MWh
56 contracts awarded to 23 companies
Estimated investment of US$4 billion
Estimated capacity of 3 068 MW

Auction 3 (22 November 2017):

5.49 TWh/y of clean energy
5.9 million CEL
Average price of US$ 20.57 (MWh including CEL):

- Wind: 45% of energy
- Solar: 55% of energy
- Firm generation capacity: 593 MW
  (turbogas 84%, solar 2%, wind 4%)

Lowest wind bid worldwide at US$ 17.70 MWh
16 contracts awarded to 8 companies
Estimated investment of US$ 2.6 billion

Source: Authors' compilation based on information from SENER, CENACE, USAID, MLED Program 2011–2018.

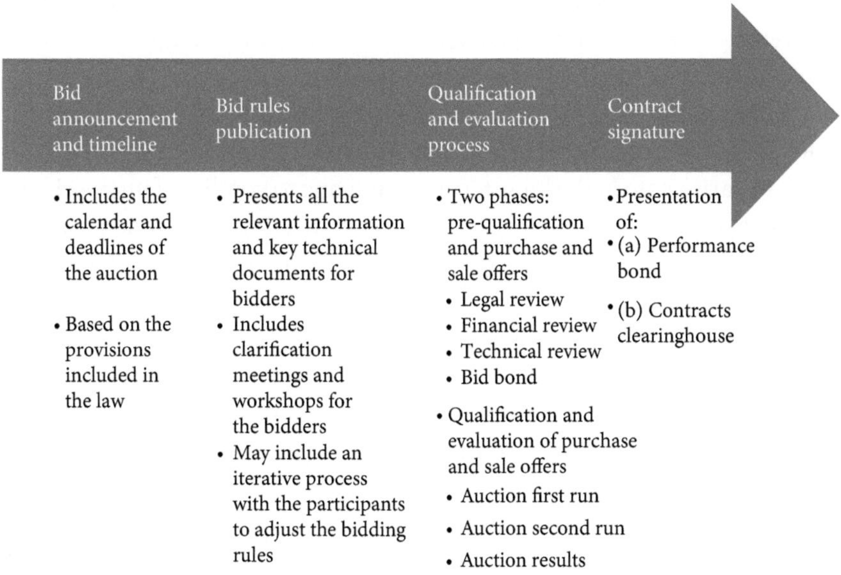

Bid announcement and timeline	Bid rules publication	Qualification and evaluation process	Contract signature
• Includes the calendar and deadlines of the auction • Based on the provisions included in the law	• Presents all the relevant information and key technical documents for bidders • Includes clarification meetings and workshops for the bidders • May include an iterative process with the participants to adjust the bidding rules	• Two phases: pre-qualification and purchase and sale offers • Legal review • Financial review • Technical review • Bid bond • Qualification and evaluation of purchase and sale offers • Auction first run • Auction second run • Auction results	• Presentation of: • (a) Performance bond • (b) Contracts clearinghouse

Figure 5.3 Auction stages

Source: Authors' compilation.

they decide to participate, they must pay an 'inscription' fee. The qualification and evaluation process is divided into two stages: the first focuses on the legal and financial capabilities of the bidders, both sellers and buyers; the second is the economic evaluation of the offers, based on an optimization model of the prices and volumes of products offered, to maximize the benefits of the auction. Finally, the winning bids submit their performance guarantees and the contracts are signed.

There is usually enough time provided between milestones. The auction timeline from the bid announcement to the contract signature is around 10 months: 6 months for the execution and award process and 4 months from award to contract signature, mainly to allow for the legal registration of the winning consortia and specific companies to be created for each of the projects. Once the contracts are signed, the projects are expected to come online in three years.

A detailed timeline for the third auction is shown in Table 5.8.

The issuing of the bid rules starts the initial stage of the auction process. These rules contain the conditions participants must adhere to and the obligations they incur by doing so. The bid rules contain all the legal, technical, and financial information required to participate in the auction and include a comprehensive annex with a set of technical documents. All the involved and related government entities provide information and support for the execution of the auction, for example, the National Institute of Archaeology and History in delivering recommendations on sensitive areas. A list of entities unable to participate in the long-term auction due to conflict of interest is also issued at this point. It is mainly focused on restricting government officers, consultants, and suppliers that deliver products or services for the auction process from participating.

If the bidders decide to participate, they must purchase the bid rules to receive a code that gives them entry to the auction through a dedicated website. The proceeds are used to cover the costs of the auction. Once the interested participants have paid for their entry, CENACE carries out the first technical workshop on the use of the dedicated website. All the legal, economic, and technical documents and products delivered for the auction are handled through this platform. The platform not only eases the delivery of the documents but also ensures the traceability of the process.

To enhance the transparency of the process, a clarification meeting is carried out, providing a full review of the bid rules with the participants in several question-and-answer rounds that seek to clarify content, modify inconsistencies, and/or add recommendations. The results of these meetings

Table 5.8 Auction calendar

Stage	Phase	Activity	Date or period
Announcement	0	Bid announcement and timeline	Day 0
Bid rules publication	1	Issue of the bidding rules to the public	Day 1
	2	Issue of the list of entities unable to participate in the long-term auction due to conflict of interest	Day 7 (deadline)
	3	Payment for entry into auction: (1) bidding rules officially submitted; (2) potential buyer registration; (3) sales offer pre-qualification requests	(1) Day 10–day 100 (90 days); (2) day 10–day 40 (30 days); (3) day 10–day 100 (90 days)
	4	First training session on the use of the dedicated website	Day 18
	5	Clarification meeting: (1) Questions about the bidding rules and the annexes; (2) Questions about the clearing house operation guide and contract model; (3) Publication of answers to questions; (4) Questions period; (5) Publication of answers to questions	(1) Day 24–day 27; (2) day 28–day 29; (3) day 35 (deadline); (4) day 36 (deadline); (5) day 41 (deadline)
	6	Issue of the final version of the bidding rules	Day 49
Qualification and evaluation process	7	Second training session and potential buyers' registration and offers initial submittal	Day 51
	8	Appointment of the social witness for transparency	Day 52
	9	Publication of the potential buyer(s) (either regulated or non-regulated)	Day 52–day 55
	10	Submittal of the regulated buyer purchase offers volume, prices, and products to CENACE	Day 77 (deadline)
	11	Publication of the regulated buyer accepted purchase offers	Day 83
	12	Submittal of the non-regulated purchase offers volume, prices, and products to CENACE	Day 92 (deadline)
	13	Publication of the non-regulated accepted purchase offers	Day 98 (deadline)
	14	Publishing of the maximum economic value threshold percentage[a]	Day 99

Continued

Table 5.8 *Continued*

Stage	Phase	Activity	Date or period
	15	Third training session on submittal of technical offers for pre-qualification	Day 120
	16	Reception of pre-qualification applications for sales offers	Day 127–day 135
	17	Submittal of bid bonds	Day 138 (deadline)
	18	Issue of pre-qualification of qualified buyers and suppliers' certificates	Day 145 (deadline)
	19	Publication of the list of pre-qualified buyers and suppliers	Day 145 (deadline)
	20	Update of the prices for purchase offers for each product based on the exchange rate (due to possible variations, CENACE may update the prices)	Day 145
	21	Fourth training session on presentation of economic offers	Day 149
	22	Reception of the first stage of economic sale offers	Day 154
	23	Reception of the second stage of economic sale offers	Day 159
	24	Review of the economic sale offers	Day 160
	25	Execution of the mathematical optimization evaluation model of the economic sale offers	Day 161
	26	Execution of the possible additional iterations of the mathematical model of the adjusted economic sale offers	Day 162
Contract signature	27	Publication of the auction results and contracts award	Day 168 (deadline)
	28	Deadline for contract signature	Day 290 (deadline)

Note: [a] If this threshold is exceeded, then the auction is achieving the expected economic benefits; if not, the auction enters into the iterative process so the sellers may lower their prices.
Source: Authors' compilation based on information from CENACE.

lead to the publication of the final version of the bid rules that are to be used during the auction.

One of the key elements developed for the third auction is the 'market clearing house'. The risks associated with having multiple qualified buyers are mitigated through this clearing house acting as a 'single buyer, single seller', meaning that all generators and off-takers sign their contracts with the clearing house. It is, in essence, 'a mechanism to manage the contracts, risks and guarantees, allowing the participation of private buyers' (CENACE, 2017).

The clearing house is included as an independent mechanism for each auction and may be operated by an accredited third party, selected through a bidding process, and assigned to an operator such as a financial trust fund or stock exchange company but with the default operation done by CENACE. Further discussion on the mechanism is included in section 5.4.1.5.

Another key element in the auction design is the inclusion of a 'social witness'. This is a specialized civil society entity focused on monitoring, tracking, and documenting the mandated compliance of the process. Usually, these witnesses are accredited non-governmental organizations. The function emanates from the constitutional mandate (Art. 134) that all acquisitions, leasing, and purchases led by public officers must be executed by public bids with legality, transparency, and impartiality.

5.4.1.1 Auction demand

Three products are auctioned: energy (MWh), generation capacity (MW), and CELs.

- Energy must be from any clean energy source. The three auctions' results only included wind and solar energy (due to the requirement of reaching commercial operation in less than three years), but they may include small hydro, efficient cogeneration from natural gas (in compliance with current methodologies), biomass, ocean tidal, and nuclear (restricted to government-controlled facilities).
- Each MWh from clean energy has an equivalent of one CEL. The offered portfolio can include integrated packages of energy and CELs, but they can also be separated products.
- Capacity can be from fossil fuel sources (the auctions are open to include either energy, capacity, or CELs, but it is not mandatory to include all of them). If no capacity was required in the auction, the ceiling price will be set at the marginal operating cost of existing projects.

The volume of the auction is dynamic and price-sensitive. Each node submits a certain volume of purchase offers with accompanying maximum (ceiling) prices. CFE, as the retail services supplier, then submits the overall purchase volume and maximum prices for generation, CELs, and capacity. CFE prioritizes certain products and nodes based on its assessment of what is needed to fulfil the requirements of regulated customers. Since the third auction, once CENACE has reviewed the purchase requirements from CFE as retail services supplier, a list of the required products is published so the potential sellers may assemble their offers. Off-takers other than CFE retail services are also allowed to submit their purchase offers, which are included in the final auction volume.

The final auction volume is based on a system optimization model that seeks to match the purchase offers and generation bids, taking into account the decommissioning of old facilities, electricity demand projections, transmission and distribution planning and constraints, fuel cost projections, clean energy requirements, and international commitments. In practice, this means that the initial nodal purchase offers most likely do not end up determining what is procured, based on the optimization of the overall system.

The CFE electricity demand requested in the third auction and associated bid ceiling prices are presented for the three products in Table 5.9 (generation capacity as requested for the three regions and electricity and CEL requirements for the country as a whole).

All these bid offers are presented to the system market operator, CENACE, which is responsible for assembling the purchase offer package presented to the sellers.

Table 5.9 Products requested in the third auction

CFE generation capacity purchase offer requests for 15 years

Region	Quantity (MW/year)	Ceiling price per MW/year US$ (MXN)
Baja California	375	$ 83,730.88 ($ 1,673,752.12)
Baja California Sur	100	$ 71,198.70 ($ 1,388,374.60)
National Interconnected System	813.10	$ 54,550.90 ($ 1,063,742.54)

CFE cumulative electricity purchase offer requests for 15 years (MWh/year)

	Quantity (MWh/year)	Ceiling price MWh/year US$ (MXN)
	5,543,896	$ 38.54 ($ 751.53)

CFE CELs purchase offer requests for 20 years (CEL/year)

	Quantity (CEL/year)	Maximum price MWh/year US$ (MXN)
	5,543,896	$ 20.75 ($404.64)

Note: US$ 1 = 19.50 MXN in July 2020.
Source: Authors' compilation with information from CENACE. The third auction included private sector purchases by two buyers (Table 5.10).

Table 5.10 Products requested from the private sector in the third auction

Purchase offer requests from the private sector			
Entity	Capacity for 15 years (MW/year)	Energy for 15 years (MWh/year)	CELs, 20 years (CEL/year)
A	77.11	35.57	9.49
B	2.42	1.12	0.3

Source: Authors' compilation with information from CENACE.

5.4.1.2 Site selection

Project developers are free to select their project sites, usually based on resource availability, land cost, and interconnection availability, and linked to the auction requirements per area (nodes) where the energy and capacity are required (based on transmission and distribution capacity and decommissioning of plants).

To aid developers, SENER provides an Atlas Nacional de zonas co Alto Potencial de Energías Limpias (National Atlas, AZEL), which includes solar radiation and wind speed data. The AZEL is also layered at a high level to the transmission grid, human settlements, roads and railroads, and excluded areas such as natural, archaeological, or social protected areas.

5.4.1.3 Qualification criteria and process

The qualification process starts with CENACE delivering the third training session on the submission of technical offers for pre-qualification—a technical workshop for the bidders to clarify questions on the format and requirements of the information, files, and documents to be submitted for qualification. The technical, financial, and legal qualification criteria are given in the following sections.

5.4.1.3.1 Technical experience

The bidder must have built and operated project(s) with similar technology in the past 10 years with a capacity equivalent to at least 33% of the size of the capacity offered in the auction. In addition, bidders must commit to maintaining direct or indirect participation in the project company for a certain period. This is to avoid the scenario where a single company presents several projects and, once awarded, sells them to other unrelated companies.

5.4.1.3.2 Financial capacity

The financial review process assesses key economic and financial indicators related to the bidders' solvency, for example, audited financial statements. Bidders also need to provide a letter of intention from lenders (banks and/or financial institutions). A key requirement is that the bidder must have obtained financing in the past of at least a similar amount to what is required by its offers in the auction.

5.4.1.3.3 Legal review

The review reduces the chance that a participant is unable to sign a PPA, obtain permits, and carry out operations in the electricity market by not meeting the minimum requirements that the local mercantile legal framework establishes. Since the third auction, the contracts have been standardized for both generators and off-takers and are signed with the clearing house.

5.4.1.3.4 Social aspects compliance

The local socio-economic development requirements are set out in the Disposiciones Administrativas de Impacto Social (Administrative Provisions for Social Impact). The regulations cover environmental and social criteria. The Environmental and Natural Resources Ministry regulates environmental compliance. The Energy Ministry regulates social compliance. The process requires the provision of data from preliminary studies, Evaluación de Impacto Social (social impact evaluations, EvIS), previous consultations, social investment, and shared project benefit plans. Preliminary studies provide inputs for EvIS and consultations. These, in turn, shape the project's shared benefits and social investment initiatives.

5.4.1.3.5 Level of project preparation

All projects are required to submit permits as part of the qualification process, including technical, environmental, interconnection, and archaeological permits, as well as information attesting to the project's financial feasibility. The exact details depend on the requirements of each permit. For example, approved grid interconnection rights are mandatory, while the environmental, social, and archaeological permit applications need to at least have been submitted to the authorities. Building, sewer, and other structural permits may be at the pre-feasibility stage.

Starting with the second auction, land lease options and proof that projects will be able to obtain permits were also required. Land lease options are effectively 'pre-contracts' on the lease and use of the site, where the owner is willing to lease the land for preliminary studies. If a project is awarded, then the whole site will be leased for the term of the life of the project. Environmental and social qualification criteria were increased for the third auction, including the submission of all key permits and assessments to mitigate environmental and social risks.

The social impact assessment must be delivered to SENER before participation in the auction and, if required, the public consultation process must be performed before initiating construction. This depends on the project profile, location, and characteristics of the local communities. The rules, methodologies, and requirements are described in the Administrative Provisions for Social Impact.

Once the sellers fulfil the pre-qualification requirements, they will receive a certificate that allows them to present their economic proposals for participation in the auction.

For transparency and traceability of the process, CENACE publishes a list of the participants that have obtained a pre-qualification certificate. This is a major milestone that ensures the integrity of the participants.

All bidders are requested to present an auction participation guarantee as a bid bond to confirm their commitment to presenting an economic proposal and to cover the total potential liabilities (TPL) related to the volume of the products intended to be delivered. The requirement is for both sellers and buyers to confirm their intention of signing the PPAs. The bond is structured in four parts and linked to Mexican investment units (UDIs)[1] established by the Mexican Central Bank. The UDI provides stability to certain markets because it is designed to retain its purchasing power without being exposed to inflation but also without the risk of an exchange rate slide. As of August 2020, 1 UDI was equal to US$ 0.30. The bid bond is structured in four parts: (i) 300,000 UDIs as an initial bond to participate in the bid process, regardless of the number of offers and products presented; (ii) 65,000 UDIs per MW of capacity offered in the auction; (iii) 30 UDIs per each MWh of electricity offered in the auction; and (iv) 15 UDIs per each CEL being offered in the auction.

If the proposed project has already been interconnected, the TPLs are reduced by 50%, and once the PPA has been signed, the auction participation guarantee is changed to a performance bond, as explained in section 5.4.1.5.

---

[1] A UDI is an index unit of funds used in Mexico. It can be traded in many currency markets because its value changes with respect to currencies. Unlike currencies, it is designed to retain its purchasing power and not be subject to inflation. Its value is published periodically by the Bank of Mexico. The value of a UDI in March 2017 was around 5.7 pesos. US$ 1 = 19.5 pesos, 300,000 UDIs = US$ 88,000. In August 2020, the value was 6.53, which is 14% above the price from 2017.

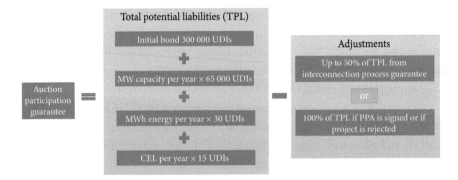

Figure 5.4 Auction participation guarantees
Source: Authors' compilation.

If the project is rejected, the bid bond is returned to the bidder. Figure 5.4 describes the guarantee mechanisms.

5.4.1.4 Bidder ranking and winner selection

The methodology for pricing includes three types of adjustments to the pay-as-bid process (del Río, 2017).

5.4.1.4.1 Nodal pricing

The regional nodal pricing adjustment is based on an hourly adjustment factor per zone, which either rewards or penalizes the zones depending on whether new generation capacity is needed or where production overcapacity exists. This internal evaluation adjustment factor does not affect the project's price but is used for the evaluation of the bid. Nodal adjustment factors are defined for each new auction.

5.4.1.4.2 Hourly adjustment

Electricity from variable clean sources is paid at the price included in the seller's bid as adjusted up or down by 'hourly adjustment factors'. This is meant to account for the expected value of the energy delivered at the inter-connection node relative to the expected average hourly price. This implies that more will be paid for electricity generated at times of higher demand and less at times of lower demand. The hourly adjustments are used for the actual payments to the winning bidders.[2]

---

[2] More information on the hourly adjustments is included in the bidding rules. Also, CENACE published a methodological note on the estimation of the marginal local prices and hourly adjustments factors; see https://www.cenace.gob.mx/Docs/MercadoOperacion/Subastas/2017/12%20Nota%20Explicativa%20de%20Metodo%20de%20Calculo%20de%20Diferencias%20Esperadas%20de%20PML%20v18%2005%202017.pdf (accessed 20 April 2023).

5.4.1.4.3 Inflation and exchange rate adjustment

The price is also adjusted to account for inflation and variations in the peso/dollar exchange rate. Each bidder may choose that its payments be indexed to Mexican inflation or the peso/dollar exchange rate. At the commercial operation date (COD), the price offered in the bid will be adjusted to account for variations in the peso/dollar exchange rate (70% weight), US inflation in proportion to the peso/dollar exchange rate variations (20% weight), and Mexican inflation (10% weight). This adjusted price is referred to as the 'initial price'. The initial price is multiplied by the average of the monthly adjustment factors (either exchange rate or local inflation as initially selected by the bidder) to calculate the adjusted monthly prices for the corresponding year.

The bid evaluation process may have two or more stages to evaluate the sale offers and prices against the purchase offers through an optimization model, considering an 'economic surplus threshold' (Figure 5.5). Once the reception of sale offers has concluded, the auction process is as follows:

- the 'electronically' sealed envelopes are opened;
- offered pay-as-bid prices are readjusted upwards or downwards based on nodal congestion price considerations;
- prices are compared and listed in ascending order;
- the lowest-priced products are selected until the entire volume of the products requested is reached;
- if a pre-established economic surplus threshold is reached or exceeded, then the auction is considered closed and the sale offers selected proceed for contract signing. The economic surplus threshold is considered as reached when the bid offers (adjusted by the optimization algorithm) meet the volumes requested at or below the price ceilings set by the purchase offers. If the threshold is not reached (meaning the volume offered is too expensive), then the auction enters an iterative process so that the bidders can lower their offered prices, after which the algorithm is run again to check whether the threshold is achieved;
- rejected sale offer participation guarantees are returned to the corresponding participants.

If a pre-established economic surplus threshold is not reached or exceeded, then the auction is considered open and a second run is activated, based on the following process: prices and volumes submitted are made public to all participants, the remaining percentage of the economic surplus threshold to be reached is made public to all participants, participants resubmit prices for

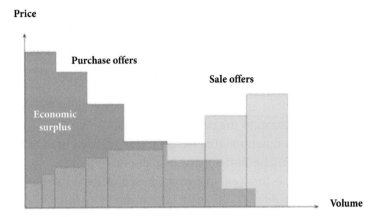

Figure 5.5 Economic surplus thresholds for a single node

Source: Montenegro Gutiérrez (2019).

the product volumes already offered, prices offered are readjusted upwards or downwards based on nodal congestion price considerations, prices are compared and listed in ascending order, the lowest prices are selected until the entire volume of the products requested is reached.

The process is repeated until the economic surplus threshold is met or until no new prices are received that are at least 1% lower than the previous iteration.

Once the results of the model are known, CENACE validates them through a review performed by academic institutions. This review process includes a social representative to guarantee transparency before the final official results are published.

At this point, the auction is considered closed and the sale offers selected proceed for contract signing. Rejected sale offer participation guarantees are returned to the corresponding participants. The auction results are published by CENACE and the participants are given enough time before contract signing for the creation of the legal entities required to represent contracts. The signature ceremony concludes the auction process.

5.4.1.5 Buyer and seller liabilities

5.4.1.5.1 Financial pre-qualification and penalties

The PPA length is 15 years covering energy and capacity and 20 years for the CELs. Projects are eligible to operate as merchant plants once the 15-year period has concluded.

In the first two auctions, the contracts were signed between CFE as the main off-taker and the generators, but since the third round of auctions, the operations are to be implemented through a contracts and guarantees management clearing house acting as a 'single buyer, single seller' (it acts as a buyer for all sellers and as a seller for all buyers), with all contracts signed within the clearing house (see section 5.4.1.6).

All participants are required to present a contract compliance guarantee (performance bond) issued at the signing date of the PPA for the duration of the contract. The performance bond will cover the following based on the auction offer: 65,000 UDIs per MW of capacity, 30 UDIs per each MWh of electricity, and 15 UDIs per each CEL.

The amount of the performance guarantee varies depending on whether certain milestones are fulfilled (option to reduce the amount) or not fulfilled (obligation to increase amount). Failure to achieve specific milestones (interconnection, operational tests) before scheduled COD will result in a 0.75% reduction in the contract price of the PPA. Delays in reaching the scheduled COD also require that bidders increase the performance guarantee by 10% (delay attributable to electricity generators), 2% (delay attributable to the federal government), and/or 5% (delay attributable to state/municipal government) for each month's delay, subject to an overall cap of two times the original guarantee amount. Generators may defer up to 12% of the contracted CELs to be delivered to the off-taker for up to two years, but any CELs so deferred shall be increased by 5% (in volume) for each deferred year. If, after deferring for two years, there is a deficiency in CELs, the generator must purchase CELs in the market. If commercial operations are not commenced by the scheduled COD, the awarded bidder must pay a penalty equivalent to 5% of the monthly payments under the PPA for every month of delay.

Since the third auction, the off-taker (buyer) must provide guarantees to be issued not later than 30 days after COD until the end of the contract: 32,500 UDIs per MW of capacity, 15 UDIs per each MWh of electricity, and 7.5 UDIs per each CEL.

For off-takers, the performance bond covers the fulfilment of the purchases and payments. If the off-taker does not pay, or is unable to take the products, the guarantees are executed through the clearing house.

5.4.1.6 Securing the revenue stream and addressing off-taker risk
The creation of a contracts clearing house, acting as a 'single buyer, single seller', helps to secure the revenue stream of the projects. For example, if a generator fails to deliver the promised energy block, the clearing house will compensate the buyers by acquiring the energy from the wholesale market until the next auction is performed and will seek to be compensated for this cost by the generator under the contractual regime. The same inverse

scenario occurs if a consumer fails to acquire the energy block stipulated in the contract.

As the clearing house is a legal entity, it can bill and collect payments. Further, it manages the guarantees and quantifies the risks on every project associated with each portfolio. It also has the ability to execute the guarantees, suspend bilateral transactions, or terminate contracts.

With regards to the auctions, the clearing house operates as follows:

(1) A project portfolio is created for each auction.
(2) The terms and guidelines for each portfolio are independent of other portfolios.
(3) The balance and payments are related to the same portfolio.
(4) Each buyer receives a proportional assignation of each of the sale offers selected as the winning offer and related to the proportional partici-pation in the auction. This is called a 'proportional assignation factor' (FAP).
(5) The FAP determines the amount corresponding to each of the prod-ucts delivered by the sellers. Figure 5.6 shows an example of the assignation in terms of capacity offered to the auction (MW).
(6) The assignation is independent in each auction. The signature of new contracts from the same participants in previous or future auctions does not alter the contract awarded in the specific auction.
(7) Each bidder will be assigned a contract to sell all its products to the clearing house. In the case of a buyer failing to fulfil its contract, the clearing house will cover its payments. Figure 5.7 shows an example of the assignation in terms of the price and payments, based on the same FAP.

It is important to mention that the clearing house is not a guarantee. It receives and manages individual guarantees and a reserve fund. This reserve fund is used to cover the immediate failures in obligations from either seller

Accepted sale offers				Accepted purchase offers		
Participation	Capacity	Generators		Buyers	Capacity	FAP
48%	100 MW	Gen 1		Retail 1	65 MW	0.30952381
36%	75 MW	Gen 2		Retail 2	45 MW	0.21428571
12%	25 MW	Gen 3		User 1	40 MW	0.19047619
4%	10 MW	Gen 4		User 2	60 MW	0.28571429

Figure 5.6 Buyers' assignation in terms of products offered

Source: Authors' compilation based on information from CENACE.

Accepted sale offers		
FAP	Annual price	Generators
0.47619048	100 MXN	Gen 1
0.35714286	75 MXN	Gen 2
0.11904762	25 MXN	Gen 3
0.04761905	10 MXN	Gen 4

Accepted Purchase offers		
Buyers	Annual price	FAP
Retail 1	65 MXN	0.30952381
Retail 2	45 MXN	0.21428571
User 1	40 MXN	0.19047619
User 2	60 MXN	0.28571429

Figure 5.7 Bidders' assignation in terms of prices offered

Source: Authors' compilation based on information from CENACE.

(by acquiring the missing products from the spot market) or buyer (by covering the missing payments). Eventually, the guarantees are executed, and the clearing house seeks to procure the missing parts in a new auction.

The clearing house is complemented by the performance bonds, a reserve fund paid by the participants in the form of an initial fee and a financial credit line to be used as an immediate response instrument.

5.4.2 Auction implementation

By legal mandate, the auctions are carried out by CENACE and led by SENER. The process is supported by other government institutions, such as the Environmental Secretariat, the Social Development Secretariat, and the Anthropology and History Institute, among others.

CENACE was selected as the technical administrator of the auctions, being the independent system and market operator with the staff to carry out the processes required, including having the legal attributes to sign and execute all the contracts. CENACE delegated its contract-signing authority (but not its legal responsibility) to the market clearing house in the third auction.

Auction participants indicated that the timely and effective implementation of the auctions reflected the capabilities of the implementing institutions. The bidding process and rules, and the legal and regulatory framework which was developed during the sector reform, also contributed to bidders' perceptions of the integrity of the process.

As noted, a 'social witness' provides oversight during the entire process, and the optimization algorithm is reviewed and audited by a renowned university to ensure the validity of the results. In addition, the auction includes a highly structured and transparent communication process (including training on the bidding platform). All auction-related information and documents are published on the SENER website and Mexico's Official Gazette.

A challenge during the implementation of awarded projects was the ability to get permits, either at a federal or state level, including construction permits and land acquisition contracts. SENER has sought to address some of these issues by requiring social impact assessments (including community consultations) as part of the bidding package.

5.5 Results from Mexico's energy auctions

Mexico's long-term energy auctions achieved some of the lowest average renewable energy prices at the time.

The combined results of the three auctions include 1,780 MW for capacity, 19,558,443 MWh/year in cumulative energy, and 24,363,975 CEL/year; combined OCGT was the predominant technology associated with providing firm generation capacity; wind and solar were the predominant technologies in cumulative energy (MWh/year) provided; and wind, solar, and geothermal were the technologies selected to deliver CELs. Table 5.11 summarizes the products awarded in the three auctions.

Table 5.12 provides the number of projects awarded by technology in each of the three auctions.

The first auction only delivered energy and CELs from renewable sources (wind, solar, and geothermal) as the auction ceiling price for capacity was low due to the surplus available at the time. The second auction included generation capacity from geothermal and combined cycle gas turbines as well as from the CFE hydroelectric plants which were already constructed but were able to deliver CELs and from wind and solar generation projects. The

Table 5.11 Summary of the products awarded in the three auctions

	Capacity (MW)	Capacity (%)	Energy (MWh/year)	Energy (%)	CEL/year	CEL (%)
Solar	194	11	11,648,653	60	1,215,9497	50
Wind	211	12	7,711,026	39	7,694,193	32
Hydroelectric	0	0	0	0	314,631	1
Geothermal	25	1	198,764	1	4,195,654	17
Combined cycle	850	48	0	0	0	0
Turbogas	500	28	0	0	0	0
Total	1,780	100	19,558,443	100	13,420,427	100

Source: Authors' compilation based on information from CENACE.

Table 5.12 Technologies awarded in the three auctions

Auction	No. of projects by technology					
	Solar	Wind	Hydroelectric	Geothermal	Combined cycle	Turbogas
First	12	6	0	0	0	0
Second	33	10	6	1	6	0
Third	9	6	0	0	0	1
Total	54	22	6	1	6	1
%	60	24	7	1	7	1

Source: Authors' compilation based on information from CENACE.

third auction was again dominated by wind and solar projects but with the participation of a turbogas plant delivering capacity.

A disaggregation by the technology and the volume of products awarded is provided in Table 5.13.

Disaggregated detail of the three auctions with the companies awarded, their associated technologies, and the volumes of products delivered is included in Table 5.14.

5.5.1 Current project situation

As of early 2022, 86% the projects awarded in the three long-term auctions are in operation. For the first auction, 1,865 MW (1,471 MW photovoltaic and 394 MW wind) were awarded, but only 78% of the capacity (1,118 MW solar and 334 MW wind) entered operation and testing. For the second auction, 2,559 MW were installed and are operating (1,773 MW photovoltaic and 786 MW wind), representing 89% of the allocated power (total of 2,892 MW between both technologies). For the third auction, 1,813 MW (1,124 MW solar and 689 MW wind) of the 2,012 MW awarded entered operation, representing around 90% of the total.

5.6 Lessons learned from Mexico's renewable energy auctions

5.6.1 Auction implementation

A well-developed legal and regulatory framework shaped the design and execution of three successful auctions. This was achieved by building on the

Table 5.13 Products awarded by technology in the three auctions

Technology	First auction			Second auction			Third auction		
	Capacity (MW)	Energy (MWh)	CEL (#)	Capacity (MW)	Energy (MWh)	CEL (#)	Capacity (MW)	Energy (MWh)	CEL (#)
Solar	–	3,772,028	3,754,955	184	4,836,597	4,933,382	10	3,0,028	3,471,160
Wind	–	1,384,021	1,384,021	128	3,874,458	3,828,757	83	2,452,547	2,481,415
Hydroelectric	–	–	–	–	–	314,631	–	–	–
Geothermal	–	–	3,996,890	25	198,764	198,764	–	–	–
Combined cycle	–	–	–	850	–	–	–	–	–
Turbogas	–	–	–	–	–	–	500	–	–

Source: Authors' compilation based on information from CENACE.

capabilities of Mexican institutions such as SENER, CRE, and CENACE and their integration as a working group seeking benefits for the electricity system at the lowest costs.

Two key characteristics of the process were important: participants' trust in CENACE's capacity and integrity, which was critical in providing accurate requirements and rules for the bidding process; and the transparency of the process, which was supported by the appointed social witness.

As a result, all the awarded projects achieved financial closure and obtained some of the lowest prices worldwide. Nevertheless, some projects are still facing environmental or social issues that need to be addressed, including in future auctions.

However, due to the current political views of the new government, the auction processes for new clean energy tenders have been halted and may face significant changes in accordance with strengthening CFE's position as the core actor in Mexico's power sector. Many of these new policies are being legally challenged.

The situation has been perceived as a negative signal to the market and to investors. Nevertheless, for the time being, the new policy still maintains the goals and commitments of adopting clean energy and mitigating climate change, complying with the legal and regulatory framework, and maintaining CENACE as an independent system and market operator.

5.6.2 Auction design

After three auctions, building upon the recently established overall sector reform, Mexico was able to meet the targets established for CELs at some of the lowest and most competitive prices worldwide at the time. As of 2020, the CEL obligations had been fulfilled by all the obligated participants.

However, the rollback of the sector reform, the social and environmental issues associated with infrastructure projects, and the technical complexities of electricity systems present challenges in terms of auction design that need to be addressed through long-term planning.

The four areas identified for the design of future auctions being considered in Mexico are discussed next.

5.6.2.1 Planning

5.6.2.1.1 Harmonization inconsistencies between market operating provisions, grid code, and other instruments

The issuing of many technical documents is a challenge in terms of harmonizing and standardizing their contents. A systematic and detailed review of the various regulatory and technical codes is thus needed. This review will help to identify aspects where the main actors—led by SENER—should intervene to establish priorities when the objectives are mutually exclusive, for example, the modernization of the infrastructure required by the Network Code and the requests of individuals to relax its application to avoid excessive costs.

5.6.2.1.2 Further integration of methodologies for grid expansion
Planning for the National Transmission Network and the General Distribution Grid continues to be reactive, considering only those projects that have already requested studies or paid the corresponding guarantees. The recommendation is for the adoption of methodologies which involve generators and infrastructure developers from the beginning in the identification of the clean energy zones to be developed.

5.6.2.1.3 Better definition and integration of markets for energy storage
There needs to be a transversal approach to incorporate storage beyond a project-level focus, thus giving way to a more comprehensive evaluation where it is deployed, strategically based on the added value to the system. To achieve this, the relevant authorities need to identify and match the services that storage offers with the operational needs of the network and then correctly classify it within or outside the market based on the services offered at a particular time and location. The payment received will then be a function of the services offered versus the operating regime and, if necessary, compensating the difference in prices between both through a 'Guarantees of Sufficiency of Income' (compensatory payments, also called 'uplifts'). Likewise, the hybrid nature and the diversity of services that storage can offer allow it to be conceived more like a collection of assets than as a technology, which opens the possibility of its inclusion as a complement in current auctions or in other specific auctions for system reliability.

5.6.2.1.4 Acceleration of transmission projects
The implementation of transmission projects needs to be speeded up by agreeing on the criteria and technical analysis used in the planning framework, including whether these projects are to be built by the private or public sector.

5.6.2.2 Auction
5.6.2.2.1 Provision of greater complementarity between generation options for better flexibility of the electricity grid
While the optimization carried out in the auctions ignores the related services demanded during the operation of the selected power plants, the

optimization carried out in the planning considers SENER's Reliability Policy as an operational restriction but not its associated costs. Most importantly, none of these optimization exercises differentiates between dispatchable firm, non-dispatchable firm, dispatchable intermittent, and non-dispatchable intermittent generation as classified by the Market Participant Registration and Accreditation Manual or the associated benchmarks. The result is that the selected generation projects do not complement each other in practice and incur higher operating costs by satisfying the same demand.

It is possible to incorporate the complementarity of the various technologies within the auctions process since CENACE has all the technical elements to do so. Each price zone, load zone, and regional control management must seek the greatest possible complementarity between the power plants in its territory to increase their response flexibility, improve coordination between balance areas, reduce the power demand, and ultimately minimize the frequency of the auctions for reliability.

5.6.2.2.2 Further definition and addressing of environmental and social requirements in the bidding rules

Several winning projects from the first auction are at risk of not being carried out because of social or environmental reasons. It is proposed to apply specific mechanisms to mitigate the additional risk in the event of not having completed the environmental and social studies at the time of participating in an auction. This could be done by requiring an additional guarantee (or an increase to the current one) that is proportional to the type of EvIS applied to the project and its degree of progress. The amount of this guarantee could then be progressively reduced as certain milestones are reached in the implementation of the project.

5.6.2.2.3 Provision of greater flexibility in contracts for greater auction participation

In its current design, the auction rules oblige all buyers to purchase the same products, in the same proportion to the energy, power, and CEL portfolio acquired by the basic service supplier(s), which is called the 'buyer's proportional allocation factor'. This rigidity has caused important market players to remain outside the auctions, considering that their needs can be better served through bilateral contracts or private auctions. The recommendation is to open the auction portfolio options to the requirements of the buyers. This could increase the number of potential participants and thus improve the economic conditions of the auctions.

5.6.2.3 Construction

5.6.2.3.1 Consideration of options of several technologies to provide greater flexibility and sufficient delivery times

According to the auction rules, the awarded projects must come online within 36 months following the contract signature. Considering 12 months of the 'pre-investment' stage of any project, only solar and wind technologies are capable of delivering clean energy in time. This situation excludes other clean technologies from participating in the auctions. This has been a cause for concern among some generator associations and the implication is that if these deadlines continue to be used, the auctions are not to be considered technology-neutral.

The recommendation is that technological neutrality should start by recognizing the intrinsic differences of each technology and adjusting the deadlines to allow them to compete on equal footing. By annualizing the financial flows of each technology according to its different maturity periods, the profitability of the different projects could be equitably compared. This modification would also make it possible to diversify the energy mix and achieve better complementarity between technologies.

5.7 Conclusion: When auctions meet political realities

Power-sector reforms take at least a decade to consolidate, and the benefits are not immediately clear to consumers. Energy auctions are designed within the local legal, regulatory, institutional, policy, strategic, market, and economic framework of the country. As a result, the following issues are identified:

- Political time frame considerations, such as elections and change of government, are important in the development of regulation and policies. Consistency is critical, regardless of the previous or current government policy or vision for the sector.
- It is critical to deliver a message to the population about the expected benefits and improvements from the auction, such as pricing, grid stability, energy availability and other socio-economic and environmental aspects.
- Auction design should incorporate social aspects associated with local and indigenous communities affected by the projects, including land, access, and participation.
- There is a need to consider alternative auction design options to meet specific objectives, such as carrying out local/regional auctions and auctions for energy storage.

Even though the change of government in Mexico has presented new challenges to the electricity industry, the momentum gained from the sector reform and the results of the energy auctions provide the framework for future decisions. The overall objectives are still to provide low-cost, reliable, and clean energy to the Mexican population.

5.8 Appendix A: Key objectives of PRODESEN

Following is a list of the key objectives included in the 2019 PRODESEN:

(1) There is sovereignty, national energy security, and sustainability.
(2) SENER carries out the planning of the National Electric System and the preparation of PRODESEN as required by law.
(3) SENER directs the planning of the National Electric System, integrating generation, transmission, distribution, commercialization, and energy transition in accordance with the requirements of national development.
(4) The supply of electricity is guaranteed in accordance with the economic growth of the country in conditions of quality and at the best price for the consumer.
(5) All the same regulations are applied to CFE and the private power producers to ensure competition, fairness, and equality of conditions.
(6) The required electricity transmission and distribution capacity are assured.
(7) Considering that electricity is a necessity, CFE is considered a public service company.
(8) The profitability and return of capital on investments made in companies participating in the electricity market is ensured.
(9) Transparency and best industrial practices are established for all participants in the National Electric System.
(10) Electricity generation with clean and renewable energies is increased and complies with international commitments regarding climate change and emissions reduction.
(11) Electricity is a necessary public service which must meet the criteria of efficiency, quality, reliability, continuity, safety, and sustainability of the electrical system.
(12) The coordination between SENER and CRE must incorporate in its guidelines for authorizations and permits the criteria put in place based on the established energy policy.

(13) A responsible balance in the electricity tariffs in relation to the costs is established, including transmission and distribution as well as generation support, including fuel prices. This will require coordination of the design of methodologies and electricity rates which allow for the profitability and sustainable development of the electricity industry as a whole as well as a quality electric service at an adequate price for users and competitive for the national economy.

(14) Optimal use is made of the CFE generation infrastructure, especially to supply the basic supply.

(15) Distribution guarantees open access within the current limits of accommodation capacity, determined for medium- and low-voltage distribution circuits.

(16) The reinforcements to the distribution network necessary for the interconnection of distributed generation power plants, whose maximum generation capacity exceeds its limits are charged to the applicant.

(17) Access to universal, efficient, quality, and reliable electrical service to all Mexicans is guaranteed.

(18) Rational and sustainable use of all available energy resources and technologies is made for national development and clean and renewable energies are integrated in an orderly, sustainable, and reliable manner into the national energy matrix, thereby promoting the generation and use of clean energies which contribute to the reduction of greenhouse gas emissions and the recovery of ecological systems.

(19) Science, technology, engineering, and national industries of services, equipment and capital goods are optimized and advantage taken of the technology transfer that reaches the country.

(20) A plan is provided to address the demand for electricity and its complement of distributed photovoltaic generation that will require the charging of electric vehicle batteries in the country in the future, for the medium and long term.

(21) The contribution of CFE to the national generation of electricity with clean energy is recognized so that it applies the same administrative and financial criteria as other private producers.

(22) The condition of fairness and fair competition between private companies and CFE in the participation of the electricity market is respected.

(23) Based on the autonomy and independence of each company participating in the electricity market, the regulations that subject other participants in the National Electric System to the subsidy or cost

charge on CFE are modified by CRE to take into account the customer subsidy allocated considering all the elements associated with the wholesale electricity market, transmission, and distribution.

(24) Intermittent renewable generation meets the criteria of not affecting the reliability of the National Electric System.

5.9 Appendix B: Definition of clean energies

Following is a list of the clean energies considered in the Mexico Regulatory Framework (Electric Industry Law):

- wind power;
- solar radiation in any form;
- ocean energy in any of its forms: tidal, wave, marine currents, and the salt concentration gradient;
- heat from a geothermal well;
- bioenergetics as specified in the Law for the Promotion and Development of Bioenergetics;
- energy generated from the heat power of methane and other gases from waste disposal sites, livestock farms, and wastewater treatment plants, among others;
- energy generated from hydrogen through combustion or use in fuel cells, whenever complying with a minimum threshold of efficiency established by CRE and the criteria from the Environmental and Natural Resources Secretariat on the life cycle of the fuel cells;
- energy from hydroelectric power plants (up to 20 MW and to a limit of 10 W/m^2—e.g., 100 MW with no flooded area greater than 10,000,000 m^2);
- nuclear power;
- energy generated with the products of the processing of agricultural waste or urban solid waste (such as gasification), when said processing does not generate dioxins and furans or other emissions that may affect health or the environment and complies with official regulations issued for this purpose by the Environmental and Natural Resources Secretariat;
- energy generated by efficient cogeneration plants in terms of the efficiency criteria issued by CRE and emissions established by the Environmental and Natural Resources Secretariat;

- energy generated by sugar mills that meet the efficiency criteria established by CRE and emissions established by the Environmental and Natural Resources Secretariat;
- energy generated by thermal power plants with geological capture and storage processes or biosequestration of carbon dioxide that have an efficiency equal to or greater in terms of kWh generated per ton of equivalent carbon dioxide emitted into the atmosphere at the minimum efficiency established by CRE and the emission criteria established by the Environmental and Natural Resources Secretariat;
- technologies considered as low carbon emissions according to international standards; and
- other technologies determined by the Energy Secretariat and Environmental and Natural Resources Secretariat, based on parameters and standards of energy and water efficiency, emissions to the atmosphere, and generation of waste, directly, indirectly or in the life cycle.

5.10 Appendix C: Projects awarded in the three auctions

Table 5.14 Companies, technologies, and products awarded in the three auctions

No.	Company	Technology	Power (MW)	Energy (MWh)	CEL (#)
First auction					
1	Aldesa Energias Renovables, S.L.U.	Wind	–	113,199	113,199
2	Aldesa Energias Renovables, S.L.U.	Wind	–	117,689	117,689
3	Consorcio Energía Limpia 2010	Wind	–	291,900	291,900
4	Energía Renovable de la Península, S.A.P.I. de C.V.	Wind	–	275,502	275 502
5	Energia Renovable del Istmo II	Wind	–	585,731	–
6	Energia Renovable del Istmo II	Wind	–	–	585,731
7	Enel Green Power México S. de R.L. de C.V.	Solar	–	972,915	972,915
8	Enel Green Power México S. de R.L. de C.V.	Solar	–	737,998	737,998

9	Enel Green Power México S. de R.L. de C.V.	Solar	–	539,034	539,034
10	Jinkosolar Investment Pte Ltd	Solar	–	277,490	277,490
11	Jinkosolar Investment Pte Ltd	Solar	–	176,475	176,475
12	Jinkosolar Investment Pte Ltd	Solar	–	48,748	48,748
13	Photoemeris Sustentable S.A. de C.V.	Solar	–	54,975	53,477
14	Recurrent Energy Mexico Development, S. de R.L. de C.V.	Solar	–	140,970	140,970
15	Sol de Insurgentes S. de R.L. de C.V,	Solar	–	60,965	60,518
16	SunPower Systems México, S. de R.L. de C.V.	Solar	–	269,155	263,815
17	Vega Solar 1, S.A.P.I. de C.V.	Solar	–	493,303	483,515
18	Vega Solar 1, S.A.P.I. de C.V.	Solar	–	246,832	241,935
Second auction					
1	Comision Federal de Electricidad	Combined cycle	374.98	–	–
2	Frontera México Generación s de R.L. de C.V.	Combined cycle	119.98	–	–
3	Frontera México Generación s de R.L. de C.V.	Combined cycle	34.99	–	–
4	Frontera México Generación s de R.L. de C.V.	Combined cycle	99.99	–	–
5	Frontera México Generación s de R.L. de C.V.	Combined cycle	99.99	–	–
6	Frontera México Generación s de R.L. de C.V.	Combined cycle	119.98	–	–
7	Enel Green Power México S. de R.L. de C.V.	Wind	–	399,129.86	399,129
8	Energía Renovable de la Península, S.A.P.I. de C.V.	Wind	14	–	–
9	Energía Renovable de la Península, S.A.P.I. de C.V.	Wind	16	–	–

Continued

Table 5.14 *Continued*

No.	Company	Technology	Power (MW)	Energy (MWh)	CEL (#)
10	Eolica de Oaxaca S.A.P.I. de C.V.	Wind	–	818,264.52	818,264
11	Parque Eólico El Mezquite S.A.P.I. de C.V.	Wind	–	820,635.81	–
12	Parque Eólico El Mezquite S.A.P.I. de C.V.	Wind	–	–	774,938
13	Parque Eólico El Mezquite S.A.P.I. de C.V.	Wind	76.74	–	–
14	Parque Eólico Reynosa III, S.A.P.I. de C.V.	Wind	–	–	1,613,416
15	Parque Eólico Reynosa III, S.A.P.I. de C.V.	Wind	–	1,613 416.80	–
16	Tractebel Energia de Altamira, S. de R.L. de C.V.	Wind	21.62	223,010.76	223,010
17	Comisión Federal de Electricidad	Geothermal	25	198,764.40	198,764
18	Generadora Fenix Sapi de C.V.	Hydroelectric	–	–	75,546
19	Generadora Fenix Sapi de C.V.	Hydroelectric	–	–	75,546
20	Generadora Fenix Sapi de C.V.	Hydroelectric	–	–	64,386
21	Generadora Fenix Sapi de C.V.	Hydroelectric	–	–	33,051
22	Generadora Fenix Sapi de C.V.	Hydroelectric	–	–	33,051
23	Generadora Fenix Sapi de C.V.	Hydroelectric	–	–	33,051
24	Alten Energías Renovables México Cuatro, S.A. de C.V.	Solar	38.59	–	–
25	Alten Energías Renovables México Cuatro, S.A. de C.V.	Solar	–	348,466.84	–
26	Alten Energías Renovables México Cuatro, S.A. de C.V.	Solar	–	373,576.95	–
27	Alten Energías Renovables México Cuatro, S.A. de C.V.	Solar	–	–	420,335
28	Alten Energías Renovables México Cuatro, S.A. de C.V.	Solar	–	–	392,082

29	Alten Energías Renovables México Cuatro, S.A. de C.V.	Solar	36	–	–
30	AT Solar	Solar	29	–	–
31	AT Solar	Solar	–	478,260.96	
32	AT Solar	Solar	–	–	478,260
33	Bluemex Power 1 S.A. de C.V.	Solar	–	249,982.32	249,982
34	Consorcio ENGIE Solar Trompezon	Solar	–	342,629.62	338,851
35	Consorcio Fotowatio	Solar	–	779,161.60	–
36	Consorcio Fotowatio	Solar	–	–	779,161
37	Consorcio Guanajuato	Solar	12	146,957.76	146,957
38	Consorcio SMX	Solar	–	278,357.76	–
39	Consorcio SMX	Solar	–	–	285,606
40	Consorcio SMX	Solar	10	–	–
41	Energia Sierra Juarez Holding s de R.L. de C.V.	Solar	–	114 115.90	–
42	Energia Sierra Juarez Holding s de R.L. de C.V.	Solar	–	–	117,064
43	Green Hub s de R.L. DE C.V.	Solar	10	72,919.11	72,919
44	HQ Mexico Holdings, S. de R.L. de C.V.	Solar	18.3	–	–
45	HQ Mexico Holdings, S. de R.L. de C.V.	Solar	–	252,444.87	–
46	HQ Mexico Holdings, S. de R.L. de C.V.	Solar	–	–	252,444
47	Kamet Energía México, S.A.P.I. de C.V.	Solar	–	–	353,466
48	Kamet Energía México, S.A.P.I. de C.V.	Solar	–	353,466.00	–
49	OPDE	Solar	–	–	213,655
50	OPDE	Solar	–	–	75,853
51	OPDE	Solar	–	213,655.15	–
52	OPDE	Solar	–	75,853.95	–
53	Quetzal Energía México S.A.P.I. de C.V.	Solar	–	–	393,611
54	Quetzal Energía México S.A.P.I. de C.V.	Solar	–	393,611.32	–
55	X-Elio Energy, S.L.	Solar	16	193,771.20	193,771
56	X-Elio Energy, S.L.	Solar	14	169,365.84	169,365

Continued

Table 5.14 *Continued*

No.	Company	Technology	Power (MW)	Energy (MWh)	CEL (#)
Third auction					
1	X-ELIO ENERGY, S.L.	Solar	10	435,354	483,727
2	NEOEN INTERNATIONAL S.A.S.	Solar	0	616,692	770,864
3	COMPAÑÍA DE ELECTRICIDAD LOS RAMONES S.A.P.I de C.V.	Turbogas	499.95	–	–
4	Canadian Solar Energy Mexico, S. de R.L. de C.V.	Solar	0	235,640	265,095
5	Canadian Solar Energy Mexico, S. de R.L. de C.V.	Solar	0	206,017	247,220
6	Canadian Solar Energy Mexico, S. de R.L. de C.V.	Solar	0	210,426	252,511
7	Consorcio Engie Wind	Wind	30.62	362,935	391,805
8	Consorcio Engie Solar 1	Solar	0	280,055	302,332
9	Consorcio Engie Solar 1	Solar	0	486,313	524,997
10	Consorcio Engie Solar 4	Solar	0	379,603	434,486
11	Enel Rinnovabile S.A. de C.V.	Wind	0	373,017	373,016
12	Enel Rinnovabile S.A. de C.V.	Wind	0	357,032	357,031
13	Enel Rinnovabile S.A. de C.V.	Wind	0	510,680	510,680
14	Enel Rinnovabile S.A. de C.V.	Wind	0	848,883	848,883
15	Consorcio integrado por MITSUI & CO., LTD y Trina Solar (Netherlands) Holdings B.V.	Solar	0	189,928	189,928
16	ENERGIA RENOVABLE DEL ISTMO II S.A. DE C.V.	Wind	52.04	–	–

Source: Authors' compilation with information from CENACE.

5.11 References

Centro (Nacional de Control de Energía) (2017). 'Cámara de Compensación de la Subasta de Largo Plazo'. June, México.https://www.cenace.gob.mx/Paginas/SIM/SubastasLP.aspx (accessed 20 April 2023).

CIA (Central Intelligence Agency). (2020). 'The World Factbook, North America—Mexico', https://www.cia.gov/the-world-factbook/countries/mexico/ (accessed 20 April 2023).

del Río, P. (2017). 'Auctions for Renewable Support in Mexico: Instruments and Lessons Learnt'. Report D4.4-MX, AURES-EU Horizon 2020 Programme.

International Energy Agency. (2018). World Energy Outlook. Paris: https://iea.blob.core.windows.net/assets/77ecf96c-5f4b-4d0d-9d93-d81b938217cb/World_Energy_Outlook_2018.pdf

Montenegro Gutiérrez, I. (2019). 'A Summary of the Mixed Integer-Programming Model Used in Long-Term Auctions for Mexico's Wholesale Electricity Market', https://almanaque.colmex.mx/wp-content/uploads/2019/11/subasta.pdf (accessed 20 April 2023).

SENER (Secretaría de Energía). (2018). 'Disposiciones Administrativas de Carácter General sobre la Evaluación de Impacto Social en el Sector Energético'. 1 June, https://www.dof.gob.mx/nota_detalle.php?codigo=5524885&fecha=01/06/2018#gsc.tab=0

SENER (2019). 'Programa de Desarrollo del Sistema Eléctrico Nacional (PRODE-SEN)'. 14 June, https://www.gob.mx/sener/articulos/programa-para-el-desarrollo-del-sistema-electrico-nacional.

6

India

The Perils of Massive Ambition

Vinay Rustagi and Mridul Chadha

6.1 Introduction: India's global renewable energy ambitions

India has one of the world's oldest and largest renewable energy (RE) auction programmes. As early as 2010, competitive bids were invited for utility-scale solar photovoltaic (PV) projects as part of the country's National Solar Mission, which set out to install 100 gigawatts (GW) of solar PV by 2022. Since then, the RE sector has grown fast. Driven mainly by falling costs, renewables accounted for 23.5% of installed capacity and 10% of total power output by early 2020—increasing from 13% and 5%, respectively, in 2015.

The auction programme is designed to fulfil two overarching objectives for the sector: to reduce the cost of renewable power and to attract private capital. A large programme size, transparent auction processes, and low barriers to entry (e.g. minimal technical and financial qualification criteria, low bid bond requirements, and the fact that 100% foreign ownership is allowed) have all been instrumental in attracting leading players from around the world. Several incentives have been put in place to encourage the construction of RE installations, particularly for solar PV. These include must-run status, exemption from inter-state transmission charges, accelerated depreciation allowances, and capital subsidies for meeting local content requirements.

In addition, in 2016, the Indian government launched its solar power park scheme that offers developers a 'plug-and-play' option, whereby government agencies take responsibility for providing land and help fund the installation of transmission infrastructure. And, in 2017, India's Ministry of New and Renewable Energy (MNRE) overhauled the auctions programme to enhance predictability and uniformity and introduce competitive bidding guidelines (CBGs) for both solar and wind power projects.

Vinay Rustagi and Mridul Chadha, *India*. In: *Renewable Energy Auctions: Lessons from the Global South.*
Edited by: Anton Eberhard and Wikus Kruger, Oxford University Press. © Oxford University Press (2023).
DOI: 10.1093/oso/9780192871701.003.0006

In 2014, the MNRE devised a multi-pronged payment-security mechanism to address the poor financial health of the country's electricity distribution companies (referred to in India as 'discoms') and the associated off-taker risk. As part of this, the wholly state-owned Solar Energy Corporation of India (SECI) was mandated to act as both a nodal agency and an intermediary procurer in national RE auctions.[1] This provided much-needed clarity for developers.

While SECI is relatively thinly capitalized and is dependent on tender fees and a power-trading margin for its revenue, developers and lenders have accepted it as a bankable counterpart. SECI has since revised the design of the tender process to improve the availability and predictability of power supply from renewable sources. Accordingly, new tenders based on hybrid and storage technologies require developers to supply power with an annual capacity utilisation factor (CUF) of as high as 85%.[2]

India's government has also taken several other steps to make the use of solar PV power attractive for off-takers. For example, thermal–solar power blending was introduced, whereby cheaper coal-based power is blended with more costly solar power under a bundled power purchase agreement (PPA). Incentives and capital subsidies linked to generation and accelerated depreciation have also been made available to reduce the cost of solar power production. However, as solar power achieves grid parity, these incentives are being phased out. In 2010, solar PV power cost US¢ 17.01/kilowatt hour (kWh)—much more than the average cost of supply for distribution companies which was then US¢ 5.31/kWh. By 2020, the cost of solar PV power had come down to US¢ 3.15/kWh; this is significantly cheaper than the average cost of supply, which was US¢ 8.12/kWh.

Overall, these measures have secured and sustained strong interest from RE developers. Competition levels remain strong, and record-breaking bid tariffs are relatively common. However, while intense bidding has resulted in lower tariffs, it has also negatively affected the financial viability of many projects. With few buffers built into financial models (for increases in equipment costs, adverse forex shifts or policy changes, such as the implementation of import duties or other tax changes), some less viable projects have been abandoned, and most of the smaller to medium-sized bidders have been squeezed out of the market.

---

[1] Although SECI's name suggests that its focus is solar power, it manages auctions for a range of RE generation projects.

[2] At the time of writing, CUF is a measurement used only in India; it is calculated as follows: energy measured (kWh)/(365 × 24 × installed capacity of the plant).

The development of India's renewables market is also hampered by a lack of planning and coordination. While the government has announced long-term plans and specified capacity and output targets as a percentage of total consumption, developers are seldom notified of upcoming tenders. In addition, tender schedules are generally dictated more by the government's ambitious targets for the sector rather than by power demand. The resulting oversupply of power has increased the risks attached to PPAs, with some discoms refusing to purchase even relatively cheap renewable power. A similar lack of planning and coordination extends into the procurement of auctioned capacity and the extension of the grid, making access to suitable sites a persistent challenge for developers, even within solar parks.

Nevertheless, India's auction programme can be considered among the most successful and ambitious in the world. It has many important lessons to share. In this chapter, we focus primarily on the design, implementation, and results of RE auctions run by SECI between August 2015 and June 2020. In section 6.2, we provide an overview of the country's power sector. In section 6.3, we describe the RE auction programme and describe the bidding process. In section 6.4, we outline the results of the auctions. The main lessons learned and some recommendations are outlined in section 6.5, while section 6.6 contains our conclusions.

6.2 Overview of India's economy

India is the world's second-most populous country, with an estimated 1.35 billion people in 2018 (World Bank, 2018b). By area, it is the seventh largest country in the world and the second largest in Asia. Politically, India has one of the more stable democracies in the world—with general elections held every five years and the transitions between administrations having been peaceful for several decades. The country has 7 centrally run regions (union territories) that are divided into a total of 29 states. The governance system is federal, with the central and state authorities having defined areas of jurisdiction.

India's economy is the seventh largest in the world (World Bank, 2018a). The country's gross domestic product (GDP) increased from US$ 1.2 trillion in 2012/2013 to US$ 1.5 trillion in 2016/2017[3] at an average annual rate of 6.9% (RBI, 2020). However, between 2012/2013 and 2019/2020, the average

---

[3] US$ 1 = INR 75.

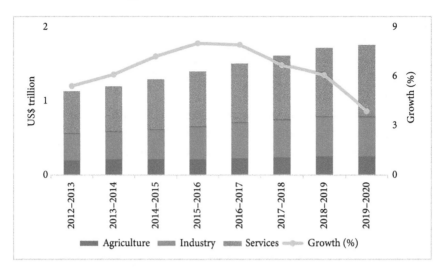

Figure 6.1 India's gross domestic product (GDP) and annual growth rate
Source: Central Electricity Authority (of India) (CEA) (2020b).

annual growth rate declined by 5.5% (see Figure 6.1). This reduction is partly related to the demonetization that occurred in 2016 (which weakened consumer demand), high leverage in the corporate sector, and increasing stress in the financial system (IMF, 2019).

Between 2012 and 2019, monthly average consumer inflation remained relatively low at 5.8%, reaching a maximum of 11.5% in November 2013. In response to low inflation and the weakening economy, the Reserve Bank of India has gradually reduced its benchmark lending rate from 8% in January 2014 to 4% by May 2020 (RBI, 2020). Over the same period, the ease of doing business in India improved significantly, and the World Bank ranked the country at 134 in 2014 and 63 in 2019.

Historically, India has relied on five-year plans for short- and medium-term planning and the implementation of government policy. In the power sector, longer-term planning (for up to 30 years) occurs but tends to lack rigour and detail. Forecasts are often highly optimistic and are essentially designed to align with government targets for economic growth, industrial investment, and tax revenue.

6.3 India's power sector

As of December 2019, India's installed power generation capacity amounted to 369 gigawatts (GW). Fossil fuels (coal and natural gas) made up 62.6% of this capacity, while renewables (including large hydro) and nuclear accounted for 37.4% (CEA, 2020b).

Coal is the dominant energy source, accounting for 55.7% (205 GW) of total installed capacity by December 2019. Large hydro projects (each with more than 25 megawatts (MW) of installed capacity) account for 12.3% (45.4 GW); wind for 10.2% (37.5 GW); and solar PV for 9.1% (33.7 GW) (see Figure 6.2).

Since 2015, RE capacity has increased by 47.1 GW, driven by both strong government support and falling costs. Solar and wind power, at 28.9 GW and 12.4 GW, respectively, account for the bulk of this capacity (see Figure 6.3 and Table 6.1). Meanwhile, the addition of new, coal-based capacity has gradually slowed due to weak power-demand growth.[4] The installation of new generation capacity using other technologies has been negligible since 2014—with nuclear power at 1 GW, large hydro at 2.8 GW, and diesel and gas (combined) at 0.3 GW.

As noted, fossil fuels still dominate India's electricity generation (at 75.1% in the 2019/2020 financial year), but this is gradually changing, having dropped from 80.4% in 2015/2016. By contrast, the share of RE (excluding large hydro) increased from 5.6% in 2015/2016 to 11.7% in 2019/2020. The share of utility-scale solar PV power increased from just 0.6% in 2015/2016

Table 6.1 Installed capacity in India's power sector

Technology	Capacity 2014/2015 (GW)	Capacity 2 2019/2020 (GW)	Capacity addition 2014/2015– 2019/2020 (GW)	Capacity change 2014/2015– 2019/2020 (%)
Coal	164.6	205.1	40.5	25
Large hydro	41.3	45.7	4.4	11
Wind	23.4	37.7	14.3	61
Solar PV	3.7	34.6	30.9	835
Gas	23.1	24.9	1.8	8
Biopower	4.4	9.9	5.5	125
Nuclear	5.8	6.8	1.0	17
Small hydro	4.1	4.7	0.6	15
Diesel	1.2	0.5	−0.7	−58
Waste	0.1	0.1	–	–
Total	271.7	370	98.3	36

Source: CEA (2020a).

[4] The impact of lower demand on solar and wind power projects is comparatively smaller due to their 'must-run' status and India's renewable purchase obligation (RPO) targets (see section 2.1.3).

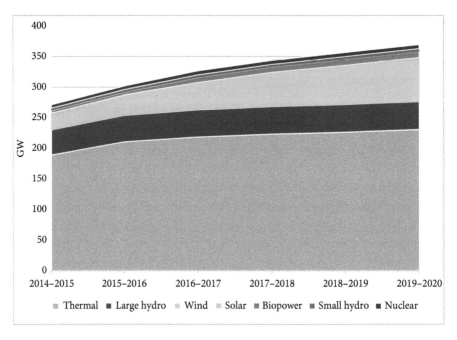

Figure 6.2 Power generation capacity in India, 2014–2020

Source: Authors' compilation.

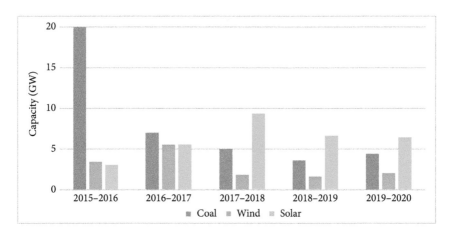

Figure 6.3 Annual GW added in India, by technology, 2015–2020

Source: Authors' compilation.

to 3.3% by 2019/2020; wind power increased from 1.9% to 5.2% in the same period.

India's steadily increasing supply of power has helped to satisfy what was once a pent-up demand for energy; that is, between 2005/2006 and

2019/2020, total power demand grew at an average annual rate of 7.5% from 631 terawatt hours (TWh) to 1,291 TWh. The reasons for this increasing demand include improved supply, higher per capita incomes (improved affordability), higher business demand, and rapid grid expansion. Between 2005 and 2018, India's per capita gross national income increased 2.5 times to US$ 7,680. Over roughly the same period (2005–2019), access to electricity increased from 67% to 99%. Per capita power consumption, while growing at an annual average rate of 4.9% throughout this period, is estimated at 1,181 kilowatt hours (kWh) per year—far below the international average, which, in 2019, was estimated at 3,012 kWh per year.

6.3.1 Power-sector structure

India's power-sector structure is complex. Constitutionally, electricity is understood to be a 'concurrent' area. This means that all 7 regional and 29 state authorities have powers to formulate laws for the sector. In addition, the states enjoy considerable leeway in deciding whether to enact policies and regulations formulated by the central government or to develop their own. The Central Electricity Regulatory Commission (CERC) acts as the national regulator, but each state also has its independent regulatory structure. Major milestones in the development of India's power sector are listed in Table 6.2, and Figure 6.4 provides an overview of the regulatory and market structure of the sector in late 2020.

In terms of ownership, 53% (196 GW) of India's power *generation* capacity was publicly owned and 47% (172 GW) was under private ownership by December 2019. In 2010, these figures were at 68% and 32%, respectively (see Figure 6.5). The rapid ingress of private companies has increased competition in the sector and driven project tariffs down.[5] As a result, power utilities have become more focused on price and more selective about signing long-term power purchase agreements (PPAs).

Private ownership of power *transmission* is much smaller—at 7.4% as of December 2019. The balance is owned by public-sector companies under central and state governments. However, new projects are now routinely tendered in open competitive bids and the private-sector share in such projects

---

[5] The biggest share of private-sector-based generation is in the RE sector. The lowest tariff bids for solar PV declined from INR 10.95/kWh (US¢ 14.6/kWh) in 2010 to INR 2.36/kWh (US¢ 3.14/kWh) in 2020. Bidding has been extremely aggressive, with internal rates of return possibly as low as 4 and 5% (rather than the 16–18% recommended).

	Centre		State/private	
Policy formulation	Ministry of Power	Ministry of New and Renewable Energy	State government	
Long-term planning	Central Electricity Authority			
Regulations	Central Electricity Regulatory Commission		State Electricity Regulatory Commission	
Generation	Centrally owned generators	Private generators	State-owned generators	Private generators
Transmission	Government-owned transmission companies	Private transmission companies	Government-owned transmission companies	Private transmission companies
System operations	NLDC	RLDC	SLDC	
Distribution			State-owned DISCOMs	Private DISCOMs
Trading	Trading licensees	Power exchanges	Trading licensees	Power exchanges
Appeal	Appellate Tribunal for Electricity			

Figure 6.4 Regulatory and market structure of India's power sector, 2020
Source: Authors' compilation.

Table 6.2 Timeline of major reforms in India's power sector

Year	Reform
1948	Electricity Act passed. State Electricity Boards set up and made responsible for power generation, transmission, and distribution.
1964	Five Regional Electricity Boards are formed to ensure grid integration and national power flow.
1975	Central power generation companies, such as the NTPC (National Thermal Power Corporation), NHPC (National Hydropower Corporation) and NEEPCO (North Eastern Electric Power Corporation), are set up.
1989	Power Grid of India established to manage inter-state transmission projects.
1991	Electricity Act of 1948 amended. Private-sector participation in generation allowed. Regional grid operators established. 100% foreign investment in power sector allowed.
1992	Regulations to determine power generation tariffs introduced.
1998	Private-sector participation in transmission allowed.
1998	Central and State Electricity Regulatory Commissions (CREC and SERCs) established.
1999	First moves to privatize power distribution.
2002	Introduction of availability-based tariff.
2003	Electricity Act 2003 introduced, leading to the separation of generation, transmission, and distribution businesses, the implementation of open access,[a] and captive power generation.
2004	Open-access regulations enforced.[a]
2006	National tariff policy issued and Renewable Purchase Obligations (RPOs) introduced.
2008	Power exchanges set up.
2010	Market for RE certificates established.
2014	Launch of nationwide rural electrification scheme.
2015	Scheme to restructure outstanding debt of distribution companies.
2016	Solar and wind power projects supplying power to distribution companies exempted from inter-state transmission charges and losses.
2017	Launch of a new scheme to ensure electricity supply to each household.
2017	Guidelines issued by the MNRE for procurement of solar and wind power via competitive auctions.
2019	Guidelines issued by the MNRE for procurement of power from hybrid solar and wind projects through competitive auctions.

Note: [a] Open access allows buyers to access distribution and transmission networks to procure electricity from suppliers other than local power distribution utilities.
Source: Authors' compilation.

is typically more than 50%. Since 2010, India's grid has expanded rapidly (extending to 421,244 circuit km) and is generally regarded as robust. Incidents of congestion have declined sharply in the past decade. Evidence of this is that the volume of electricity traded at power exchanges that could not be delivered due to congestion declined from 17% in the 2012/2013 financial year to less than 0.4% in the 2019/2020 period (CERC, 2020).

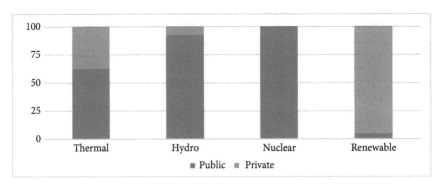

Figure 6.5 Ownership of power generation assets in India, March 2020 (%)
Source: Author's compilation.

Electricity *distribution* is dominated by around 60 public distribution companies, known as discoms, that operate as monopolies in their assigned areas.
Private-sector participation in this sector is limited either to franchise agreements or public–private partnerships. Mumbai is the one exception; here,
distribution is entirely privately owned.

Key government institutions responsible for India's electricity sector are
listed and briefly described in Table 6.3. The MNRE is the ministry dedicated
to the promotion of RE technologies in India. It has a separate budget, which
means that it has the independence to formulate and implement policies. This
has also enabled it to set up institutions such as SECI, which spearheads the
country's auction programme.

6.3.2 Tariff setting and financial sustainability

Retail electricity tariff determination processes are subject to various forms
of political intervention at the state government level. State regulators are
expected to determine tariffs annually using a cost-plus model to ensure full
cost recovery for discoms. In practice, however, the discoms are rarely able to
recover full costs as local governments exert pressure on the regulators and
the discoms to keep tariffs low to appease their electorates.[6] In 2018/2019, the
average cost of power supply was INR 6.09/kWh, but the average tariff was set
at INR 0.52/kWh lower, even after accounting for a subsidy-inclusive average

---

[6] State authorities make all decisions regarding the appointment of members of state regulatory bodies.
Certain state authorities are known to have exerted direct intervention in the tariff-determination process,
but how they assert control over other regulatory decisions is unclear.

Table 6.3 Key state institutions in India's electricity sector, 2020

Ministry of Power (MOP)	Responsible for formulating national electricity policy
Ministry of New and Renewable Energy (MNRE)	Nodal ministry for the promotion and deployment of RE
Solar Energy Corporation of India (SECI)	Nodal agency for facilitating the implementation of various solar and wind energy schemes and for organizing auctions for RE projects
Central Electricity Authority (CEA)	Statutory body under MOP that is responsible for preparing a national electricity plan every five years. Also the nodal agency for development of hydro power.
Appellate Tribunal for Electricity (APTEL)	Statutory body constituted for the purpose of hearing cases against the orders of the regulatory commissions
Central Electricity Regulatory Commission (CERC)	Statutory body responsible for setting inter-state generation and transmission tariffs. Also creates regulations for power-market operations, grants trading licences, and deals with disputes.
State Electricity Regulatory Commissions (SERCs)	Statutory bodies with responsibilities similar to the CERC but with jurisdiction for a particular state
National Load Dispatch Centre (NLDC)	National grid operator that supervises all inter-regional power flows
Regional Load Dispatch Centres (RLDC)	Responsible for optimal grid operations at a regional level and supervising inter-state power flows
State Load Dispatch Centres (SLDC)	Responsible for optimal grid operations at state level and for supervising intra-state power flows
Power Grid Corporation of India Ltd	The state-owned central transmission utility (CTU) that undertakes inter-state electricity transmission and is responsible for planning and coordinating inter-state transmission systems

Source: Authors' compilation.

tariff of INR 5.57/kWh by the state governments.[7] Political influence is mainly wielded in the form of cross-subsidization across consumer categories and the limiting of justifiable tariff increases.[8]

[7] At July 2020 values, INR 75 was worth US$ 1.
[8] For example, high-income residential, industrial, and commercial consumers pay higher tariffs than low-income residential and agricultural consumers. Some residential and most agricultural consumers are supplied with 'free' electricity.

The poor financial health of power distribution companies has been a long-standing concern. Discoms are expected to operate on a cost-plus model, but high levels of political interference and poor governance limit operational and financial performance. High technical and commercial losses (22% in 2018/2019), and the under-recovery of costs are also delaying attempts to modernize the network (see PTI, 2019, 2020).

Accordingly, although performance can differ dramatically from state to state, the financial performance of discoms is generally deteriorating. In the 2018/2019 financial year, cumulative losses amounted to US$ 6.6 billion—up from US$ 3.9 billion in the previous year. In addition, debt levels increased from US$ 60.6 billion in 2015 to US$ 63.7 billion in 2019, and outstanding dues to power producers reached US$ 26.5 billion in March 2019—up from US$ 6.7 billion in 2010 (see Figure 6.6). The average time taken to clear such dues also increased to five months.

The Ministry of Power (MoP) and the Power Finance Corporation, with the help of certain external agencies, rank the discoms annually against various parameters, including operational and financial competence. In 2019, discoms in only 9 of 24 surveyed jurisdictions reported an annual profit. Of the 24 states, 5 of those surveyed account for 53% of dues outstanding to power producers. Nevertheless, most discoms were accorded high ratings (Power Finance Corporation, n.d.). As long as the ranking process is carried out under the aegis of the government, it seems unlikely that these evaluations will be objective.

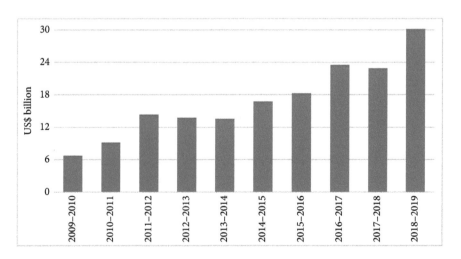

Figure 6.6 Payments owed by DISCOMs to power generation companies, 2009–2019
Source: Power Finance Corporation (n.d.).

6.3.3 Regulatory and policy framework on renewable energy

India's RE programme is guided by its 'National Action Plan on Climate Change', published in 2008 (Government of India, 2008). The plan set targets for *RE capacity* at 175 GW and *RE consumption* at 21% by 2022; the latter takes the form of renewable purchase obligations (RPOs).

RPO targets apply to all power utilities and bulk power consumers that have captive power plants and/or obtain power from open-access sources. The targets were designed when renewable power was two to three times more expensive than conventional power and have not yet been changed, even though RE is now cheaper.

States are also free to set their own RPO targets, and this has led to wide variations between states. Entities that fail to meet their targets are required to purchase RE certificates that are generated by RE power producers and can be traded on the national stock exchange. In general, however, compliance rates remain low and enforcement processes lax. In 2019, for example, the MNRE reported that 27 states and union territories had met only 60% of their RPO targets. In addition, discoms can ask state regulators to issue dispensations that retrospectively relax RPO targets or carry over their unmet obligations into future years.

6.3.4 Renewable energy procurement through competitive bidding

Apart from the RPOs, India's government has implemented several supporting policies and regulations to support the growth of the RE sector and to achieve national targets.

- *Competitive bidding guidelines* (CBGs) are issued by the MNRE for the procurement of solar and wind power. These provide a framework for the procurement of renewable power by all government agencies and power utilities across the country. The objective is to provide guidance to both procurement agencies and the private sector and to ensure consistency in procurement across states. Deviations from the guidelines have to be approved by the relevant regulators. Separate sets of guidelines have been issued for solar, wind, and hybrid RE projects, covering all the critical aspects of project procurement, including PPA tenor, tariff structure, technical standards, eligibility criteria, and contractual provisions such as termination events, penalties, *force majeure*, and legislative shifts. The guidelines are updated frequently in response to evolving market parameters. For example, land acquisition requirements have been amended twice since 2017 so where developers initially had 7 months to acquire land after signing the PPA, they now have up to 18 months. Project commissioning deadlines have also been amended twice since 2017 so where developers initially had 15 months to commission solar power projects after signing a PPA, they now have up to 18 months.

- All RE power plants (other than biomass and large hydro plants) have *must-run status* and are not subject to merit-order dispatch. The must-run directive applies in all circumstances except where the grid has to shut down for technical or safety reasons. However, because no clear protocols exist for determining the presence of 'technical or safety reasons', many states openly breach this requirement when demand is low or cheaper power is available. The MNRE has amended the bidding guidelines to address curtailment risk and allow developers to benefit from a provision for 'deemed generation', but this has not yet been successfully invoked (see Table 6.13). Some project developers have therefore challenged regulators through the courts.
- The *solar parks scheme* was launched in 2014 with a target of 20 GW that was later expanded to 40 GW in 2017 (see section 6.4.1.3).
- Solar and wind projects in resource-rich states have been encouraged to sell power to other states. Those projects that have been awarded through competitive bidding and that achieve commercial operation before 31 December 2022 are *exempted from inter-state transmission charges*.
- To improve the predictability and integration of variable renewable power into the grid, the government has mandated that solar and wind projects *forecast and schedule their daily power* output in 15-minute blocks. Moreover, penalties are imposed for the over- and under-injection of power under a deviation settlement mechanism (DSM). These regulations were first introduced centrally in 2015, with states following suit over the next few years. By 2020, 15 states had formulated DSM regulations for solar and wind projects. However, several developers are opposed to project-level generation forecasts and penalties. In particular, those that were awarded projects before the implementation of the regulations had not allowed for the financial costs of compliance. They have instead recommended state-level generation forecasting with limited or no penalties for individual project developers.

- The government provides several *financial incentives* to keep RE afford-able and financially attractive to purchasers. These incentives include capital subsidies, allowances for accelerated depreciation, a concessional rate for goods and services tax (GST), and a lower rate for income tax. Some of these incentives are gradually being phased out as capital costs have come down and the price of RE has become more competitive with thermal power.[9]
- To *simplify and expedite project development*, several states have waived various permits and approvals required by RE projects. Some states also offer a single-window, project-approval clearance, which combines all approvals related to land acquisition and use, environmental impact mitigation, job creation, etc. A foreign direct investment policy has also been created that allows automatic approval to international investors who wish to own 100% equity in projects.

6.4 The design of India's renewable energy auctions

India held its first solar power auction in 2010. The auction programme was designed to increase transparency in procurement processes, reduce power costs, and attract a high level of investment. To improve afford-ability, the government initially also created various ad hoc schemes, such as capital subsidies and options of blending RE with cheaper thermal power.

Since 2014, SECI, under the aegis of the MNRE, has been the nodal agency for all national-level solar and wind energy tenders (see Table 6.4). However, companies, such as NTPC (a state-owned thermal power distribution com-pany) and NHPC (a state-owned hydropower company) have also issued national solar and wind energy tenders, and state authorities are free to procure power from central government schemes or run their own auction programmes. In this chapter, we focus on auctions run by SECI between 2015 and early 2020.

The CBGs cover the procurement of solar and wind power plants (MoP, 2017). They attempt to create a degree of homogeneity in auction processes run by various procurement agencies and ensure that all developers and investors receive the same treatment. Aspects of the guidelines have since

[9] For utility-scale projects, capital subsidies have been almost completely phased out. Currently, they are offered only under the public-sector undertaking (PSU) scheme, which has a mandatory local-content clause (see Table 6.5). The maximum capital subsidy offered under this scheme is INR 7 million/MW (US$ 93,300), which is roughly equivalent to the extra cost of using domestically manufactured panels but is subject to bids by PSUs. The government has not defined any methods for setting the maximum limit.

Table 6.4 Stand-alone solar and wind power tenders
issued by SECI in India, August 2015–June 2020

	Solar	Wind
Number of tenders issued (excluding cancelled tenders)	31.0	8.0
Capacity auctioned (GW)	24.3	11.4
Capacity received (GW)	44.6	17.8
Capacity allocated (GW)	19.1	9.3

been amended, primarily to address project implementation challenges and
to reduce the risks facing developers and investors (MNRE, 2019; MoP,
2019a, b).

6.4.1 Auction designs and processes

As shown in Table 6.5, SECI has developed several procurement schemes,
taking into account different facets of project development (available
resources, transmission options, and technologies) as well as the nature of
power demand and the government's objectives for the RE sector. Some
schemes have been designed specifically to promote the domestic manufac-
ture of solar PV cells and panels, while others have been designed to provide
stable power output by combining RE and thermal power.

Procurers usually issue a request for proposals (RfP) that interested
investors can obtain online for a nominal fee. The auctions have two rounds—
technical and financial; bids that qualify in the technical round are eligible to
participate in the financial round (see section 6.1.1.4). Bids that qualify are
then required to specify capacity and an initial price. The bids are then ranked
and stacked in price order, and the cheapest 80% of the bids proceed to an
electronic auction round (section 6.4.1.5).

In most auctions held so far, SECI and other central agencies have
taken a pay-as-bid approach. However, SECI recently proposed a uniform
pricing approach that would have required all developers to match the
lowest bid tariff. Following opposition from developers, the proposal was
withdrawn.

With regard to time frames and milestones, the bid guidelines and tender documents define clear deadlines for project execution (see Table 6.6).
However, SECI accepts feedback from stakeholders on proposed timelines
and is willing to amend these for specific tenders. For example, if bidders

Table 6.5 Types of renewable energy auctions in India

Energy source	Auction details
Solar, wind, and hybrid interstate transmission system (ISTS) projects	Project developers can set up projects anywhere in the country. They retain responsibility for land acquisition and grid connectivity. Most auctions have been run under this scheme.
Solar/RE parks	Project developers are required to set up projects in designated RE parks. Land and transmission infrastructure, usually developed by SECI or other public companies in partnership with state governments, is provided to project developers at a fixed price.
Manufacturing-linked project developments	Developers are required to set up solar PV cell and panel manufacturing facilities, in direct proportion to assigned power development capacity.
Public-sector undertaking (PSU) schemes	Projects issued under this scheme may be developed only by government entities and publicly owned companies for captive consumption or the supply of power to other PSUs. The developers are given viability-gap funding (based on the bids submitted) and are mandated to use locally manufactured RE equipment.
Solar and wind power blended with fossil fuel	Developers can supply solar and wind power blended with power from coal-based power plants. The minimum share of renewable power capacity allowed is 51%.
Agriculture-focused KUSUM programme[a]	This is designed to provide solar power to farmers for their own consumption to help them earn an income from the sale of surplus power to local utilities. The programme has the benefit of reducing grid losses in that power is produced closer to where it is consumed.

Note: KUSUM = Kisan Urja Suraksha evem Utthan Mahabhiyan (Farmers' Energy Security and Upliftment Project).
Source: Authors' compilation.

require time to visit proposed project sites, bid submission deadlines can be extended.

In practice, however, given the uncertainties surrounding off-taker demand, as well as access to land and transmission infrastructure, the timeline from the request for proposals[10] to bid submission has become unpredictable. For instance, a 7.5 GW solar power tender issued by SECI in December 2018 never reached the auction stage, in spite of multiple extensions, and was cancelled in January 2021. In this case, a lack of transmission

[10] Note that in India, an RfP is often referred to as an RfS, meaning *request for selection*.

Table 6.6 Timeline for tender processes across technologies, India 2020

Event	Timeline
Request for proposals (RfP)	–
Pre-bid meeting	Undefined
Bid submission	Usually within 30–45 days of the RfP
Auction	Usually within 15–30 days of bid submission
Letters of award issued	Within 60–120 days of auction date
Signing of PPA	Within 30–90 days after letters of award are issued
Regulatory approval	Within 60 days of filing for approval
Financial close	Solar: within 9 months of signing PPA if project located in a solar park; otherwise 12 months Wind: within 7 months of signing PPA
Commercial operation date	Solar: within 15 months of signing PPA if project located in a solar park; otherwise 18 months Wind: within 18 months of signing PPA

Source: Authors' compilation.

evacuation infrastructure in the proposed location has led to tender cancellation. By contrast, the RfP for SECI's Tranche VIII 1.2 GW solar power tender was issued on 3 January 2020, and the auction was completed on 28 February 2020.

6.4.1.1 Auction demand

Actual auction demand often tends to diverge from official plans or announcements. In 2017, the MNRE announced a roadmap for the issuing of solar power auctions with a projected capacity of 30 GW in 2018/2019 and 2019/2020. In fact, in 2018/2019, tenders were issued for over 49.5 GW of solar power, and in 2019/2020, tenders were issued for 29.8 GW. Similarly, the MoP announced that wind power tenders of 10 GW would be issued in 2017/2018 and 2018/2019. The wind capacity tendered in 2018/2019 was only 6.6 GW, and in 2019/2020, the capacity was just 3 GW.

No clear plan or schedule exists for the issuing of tenders. In practice, this means that bidders don't know when tenders will be issued. SECI seems to issue tenders when under pressure from the MNRE, and based on its assessment of power demand/supply, the availability of solar/RE park infrastructure, and the results of previous tenders. While SECI maintains regular dialogue with discoms across the country, it receives no binding commitments for the purchase of power until after auctions are completed. The lack of firm demand means that even if auctions are successful, projects might fail to find off-takers. This was the case for several auctions held in 2019.

6.4.1.2 General conditions related to auctions

The bid guidelines state that procurers can invite bids for generation capacity (MW) or energy output (MWh). Thus far, all RE auctions held in India have been for capacity. The minimum bid size has been set at 50 MW, and procurers are at liberty to set their own maximums. For solar and solar park tenders linked to interstate transmission systems, the maximum bid size is usually equal to the total offered capacity. The largest project size offered by SECI so far is 3 GW, with the average being around 1.5 GW (see Figure 6.7).

To ensure that no project can walk away with the entire capacity, SECI generally sets a maximum project size for wind power tenders of between 15% and 50% of the tendered capacity. This changed when the wind tender for Interstate Transmission System (ISTS) IX was issued in March 2020 (SECI, 2020); the maximum project size was set at 100% of offered capacity, which was 2 GW (see Figure 6.8).

The background to this is that larger developers put pressure on SECI to allow bids for the entire tender capacity, while smaller developers have pushed for smaller caps on maximum bid size. As a result, SECI often tinkers with minimum and maximum bid sizes as they try to balance their wish to attract a large number of developers with their aim of keeping tariffs low and

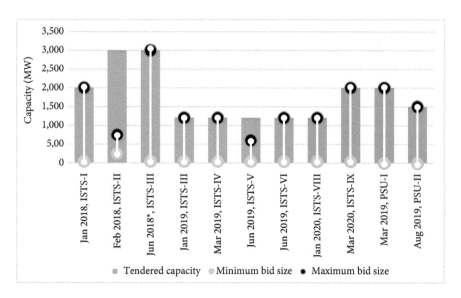

Figure 6.7 Bid size and capacity of the solar interstate transmission system and public sector auctions, 2018–2020

Note: * Tender cancelled.
Source: Authors' compilation.

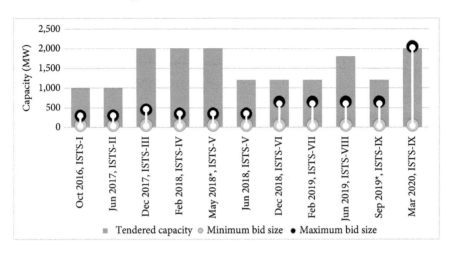

Figure 6.8 Bid size and capacity in wind interstate transmission system tenders, October 2016–March 2020

Note: * Tender cancelled.
Source: Authors' compilation.

enabling developers to benefit from the economies of scale associated with large projects.

The CBGs allow procurers to set tariff caps but do not specify how these should be determined. Before 2017, caps were set according to generic tariffs determined by CERC. However, CERC stopped its generic tariff determinations in 2017/2018. Since then, procurers have been trying to push tariff caps down to reduce the price of power. Developers have resisted this, and several tenders with unrealistically low tariff caps have been undersubscribed, and some have even been cancelled. In 2018, SECI responded to calls by developers to increase tariff caps in some tenders (Chandrasekaran, 2018). Understandably, more developers are likely to participate in tenders that have higher tariff caps (see Figure 6.9).

As recently as November 2019, the MNRE stated its opposition to the removal of tariff caps (Ramesh, 2019). However, by March 2020, poor responses to several tenders and repeated developer demands had forced SECI to remove all tariff caps (Chatterjee, 2020). Interestingly, solar tariffs have fallen anyway because market competition is so intense and because equipment prices continue to fall.

Tariffs set via auctions still have to be approved by the relevant central and state regulatory authorities. However, discoms and tender-issuing agencies

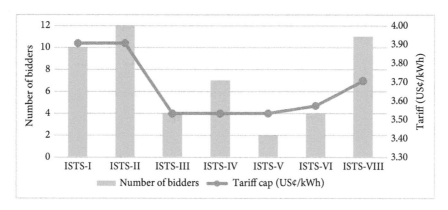

Figure 6.9 Tariff caps set by the Solar Energy Corporation of India (SECI) in interstate transmission system tenders for solar power projects

Source: Authors' compilation.

regularly seem to miss deadlines set for securing the necessary tariff approvals from regulators. Some projects have been cancelled as a result.[11]

A feed-in tariff regime is still followed for biomass and biogas, small hydropower (less than 25 MW), and small solar and wind energy projects. State regulators determine these feed-in tariffs annually, using the prevailing standard inputs for project costs, interest rates, and operations and maintenance costs, as well as for returns on equity.

Commissioning timelines are shown in Table 6.7 and, as specified in the CBGs, have been modified following feedback from developers. For wind tenders, procurers are free to set commissioning timelines longer than those prescribed in the guidelines. In a tender issued in March 2020, SECI increased the commissioning timeline to 24 months. This decision was influenced by project execution challenges facing the developers and by the poor response to three preceding wind power tenders that were undersubscribed by between 50% and 100%.

Between January 2017 and April 2020, 403 solar and 31 wind power projects awarded through auctions were commissioned (see Figure 6.10). Of these, only 152 solar power projects and 8 wind power projects were commissioned on time. The average delay in the commissioning of solar projects

---

[11] In most cases, it seems that discoms and state governments work behind the scenes to influence cancellations if demand or prices come down and they are no longer interested in buying power at the awarded price. However, if regulators can find cheaper tariffs elsewhere, they have also been known to take a stand and reject agreed tariffs.

Table 6.7 Commissioning deadlines for solar power projects, India 2017–2019

2017	Projects inside a solar park: 13 months from date of signing PPA Projects outside a solar park: 15 months from date of signing PPA
2018	Projects inside a solar park: 21 months from date of signing PPA Projects outside a solar park: 24 months from date of signing PPA Additional 2–3 months allowed for projects above 250 MW
2019	Projects inside a solar park: 15 months from date of signing PPA Projects outside a solar park: 18 months from date of signing PPA Commissioning deadline can be extended by up to a year in cases where delays occur in the transfer of land by government or the approval of tariffs by regulatory authorities.

Source: MNRE (2019).

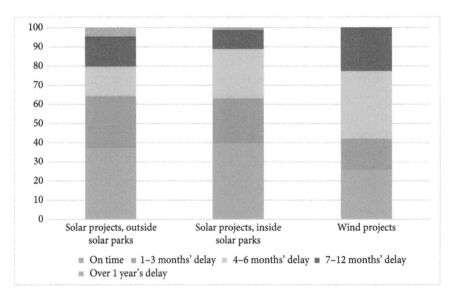

Figure 6.10 Delays in solar and wind project commissioning, India, 2020 (%)
Source: Authors' compilation.

located outside and inside solar parks was 6 months and 4.5 months, respectively. The average delay with regard to the commissioning wind projects was 5 months. However, these delays seem to be getting longer.

In theory, however, the CBGs allow for the partial and early commissioning of projects. Developers have to commission at least 50 MW to claim partial commissioning, and the commercial operation date is declared when the entire project capacity is commissioned, which can be before the scheduled date. The guidelines allow for the sale of power from partial or full capacity commissioned before the scheduled date at 75–100% of PPA tariffs (Ministry of Power, 2019a, b).

6.4.1.3 Access to land and transmission infrastructure

While developers were initially required to prove land ownership before submitting bids, this changed in 2018 and again in 2019 (see Table 6.8). Given the uncertainties related to tender scheduling and the auction programme, developers were understandably reluctant to commit capital and complete land acquisition before submitting bids. The decision was then made to relax ownership requirements to increase competition and allow new and foreign companies to compete for tenders, regardless of whether or not they own land.

Even so, the completion of land-acquisition formalities within the (now permitted) project execution timeline of 12–18 months remains a major challenge. Non-uniform obligations under state policies, complex acquisition regulations that vary across states, poorly maintained land records, and lengthy approval processes can create complex and gruelling obstacles (Bridge to India, 2015; Kumar and Thapar, 2017). The resulting delays can result in penalties, the calling of bid bonds, and even the cancellation of PPAs. Some project developers have themselves attempted to terminate PPAs, citing *force majeure* related to delays in land procurement.

To address the difficulties with land acquisition and transmission infrastructure, the MNRE announced the development of solar parks and ultra mega solar power projects in 2017, along with plans to add 40 GW of solar capacity through the scheme by 2022. Under the scheme, state authorities can acquire land and build transmission infrastructure and offer these to RE developers on a 'plug-and-play' basis. Similarly, public-sector companies that already have large landholdings are being offered incentives to set up solar power parks (MNRE, 2018). In addition, the central government has undertaken to provide financial assistance for the preparation of detailed project reports plus a subsidy of US$ 0.03 million/MW for the development of infrastructure (MNRE, 2017).

Table 6.8 Initial guidelines and subsequent amendments regarding land acquisition

Initial guidelines, 2017	Developers must identify all land required in their bid submissions. They must show possession of 100% of the land within seven months of signing the PPA.
1st amendment, 2018	Developers are no longer required to identify land in bid submissions but must show possession of 100% of the land within 12 months of signing the PPA.
2nd amendment, 2019	Developers have up to 18 months to show possession of 100% of the land.

Sources: MNRE (2018, 2019); MoP (2017, 2019a, b).

In return, developers are required to pay a mix of upfront and recurring annual charges for the use of solar park sites. The minimum installation size set by the MNRE is 500 MW, but this can be reduced if contiguous land is not available. The largest solar power park approved so far has a capacity of 5 GW.

The solar park scheme has proven especially popular with international developers, for whom land acquisition was a major hindrance. The scheme has also helped in scaling up project sizes and accelerating project execution—on average, project implementation inside solar parks is shorter by three months. However, the scheme has faced challenges. Developers complain of high charges, poor site conditions, and excessive delays, with around 37% of projects in solar parks reportedly missing their commissioning deadlines by more than three months (Seetharaman and Chandrasekaran, 2019).

According to the initial plan, the MNRE hoped to see solar park projects deliver 20 GW of new capacity by 2019 (MNRE, 2018). Our calculations indicate that solar parks were contributing just 9.7 GW by early 2020. The MNRE has therefore modified the scheme to include a financial incentive (US$ 0.6/MWh for host states that export power to other states) and to remove the obligation on host states to procure at least 20% of the power generated by solar parks. These measures seem to have prompted certain states to host more solar parks, which are now evolving into RE parks (SECI, 2019).

Responsibility for the development of deep and shallow transmission infrastructure varies depending on the presence of RE parks. Figures 6.11–6.13 show which agencies are responsible for infrastructure development in *intra*state, *inter*state, and RE parks. As indicated, where park-related infrastructure is unavailable, developers are responsible for the costs and construction of shallow transmission facilities. In all cases, the state and central transmission utilities (STUs and CTUs) are responsible for developing deep/shared transmission infrastructure. In practice, project construction and the installation of transmission infrastructure are seldom synchronous, resulting in massive delays in some cases as well as under-subscription of several large tenders (Bridge to India, 2019).

The MNRE has sought to address the issue of transmission infrastructure delays by amending the bid guidelines such that if delays occur, project developers cannot claim any direct compensation. Instead, to compensate developers for revenue loss, procurers can be required to purchase any power that exceeds the maximum allowed in the PPA over the first three years. Penalties levied on the entity responsible for the construction of transmission

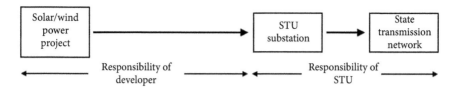

Figure 6.11 Agencies responsible for setting up infrastructure for *intra*state transmission, India, 2020

Source: Authors' compilation.

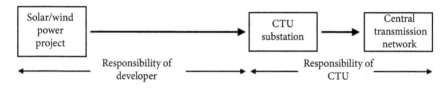

Figure 6.12 Responsibilities for setting up infrastructure for *inter*state energy transmission, India, 2020

Source: Authors' compilation.

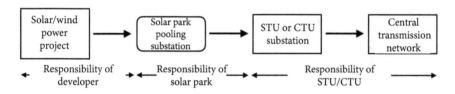

Figure 6.13 Responsibilities for setting up transmission infrastructure related to renewable energy (RE) parks, India, 2020

Source: Authors' compilation.

infrastructure can also be used to compensate the developers (MoP, 2019b). In practice, by early 2020, no compensation had yet been paid to developers.

In cases where transmission infrastructure has been developed on time but RE projects have been delayed, the central or state transmission utilities tend to encash bank guarantees submitted by project developers as part of their transmission connectivity applications (CERC, 2019). Transmission connectivity obligations and approval processes are, however, beyond the scope of the CBGs.

6.4.1.4 Qualification criteria and bid processes

Tender packs typically consist of the basic RfP plus drafts of the PPA and power sales agreement (PSA).[12] Where land or RE parks are available, lease- and implementation-agreement templates are also included. Besides key details, such as total capacity, technology (solar, wind, or hybrid) and location, the RfP defines all relevant terms and conditions for the tender, including:

- eligibility criteria;
- bid submission procedures;
- bid evaluation and auction processes;
- templates for the details that bidders have to submit about their corporate structure, financial viability, technology choices, and capital costs;
- tariff-cap specifications;
- minimum and maximum project size;
- obligations to use locally manufactured goods, if any;
- minimum annual CUF to be guaranteed by the developer;
- bid-bond requirements;
- project timeline and related penalties;
- required clearances and approvals;
- key contractual provisions regarding legislative changes, instances of excess power generation, transmission (un)availability, and grid back-down, etc.

Note that no clearances or approvals are required when the initial bids are submitted. See Table 6.9 for a list of the documents bidders have to submit as they proceed through the rest of the bid process.

The CBGs clearly state that developers must apply for all approvals and clearances within 90 days of issuance of the letter of award and must continuously follow up with the relevant authorities. This process tends to be plagued with bureaucratic delays, and clearances typically take up to eight months to secure. On request from developers, SECI will write to concerned authorities to ask them to speed up the process, and in some cases, state governments have waived certain clearances as an incentive to the RE sector. Nonetheless, RE project developers are required to obtain several clearances and approvals (see Table 6.10) before construction can begin. In the case of solar parks, the implementing agency can help developers to obtain clearances linked to the

---

[12] A PSA is a back-to-back agreement, whereby SECI (or other intermediary off-takers) sell power to Discoms.

Table 6.9 Documents RE developers have to submit to participate in an RE auction, India 2020

At bid submission

Documents that prove technical capability
Documents that prove financial resources
Details of project capacity and technologies proposed
Estimated annual generation
Initial financial bid
Earnest money deposit
Initial project cost estimates

Within 70 days of issuance of letter of award
Performance bank guarantee

At signing of PPA
Final project configuration

At financial close
Details of debt secured
Detailed project report
Proof of having secured required clearances and permits to generate and supply power
Details regarding ownership and structure of power generating company

At project commissioning
Proof that land arrangements have been secured
Plant layout
Connectivity and transmission agreements
Approval of metering scheme
Project synchronisation certificate from relevant body

Source: SECI (various).

solar park area, but developers have to obtain all 'external' clearances, such as those related to inter-state transmission.

6.4.1.4.1 Technical and financial criteria

The CBGs provide no quantifiable technical qualification criteria. To promote competition, tenders issued by SECI and other agencies require only experience in 'commercially established and operational technologies'. Bidders are not required to demonstrate any level of previous RE development or operational experience. Fortunately, this does not seem to have had any material adverse effect on the sector. RE technology is easily available and, as compared with thermal power plants, the technical/construction requirements are relatively straightforward.

The financial criteria specified in the CBGs are fairly standard, and the thresholds have been kept relatively low to promote competition and ensure high participation from developers. Bidders are required to have a net worth of at least 20% of the generic project cost and must provide proof of their

Table 6.10 Clearances and approvals required by solar and wind project developers, India 2020

Project step	Process/ tasks
Land acquisition	Lease or purchase agreement and land-use permission changed to 'industrial'
Clearances and approvals	Consent of State Pollution Control Board Certificate of no-objection from district administrator Certificate of no-objection from village administration authority Approval for water usage (applicable to solar thermal projects only) Permission from chief electrical inspector to lay power evacuation lines Certificate of no objection from the state energy department Clearance from forest department if the project is proposed on forest land Clearance from defence ministry if the project is proposed on defence-force property

Source: Pawar (2014).

financial resources in terms of their minimum annual turnover and profit level or a letter of credit.

The industry has persistently and successfully pushed for relaxation of these criteria to allow developers to bid for larger power plants. In practice, the requisite values have declined anyway in line with reductions in project costs. For example, the net worth requirement for solar power projects has declined from US$ 0.15 million per MW in 2018 to US$ 0.11 million per MW in 2020. Similarly, the minimum annual turnover requirement declined from US$ 0.07 million per MW to US$ 0.05 million per MW over the same period. In isolated cases, amounts have been lowered for specific tenders in an attempt to attract more bidders. In general, however, as with the technical criteria, the relatively low financial qualification criteria do not appear to have had a materially adverse effect on the sector. So far, developers have been able to raise money relatively easily, subject to project viability.

6.4.1.4.2 Local content
To help create a market for local manufacturers, the Indian government has pushed for the use of domestically manufactured equipment since its RE auction programme began in 2010. India's first solar power auction required developers to use Indian-made panels.

In 2014, a 750 MW solar power tender was issued where 50% of the capacity to be awarded was reserved for locally made panels. The United States then challenged this stipulation at the World Trade Organization (WTO). In 2016, the WTO ruled against India, forcing the country to stop taking these measures. To circumvent the ruling, the Indian government announced the PSU scheme (see Table 6.4). Projects auctioned under this scheme must use Indian cells and panels, but the power they generate can be used only by government-owned companies.

India's manufacturing capacity in the RE sector has grown substantially since 2010. By early 2020, solar PV cell and panel manufacturing capacity were at 3 GW and 11 GW, respectively (see MNRE, n.d.). So far, however, the utilization of this capacity averages between 2.5 and 3 GW per annum. Part of the reason for the slow uptake of locally manufactured products is that the developers perceive imported equipment to be both cheaper and based on better technology.

To support domestic manufacturers, the government has also imposed safeguard duties on imports of solar equipment. As a result, domestic manufacturers' market share increased from around 12% to 30% between 2017 and 2019 (Ministry of Commerce and Industry, 2020). Further duties are being considered alongside the possible introduction of financial incentives for domestic manufacturers because the government sees the slow development of manufacturing capacity as inconsistent with the aim of growing the RE sector.

The CBGs do not mandate the use of local content in RE projects. However, the MNRE and SECI have made the use of local content a qualifying criterion in several auctions—the PSU scheme being one example. In addition, the CBGs require that solar panels and inverters conform to specifications issued by the Bureau of Indian Standards. Accordingly, the MNRE has published lists of solar PV cells as well as other solar and wind-turbine technologies that conform to these specifications.

6.4.1.5 Bidder ranking and winner selection

Bidders that qualify in the technical round are invited to bid again in the financial round. To ensure that the process remains competitive, bidders accounting for only 80% of the total bid capacity with the lowest tariffs are invited to participate in this round. No other weighting or preference is accorded to bidders with greater experience in installed capacity or, indeed, in any other regard.

The auction process takes place electronically so that each bidder can see the capacity and tariffs proposed by other bidders on an anonymous basis. The auction window is initially opened for 30 minutes and is extended by 8 minutes each time a new bid is submitted. The auction window can be

extended an unlimited number of times. The starting bid for each participant is the price quoted in their original bid submission, but bids are awarded
based on the capacity they put forward in the electronic bidding process.
In other words, capacity is awarded to bidders in ascending order of tariff
amounts submitted (see Table 6.11).

6.4.1.6 Buyer and seller liabilities

To bid, developers have to meet two separate financial requirements. The first
is an 'earnest money' deposit (EMD) of about 1% of the capital cost of their
project as proposed in their bid submission. This is the equivalent of a bid
bond and takes the form of a bank deposit, a bank draft, or a bank guarantee
issued by a commercial bank. These deposits are returned to unsuccessful
bidders once the auction process is complete and are forfeited if successful
bidders fail to sign the PPA or submit the required performance guarantee
within the stipulated time.

The second requirement is the provision of a performance guarantee (PBG)
issued by a commercial bank when the PPA is signed. The value of the guarantee has to be 2% of the estimated project cost and can be encashed by the
procurer if a developer fails to achieve financial close, commission projects
by the stipulated deadline, or meet guaranteed generation levels.

The value of bank guarantees as a percentage of the project cost has reduced
sharply in recent years. The RE industry has persistently and successfully
pushed for a relaxation in bid-bond requirements to allow developers to bid
for larger capacities. Given the many challenges developers face in obtaining guarantees from commercial banks, SECI has decided to allow bidders
to submit a payment-on-order instrument (POI) instead (Bridge to India,

Table 6.11 An example of the bucket-filling approach to awards where the total offered capacity is 1,000 MW

Developer	Tariff bid (US¢/kWh)	Bid capacity (MW)	Capacity awarded (MW)
A	3.33	300	300
B	3.35	200	200
C	3.36	300	300
D	3.36	100	100
E	3.37	200	50
F	3.37	300	50
G	3.39	100	0

Source: Authors' compilation.

2020a). A POI is an undertaking by a government-owned financial institution to pay the procurer in scenarios where a bank guarantee becomes liable for encashment.

Although project delays are common, bank guarantees are rarely encashed. To date, SECI has been very accommodating of the challenges facing developers about accessing land, transmission infrastructure, necessary permits, etc.

6.4.1.6.1 Delayed commissioning

The commissioning timetable allows a maximum of six months' extension beyond the specified completion date, and developers are obliged to pay liquidated damages during this period. These damages are claimed by encashing part of the performance guarantee on a per-day basis in proportion to capacity not commissioned.[13] If a developer fails to commission the project six months after the specified completion date, contracted capacity is reduced to commissioned capacity (minimum 50 MW) as per that date.

Again, in practice, developers often approach SECI to seek an extension in scheduled completion dates because delays are attributable to factors beyond their control. SECI usually takes a flexible view and issues ad hoc extensions to developers.

6.4.1.6.2 Generation guarantees and penalties

To date, all RE tenders issued by SECI and other central government agencies have required developers to bid for capacity rather than energy. However, developers are required to guarantee a minimum annual CUF (typically 17% for solar projects and 22% for wind projects). Any shortfall in CUF (and thus generation) makes developers liable for penalties, and these have been set at 25–50% of the PPA tariff for the output shortfall.

As part of bid submissions, developers are required to provide annual generation estimates for their projects. They are also required to fulfil minimum annual CUF levels as tendered and maintain the annual CUF to within +10% and −15% of the figure proposed.

As per the terms of the tender and the PPA, procurers are required to pay bills presented to them by IPPs within the stipulated timeframes. Procurers are given 30 days beyond the due date to clear the dues. After this, a late-payment surcharge is levied at 15% per annum, calculated on a simple interest basis. Procurers must also submit a revolving letter of credit covering 105% of the project's average monthly revenue. This letter of credit can be partially or

---

[13] The CBGs contain no pre-defined amounts for liquidated damages.

fully cashed if the procurer fails to clear outstanding dues within the 30-day period. As an intermediary procurer, SECI also has the right to sell power to a third party if the distribution company (as the final procurer) fails to fulfil its obligations.

Provisions made for the sale of excess energy state that the procurer enjoys the first right of refusal on the sale of power to other consumers and can procure surplus power at 75% of the PPA tariff (see Table 6.12). In theory, developers can sell excess power to other consumers, but no such cases have been reported yet. No penalties are levied on developers if shortfalls in power delivery result from the unavailability of transmission infrastructure.

Delays in the commissioning of required transmission infrastructure have led to several projects being deferred. As a result, the MNRE has made major changes to the CBGs (Bridge to India, 2018). These include broadening the scope of factors that make compensation payable to developers and increasing the amounts of compensation payable (see Table 6.13).

In practice, no records are kept of the reasons for grid unavailability. Discoms and state transmission companies are notorious for curtailing power on grounds of 'grid security'. This has become a contested issue with developers, who have made representations requesting that the reasons for grid unavailability are authenticated. Projects connected to the national grid seldom experience this problem since discoms don't have the authority to issue curtailment instructions to the national grid operator.

6.4.1.6.3 Compensation for changes in the law

As part of the PPA, developers can claim compensation if legislative or tax-rate changes impact negatively on project development. To seek such

Table 6.12 Generation guarantees required from solar and wind power generators, India 2020

Technology	Minimum annual CUF	If output is below committed CUF	If generation is above committed CUF
Solar	At the procurer's discretion but typically 17%	Generator pays a financial penalty of at least 25% of PPA tariff	Procurer has first right of refusal and may procure excess power at 75% of PPA tariff
Wind	22%	Penalty is at least 50% of PPA tariff (revised down from 75%)	Procurer has first right of refusal and may procure excess power at 75% of PPA tariff

Source: Authors' compilation.

Table 6.13 Compensation defined as per MNRE bid guidelines, India

Technology	Transmission infrastructure not ready	Grid becomes unavailable while the project is operational	Grid operator asks generator to curtail output
Solar	Generation loss is calculated proportionally at 19% of CUF or committed CUF, whichever is lower. Procurer is liable to purchase excess generation equal to generation loss over the first three years of operations.	Generation loss is determined on the basis of the number of hours that the grid is unavailable and the average hourly generation in a year. Excess generation equal to generation loss is procured over three years at the PPA tariff.	No compensation if generation is curtailed to ensure grid security. Deemed that generation compensation is paid in all other instances.
Wind	No specific clause on compensation in the CBGs or tender documents.	Compensation is payable if the grid is unavailable for more than 50 hours in a year. Generation loss is determined by the number of hours that grid is unavailable and average hourly generation in a year. Excess generation equal to generation loss is procured over three years at the PPA tariff.	No compensation is paid if generation is curtailed to ensure grid security Deemed that generation is paid as compensation in all other instances.

Source: Authors' compilation.

compensation, developers have to approach the regulatory authorities and demonstrate the impact on project costs. Once approved by the regulator, the off-taker and developer usually agree to an annuity plan for the payment of compensation. Developers have successfully sought compensation for increased project costs resulting from the introduction of the GST as well as safeguard duties on solar cells and panels.

6.4.1.6.4 Socio-economic and environmental obligations
RE project developers in India are subject to very minimal environmental or social obligations. Neither SECI nor other government agencies require environmental impact assessments (EIAs). At first, developers were required to secure 'consent to establish' and 'consent to operate' from the State Pollution Control Boards (SPCBs). These consents were given after evaluating the

potential environmental impacts of the likely emissions and effluents linked to projects. In 2016, as part of efforts to improve the 'ease of doing business' for RE developers, the government removed the need for developers to obtain SPCB consent. Instead, projects are now require merely to inform SPCBs of the development (Ministry of Environment, Forest and Climate Change, 2016).

The only other environmental obligation mentioned in the CBGs is the 'end-of-life' disposal of solar panels in accordance with the government's Hazardous and Other Waste Rules published in 2016 (Aggarwal, 2017). However, these regulations do not even cover the treatment of solar PV waste.

Indian lenders, who provide an estimated 80% of the total primary debt financing in the RE sector, do not require EIAs as part of their due diligence process either. EIAs are therefore undertaken only when international agencies, such as the International Finance Corporation, the Asian Development Bank, the European Investment Bank, and the German state's development bank, KFW, get involved in project financing.

6.4.1.6.5 Termination compensation

Failure to commission projects within stipulated timelines or supply power as per the terms of the PPA terms, along with bankruptcy and changes in project control or shareholding, are considered to be developer defaults. In such cases, procurers are entitled to compensation equivalent to six months of the PPA tariff for the contracted capacity. The procurer also has the right to acquire project assets at 90% of outstanding debt.

In cases of natural *force majeure*, no termination compensation is payable by either party. In case of non-natural *force majeure* events, such as war, strikes, or the nationalization of assets, procurers have to take over project assets and pay the developer's outstanding debts plus 110% of the adjusted equity.

6.4.1.7 Securing the revenue stream and addressing off-taker risk

6.4.1.7.1 Payment security mechanism

India's distribution utilities are in a state of chronically poor financial health, and this has created long delays in paying power generators (refer to section 6.3). Various clauses in the CBGs protect the financial interests of power generators so that if a discom defaults on payment, a three-pronged payment-security mechanism kicks in (see Table 6.14).

The Payment Security Fund was initially funded through a budgetary allocation by the central government (ICRA Ltd, 2020). However, a 2020 revision of the CBGs created an alternate mechanism to create a corpus for the fund.

The revision states that, at the time of bid submission, project developers must pay SECI US$ 6,667 per MW[14] as a contribution to the fund. Thus, the charges are effectively passed on to the procurers and, ultimately, to consumers.

State-government guarantees can be exercised only after the two other measures have been exhausted (MNRE, 2019). In practice, however, the payment security mechanism does not seem to have been invoked yet; developers probably fear the possible consequences of escalating disputes with discoms and state governments.

Failure to make timely payments or to honour PPA obligations are the main default events for procurers. In such cases, a procurer can transfer its rights and responsibilities under the PPA to a third party, subject to the approval of the generator. If the transfer is not possible, the procurer is required to either acquire project assets at an amount equal to outstanding debt plus 110% of 'adjusted equity' or pay compensation equivalent to six months of the PPA tariff for the contracted capacity. As of mid-2020, even though distribution companies owe millions of dollars in outstanding payments to power generation companies, no procurer had transferred its rights, acquired project assets, or made any compensatory payment to developers.

Tariffs are denominated in the local currency, and the tariff structure is left to procurers' discretion. A procurer may opt for a PPA with a fixed tariff for its entire duration or set an annual escalation rate for all or part of the PPA term. Setting a fixed tariff for the duration of the PPA is the dominant practice but, if applied, annual escalation rates have to be mentioned in the RfP. However,

Table 6.14 Three kinds of payment security for RE power generators

Letter of credit	Payment Security Fund	State government support
A revolving letter of credit equivalent to 105% of one month of average revenues for the project	A cash-funded reserve equivalent to three months of average project revenues	A guarantee from the relevant state government or a three-way agreement between SECI, the Reserve Bank of India, and the state government allowing SECI to access monies from state government's share of tax revenue[a]

Note: [a] Discoms are required to pay an additional tariff of US¢ 0.13/kWh if a state government cannot provide a guarantee.
Source: Authors' compilation.

[14] As at July 2020, US$ 1 was INR 75.

escalation rates are generally not linked to any market instruments and the CBGs do not oblige procurers to explain how the escalation rate will be set.

6.4.1.7.2 Project finance

Most of the lending to solar and wind power projects in India comes from public and private non-banking financing companies (NBFCs). In 2018, 75% of estimated RE project funding in India (around US$ 3.25 billion) was channelled through commercial banks and private non-banking financial institutions (CENFA, 2019). Since then, the share of public NBFCs in total project financing has soared—private financiers have been hit by liquidity crises in the local financial system, and concerns about asset quality have increased. Commercial banks have also cut back on their exposure to renewable power. This is partly because of concerns around discom finances and partly because banks have suffered huge losses from their exposure to conventional power projects. Multilateral funding agencies such as the International Finance Corporation (IFC) and the Asian Development Bank are selectively involved in lending to the sector.

6.4.2 Auction implementation

As noted, RE auctions in India were initiated in 2010 as part of the country's 'National Action Plan on Climate Change' (Government of India, 2008). Initially, solar power was procured using a mix of feed-in tariffs and auctions. However, because of various large corruption scandals around the allocation of coal mines and telecom spectrum around that time, the central government began to favour auctions as these were seen as more transparent.

Having a separate and dedicated ministry—the MNRE—for the promotion of RE technologies has been critical to the implementation of India's RE auctions. Established as early as 1992, the ministry has had the budget and the freedom to develop long-term policy and regulatory frameworks that promote RE. From this, institutions such as SECI and the National Institute of Wind Energy have emerged, while financial institutions, such as the Indian Renewable Energy Development Agency, have grown stronger. The MNRE also helped implement early financial support programmes, including tax and generation-linked incentives, which were critical to the expansion of RE power generation capacity in India before the auction programmes kicked in.

In 2015, the RE capacity target was increased from 20 GW to 100 GW by 2022. To achieve this ambitious target, SECI was set up under the direct control of the MNRE as the nodal agency for procurement and programme administration. Designed to be free of any potential conflicts of interest, SECI's core operations are limited to RE auctions. SECI has since become India's main tendering agency for RE projects, and the role of other centrally controlled state-owned entities, such as NTPC and NHPC has diminished. Several states have cut back on their procurement schemes because bidders are increasingly reluctant to bid for projects in states where discoms are a direct risk. Nevertheless, SECI does not hold exclusive rights to hold RE auctions, and no clear rationale or plan exists for the split of tenders between SECI and other public-sector agencies.

In running RE auctions, SECI has three key responsibilities. The first is to coordinate input from the MNRE, project developers, off-takers, transmission network planners, grid operators, and other stakeholders on the design of new tenders and RE procurement programmes. The second is to issue tenders and then engage with potential bidders through pre-bid meetings where objections and points of clarification can be raised. These meetings are usually unstructured, and no formal notes are issued. (As noted in section 6.4.2, the timetable from tender issuance to auction is fluid and, according to members of the industry, SECI frequently revises its bid timetables.) The third responsibility is to act as the intermediary procurer between project developers and off-takers (discoms).

Document submission, as well as competitive financial auctions for SECI-issued tenders, are conducted online. All documents and bids are electronically encrypted, with users required to set their own passwords. SECI claims that bids cannot be decrypted, even if the tender-opening officers of the buyer organization and the personnel of the e-tendering service provider were to connive (SECI, 2020). The auction results are made publicly available on SECI's website within 30 days of the auction's completion.

While SECI is relatively thinly capitalized and has comparatively little operational or financial experience, it enjoys a strong credit rating of AA+ by virtue of being 100% owned by the government of India and because it is the nodal agency for a critical sector. Despite some concerns around SECI's financial capabilities in the earlier years, Indian and international financiers alike now see the agency as a bankable counterpart.

SECI's balance sheet is still relatively small, given its commitments in several PPAs. But its 100% government ownership, its tripartite agreements with state governments and the Reserve Bank of India, and its gradually strengthening payment-security mechanisms have made it acceptable to developers as an intermediary procurer. So far, SECI has paid project developers on time even where discom payments to SECI have been delayed. Informally, SECI has alerted developers that if discom delays increase, their payments might be less timely in future. So far, this has not resulted in any deterioration in its credit rating.

SECI is almost entirely self-funded. It earns income from bid-processing fees (of up to US$ 0.2 million per project), success charges (US$ 13.330 per MW), and forfeited bid bonds. It also charges discoms a trading margin of up to US¢ 0.9/kWh when it acts as an intermediary procurer. For the financial year ending 31 March 2019, SECI reported revenue of US$ 434.7 million, which was up by 178% year on year. For the same period, it also reported a profit after tax of US$ 17.3 million (up 101% year on year) and a cash balance of US$ 222.7 million as of 31 March 2019 (SECI, 2019).

SECI is staffed largely by government officials seconded from other departments and public-sector organizations. For example, at the time of writing this chapter, its managing director was a senior bureaucrat in the government. The technical director has been seconded from the Power Grid Corporation, the national grid developer and operator. The organization is operationally stretched, and there are rumours of short-staffing, lack of expertise, and delayed timelines. No external audits of the bidding process or results occur, but SECI itself is subject to a general audit by India's auditor general. So far, no bidders or off-takers have accused SECI of mismanagement or impropriety, and no disputes relating to auctions have surfaced.

6.5 Results from India's renewable energy auctions

Since 2015, SECI has awarded around 43.5 GW of RE generation capacity.[15] The following analysis is restricted to auctions for stand-alone solar and wind power generation only, which account for 28.4 GW of the allocated capacity.

Between August 2015 and June 2020, SECI allocated a solar power capacity of 19.1 GW across several states (Table 6.15). Over the same period, SECI also auctioned another 9.3 GW of wind energy capacity (Table 6.16).

Until 2017, almost all SECI tenders were issued on a state-specific basis. Projects were expected to be developed within each state to supply power to their respective discoms. However, in 2018, the ISTS scheme was introduced to develop projects in the states that have the most solar and wind resources (mainly Rajasthan and Gujarat). The plan is for these projects to supply states with relatively poor RE resources and/or limited land availability via the

---

[15] Prior to this, SECI had issued only one utility-scale tender.

Table 6.15 Solar auctions completed by SECI, India, September 2015–June 2020

Tender issued	Project location	Tendered capacity (MW)	Subscription (x)	Lowest tariff bid (US¢/kWh)
August 2015	Maharashtra	450	2.3	5.91
August 2015	Maharashtra	50	1.0	5.91
November 2015	Uttar Pradesh	390	NA	5.91
January 2016	Andhra Pradesh	400	1.6	5.91
February 2016	Karnataka	1000	1.1	5.91
March 2016	Chhattisgarh	100	1.6	5.91
March 2016	Gujarat	225	NA	5.91
March 2016	Gujarat	25	NA	5.91
April 2016	Odisha	300	1.0	5.91
April 2016	Uttar Pradesh	160	1.6	5.91
June 2016	Maharashtra	50	2.0	5.91
June 2016	Maharashtra	450	2.4	5.91
November 2016	Rajasthan	250	5.6	3.49
November 2016	Rajasthan	500	4.6	3.25
June 2017	Rajasthan	250	5.4	3.31
June 2017	Rajasthan	500	6.2	3.29
January 2018	Andhra Pradesh	750	1.7	3.60
January 2018	Karnataka	200	2.0	3.76
January 2018	Pan India (ISTS)	2000	1.9	3.25
February 2018	Pan India (ISTS)	3000	1.7	3.25
April 2018	Uttar Pradesh	150	1.0	4.39
August 2018	Rajasthan	750	3.2	3.31
August 2018	Maharashtra	250	1.6	3.83
January 2019	Pan India (ISTS)	1200	1.3	3.40
March 2019	Pan India (ISTS)	1200	1.8	3.39
March 2019	Pan India (ISTS)	2000	0.6	4.67
March 2019	Rajasthan (ISTS)	750	1.5	3.33
June 2019	Pan India (ISTS)	1200	0.5	3.37
June 2019	Pan India (ISTS)	1200	1.0	3.61
August 2019	Pan India (ISTS)	1500	1.0	4.67
January 2020	Pan India (ISTS)	1200	3.3	3.33
March 2020	Pan India (ISTS)	2000	2.6	3.15

Note: The lowest tariff is recorded at US¢ 5.91/kWh for tenders up to June 2016. For all these tenders, the tariff for the sale of power to the discoms was fixed at this level. The bidders were instead required to bid for the capital subsidy required to make this tariff acceptable to them. Two similar tenders were issued in 2019 with tariffs fixed at US¢ 4.67/kWh.
Source: Authors' compilation.

national grid. The scheme has helped to scale up procurement immensely, and tariffs have lowered in response to the large tenders and project sizes. With SECI coordinating the procurement process as both the lead agency and intermediary off-taker, competition between developers to build project

Table 6.16 Onshore wind tenders issued by SECI, October 2016–June 2019

Tender issued	Project location	Tendered capacity (GW)	Subscription (x)	Lowest tariff bid (US¢/kWh)
October 2016	Pan India (ISTS)	1,000	2.6	4.61
June 2017	Pan India (ISTS)	1,000	2.9	3.52
December 2017	Pan India (ISTS)	2,000	1.9	3.25
February 2018	Pan India (ISTS)	2,000	1.5	3.35
June 2018	Pan India (ISTS)	1,200	1.8	3.68
December 2018	Pan India (ISTS)	1,200	1.9	3.76
February 2019	Pan India (ISTS)	1,200	0.5	3.72
June 2019	Pan India (ISTS)	1,800	0.3	3.77

Source: Authors' compilation.

pipelines has been intense, and investment capital has flowed in from around the world. However, the scheme has also exacerbated challenges linked to the availability of land and transmission infrastructure in states where these projects are located.

6.5.1 Tariff issues

While bid tariff levels are somewhat volatile, the general trend has been downwards. Between January 2017 and June 2020, the lowest solar and wind tariffs declined by 4.8% and 18.2%, respectively. The auctions have helped to make RE the cheapest source of power generation. While the average cost of power procurement by discoms increased from US¢ 5.49/kWh in 2015/2016 to US¢ 6.31/kWh in 2018/2019, the price of RE has fallen from US¢ 5.91/kWh in 2015 to US¢ 3.15/kWh in 2020.

The falling cost has attracted increasing demand from discoms but also created expectations that tariffs will remain low or continue to fall indefinitely. Arbitrary and unreasonably low ceiling tariffs have derailed many tenders. Several auctions have also been cancelled after tariffs failed to meet discoms' expectations, even though developers explained that their project costs increased because of factors such as poor site conditions, connectivity challenges, and tax increases.

Falling tariffs have also created resentment among some of the early procurers of renewable power. The MNRE guidelines allow procurers to sign PPAs of 25 years or more. In practice, most PPAs are limited to 25 years. In rare cases, longer durations are considered as a means of reducing bid tariffs of projects with high capital costs.[16] However, the states of Gujarat, Andhra Pradesh, and Punjab, which established RE installations some years ago, have found themselves locked into agreements with relatively high tariff rates and have threatened to renegotiate these PPAs. Affected developers have approached the regulators and the courts for protection against these threats. Following intervention from the central government, the state of Andhra Pradesh agreed to honour the PPA tariff. In Gujarat, the state regulator sided with the developers, and no changes were made to the PPAs. However, Gujarat has since cancelled several tenders after bidders refused to reduce tariffs in the financial bidding rounds. The state of Punjab also recently asked operational projects to reduce tariffs, citing revenue loss linked to reductions in power demand caused by the COVID-19 pandemic.

6.5.2 Competition levels

As shown in Tables 6.15 and 6.16, most tenders were heavily oversubscribed in the period 2015–2018. Competition has since waned somewhat, with several large tenders in 2019 and 2020 being undersubscribed. Of the 32 solar tenders awarded between August 2015 and March 2020, 22 were oversubscribed, 4 were fully subscribed, and 6 were undersubscribed. Of the 8 wind tenders awarded by SECI since October 2016, 6 were oversubscribed and 2 were undersubscribed.

In the face of the multiple challenges involved in RE tenders, most small and mid-sized RE developers have left the tender market. Factors contributing to their exit include falling returns, delays in project commissioning, tighter working-capital conditions (caused by delays in the processing of 'change-in-law' claims linked to higher taxes and duties), decreasing availability of debt financing, delayed payments from discoms, aggressive ceiling tariffs, and increases in minimum project size.

6.5.3 Tender design and issuance

Weakening power-demand growth and poor enforcement of RPOs mean that discoms are increasingly reluctant to procure additional renewable power plants. Simultaneously, many discoms are complaining about the variability of renewable power output and the higher transmission and balancing

[16] For example, the proposed PPA for a 7.5 GW solar project in the Ladakh region is for 35 years; in this case, the project's capital costs are higher because integrated transmission works are included.

costs that this creates. Furthermore, the inability of RE generation to meet the evening peak load forces discoms to buy expensive power from the exchanges. Despite these problems, SECI is under pressure to meet political targets and has therefore pushed through new tenders. This has created a misalignment between RfPs and demand from discoms, leaving several tenders in limbo.

The MNRE and SECI have had to find ways to meet peak demand and provide round-the-clock power. One solution has been to blend RE with energy storage and thermal power installations. Hybrid projects that harvest both solar and wind resources are also gaining popularity because they have the potential to deliver a more even supply of power.

6.5.4 Shifts in the businesses involved

Just 10 RE developers accounted for 68% (28.4 GW) of the solar and wind power capacity awarded in India between 2015 and 2020 (see Table 6.17). Of this, the top two companies, Renew Power and SB Energy, accounted for 26% of awarded capacity. Both companies are backed by foreign investors and are therefore equipped to raise capital for large projects. The average bid sizes submitted by Renew Power (212 MW) and SB Energy (265 MW) are substantially larger than those submitted by other project developers, which average out at 133 MW.

Table 6.17 Concentration of stand-alone solar and wind power capacity awards, India, August 2015–March 2020

Developer	Awarded capacity (MW)	Share of awarded capacity (%)
Renew Power	3,815	13
SB Energy	3,704	13
Adani Green Energy	2,410	8
Acme Cleantech	2,085	7
NTPC	1,952	7
Azure Power	1,860	7
Hero Future Energies	1,000	4
Eden Renewables	900	3
Ayana Renewable	850	3
Sembcorp	800	3

Source: Authors' compilation.

Although many smaller developers no longer participate in RE auctions, new developers continue to enter the market. Leading international investors have committed large amounts of equity capital to India's RE sector. In 2019 alone, these included pension fund managers (CDPQ and CPP Investment Board); sovereign wealth funds (Abu Dhabi Investment Authority (ADIA), GIC, Temasek, Masdar, the CDC Group, the Department for International Development (DFID), Norfund); oil and gas companies (Total, Shell, Petronas); energy utility companies (Engie, EDF Energy, JERA, Sembcorp, CLP, Enel, Fortum); and private equity funds (Actis, Global Infrastructure Partners, and the Everstone Group). Several new development platforms have been created and the overall investment mood remains buoyant.

6.5.5 Bidding and commissioning timelines

As noted, several uncertainties surround tender and project commissioning timelines. Thus, by early 2020, only one-quarter of the solar power capacity awarded by SECI since August 2015 had been commissioned. Indications are that construction delays are even more serious for wind projects. In some instances, discoms are not coming forward to implement power sale agreements even though auctions have been completed and letters of award sent out. Rough estimates, based on informal communications, are that up to 15,000 MW of RE generation is affected by these issues.

The lack of power demand from discoms, combined with SECI's constant tinkering with project sizes, location, technology mix in auction designs, uncertainties about import duties, and growing site-related challenges, mean that project construction is generally delayed. So far, the government has granted ad hoc extensions to developers, and contractual penalties have seldom, if ever, been enforced.

6.6 Lessons learned from India's renewable energy auctions

6.6.1 Auction implementation

The formulation of CBGs has been immensely helpful in ensuring transparency and predictability of the programme. Backed by strong central government support and ambitious targets, India's RE programme has attracted substantial investment.

The central government's ongoing engagement with off-takers and project developers—to update and modify rules in ways that address market concerns and playing the role of mediator and arbiter—has been invaluable. Although some organizations have expressed concerns about SECI's organizational capability and staffing levels, the auctions have run reasonably smoothly so far. This is especially notable given the size of the programme and the amount of interaction required with state and central governments, including the departments of finance, transmission, industry, labour, and the environment.

Other important lessons learned so far can be summed up in three main points.

- SECI plays a crucial role. SECI's role as intermediary off-taker has shielded project developers from direct discom risk and has been instrumental in addressing off-taker concerns. This is evident in the fact that participation levels in SECI tenders are higher than in tenders issued by discoms. SECI's involvement as a bankable counterpart is critical in attracting bidders.
- More planning and coordination would solve a raft of problems. Tender issuers, transmission network developers, regulators, and off-takers tend to plan in separate silos. This creates delays in the construction of transmission networks, the identification of off-takers, the identification and acquisition of suitable sites, and tariff adoption by regulators. Measures taken to mitigate these challenges include the development of solar parks and the involvement of tender-issuing agencies in transmission planning. Provisions for compensation to developers where power evacuation systems are delayed have also been strengthened. However, integrated planning remains necessary to address the uncertainties related to project implementation.
- Detailed schedules and further safeguards would benefit the sector. So far, neither SECI nor any other tender-issuing agencies have published tender schedules. It seems that this is at least partly designed to maintain high levels of competition between developers. What it means is that developers have little time for strategic planning; instead, they are forced to participate in bid processes that occur at ad hoc and erratic intervals. Many developers bid aggressively, for fear of missing out, but then fail to commission projects on time and/or later seek to cancel PPAs. The sector as a whole would benefit if tender agencies provided basic information about tender schedules and put stronger safeguards in place against awards being made on unrealistic bids. Possible safeguards could

include higher bid bonds as well as independent evaluations of proposed tariffs and project viability.

6.6.2 Auction design

The Indian government's view is that renewable power is a mature and relatively simple technology. For this reason, very low technical and financial qualification criteria were set for developers. Initially, this attracted a large number of bidders and created high levels of competition with aggressive tariffs proposals. As the sector matured and project sizes increased, smaller developers have tended to exit the auction programmes, leaving only large and well-funded developers to bid.

The tendering schedule has been dictated more by the government's ambitious targets for the sector than by power demand. Thus, while power demand has slowed, and discoms are reluctant to sign new PPAs because they have excess supply, SECI and other government agencies have continued to issue large new tenders. Many projects have been cancelled or delayed as off-takers fail to sign PPAs and regulators refuse to approve tariffs. These problems could be prevented if tendering agencies were obliged to obtain reliable information about power demand in specific states before issuing new tenders.

The CBGs provide considerable flexibility on certain key bidding parameters, including technical and financial qualification criteria, ceiling tariffs, and project size. They also make provision for legislative changes. Frequent and ad hoc changes to these parameters have created fluidity in tender schedules and given developers the latitude to lobby SECI to make changes in their favour. The resulting uncertainties that now prevail must be addressed; that is, bidding parameters must be set consistently and ad hoc changes should no longer be allowed.

6.7 Conclusion: The need to match ambition with planning

India was among the first countries in the world to launch an RE auction programme in 2010. The programme is also among the world's largest, and its capacity targets are ambitious. So far, the auction programme has worked well; combined wind and solar power capacity grew from 18.4 GW in March 2012 to 72.2 GW in March 2020.

India's auction programme has been designed to achieve two primary objectives—to reduce the cost of renewable power and to attract private capital to the sector. Based on these two parameters, the programme has been successful. Aggressive bidding has led to a sharp decline in tariffs, while transparent bidding rules, above-board processes (important in a country prone to corruption), and the scale of the programme have attracted leading players from around the world.

The programme has evolved significantly as a result of issues facing developers and off-takers as well as changes in the technologies. As Figure 6.14 shows, sectoral growth has been uneven, indicating the impact of various challenges related to project implementation.

At the heart of many of these challenges is the tension between the ambitions of central government and realities at state level. India's central government adopted an ambitious renewable capacity target and backed it up with a slew of policy measures, but the state governments and discoms have to focus on actual power demand and the relative costs of different generation options. As a result, enthusiasm for RE among state authorities is more muted. Many of the critical decisions and regulatory processes, including the terms of PPAs, site availability, and RE park development, are determined at state level. Tensions between the priorities of central and state governments are creating significant policy conflicts and uncertainty on the ground.

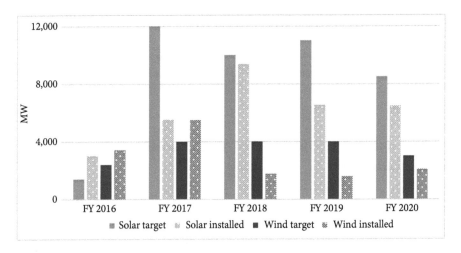

Figure 6.14 Solar and wind capacity additions in India, 2016–2020
Source: Authors' compilation.

At the same time, SECI has been instrumental in dealing with many of the off-taker concerns expressed by private-sector developers. Thus, although many states run their own auctions, developers prefer SECI-run auctions, and this has substantially increased the role that SECI and other central government agencies play in RE auctions.

The other notable feature of the auction programme and the CBGs is their fluidity. The government has formally amended the CBGs several times to address challenges in project execution and respond to changing market conditions. In addition, various other parameters have been altered in seemingly ad hoc and experimental ways. Changes in manufacturing policies and the structure of import duties and tax rates, for example, combined with shifts in financial markets due to macroeconomic weakness, have adversely affected the sector.

Consequently, tender and project implementation schedules have been delayed. Many tenders have been cancelled outright because of low subscription rates, and some projects have been abandoned after auctions either because the discoms did not come forward to sign PPAs or because developers found that projects were unviable. The government's decision to issue tenders without being certain of demand and its unwillingness to evaluate project viability as outlined in bid proposals have been major failures. To improve RE project execution and operation, integrated planning across concerned agencies must be undertaken.

Finally, the programme's strong focus on tariff reductions has led to two major changes in tender design. The first is that tender and project sizes increased over time because the economies of scale achievable by larger projects are believed to result in lower tariffs. The second is that more projects are being located in the two or three states where RE resources are good, the land is cheaper/more available, and cost-efficient connections to the national grid are achievable. The high concentration of capacity in particular states has exacerbated some of the execution challenges related to the availability of land, grid connections, water, and other resources necessary for project construction and operation. It can be argued that the promotion of smaller projects across the country would be beneficial for grid resilience and job growth while reducing transmission losses.

To sum up, India's RE auction programme has had mixed success. The programme has resulted in massive RE capacity additions at very low costs. However, its implementation has also created stress in the sector, especially for smaller companies, and highlighted tensions between the state and central governments' various priorities. For example, the government has been prevented from encouraging domestic manufacturing to keep import tariffs low and secure higher tax revenues. Perhaps, for this reason, private investors across the value chain cite instability in the policy framework as one of the key challenges facing the sector.

6.8 References

Aggarwal, M. (2017). 'Government Eases Environmental Clearance Rules for Solar Power Projects, Parks'. *Mint*, 23 August, https://www.livemint.com/Politics/QW4cJ9yjhmvUtOZCPyOt3J/Govt-eases-environment-clearance-rules-for-solar-projects.html (accessed 21 April 2023).

Bridge to India (2015). 'Will Land Be the Main Hurdle for India's Solar Dreams?' Blogpost, 22 April, https://bridgetoindia.com/will-land-be-the-main-hurdle-for-indias-solar-dreams (accessed 21 April 2023).

Bridge to India (2018). 'ISTS Tenders Face Long Delays'. Blogpost, 7 May, https://bridgetoindia.com/ists-tenders-face-long-delays (accessed 21 April 2023).

Bridge to India (2019). 'Project Execution Slowdown to Continue'. Blogpost, 1 October, https://bridgetoindia.com/project-execution-slowdown-to-continue (accessed 21 April 2023).

Bridge to India (2020a). 'Waiving Bank Guarantees Not Desirable'. Blogpost, 20 March, https://bridgetoindia.com/waiving-bank-guarantees-not-desirable (accessed 21 April 2023).

CEA (Central Electricity Authority) (2020a). 'Executive Summary of Power Sector: March 2020', http://www.cea.nic.in/reports/monthly/executivesummary/2020/exe_summary-03.pdf (accessed 21 April 2023).

CEA (2020b). 'Generation Reports', http://www.cea.nic.in/monthlygeneration.html (accessed 21 April 2023).

CENFA (Centre for Financial Accountability) (2019). 'Coal vs Renewables: Financial Analysis, India 2018', https://www.cenfa.org/wp-content/uploads/2019/08/India-2018-Coal-vs-Renewables-Finance-Analysis.pdf (accessed 21 April 2023).

CERC (Central Electricity Regulatory Commission) (2019). 'Petition No. 23/MP/2019'. 9 August, http://www.cercind.gov.in/2019/orders/23_MP_2019.pdf (accessed 21 April 2023).

Chandrasekaran, K. (2018). 'SECI Increases Ceiling Price for Two Tenders to Woo Developers'. *Economic Times*, 12 November, https://economictimes.indiatimes.com/industry/energy/power/seci-increases-ceiling-price-for-two-tenders-to-woo-developers/articleshow/66583453.cms (accessed 21 April 2023).

Chatterjee, A. (2020). 'Govt Removes Tariff Caps for Solar, Wind Power Auctions'. *Financial Express*, 7 March, https://www.financialexpress.com/economy/govt-removes-tariff-caps-for-solar-wind-power-auctions/1891366 (accessed 21 April 2023).

Government of India (2008). 'National Action Plan on Climate Change', https://static. pib.gov.in/WriteReadData/specificdocs/documents/2021/dec/doc202112101.pdf

Hochberg, M., and Poudineh, R. (2018). 'Renewable Auction Design in Theory and Practice: Lessons from the Experiences of Brazil and Mexico'. Oxford Institute for Energy Studies, https://www.oxfordenergy.org/publications/renewable-auction-design-theory-practice-lessons-experiences-brazil-mexico (accessed 21 April 2023).

ICRA Ltd. (2020). 'Solar Energy Corporation of India Ltd: Ratings Reaffirmed, Outlook Revised to Stable; Rated Amount Enhanced'. 29 January, https://www.icra.in/Rationale/ShowRationaleReport/?Id=91959 (accessed 21 April 2023).

IMF (International Monetary Fund) (2019). 'India: 2019 Article IV Consultation'. Press release, staff report, staff statement, and statement by the executive director for India, 23 December, https://www.imf.org/en/Publications/CR/Issues/2019/12/23/India-2019-Article-IV-Consultation-Press-Release-Staff-Report-Staff-Statement-and-Statement-48909 (accessed 21 April 2023).

Kumar, A., and Thapar, S. (2017). 'Addressing Land Issues for Utility-Scale Renewable Energy Deployment in India'. December, https://shaktifoundation.in/wp-content/uploads/2018/01/Study-Report-Addressing-Land-Issues-for-Utility-Scale-Renewable-Energy-Deployment-in-India.pdf (accessed 21 April 2023).

Ministry of Commerce and Industry (2020). 'Final Findings of Review Investigation for Continued Imposition of Safeguard Duty on Imports of "Solar Cells, Whether or Not Assembled in Modules or Panels" into India: Proceedings under the Customs Tariff Act, 1975 and the Custom Tariff'. Directorate General of Trade Remedies, 18 July, https://www.eqmagpro.com/final-findings-of-review-investigation-for-continued-imposition-of-safeguard-duty-on-imports-of-solar-cells-whether-or-not-assembled-in-modules-or-panels-into-india/

Ministry of Environment, Forest and Climate Change (2016). 'Environment Ministry Releases New Categorisation of Industries'. Press release, 5 March, https://pib.gov.in/newsite/printrelease.aspx?relid=137373 (accessed 21 April 2023).

MNRE (Ministry of New and Renewable Energy) (n.d.). 'Solar PV Manufacturing', https://mnre.gov.in/solar/manufacturers-and-quality-control (accessed 2 October 2020).

MNRE (2017). 'Administrative Sanction for Implementation of Scheme for Enhancement of Capacity from 20,000 MW to 40,000 MW for "Development of Solar Parks and Ultra Mega Solar Power Projects'. 21 March, https://www.eqmagpro.com/administrative-sanction-for-implementation-of-the-scheme-for-enhancement-of-capcity-from-20000-mw-to-40000-mw-for-development-of-solar-parks-and-ultra-mega-solar-power-projects/(accessed 21 April 2023).

MNRE (2018). 'Modifications in Scheme for Development of Solar Parks and Ultra Mega Solar Power Projects'. 18 September, https://mnre.gov.in/img/documents/uploads/file_f-1592551752084.pdf (accessed 21 April 2023).

MNRE (2019). 'Amendments to the Guidelines for Tariff-Based Competitive Bidding Process for Procurement of Power from Grid Connected Solar PV Power Projects'. 22 October, http://www.indiaenvironmentportal.org.in/content/474004/amendment-to-the-guidelines-for-tariff-based-competitive-bidding-process-for-procurement-of-power-from-grid-connected-re-power-projects/ (accessed 21 April 2023).

MoP (Ministry of Power) (2017). 'Guidelines for Tariff-Based Competitive Bidding Process for Power Procurement from Grid-Connected Wind Power Projects'. 8 December, http://164.100.94.214/sites/default/files/schemes/guideline-wind.pdf (accessed 21 April 2023).

MoP (2019a). 'Amendment to the Guidelines for Tariff-Based Competitive Bidding Process for Power Procurement from Grid-Connected Wind Power Projects'. 16 July, https://www.mercomindia.com/mnre-hybrid-bidding-guidelines-amends (accessed 21 April 2023).

MoP (2019b). 'Second Amendment to Guidelines for Tariff-Based Competitive Bidding Process for Procurement of Power from Grid Connected Solar PV Power Projects'. 3 August, https://indiasolarnavigator.com/public/tender_uploads/utility_policy-5e1432de29928.pdf (accessed 21 April 2023).

Pawar, M. (2014). 'Environmental and Social Clearances for Renewable Energy Projects in India'. *Energetica India*, January–February, 4–6.

Power Finance Corporation (n.d.). 'Performance Report of State Power Utilities', https://www.pfcindia.com/Home/VS/29 (accessed 21 April 2023).

PTI (Press Trust of India) (2019). 'Power Discoms Suffered Losses Worth Rs 27,000 Crore in 2018–19: R.K. Singh'. *Business Today*, 2 October, https://www.businesstoday.in/current/economy-politics/power-discoms-suffered-losses-worth-rs-27000-crore-in-2018-19-rk-singh/story/392794.html (accessed 21 April 2023).

PTI (2020). 'Discoms' Outstanding Dec Dues to Power Gencos Up Nearly 50% to Rs 88 177 Cr'. *Business Standard*, 17 February, https://www.business-standard.com/article/pti-stories/discoms-outstanding-dues-to-power-gencos-rise-nearly-50-pc-to-rs-88-177-cr-in-dec-120021600245_1.html (accessed 21 April 2023).

Ramesh, M. (2019). 'Renewable Energy Ministry Rules Out Removal of Tariff Caps'. *Business Line*, 13 November, https://www.thehindubusinessline.com/news/renewable-energy-ministry-rules-out-removal-of-tariff-caps/article29963990.ece# (accessed 21 April 2023).

RBI (Reserve Bank of India) (2020). 'Database on Indian Economy'. 16 May, https://dbie.rbi.org.in/DBIE/dbie.rbi?site=home (accessed 21 April 2023).

SECI (Solar Energy Corporation of India) (2019). Annual *Report* 2018–19 (Gurugram: SECI).

SECI (2020). 'Request for Selection (RfS) Document for Setting Up of 1200 MW ISTS-connected Wind–Solar Hybrid Projects: Tranche-III'. 14 January, https://seci.co.in/web-data/docs/tenders/RfS_ISTS%20Wind-Solar%20Hybrid%20Power%20Developers_1200MW%20T-III_final%20upload.pdf (accessed 21 April 2023).

Seetharaman G., and Chandrasekaran, K. (2019). 'Government's Solar Park Push Is Running into Land Acquisition and Transmission Challenges'. *Economic Times*, 28 April, https://economictimes.indiatimes.com/industry/energy/power/governments-solar-park-push-is-running-into-land-acquisition-and-transmission-challenges/articleshow/69074597.cms (accessed 21 April 2023).

World Bank. (2018a). 'GDP (Current US$): India', https://data.worldbank.org/indicator/NY.GDP.MKTP.CD?locations=IN&most_recent_value_desc=true (accessed 21 April 2023).

World Bank. (2018b). 'Population, Total: India', https://data.worldbank.org/indicator/SP.POP.TOTL?end=2018&locations=IN&start=2009&view=chart (accessed 21 April 2023).

7

South Africa

A Regional Trailblazer Seeking Transformation

Wikus Kruger, Anton Eberhard, Anna V. Filipova, and Raine Naude

7.1 Introduction: The timely genesis of a transformative auction programme

The Department of Energy (DoE) established the South African Independent Power Producer Procurement Programme (IPPPP) in late 2010 to diversify electricity generation and urgently address the power shortages that had been affecting the country since 2008. The programme was also, to a large extent, a mechanism for demonstrating South Africa's political commitment to introducing renewable energy at the fifteenth UN Climate Change Conference (COP 15), when President Zuma voluntarily committed to reducing the country's carbon emissions by 42% by 2025, and at COP 17, which was hosted in Durban.

The Renewable Energy Independent Power Producer Procurement Programme (REI4P) and the Small Projects Independent Power Producer Procurement Programme (SP–I4P), subsets of the IPPPP, were specifically set up to procure renewable energy capacity from the private sector. The programmes replaced the Renewable Energy Feed-in Tariff (REFiT) mechanism, previously developed by the National Electricity Regulator of South Africa (NERSA) after an independent legal assessment concluded that a feed-in tariff violated South Africa's procurement regulations.

As competition increased over successive bidding rounds, project costs have fallen dramatically. On average, this has reduced by more than 50% for wind projects and 70% for solar PV projects between 2011 and 2015. The latest round of procurement saw projects secured at prices below Eskom's average cost of supply. These projects have been instrumental in enhancing energy security and diversifying the country's energy mix.

REI4P has had significant positive economic and environmental impacts. The programme attracted private-sector investments to the value of US$

Wikus Kruger, Anton Eberhard, Anna V. Filipova, and Raine Naude, *South Africa*. In: *Renewable Energy Auctions: Lessons from the Global South*. Edited by: Anton Eberhard and Wikus Kruger, Oxford University Press. © Oxford University Press (2023).
DOI: 10.1093/oso/9780192871701.003.0007

14,27[1] billion, 20% of which is foreign investment. This equates to more investment in independent power producers (IPPs) than the rest of sub-Saharan Africa has managed to attract as a whole over the past two decades. The programme has also made economic development contributions, with the creation of 42,374 job years for South African citizens and economic and enterprise development contributions amounting to US$ 98.1 million by the end of June 2019. It is estimated that the programme has also contributed to South Africa's climate change mitigation and adaptation objectives by reducing carbon emissions by 38.8 metric tons and achieving water savings of 45.8 million kilolitres since its inception (DoE, 2019b).

Despite its achievements, REI4P has faced several implementation challenges in recent years. The influence of vested interests, threatened by the programme's success, delayed the implementation of later rounds of the programme and has limited the scope of its impacts (Montmasson-Clair and das Nair, 2017). The programme has specifically experienced significant (three plus years') delays in the signing of the key off-taker contracts (power purchase agreements) for projects awarded in 2015 under bid window 4. Further project awards have either been cancelled, in the case of the expedited REI4P bid window, or ignored, as in the case of SP–I4P. New rounds of procurement were implemented in 2021, including for a controversial 'Risk Mitigation IPP procurement programme', but none of these projects have reached financial close, despite the country facing electricity blackouts (load shedding) on an increasingly frequent basis. Investor confidence has been further eroded by prolonged policy uncertainty and the deterioration of Eskom's financial and operational status.

This hiatus in procurement and investment is all the more concerning when one considers what has been lost. Several countries in sub-Saharan Africa have now procured renewable energy projects at prices below those achieved in REI4P, largely thanks to the procurement model pioneered in South Africa. The capacities developed to service REI4P in South Africa—whether project developers, transaction advisers, or a host of other skilled blue-collar and white-collar professionals—have now been forced to leave South Africa or the industry, representing a real loss of skills and knowledge for the country. South Africa has also squandered investors' and lenders' growing comfort with the programme that could have opened the door to less onerous and less costly risk-mitigation requirements. And many of the local manufacturing and job creation ambitions driving the programme have ground to a halt as factories and project developers had to close their doors or lay off workers.

---

[1] Based on a USD/ZAR exchange rate of 1:14.7.

Recent belated progress in electricity system planning has unfortunately not translated into procurement certainty. In October 2019, the Department of Mineral Resources and Energy (DMRE, previously known as the DoE) approved and published the first update of the Integrated Resource Plan (IRP) since 2010—despite policy requiring an update every two years. While the IRP 2019 states that South Africa urgently needs to procure generation capacity, ministerial determinations for capacity, which signify the start of a new procurement process and, most importantly, contribute to investor certainty, were only issued in 2020. This is all the more concerning considering that the country experienced its worst period of rolling electricity blackouts (load shedding) ever in late 2019, with power system stability a daily concern.

Contributing to this sense of uncertainty are the important but complex changes underway in the country's power sector. South Africa has not been exempt from the socio-technical changes occurring in energy sectors globally, where a rapid transition towards low-carbon, decentralized electricity markets is underpinned by the falling costs of renewable energy technologies. This has important implications—many of which are still unclear—for a country built on a coal-based power system, both at the national and local level. In addition, Eskom's ongoing financial and operational crisis has triggered a process of reforming the current organizational structure of the power sector. While this is a welcome and much-needed development, the pace of reforms has been slow and the process has met with fierce opposition by many in the industry.

Despite its current challenges, South Africa has demonstrated that it is possible to introduce renewable energy IPPs at scale in a highly centralized, vertically integrated power sector (IRENA, 2018). It has also shown that rapid, low-cost generation capacity expansion can be achieved in the African context, while also contributing to socio-economic objectives. As seen from REI4P outcomes to date, these competitive tender processes are able to secure a pipeline of high-quality projects within a short time, while rigorous compliance requirements ensure transparency and minimize opportunities for rent-seeking.

This chapter details the design features and implementation structures of REI4P and SP–I4P and describes how these have contributed to their outcomes. It also delves into the current policy uncertainty and implementation challenges in order to consider how these affect the future design and sustainability of the programmes. This chapter begins by outlining the political and socio-economic context surrounding South Africa's electricity sector (section 7.2) and then describes the two key renewable energy procurement programmes and their underlying qualification and evaluation criteria and processes (section 7.3). Section 7.4 discusses the key actors and stakeholders involved in the governance and implementation of REI4P and SP–I4P, whilst section 7.5 discusses the key sources of project funding and mechanisms for risk mitigation. In section 7.6, the current risks and opportunities for the future of the two programmes is outlined; and, finally, section 7.7 draws on lessons from both the successes and challenges of REI4P and SP–I4P.

7.2 South Africa's power sector

With a gross domestic product (GDP) of US$ 366 billion in 2018, South Africa is the second-largest economy in Africa and is classified as an upper-middle-income economy (Trading Economics, 2019). Economic growth has been meagre in recent years. GDP grew by 1.3% in 2017 and 0.8% in 2018 and has failed to keep up with population growth. Finance, real estate, and business services are the largest contributors to GDP (22.4%), followed by general government services (16.7%). The most energy-intensive economic sectors are industry and transport at 36% and 27% of total energy demand. respectively. Within the industrial sector, the most energy-intensive activities are connected to iron and steel processing (19% of total demand), mining and quarrying (16%), and chemicals and petrochemicals processing (12%). Based on global rankings, South Africa is the fourteenth largest emitter of green-house gases in the world (Carbon Brief, 2018), primarily due to its reliance on coal for electricity generation.

South Africa faces the triple challenges of unemployment, poverty, and inequality. Official unemployment reached 29% in the second quarter of 2019, one of the highest levels in the world (StatsSA, 2019b). Based on South Africa's lower-bound poverty line, 40% of South Africans were categorized as poor in 2015, an increase from 36.4% in 2011 (StatsSA, 2017). Inequality, measured by the GINI coefficient, stood at 0.68 in 2015 (StatsSA, 2017). Sluggish economic growth, high unemployment rates, decreased investment, low commodity prices, and policy uncertainty are just some of the factors that contribute to these continued trends.

The South African power sector is dominated by the vertically integrated, state-owned, national power utility—Eskom—controlling the generation, transmission, and much of the distribution of electricity. Since 2011, privately owned IPPs have been able to enter the market but produce less than 5% of the country's electricity. Eskom supplies electricity directly to some of the largest electricity consumers in industry and mining while also supplying medium-voltage electricity to municipal distributors (Figure 7.1). The electricity distribution network is shared between Eskom (58%) and

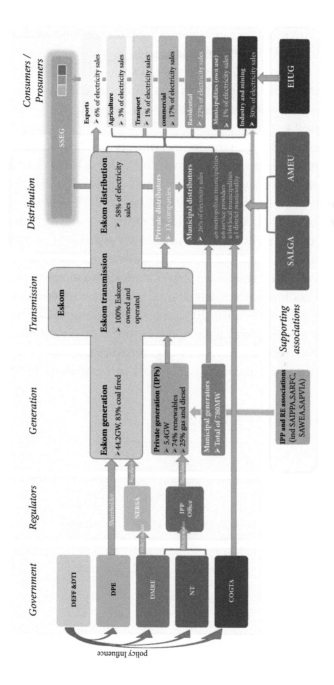

Figure 7.1 Structure of the South African electricity sector and key sector entities
Source: OneWorld.

municipal distributors (42%) (NERSA, 2012; Eskom, 2019a). There are 188 distributors of electricity in South Africa, licensed according to the Electricity Regulatory Act (ERA), including 6 metropolitan municipalities, 2 metropolitan electricity service providers (City Power in Johannesburg and Centlec in Buffalo City), 164 local municipalities, 1 district municipality (uMkhanyakude), 13 private distributors, and Eskom (StatsSA, 2016).

Eskom's severe structural, operational, and financial crises have resulted from a process of deterioration since 2007, as measured by key indicators presented in Table 7.1.

Electricity sales have been on the decline, while revenue has stagnated and operational costs (employee and coal costs) have skyrocketed. Despite the fact that generation capacity has increased only slightly by 3.5%, Eskom's debt has risen by 988% to reach US$ 30.6 billion[2] in 2019 (Eskom, 2019a). Eskom has accumulated unsustainable levels of debt—mainly in pursuit of building the Medupi and Kusile mega coal power stations—but only generates enough cash to cover 47% of its debt obligations. As South Africa's biggest state-owned enterprise (SOE), Eskom represents a massive risk to the fiscus and the economy. Eskom's operational crisis has also led to ongoing load shedding in 2018, 2019, 2020, 2021, and 2022, with significant negative consequences for South Africa's economic growth and development.

Eskom is also still reeling from a serious governance crisis based on facilitated rent-seeking and corruption (Godinho and Hermanus, 2018). This

Table 7.1 Eskom key indicators: 2007 vs 2019

Indicator	2007	2017	2019	Change 2007–2019
Generation capacity (GW)	42.7	44.1	44.2	3.5%
Employee costs (billion Rand)	9.5	33.2	33.3	250.5%
Employees (number of people)	32,674	47,658	46,665	42.8%
Coal costs (billion Rand)	10	50.3	58.5	485%
Coal purchases (million tonnes)	1,174	1,203	118	0.8%
Electricity sales (GWh)	218,120	214,121	208,319	−4.5%
Revenue (billion Rand)	39.4	177.1	177	356.6%
Debt (billion Rand)	40.5	355.3	440.6	987.9%
Debt service cover	–	–	0.47	–
Average tariff (Rc/kWh)	18.38	83.6	98.01	433.4%[a]

Note: [a] Nominal increase.
Source: Burkhardt and Cohen (2019); Eskom (2019a, b).

[2] At current exchange rate of US$ 1:ZAR 14.7 equivalent to about ZAR 450 billion.

has hollowed out skills at all levels, which will take years to rebuild and which has also negatively affected its ability to secure funding (Eskom, 2019a).

Eskom's poor financial and operational health, coupled with its position as single off-taker of IPP power, exposed private-sector investors to increasing off-taker (payment) risk. Despite its deep crisis, Eskom, as the dominant entity in the electricity sector, is considered too big to be allowed to fail, and it therefore received (and continues to receive) significant government support, including multiple financial bail outs (Hartley and Mills, 2019; Paton, 2019). At the same time, its near-monopoly status undermined interventions to restore its financial health and allowed it to prevent access by private-sector players to the national transmission network.

President Ramaphosa's Eskom Sustainability Task Team formulated a restructuring proposal, some of which was taken forward by the Department of Public Enterprises (DPE) in the Roadmap for Eskom in a Reformed Electricity Supply Industry (DPE, 2019). The roadmap outlined specific steps and timelines for restructuring Eskom, including the incremental process of separating Eskom into three state-owned subsidiaries: Generation, Transmission, and Distribution. The first step outlined by the document is the creation of a fully Eskom-owned transmission subsidiary, responsible for purchasing, system operation, and grid management. The roadmap set timelines for the functional separation of a transmission subsidiary to be completed by March 2020, while the legal separation of the Generation, Transmission, and Distribution entities was to be completed by 2020/2021. By the first quarter of 2022, none of these deadlines had been met.

The emergence of distributed generation, or small-scale embedded generation (SSEG), is further disrupting and changing the landscape of the power sector. SSEG occurs at both the consumption and the distribution level of the value chain as it is implemented both by municipalities and by electricity consumers (creating what is known as prosumers or consumers who also produce electricity). SSEG allows for decentralized energy generation, thus blurring the traditional lines between the roles of distribution, generation, and consumption along the value chain. SSEG allows for additional actors to take on roles previously controlled by Eskom. Unlike large-scale IPP projects, SSEG is less dependent on centralized decision-making. Despite the lack of a clear national-level regulatory framework, SSEG has emerged as a disruptive force for the vertically integrated structure of the South African electric power sector, from the subnational level. There is currently just under 1 gigawatt (GW) of installed SSEG capacity nationally, projected to reach 7.5GW by 2035 (GreenCape, 2019).

Much of the blame for the South African power sector's current state of affairs can be laid at the doors of a handful of strategically important public-sector entities (Table 7.1). Key among these are the Department of Mineral Resources and Energy (DMRE), the DPE, Eskom, and the National Energy Regulator of South Africa (NERSA) (Table 7.2). The ministries, parastatal, and regulator have all been subject to massive instability and lost significant capacity over the past decade, in large part due to the coordinated, deliberate repurposing of South Africa's public sector and, in particular, state-owned enterprises to facilitate rent-seeking and corruption (Godinho and Hermanus, 2018). For example, the Department of Energy (renamed Mineral Resources and Energy in 2019) has had six ministers since 2012, while Eskom has had 13 chief executive officers (CEOs) in the past decade. NERSA has also recently been taken to court by Eskom regarding its regulatory decisions, which effectively wiped out a crucial bail out from the state. The result is a sector stumbling from one crisis to the next, propped up by a few remaining pockets of excellence in the National Treasury and certain sections of Eskom, among others. President Ramaphosa's administration has done much to start reversing this trend, but a massive amount of work remains to be done to change the political economy of the sector and rebuild what was destroyed.

South Africa has developed an unfortunate reputation for being able to develop world-class policy yet struggle to implement the same policies (Kruger, 2012; Trollip and Boulle, 2017). Table 7.3 provides an overview of the legislation and policies that govern South Africa's power sector. It shows that the policy and legislative basis for a more decentralized, renewable energy-based power sector has long been in place—starting with the White Paper on Energy Policy (1998). It nevertheless required an extraordinary set of circumstances (discussed in section 7.3) to realize at least some of these policy objectives. This disconnect between stated intent and action has long plagued the sector and continues to impede progress.

7.2.1 Supply and demand

South Africa's power system (49,2 GW—Figure 7.2) is the biggest in sub-Saharan Africa by some margin, representing about half of the installed capacity of the entire region. Coal dominates, with 37 GW (less than 70% of which is available at any one time), followed by renewable energy with 3.9 GW. Nuclear and hydropower (hydro) contribute around 4% of generation capacity each (DoE, 2019d). There are three main groups of electricity generators: (i) Eskom, which operates 89% of total generation capacity in South

Table 7.2 Key institutions in South Africa's electricity sector

Institution	Key features
National Treasury (NT)	Manages government spending and approves budgets of all government departments. Its powerful influence enabled it to build a strong foundation of political support and buy-in necessary for implementation of the REI4P programme (Morris and Martin, 2015).
The Department of Mineral Resources and Energy (DMRE), changed from Department of Energy (DoE) in 2019	Secures provision of energy and mineral resources to promote socio-economic development. Drafts electricity sector legislation, policies, and plans and oversees the Integrated National Electrification Programme (INEP); sets the Electricity Pricing Policy against which NERSA regulates and sets tariffs; provides oversight of the Central Energy Fund (CEF) and the IPP Office. Develops energy policy and plans (including IEP and IRP). The minister also initiates procurement of new-generation capacity by issuing ministerial determinations and specifying the technologies, capacity, and entities (public vs private) responsible for building new capacity.
Independent Power Producers Office (IPPO)	Designs and runs competitive procurement programmes or auctions for IPPs to contribute to renewable and non-renewable sources of new electricity generation capacity. Set up through an MOU between the DMRE, the NT, and the DBSA.
Department of Public Enterprises (DPE)	Provides oversight of all SOEs and is the sole shareholder of Eskom, with its primary mandate being to ensure Eskom's efficiency and sustainability. It has, from time to time, been less than supportive of competition and the entry of IPPs (Morris and Martin, 2015).
Department of Environment, Forestry and Fisheries (DEFF)	Promotes clean and efficient energy use in South Africa, in line with international climate objectives. Negotiates and determines South Africa's international greenhouse gas mitigation commitments (NDCs).
Department of Trade and Industry (DTI)	Promotes inclusive and equitable economic and industrial development. It plays a small but critical role in the energy sector, including in the design process of REI4P.
Eskom	South Africa's power utility, a parastatal. It is regulated by NERSA and the National Nuclear Regulator and is currently in a deep operational, structural, and financial crisis, unable to service its debt obligations, which exceed US$ 30,6 billion[a] (Eskom, 2019a). The President appointed the Eskom Sustainability Task Team in early 2019 to provide expert support and
National Energy Regulator (NERSA)	Regulates and determines electricity tariffs; grants licences for generation, transmission, and distribution of electricity; establishes and monitors technical supply and service standards.

Continued

Table 7.2 *Continued*

Institution	Key features
Local government/ municipalities	The electricity distribution network is shared between Eskom and municipal distributors, with municipalities distributing 42% of electricity sold (NERSA, 2012; Eskom, 2019a).
	The Constitution of the Republic of South Africa (1996) mandates municipalities to distribute electricity in their areas of jurisdiction, subject to national and provincial legislation and regulation.
South African Development Finance Institutions (DFIs)	The Development Bank of Southern Africa (DBSA) is wholly owned by the South African government; its objective is to enhance sustainable development in the Southern African Development Community (SADC) by driving financial and non-financial investments in the social and economic infrastructure sectors; the DBSA entered into a memorandum of agreement (MOA) with the National Treasury and the DoE to provide funding for the REI4P programme.
	The Industrial Development Corporation (IDC), owned by the South African government, under the supervision of the Economic Development Department, was set up to promote economic growth and industrial development; it played a significant role as a debt financier for REI4P as well as an equity investor, providing support to community trusts and B-BBEE companies to purchase their share of equity.

Note: [a] At current exchange rate of US$ 1:ZAR 14,7 equivalent to about ZAR 450 billion.
Source: Authors' compilation.

Africa; (ii) municipal generators (with about 1%); and (iii) IPPs and private generators (with about 10%), including cogeneration. In kilowatt hour (kWh) terms, IPPs contribute less than 5% of total electricity.

The country's power sector has historically been built on a highly centralized model that prioritized scale and the close alignment of mining and energy interests, resulting in what has been termed the minerals-energy complex (Baker et al., 2014; Baker, 2015). South Africa's coal-fired power stations are clustered in the northeast of the country, close to the coal-mining belt (Figure 7.3). Eskom's newest mega coal power stations, Medupi and Kusile, have experienced multiple delays and disastrous cost overruns (McCann, 2019). The associated debt burden has resulted in steep annual electricity tariff increases and represents the single biggest threat to South Africa's fiscal health. To compound matters, these stations are performing poorly, operating at less than two-thirds of design capacity (DoE, 2019d; McCann, 2019).

Table 7.3 Legislation and policies

Policy	Key features
National Development Plan 2030 (NDP), 2013	Long-term strategic development plan focuses on reducing poverty and inequality by 2030 (NPC, 2011).
Nationally determined contribution to the UNFCCC, 2015	Aligns with objectives of the NDP; outlines South Africa's climate change commitments (targeted GHG emission reductions following a peak, plateau, and decline trajectory).
	Identifies energy efficiency, renewable and nuclear energy, and advanced biofuels as key mechanisms for achieving the country's mitigation objectives (DoE, 2015b). It articulates diversification and transformation of the electricity mix.
Electricity Regulation Act (ERA), 2006	Empowers the Energy Minister to make 'determinations' on how much electricity should be procured and when, by whom, and who should be the buyers. It defines NERSA's powers and functions, including tariff setting, licensing, and technical standards.
Electricity Pricing Policy of 2008	Provides electricity pricing guidelines and a methodology for determining electricity tariffs (Amra, 2013).
White Paper on Energy Policy, 1998	Aimed to increase access to affordable electricity, post-1994, and to improve energy governance, stimulate economic development, and diversify the supply of electricity.
	Two key objectives were to introduce IPPs and to restructure the electricity distribution industry.
Eskom Conversion Act No. 13, 2001	Converted Eskom into a public company in terms of the Companies Act, making government ownership of Eskom explicit, with Eskom no longer able to operate under its own special legislation (Maroga, 2009).
Renewable Energy Policy Paper, 2003	Established a target of 10,000 GWh of renewable energy to be achieved by 2013 (DME, 2003a).
Roadmap for Eskom in a Reformed Electricity Supply Industry, 2019	Published by the DPE in October 2019 and provides a roadmap and institutional arrangements for separating Eskom into three subsidiaries: generation, transmission, and distribution. Provides timelines to complete the unbundling process by 2020/2021 and provides for financial support to Eskom through two fiscal injections over the period.
	Eskom will be allowed to operate and own its own renewable energy capacity.
Integrated Energy Plan (IEP), 2016 and Integrated Resource Plan (IRP)	The IEP is the overall energy plan for the sector, covering liquid fuels (diesel, petrol, paraffin) and electricity and gas, while the IRP provides a detailed plan for future electricity generation options (DoE, 2016b). The IRP provides the legal basis for electricity generation procurement and investments in the electricity sector and establishes the country's energy mix.
	The IRP 2010–2030 set a target of approximately 17,88 MW of new power generation capacity to be derived from renewable energy sources. The IRP is meant to be updated every two years. IRP 2019 is discussed in more detail

Source: Authors' compilation.

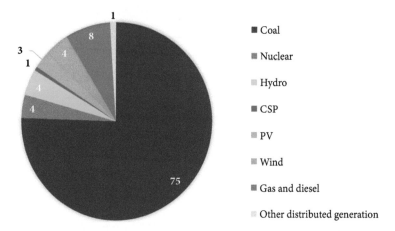

Figure 7.2 Breakdown of South Africa's total generation capacity (%)
Source: Department of the Environment (DoE) (2019b).

South Africa is facing a major transition in the energy system, mainly driven by the economics of increasingly cost-competitive renewable energy technologies and the declining dominance of coal. Global investments in coal power have fallen around 25% between 2015 and 2017 (IEA, 2018), and the transition away from fossil fuels is impacting South Africa as global coal demand weakens. This is already dramatically altering the geography of South Africa's power sector (Figure 7.3) (StatsSA, 2018a; Eskom, 2019a). The transition is also impacting coal-mining towns and workers, resulting in job losses and devastating local economic impacts, and is set to accelerate in coming years. Recent analyses estimate that mitigating these impacts to ensure a 'just transition' will cost South Africa in the region of US$ 400 million—a fraction of the costs of the Medupi and Kusile power stations (Cruywagen et al., 2019).

South Africa has experienced rolling power cuts over the past 12 years, initially caused by insufficient generation capacity to meet demand. More recent rounds of load shedding are mainly attributable to maintenance issues linked to Eskom's ageing power plants and coal supply problems, preventing optimal plant operation and destabilizing electricity supply. As projected by the IRP 2019 and Eskom's medium-term system adequacy reports, there is a high risk of energy shortages as Eskom's energy availability factor (EAF) remains low (60–70%), and non-compliance with the National Environmental Management Act (NEMA) in terms of air pollution from its coal-fired power plants could result in shutdowns of power plants (DoE, 2019d).

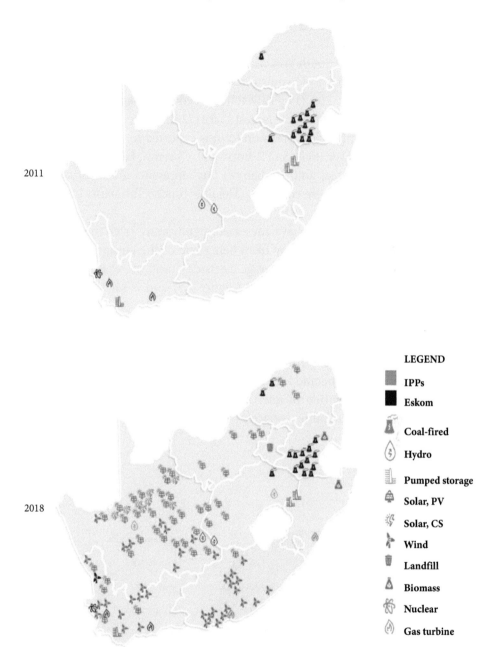

Figure 7.3 Geographic distribution of South Africa's power stations, 2011 vs 2018
Source: Authors' compilation.

7.2.2 Electricity sales and tariffs

Over the past decade, South Africa's electricity sales have been declining due to higher tariffs and a slowdown in economic growth. In 2019, Eskom electricity sales totalled 208,319 gigawatt hours (GWh), compared to around 215,000 GWh in 2009. Of this, the largest share (42%) was sold to municipalities (Figure 7.4). Only a small portion (6%) is exported to members of the Southern African Power Pool (SAPP, Botswana, eSwatini, Lesotho, Mozambique, Namibia, Zambia, and Zimbabwe) but represents a critical source of electricity supply to these countries (Deloitte Touche Tohmatsu Limited, 2017; Eskom, 2019a).

Eskom's electricity tariffs have increased significantly over the past 10 years, shifting South Africa away from being one of the cheapest electricity providers in the world. The average electricity tariff increased by 120% in real terms between 2008 and 2018 (Figure 7.5) and is set to continue. This is partly caused by NERSA failing to award cost-reflective tariffs, which increases Eskom's cost of borrowing—exacerbating the already unsustainable debt burden—and undermines maintenance, leading to steeper tariff hikes as Eskom's costs increase. Price increases amplify the problem of affordability, especially for low-income households already in energy poverty. But it also threatens the retention of intensive energy investors, who are implementing their own generation capacity projects or moving their businesses offshore.

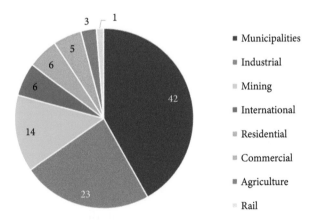

Figure 7.4 Eskom electricity customers (%)
Source: Eskom (2019a).

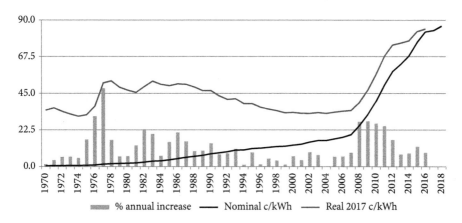

Figure 7.5 Eskom average tariff increases, 1970–2018 (%)

Source: Eskom.

7.2.3 The Integrated Resource Plan (IRP)

The 2019 IRP indicates a need for 39.7 GW of new electricity generation capacity between 2019 and 2030. It identifies the decommissioning of old coal power plants as the opportunity for creating a completely different mix of generation sources to the current one, with a predominant need for modular and flexible capacity to complement the existing inflexible capacity in the period up to 2030 (DoE, 2019d).

The long-term plan envisages the following interventions (DoE, 2019d):

- the addition of 7,2 GW of new coal generation capacity, of which 5.7 GW has already been contracted—combined with the decommissioning of 11 GW of old, coal-fired power stations, this results in an overall reduction in the share of coal generation capacity to 43% of the country's total by 2030;
- the extension of the plant life of Koeberg Nuclear Power Station—the IRP recommends extending this until 2044;
- the addition of 2.5 GW of hydroelectric generation capacity;
- the addition of 22.9 GW of renewable energy generation capacity, including wind (15.8 GW), solar photovoltaic (PV) (6.8 GW), and concentrated solar power (CSP) (300 megawatts (MW)). Out of this, 10.8% has already been contracted, while commissioning the remaining 20.4 GW is 'smoothed out' across the 12 years until 2030. The plan acknowledges renewable energy as an opportunity to diversify the electricity mix and demonstrates that the least-cost unconstrained scenario would

build only solar PV, wind, and gas plants. However, the published IRP puts annual limits on new capacity of solar PV (1 GW) and wind (1.6 GW);

- the addition of 2 GW of storage capacity—the IRP 2019 envisages storage as a disruptive technology, which can be used to harness the full potential of variable renewable energy;
- an additional 3 GW of gas and diesel turbine generation capacity to provide the flexibility needed to complement variable renewable energy;
- an additional 500 MW of other generation capacity every year between 2023 and 2030, including distributed generation, cogeneration, biomass, and landfill gas.

The IRP has been characterized as a political compromise document that tries to accommodate all interests (Eberhard, 2019). It is not based on the least-cost scenario—which would be based on wind and solar PV complemented by flexible resources such as natural gas or, possibly, storage. Rather, it includes several policy adjustments aimed at incorporating 'new, innovative technologies that are not currently cost competitive' and minimizing the 'impact of decommissioning of coal power plants and the changing demand profile' (DoE, 2019d: 93). The policy-adjusted scenario of IRP 2019 results in a 5% higher tariff in 2030 compared to the least-cost test scenario, mainly due to the inclusion of coal and hydro power and the envisaged need to continue to utilize Eskom's diesel-fired capacity to address supply shortages in the immediate term (DoE, 2019d).

While far from ideal, the 2019 IRP offers some certainty to the sector by charting a way forward and establishing the legislative basis for new procurement decisions. The cabinet-approved IRP indicates that new generation (apart from nuclear) will be built by third parties (i.e. the private sector) and provides indicative timelines in terms of when this new capacity will be required. Unfortunately, it seems that there is little urgency about these decisions, despite the severe energy security challenges facing the country (Eberhard, 2019).

7.3 The design of South Africa's renewable energy auction programmes

7.3.1 The Renewable Energy Independent Power Producer Procurement Programme

REI4P is a competitive tender process aimed at facilitating private investment into utility-scale, grid-connected renewable energy projects (IRENA, 2018).

Under this programme, IPPs could submit bids for renewable energy generation projects using wind, solar PV, CSP, small hydro, biomass, biogas, or landfill gas. The electricity supply constraints experienced in the 2008–2011 period as well as the need to demonstrate a political commitment to climate change mitigation; when South Africa hosted international climate change negotiations at the COP in Durban in 2011, it opened up the political space for the rapid implementation of the programme (Morris and Martin, 2015; IRENA, 2018).

REI4P was designed as a single-stage bidding process with no pre-qualification round, mainly driven by the need to speed up the procurement process (IRENA, 2018). There have been six rounds of bidding for large-scale renewable energy (RE) projects, referred to as bid windows 1, 2, 3, 3.5 (limited to CSP), 4, and 5 (IPP Office, 2019). The programme attracted fierce competition and led to significant reductions in bid prices. The latest prices of awarded bids indicate that solar PV and wind energy are now cheaper than Eskom's average cost of supply and far below the cost of new coal power stations (Eberhard and Naude, 2017). The low prices submitted in bid window 4 prompted the DoE to double the awarded capacity. An expedited bid window was also introduced in 2015 aimed at giving a second chance to all bids that had not been successful during previous rounds.

7.3.2 The Small Projects Independent Power Producer Procurement Programme

In 2013, the DoE introduced SP–I4P as a subset of REI4P, with the objective of procuring 200 MW of generation capacity from small (1–5 MW) projects. This included projects using onshore wind, solar PV, biomass, biogas, and landfill gas (Eberhard and Naude, 2017). SP–I4P was designed to be less costly and simpler than REI4P, with the purpose of attracting emerging South African small and medium enterprises (SMEs) who were crowded out by large, international companies in the REI4P process. These smaller IPPs faced a number of barriers to entry into REI4P, including the cost of bidding, the ability to meet financial qualification criteria, and the difficulty of competing with large, international firms. By reducing the project sizes and adjusting the bidding process and qualification criteria, the DoE hoped to deepen the programme's economic development impact. SP–I4P ran two bid windows, which resulted in 99 MW of generation capacity being awarded to 20 small-scale renewable energy projects (IPP Office, 2019). None of the contracts approved under SP–I4P have been signed to date, which is surprising considering that these projects faced the same impasse that prevented the bid window 4 projects from advancing and which was resolved in 2018.

7.3.3 Auction design

7.3.3.1 Auction demand

Consistent and predictable planning is an important contributor for attracting private-sector investment in new generation capacity (Eberhard et al., 2017). As noted above, in South Africa, the IRP is the key electricity sector planning tool which determines the long-term electricity mix of the country. Based on the IRP, the Minister of Mineral Resources and Energy issues ministerial determinations which define the capacity that can be procured from a particular type of technology as well as the timelines for implementation and specifications of the ownership structure of the new generation capacity (Table 7.4).

Following a public consultation process,[3] NERSA is bound to issue licences as per these determinations, and the requests for proposals (RfPs) issued by REI4P and SP–I4P are also required to align with these determinations in terms of the amount of generation capacity to be procured.

Renewable energy allocations, which drive REI4P procurement, are differentiated by technology type and include onshore wind, CSP, solar PV, biomass, biogas, landfill gas, and small hydro (less than 40 MW) (IRENA, 2018). Allocations for SP–I4P, however, are not technology-specific, placing different technologies in a position to bid against one another for the available capacity (IPP Office, 2019).

7.3.3.2 Site selection

The South African approach to project site selection and preparation, which is mainly private-sector led, remains a relative anomaly in the sub-Saharan

Table 7.4 SP–I4P (pre-)qualification criteria

Evaluation criteria	Stage 1	Stage 2
Legal criteria and evaluation	✓	✓
Land (acquisition and use rights)	✓	✓
Environmental criteria and evaluation	✓	✓
Technical criteria and evaluation	✓	✓
Economic development criteria	✓	✓
Financial criteria and evaluation		
Structure of the project		
Value for money		

Source: Naude and Eberhard (2017).

[3] The initial determinations that underpinned REI4P were not subject to the same public consultation process, although a public participation process was required for the licensing of each awarded project.

context. In most other auction programmes in the region, project sites are usually 'provided' by the state with the intention of reducing bidding costs and project development timelines. In reality, this intention is often subverted by poorly selected and developed sites, leading bidders to prefer finding and preparing their own project sites (Kruger et al., 2019).

Under REI4P, bidders were responsible for carrying out their own respective site selection processes and thereafter had to submit adequate proof of land acquisition. The bidder was required to give the coordinates of the proposed project site and details of the registered owner (if the bidder was not the owner of the land). This associated submission could involve a notarial lease or title deeds for the project site; an unconditional land option, sale, or lease of land agreement; or a conveyancer's certificate (in the event that the title deeds were unattainable at the time of submission). Following legal advice, the bidder needed to provide a report which detailed land use change, zoning applications, subdivisions, and other relevant factors pertaining to the site. If a bidder intended to use landfill gas or municipal land for the site, they needed to submit a letter of approval from the relevant municipality (Eberhard and Naude, 2017).

This process proved to be arduous and costly for unsuccessful bidders, prompting a change from bid window 4 onwards. Bidders were no longer required to submit applications for subdivision, zoning, and land use change as proof of land acquisition. But bidders could provide proof of a land lease option, including requirements (but not approved applications) related to subdivision and zoning applications as well as land use change.

SP–I4P site-related bid requirements were much lighter. Bidders only needed to submit a letter from the land owner indicating that they were willing to enter into negotiations with the project owner, if the project was awarded, and a letter indicating the types of legal authorization that would be required with respect to the site.

Under REI4P and SP–I4P, responsibility for securing grid access lay primarily with the bidder, who needed prior confirmation from the grid provider (Eskom) that the relevant substations and transmission and distribution lines had enough capacity to accommodate the proposed project. A project could either connect to the transmission system (i.e. through the Eskom transmission business unit) or to the distribution system (i.e. through the Eskom distribution business unit or the local municipality), depending on the project's location and on the location of the point of connection. Successful bidders included either a transmission or distribution agreement with the respective grid provider as part of their power purchase agreement (PPA). Bidders were also responsible for acquiring all land needed for the installation of power lines that were required. These lines often spanned many kilometres and crossed multiple properties. It is also worth noting that, in the event of a municipality being the grid provider, bidders were required to provide relevant agreements (i.e. an implementation protocol and an amendment agreement to the electricity supply agreement), prepared ahead of financial close.

Generally, the grid operators were responsible for 'deep connection works' (connection works on shared assets) and bidders were responsible for the 'shallow connection works' (works for the dedicated customer connection of the facility to the system). Shallow connection works could be done in one of three ways: (i) they could be Eskom-built, (ii) they could be own-built (in a case where the bidder held ownership of the connection works, requiring another transmission or distribution license), or (iii) they could be self-built (in a case where the bidder had built the connection works and thereafter transferred it to the grid provider). Bidders were required to provide a letter affirming their ability to comply with grid codes ahead of the commercial date of operation, and they also needed to specify which part of the grid connection works they would perform. Bidders needed to submit a cost estimate letter (CEL) from the municipality or Eskom at their own cost, providing an indicative timeline, together with costs required for the deep connection works. This had to be replaced by budget quotes after preferred bidder award. There were major discrepancies between the CELs and budget quotes in many instances, with the latter being several times more expensive than was originally indicated in the CEL. This was problematic since bidders had bid on the basis of the CEL costs and could not adjust their bids based on the actual costs incurred.

As part of the REI4P process, bidders needed to provide evidence that all required environmental approvals had been received before the bid submission. In general, the key requirement across the technology spectrum is an environmental authorization, as stipulated by the South African NEMA. Depending on the power plant's size and capacity, this authorization is either in the form of a basic assessment report (BAR) or an environmental impact assessment report (EIAR). This proved to be one of the most costly and time-consuming requirements of the bidding process; for example, for wind projects, at least 12 months of costly bird and bat monitoring data was required.

In an effort to mitigate this risk and minimize such costs, the government established a coordination plan for renewable energy generation and transmission planning. In 2016, eight renewable energy development zones (REDZs) and five power corridors were approved through strategic environmental assessments (SEAs) to serve as a guideline for future locational selections. Three additional REDZs were proposed in the second phase of the wind and solar PV SEA, in line with the provisions for new renewable energy capacity in IRP 2019. The REDZs have the potential to stimulate the development of renewable energy projects in specific areas. This proposal could thus contribute to coal mine rehabilitation and support a just energy transition in areas where the government is planning the decommissioning of 12 GW of existing coal power stations by 2030 (CSIR, 2019).

The environmental permitting requirements for SP–I4P were generally less onerous than for REI4P, only requiring an EIAR if deemed necessary by an independent, qualified practitioner. If the potential project would not cause major environmental impacts, the independent practitioner simply needed to present a document verifying this.

7.3.3.3 Qualification and compliance requirements

Both REI4P and SP–I4P had stringent qualification criteria for screening potential bidders and has been described as 'the most onerous bidding programme in the world'. This process aimed to ensure that only committed and highly capacitated bidders were selected and that projects had a high likelihood of being built on time.

SP–I4P generally followed a similar process to that of REI4P for bid qualification and evaluation. However, SP–I4P utilized a two-stage bidding process aimed at limiting the cost-at-risk incurred by bidders, unlike the single-stage REI4P (Eberhard and Naude, 2017). Under the two-stage process, only bidders who met the high-level stage 1 qualification criteria and were awarded 'selected bidder' status could prepare and submit bids for stage 2 of the process. Unfortunately, the qualification criteria for stage 1 were set so high that this process made little difference to the cost of bidding, with many arguing that, in fact, it increased transaction costs for both the bidders and the procuring authority (Table 7.5).

In order to prevent large IPPs detracting from the objectives of SP–I4P, they were not permitted to split up existing large projects and submit these as several small ones.

Figure 7.6 presents a timeline of the REI4P and SP–I4P rounds launched and completed up to bid window 4. There were usually three months between the RfP release date and the final date for submission of bids. Once the evaluation consultants had completed the screening for compliance with qualification criteria and general requirements and bidders were awarded, the preferred bidders were expected to reach financial close of their projects within 9–12 months. Commercial operation date (COD) was expected within 24–30 months after financial close. Despite these pre-defined timelines, and

Table 7.5 Contracted capacity permitted per project

Technology	Minimum capacity (MW)	Maximum capacity (MW)
Onshore wind	1	140
CSP	1	75
Solar PV	1	100
Biomass	1	25
Biogas	1	10
Landfill gas	1	20
Small hydro	1	40

Source: IRENA (2018).

the fact that penalties were envisioned for delays in implementation, the DoE sometimes allowed for delays in these timelines. As can be seen from Figure 7.6, in reality, most projects exceeded these timelines.

7.3.3.3.1 Legal compliance
In order to comply with REI4P legal qualification requirements, bidders had to establish a special-purpose vehicle (SPV) ahead of submitting their bid. The purpose of this SPV was to ensure that the project was 'ring-fenced' in terms of the South African Companies Act. This condition was relaxed with the launch of bid window 4 in 2014. It was no longer necessary to create an SPV before bid submission, but an undertaking was required which indicated that if the bid was awarded, the company would be established as such. Bidders, as well as their investors and lenders, were also required to confirm their acceptance of the conditions of the PPA, implementation agreement (IA), and connection agreement (CA) (IRENA, 2018).

7.3.3.3.2 Technical compliance
Technical compliance requirements differed significantly between REI4P and SP–I4P. Technological differences between projects resulted in variations between PPAs and variations in size constraints.

Under REI4P, bidders were required to provide energy sales report forecasts, reviewed by an independent, third-party body. The forecast minimum requirements differed per technology, with, for example, at least one year of site-specific data required for onshore wind projects and 10 years for solar PV. In the case of biomass and biogas projects, bidders needed to provide fuel supply agreements or market studies covering at least two years of the

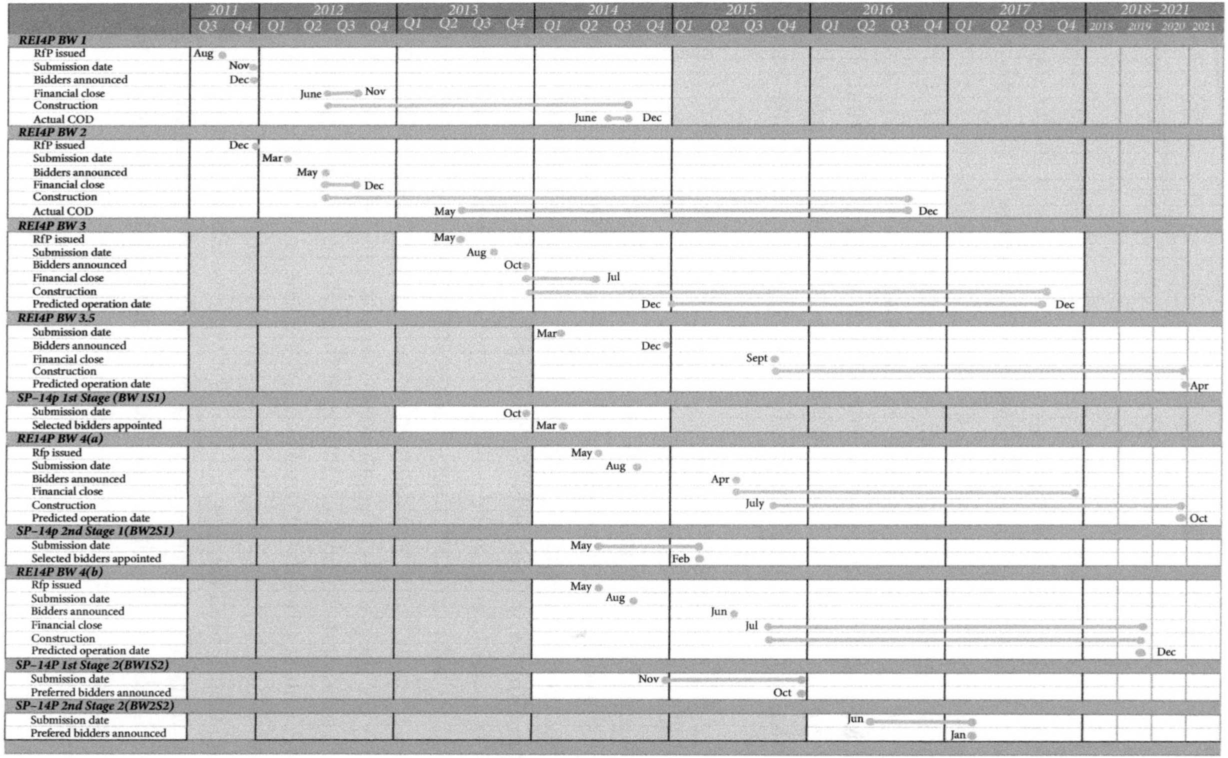

Figure 7.6 Timeline of Renewable Energy Independent Power Producer Procurement Programme (REI4P) and Small Projects Independent Power Producer Procurement Programme (SP-I4P), 2011–2018

Source: Authors' compilation.

project's operation as documentary evidence of energy resource certainty (IRENA, 2018).

Under REI4P, bidders were also required to submit evidence that the equipment met international standards and adhered to prescribed certification programme designs. Bidders also needed to provide proof that the proposed projects met prescribed technical availability standards. Prescribed standards were specified according to the underlying technology type, and technology-specific PPAs were provided as part of the RfP documentation.

The REI4P process put technology-differentiated limitations on the maximum contracted capacity per project (Table 7.6). The purpose of the capacity constraints was to promote competition by preventing companies who were able to invest in large-scale projects from dominating the procurement process (IRENA, 2018). There were, however, no limits on the number of projects that one bidder could submit or be awarded in the same REI4P round. The result has therefore been a process that limits the cost-benefits associated with economies of scale without necessarily increasing competition between bidders.

Technical requirements were relaxed slightly for SP–I4P, although the procurement conditions were fairly similar to those under REI4P. The small projects procurement programme did not require bidders to provide evidence that technologies had a 'proven' track record, as was the case in REI4P. SP–I4P did not require international certification of equipment, although the South African Bureau of Standards (SABS) and Grid Code compliance was still needed. In order to ensure the viability of projects where the equipment was not internationally certified, the DoE suggested that bidders engage with potential lenders early in the process in order to ensure that they were willing to lend money for the particular equipment (Eberhard and Naude, 2017).

Energy sales forecast requirements were, at first glance, also less stringent under SP–I4P: only six months of wind data, versus one year, was required for onshore wind projects during stage 1. However, stage 2 required 12 months of data. In addition, SP–I4P required that the wind assessment expert had at least three years of experience, versus a minimum five-year requirement under REI4P. Under SP–I4P, there was also no requirement for an additional independent review of the forecast data as long as this was provided by an independent expert.

7.3.3.3.3 *Financial and commercial capability*
To assess the financial standing of bidders, REI4P had standard requirements for commercial bids, including audited financial statements, net asset tests, and/or track record tests of all finance and equity providers (IRENA,

2018). In the first rounds of REI4P, these documents were also required with regards to subcontractors, including a signed contract with engineering, procurement, and construction (EPC) contractors and operations and maintenance (O&M) providers, but this requirement was relaxed in later bid windows. Bidders were also required to provide a detailed breakdown of all funding sources, including equity finance, corporate finance, and external debt requirements and how these funds would be allocated. Financial due diligence plans, accompanied by risk-mitigation strategies, were also required to establish the funding proposal's robustness and viability.

Under REI4P, debt-funded project bids had to be accompanied by credit committee-approved commitment letters and term sheets from lenders. This assured the IPP Office that by the time bids were submitted, a stringent due diligence process had already been completed. Lenders played a pivotal role in shaping REI4P and the structure and contents of the underlying contracts. In an effort to ensure that the awarded projects would be bankable, the IPP Office tested all contracts with lenders prior to going to market. This was one of the reasons why only 'proven technologies' were included in the procurement process and why the bidding documents were non-negotiable.

Funders needed to agree to the assigned risk allocation by accepting the relevant provisions in the PPA, IA, and direct agreement (DA). In order to prove the robustness of their financial models, bidders were also asked to submit two financial models, which needed to include a foreign exchange exposure sensitivity analysis, tax and accounting treatment disclosures, and a list of all underlying assumptions. A success payment declaration also had to be submitted, outlining those costs incurred during the bid preparation process that would be eligible for reimbursement should the project reach financial close (IRENA, 2018).

The stage 1 qualification process under SP–I4P did not involve any financial compliance requirements. In stage 2, bidders were assessed against two sets of financial criteria, the first being price, similar to REI4P. The second financial criterion related to the viability and robustness of the funding proposal and assessed the project in terms of underlying funding sources, including equity finance and debt funding. To this end, each of the equity holders had to submit a letter of support certifying that due diligence had been completed. In contrast, senior and mezzanine debt financiers were only required to submit a letter indicating credit approval of preliminary term sheets and a detailed plan for reaching final credit approval. Similar to REI4P, a schedule had to be submitted of all project development costs that were subject to reimbursement through success payments once the project reached financial close. However, reimbursements were limited to only 2.5% of the total costs, with the objective of ensuring that project preparation costs remained low for small projects (Eberhard and Naude, 2017).

A bid bond guarantee mechanism was required by REI4P in order to ensure that awarded bidders fulfil their commitment to contract signing. Bidders were required to submit a bond guarantee of R 100,000 per MW (equivalent to about US$ 6,800/MW), which selected bidders were required to double before being officially awarded preferred bidder status, effectively making it a performance guarantee. In contrast, no bid bond was required under SP–I4P, but a performance guarantee was required from the preferred bidder once they were qualified. The performance guarantee was meant to be in place until COD to act as an incentive for the project to reach COD on time. The IPP Office did, however, waive this requirement for awarded/announced SP–I4P projects since there has been such uncertainty around their final awards.

7.3.3.3.4 Economic and socio-economic development

Economic development requirements under REI4P and SP–I4P were designed to incentivize the promotion of job creation, local industrialization, community development, and black economic empowerment through the implementation of renewable energy projects. In this way, the programmes were designed not only as a mechanism for procuring new energy generation capacity but also as a tool for contributing to broader national development objectives through stimulating an indigenous renewable energy industry, which creates employment opportunities, uplifts society, and diversifies ownership (IPP Office, 2019). These requirements generated conflicting responses, with some bidders finding them too subjective and stringent, while labour unions viewed them as not stringent enough to generate real change (Eberhard et al., 2014). However, they were instrumental in generating critical political support for the programme (Eberhard et al., 2014).

Bidders needed to pass two primary economic development (ED) thresholds in order to qualify to participate in the auction process under REI4P. The first threshold set a minimum of 40% 'South African Equity Participation' in the bidding entity, with the initial definition stating that, in order to qualify as South African, the company had to be based and registered in the country and involve shareholding by South African citizens. From bid window 3, the definition was narrowed to a requirement for participation of South African citizens in the entity as direct or indirect shareholders in the project company (IRENA, 2018).

The second economic development threshold required that bidders demonstrate a broad-based black economic empowerment (B-BBEE) contributor status level (CSL) of at least five. CSL is determined in accordance with B-BBEE codes as dictated by the South African BBBEE Act (53/2003). The purpose of the Act and this qualification requirement is to promote the achievement of higher economic growth, increased employment, and more equitable income distribution through increased broad-based and effective participation of (historically disadvantaged) black people in the South African economy.

In addition to the two primary thresholds, bidders were also required to meet, or exceed, the minimum thresholds indicated in the economic development scorecard, with supporting evidence. These thresholds differed for REI4P and SP–I4P (Table 7.6), with economic development qualification requirements significantly reduced for small renewable energy projects (IRENA, 2018).

As part of the local content criteria, a share of the total project cost needed to be spent in South Africa (45% for solar PV projects and 40% for all other technologies). This constituted 25% of the economic development score (discussed in more detail in the following sections), and both thresholds and targets were increased over the bidding windows.

Local content requirements were a key driver under SP–I4P and were generally set at higher levels across all technologies compared to REI4P. Bidders were required to have a 40% South African entity participation at bid submission. This needed to increase to 60% within no more than one-third of the scheduled operating period (Eberhard and Naude, 2017). Similarly, in order to stimulate SME participation, bidders were required to show SME shareholding of at least 10% at bid submission and to increase this to 30% within one-third of the scheduled operating period (Eberhard and Naude, 2017). Bidders were also required to submit a plan for achieving the increases within the stipulated timeframe. As in REI4P, bidders were required to submit documentation to prove a minimum Level 5 BBBEE CSL.

7.3.3.4 Bidder ranking and winner selection

Projects under REI4P and SP–I4P were evaluated based on a multicriteria 70:30 split between price and economic development criteria, respectively. This split, which was unique to the South African renewable energy auction, placed significant weight on economic development criteria. This was notably different from the general South African government procurement policy split of 90:10 (for projects of this size), which favours the price criteria significantly. In order to apply the weighting, the IPP Office had to obtain an exemption from the Public Preferential Procurement Framework Act in

Table 7.6 Economic development minimum thresholds for REI4P and SP-I4P bidders

Element	Description	REI4P		SP-I4P	
		Threshold %	Target %	Threshold %	Target %
Job creation	South Africa-based employees who are citizens	50	80	–	90
	South Africa-based employees who are black people	30	50	–	60
	Skilled employees who are black people	18	30	–	50
	RSA-based employees who are citizens and from local communities	12	20	–	30
Local content	Value of local content spending	40 (45 for solar PV)	65	50	70
Ownership	Shareholding by black people in the seller (bidder)	12	30	–	40
	Shareholding by local communities in the seller	2.5	5	–	10
	Shareholding by black people in the construction contractor	8	20	–	30
	Shareholding by black people in the operations contractor	8	20	–	30
Management control	Black people in top management	–	40	–	40
Preferential procurement	B-BBEE procurement as percentage of total procurement spend	–	60	–	70
	Qualifying small enterprises and SME procurement as percentage of total procurement spend	–	10	–	20
	Women-owned vendor procurement as percentage of total procurement spend	–	5	–	10
Enterprise development	Enterprise development contributions as a percentage of revenue	–	0.6	–	1
	Adjusted enterprise development contributions as a percentage of revenue	–	0.6	–	1
	Enterprise development contributions on SMEs	NA	NA	0.5	1
Socio-economic development	Socio-economic development contributions as a percentage of revenue	1	1.5	–	3
	Adjusted socio-economic development contributions as a percentage of revenue	1	1.5	–	3
SME participation	Key components and/or equipment and balance-of-plant spend on SMEs	NA	NA	50	70

Note: NA = not applicable.
Source: IRENA (2018).

order to maximize economic development objectives. The strong focus on economic development criteria attracted some criticism due to fears that it would lead to higher bid prices. The bid tariff outcomes (Table 7.11), however, indicate that while tariffs might have been lower in the absence of these requirements, REI4P still saw a significant decline in prices throughout the process (IRENA, 2018).

A price ceiling mechanism was applied and made public prior to the bid submission deadline. Table 7.7 presents the price caps across the different REI4P bid windows as well as the average price outcome by technology type. Price caps were adjusted downwards in each round, based on local and global influencing factors. Price caps were removed for solar PV- and wind-based projects in bid window 4 due to the significant cost decreases for these technologies.

The weighting assigned to different elements of economic development are presented in Table 7.8, comparing REI4P weighting to SP–I4P weighting. SP–I4P differed from REI4P in terms of assigning less weight to job creation and local content elements. It also has an additional element which measures SME participation. Economic development contributions were evaluated and scored on an absolute, points-based basis in earlier rounds. In later rounds, the programme used relative scoring: all bids were evaluated against the bid with the highest economic development score, which met or exceeded all economic development targets (Table 7.8). The IPP Office published quarterly reports on the REI4P programme, which indicate that all contracted projects either reached or exceeded economic development commitments, noting that the data provided still needed to be audited and verified (IRENA, 2018).

7.3.3.5 Securing the revenue stream and addressing off-taker risk

In order to ensure investment in REI4P, a secure revenue stream and limiting off-taker risk was essential. REI4P put various mechanisms in place to ensure this, such as sovereign guarantees, as well as limiting foreign exchange risk. More recently, foreign project owners have also secured guarantees from the World Bank's Multilateral Investment Guarantee Agency (MIGA), in an effort to mitigate political risk.

In order to limit the exposure of bid prices to inflation risks, bidders were required to submit fully and partially indexed prices according to the South African consumer price index (CPI) for the 20-year period of the PPA. Bidders would be paid in South African Rand (ZAR) on a take-or-pay basis: the off-taker (e.g. Eskom) was obliged to either take delivery of electricity—regardless of whether it was needed—or to pay the amount that the IPP

Table 7.7 Price caps and average bid tariffs for bid windows (BWs) 1–4 (in US$/MWh)

Bid window (BW)	BW 1		BW 2		BW 3		BW 4 (b)		BW 4(a)	
Technology	Price cap	Bid tariff	Price cap	Bid tariff	Price cap	Bid tariff	Price cap	Bid tariff	Price cap	Bid tariff
Onshore wind	140	140	150	110	100	80	70	60	–	50
Solar PV	360	350	360	210	140	100	80	70	–	70
CSP	360	340	360	320	170	170	130	–	140	–
Biomass	130	–	140	–	140	140	140	–	120	120
Biogas	100	–	100	–	80	–	140[a]	–	-a	–
Landfill gas	80	–	110	–	100	100	90	–	80	–
Small hydro	130	–	130	130	90	–	110	–	90	90

Note: [a] No biogas capacity was made available for tender under bid window 4.
Source: IRENA (2018).

Table 7.8 Weighting of the elements of economic development criteria under REI4P and SP–I4P

Element	Description	REI4P weighting (%)	SP–I4P weighting (%)
Job creation	RSA-based employees who are citizens	25	20
	RSA-based employees who are black people		
	Skilled employees who are black people		
	RSA-based employees who are citizens and from local communities		
Local content	Value of local content spending	25	20
Ownership	Shareholding by black people in the seller	15	15
	Shareholding by local communities in the seller		
	Shareholding by black people in the construction contractor		
	Shareholding by black people in the operations contractor		
Management control	Black people in top management	5	5
Preferential procurement	B-BBEE procurement as percentage of total procurement spend	10	10
	Qualifying small enterprise and SME procurement as percentage of total procurement spend		
	Women-owned vendor procurement as percentage of total procurement spend		
Enterprise development	Enterprise development contributions as a percentage of revenue	5	5
	Adjusted enterprise development contributions as a percentage of revenue		
Socio-economic development	Socio-economic development contributions as a percentage of revenue	15	15
	Adjusted socio-economic development contributions		
SME participation		–	10

Source: Authors' compilation.

would have been paid had Eskom been able to take the power. This is a standard requirement for renewable energy projects, most of which are not dispatchable due to the variable nature of the resource.

While sellers were exposed to some foreign exchange risks for upfront capital expenditure, the prescribed spot price (and corresponding bid tariffs, which were submitted in the bid at financial close) could be adjusted for capital expenditures. Bidders indicated an electricity price at bid submission based on a forex rate stipulated by the DoE/IPP Office at the time. During the time between bid submission and financial close, there would have been forex fluctuations. Bidders were allowed to adjust their submitted price (up to a maximum of 60% due to the 40% local content requirement) based on the changes in the exchange rate between bid submission and financial close.

Preferred bidders signed an IA with the DoE that functioned as a sovereign guarantee but also formed the contractual basis for the bidders' socio-economic development commitments. The contingent liability presented by the sovereign guarantees was seen by the National Treasury as presenting a very low risk because of an intergovernmental framework agreement between NERSA, Eskom, and the National Treasury. This agreement essentially ensured that NERSA passed through the costs of the PPAs to Eskom customers—without affecting Eskom's allowed tariffs.

Additional risk-mitigation instruments have also become involved more recently, specifically to insure against political risk. There has been an increase in cover provided by the World Bank Group's MIGA for foreign investors, with REI4P projects now being MIGA's biggest exposure in Africa. MIGA provides break-of-contract cover, which comes at a significant cost to the project (Mayer, 2018). This has been motivated by worries about announcements from NERSA and the relevant ministries that the tariffs from the earlier bid windows will be renegotiated (Creamer, 2019).

7.3.3.5.1 Assigned liabilities for transmission delays

The costs of extending the grid from the generation facility to the main network delivery point ('shallow' connection works) were borne by the project developer, with the grid interconnection works beyond the delivery point ('deep' connection works) remaining the responsibility of the grid operator (e.g. Eskom) upon COD. If transmission was not provided by Eskom as stated in the budget quote, it was classified as a system event. This meant that the project would be paid for the energy that it would have delivered, and the last-stop COD would be moved out in accordance with the delay.

7.3.3.5.2 Delay and underbuilding penalties

Bidders for REI4P were not required to provide any completion or performance bonds. However, if construction had not started within 180 days of the effective date, the project would be terminated. Furthermore, the PPA stated that for each day that construction went beyond the scheduled COD, the operating period of the contract was decreased by one additional day; that is, for each day's delay, two days' worth of revenue was lost (IRENA, 2018).

A project could also be terminated or fined if it failed to comply with its ED obligations. Projects were awarded financial penalties and/or half a termination point for performance below 65% on any ED obligation, which are reported on quarterly (IRENA, 2018). There is anecdotal evidence that some bidders included the cost of penalties/non-compliance in their bids as part of a bidding strategy aimed at maximizing ED scores in the evaluation process. If an IPP received more than 9 termination points over a 12-month period, the PPA could be terminated—something which has not happened to date. Most termination points awarded to date have been for projects failing to comply with their 'women-owned businesses' commitments.

7.3.4 Auction implementation

In order to ensure that potential bidders trusted both the agency and the auction process, there was a need to match existing institutional resources with the bidders' needs and expectations. Auction success, in general, is as much dependent on bidder trust in the auction process and in the implementing unit, which is built on the underlying institutional framework, as on good auction design. The presence of a clearly mandated, credible, well-capacitated, and well-resourced agency responsible for managing and implementing the auction process was a critical success factor.

The initial step in procuring renewable energy generation in South Africa was the design of a renewable energy feed-in tariff (REFiT). The Electricity Regulatory Division at NERSA initiated and lead this process in 2007 (Figure 7.7), as a way of meeting the target of 10,000 GWh of renewable energy by 2013, as set out in the 2003 Renewable Energy White Paper (Baker, 2016). A number of government departments provided support, including the National Treasury, the DPE, and the Department of Environmental Affairs (DEA), as well as various bilateral donors. The process of designing the programme and determining the tariff levels involved a prolonged negotiation process, with NERSA, various government departments, funders, and project developers, as well as civil society representatives, involved.

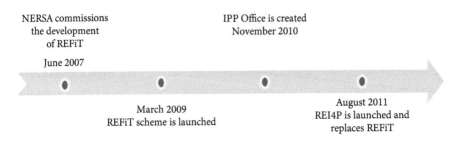

Figure 7.7 Timeline of Renewable Energy Feed-In Tariff (REFiT) and REI4P

Source: Authors' compilation.

REFiT was launched in March 2009, despite significant opposition to renewable energy within NERSA itself. There was also opposition from the DoE and Eskom and disagreements around the level of tariffs, mistrust of renewable energy, and perceived financial and political risks (Baker and Wlokas, 2015). The NERSA REFiT consultation paper, published in 2008, was South Africa's first mechanism intended to attract renewable energy investments and marked the first time that global renewable energy investors turned their eyes towards South Africa as an investment destination (Baker and Wlokas, 2015).

National Treasury finally declared REFiT illegal, following an assessment by legal advisers, who found that a predetermined feed-in tariff would be against South Africa's procurement rules (Baker and Wlokas, 2015). In addition, the National Treasury and the DoE expressed concern that NERSA did not have the financial or technical capabilities to run REFiT, putting the scheme at risk of corruption, given the high tariffs set by the regulator (Baker, 2016). As a result, in 2010, the DoE was mandated with replacing REFiT with a competitive bidding system in the form of REI4P (Eberhard et al., 2014).

To ensure the success of REI4P, and to avoid similar institutional capacity shortfalls to those experienced by NERSA, the DoE sought the assistance of the National Treasury's public–private partnership (PPP) unit to help manage the process of setting up the programme. The PPP unit was established in 2000 and, since 2007, had been working with the private sector, helping to promote IPPs. It was widely viewed as a highly capable, well-capacitated team that had a proven track record and understood both the public and private sectors' objectives, needs, and concerns. In November 2010, a small team from the PPP unit and the DoE together created the IPP Office, overseen by the DoE. The office had the advantage of being highly respected by both private- and public-sector stakeholders, and it enjoyed high-level public-sector support, which enhanced its credibility and, as a result, that of REI4P.

An important and highly valued aspect of the programme was the degree of autonomy enjoyed by the IPP Office. The IPP Office's primary responsibility was to provide procurement opportunities for IPPs (PMG, 2018). Despite the IPP Office reporting to the DoE, it was mandated with facilitating and running the entire REI4P process and was allowed to operate fairly independently (Figure 7.7), outside the regulatory and funding scope of the DoE. This created credibility and flexibility for this dedicated unit, which allowed the office to focus more on practical problem-solving rather than compliance with standardized governmental policies and procedures.

Coordination among government entities was key to the success of REI4P. The IPP Office ran the REI4P bidding process, selected the preferred bidders, and submitted a motivated list to the DoE. The DoE then approved the list of preferred bidders. Once preferred bidders had been selected, NERSA was mandated to provide them with generation licences. Other government departments, including the DTI, also needed to provide their input on qualification criteria, such as local content requirements and B-BBEE legislation compliance. IPP project developers prepared and submitted bids through the IPP Office. This process also required the involvement of relevant provincial and municipal departments to provide authorization to meet the bid qualification criteria (Eberhard and Naude, 2017).

Licensing was, at times, an onerous process for some government departments, given the number of bids submitted in each round. For example, between late 2010 and 2013, the DEA received 1,500 environmental authorization applications, putting enormous pressure on the capacity of the department (Eberhard and Naude, 2017). Eskom had to issue CELs of both the feasibility and approximate cost of connecting these projects to the grid to all the projects that had submitted bids (Eberhard and Naude, 2017). This required an extensive assessment of each project in order to issue the CEL. Given the increasing numbers of bidders that have applied for each successive round, this has become an extremely laborious process for Eskom and other governmental departments. To minimize the administrative burden that accompanied REI4P, the Department of Water Affairs (DWA), for example, only considered water use licence applications of preferred bidders, as opposed to all bidders, in order to limit the number of licensing applications submitted (Eberhard and Naude, 2017). Once preferred bidders have been selected, approved, and granted the necessary licences, Eskom then signed PPAs which allows these projects to reach financial close and construction to begin.

Securing sufficient funding for designing and implementing the programme has been essential. The DoE, National Treasury, and Development Bank of Southern Africa (DBSA) entered into a memorandum of understanding (MoU) to provide funding for the REI4P programme. The DBSA provided US$ 4.6 million[4] in financing for the IPP Office to hire transaction advisers, set up a project office, and facilitate capacity building (Eberhard et al., 2014). The National Treasury provided a further US$ 6.8 million to the IPP Office to repay the DBSA and ensure the smooth running of REI4P through bid windows 1 and 2 (Martin and Winkler, 2014). Subsequent to this, on signing of implementation agreements, successful IPP companies paid a bidder registration fee, as well as a project development fee totalling 1% of the total project costs, into a project development fund for renewable energy projects. This fund effectively provides financing for the IPP Office and all its activities. This fund is managed by the DoE (now DMRE) and ensures that the REI4P programme is not attached to the formal government budget. The funding covers the current and future costs of REI4P, including the oversight costs of the REI4P programme (Eberhard et al., 2014).

The financial independence of the office ensures greater flexibility, credibility, and transparency in decision-making, as well as in hiring and compensation decisions. Various bilateral donor agencies representing the United Kingdom, Spain, Germany, and Denmark also provided funding for technical assistance to establish this programme. A grant of US$ 6 million from the Global Environment Facility (GEF), for example, was made available by the World Bank to fund advisory services under the Renewable Energy Market Transformation Project. Donor agencies also provided advice on setting up the REI4P tender process based on a review of international good practice and tender processes that had been conducted in Brazil, Germany, France, India, and Spain, amongst other countries (Eberhard et al., 2014).

The IPP Office contracted various local and international financial, legal, and technical transaction advisers to provide technical support in setting up and running REI4P. In the initial design stages of the programme, 50 advisers with knowledge and expertise in auction design international best practice provided input into the development of REI4P. This grew to over 100 representatives from 13 professional firms (Eberhard et al., 2014). The IPP Office also hired external professional firms (Table 7.9) to independently evaluate the procurement process and its outcomes. This independence was widely acknowledged by bidders as being an important driver of their decision to participate in REI4P (Eberhard et al., 2014).

---

[4] At current exchange rate of US$ 1:ZAR 14.7, equivalent to about ZAR 80 million.

Table 7.9 REI4P evaluation consultants

Function	Firm
International reviewers	Legal: Linklaters (United Kingdom (UK)) Technical: Tony Wheeler Consulting (UK) Governance: Ernst & Young (South Africa (SA))
Project management	SPP Project Solutions (SA)
Legal evaluation	Bowman Gilfillan (SA) Edward Nathan Sonnenbergs (ENSafrica) Ledwaba Mazwai (SA) Webber Wentzel (SA)
Technical evaluation	Mott MacDonald (SA)
Financial evaluation	Ernst & Young (SA) PricewaterhouseCoopers (SA)

Source: Adapted from Eberhard et al. (2014)

From November 2010, the IPP Office was given nine months to prepare all the necessary bid documentation and associated legal contracts for the launch of the REI4P programme. South Africa had never before run a competitive renewable energy tendering process. It was therefore critical that the IPP Office was comprised of experienced and respected team members. Karen Breytenbach, a senior manager from the PPP unit was appointed to lead the IPP Office. Her extensive experience working with the private sector, managing consultants, and working with PPP contracts made her an ideal candidate to manage this process (Eberhard et al., 2014).

Other members of the unit included technical and legal experts, all with a recognized track record in closing IPP contracts. This team was viewed favourably in both the public and private sectors and, cumulatively, had a reputation for being problem-solvers and facilitators as opposed to regulators. The experts in the team were well known to the bankers, lawyers, and consultants working in private-sector infrastructure projects in South Africa. There was therefore less of the typical mistrust from private-sector businesses that often accompanies the workings of government agencies in South Africa (Eberhard et al., 2014). Furthermore, dialogue and engagements with private-sector counterparts on critical components of REI4P design and implementation began almost immediately with the launch of the office. This engagement continued throughout the REI4P process and catalysed enthusiastic participation from private-sector players from the start (Eberhard and Naude, 2017).

Despite the programme's initial success, implementation has been hampered by industry incumbents. Eskom has played a major role in this regard.

Eskom's top management refused to sign 37 PPAs awarded in bid window 4 and the first SP–I4P bid window. This impasse lasted until April 2018, causing a three-year delay. This undermined investor confidence in the sector and created uncertainty regarding the future of South Africa's IPP Programme (Creamer, 2017). Given that the IPP Office derives funding from IPPs through the Project Development Fund for Renewable Energy projects and is not dependent on government budgets, a hiatus in the signing of PPAs also reduced funding for the programme between 2015 and 2018 (Figure 7.8). The impasse was only resolved after a series of appointments of new people in key positions, including a new Minister of Energy, a new Minister of Public Enterprises, and a new Eskom board and management team.

Another event which highlights vulnerabilities in the IPP Office's institutional set-up was the attempt of the Minister of Energy to move it out of the DoE and house it under the Central Energy Fund (CEF). CEF was initially set up under the apartheid regime as a sanctions-busting fund to ensure South African energy security. In 2017, during a speech in Parliament, former Energy Minister Mmamoloko Kubayi announced that the IPP Office would move to CEF because of the financial constraints facing the IPP Office and in order to ensure the sustainability of the IPP programme (DoE, 2017b). This decision was queried extensively by Members of Parliament, given that two

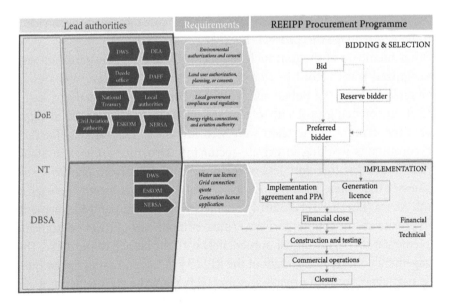

Figure 7.8 Institutional set-up and governance structure of REI4P

Source: Adapted from Eberhard and Naude (2017).

CEF companies, PetroSA and the Strategic Fuel Fund (SEF), were both facing severe financial and governance issues. These financial and governance issues could impact on the sustainability of CEF and, therefore, housing the IPP Office in CEF had the potential to undermine the sustainability of REI4P (Creamer, 2017). The move was also fiercely opposed and resisted by the IPP Office. Jeff Radebe, who became Minister of Energy in early 2018, stated, in a meeting with the Portfolio Committee on Energy in May 2018, that the Ministry had no intention of moving the IPP Office. Furthermore, he said that REI4P was one of the best programmes of its kind globally and, in fact, that the role of the IPP Office should be enhanced and its independence maintained (PMG, 2018; Omarjee, 2019a). He enforced the signing of the outstanding PPAs and reaffirmed the government's commitment to REI4P.

Despite the tumultuous years from 2015 that have prevented REI4P from reaching its full potential, the signing of bid window 4 PPAs allowed projects to reach financial close after four years, and the finalization of the IRP signalled a renewed era for REI4P and IPPs. It is imperative that strong leadership, stemming from the IPP Office, continues to underpin the I4P process to ensure consistency and maintain investor confidence necessary for continued growth.

7.4 Results from South Africa's renewable energy auctions

Outcomes from the first four REI4P bid windows have been impressive. Between bid windows 1 and 4, the average price for wind projects declined by 50% from R 1.75/kWh to R 0.,88/kWh, while the average price for solar PV projects declined by 75% from R 4.22 to R 1.06/kWh (in 2019 prices) (IPP Office, 2019). As of June 2019, there are 91 active projects[5] (6.3 GW—Table 7.6), of which 64 are in operation, representing 4 GW of installed capacity.

Eskom claims that it has struggled to manage integration of RE due to the variable nature of generation (Pombo-van Zyl, 2014). However, the utility-scale variable renewable energy (VRE) fleet proved to be vital in limiting the extent of load shedding in 2019. This was the most intensive load-shedding experienced in South Africa, with 595 GWh of load shed in March 2019 alone, of the total 769 GWh in the first quarter of 2019 (there was 1,325 GWh

---

[5] Projects that have begun construction (Wright and Calitz, 2019a).

of load shedding throughout 2015) (Wright and Calitz, 2019a). VRE con-tributed 2.975 GWh (5.3%) to the power system in the first quarter of 2019, with monthly contributions ranging from 4.9% to 6.0%, weekly contributions from 4.1% to 7.0%, and daily contributions from 2.9% to 7.7%. During load-shedding periods, VRE contributed 357 GWh of the total 2,975 GWh during the first quarter of 2019; that is, load shedding could have increased from 769 GWh to 1,126 GWh (a 46% increase). Instantaneous contributions from the VRE fleet during load-shedding periods was up to 2.3 GW, meaning that, without the VRE fleet, load-shedding stages 5 and 6 (5,000 MW and 6,000 MW load reduction, respectively) could have occurred (Wright and Calitz, 2019a). The project contracts and agreements contained no provision for increasing the contracted capacity, which led the local wind industry associa-tion to call for a relaxing of these provisions in the face of severe load shedding in late 2019, which would allow wind IPPs to inject an additional 500 MW into the system (IRENA, 2018; SAWEA, 2019).

The statistics from Table 7.10 suggest that market readiness for bid win-dow 1 was overestimated significantly: only 41% of tendered capacity was awarded, compared to 82% in bid window 2. This resulted in limited com-petition and high prices. The tendered volume was reduced in subsequent auctions, thus increasing competition and lowering winning prices (IRENA, 2018).

Table 7.11 provides detail on the capacity procured under SP–I4P by type of technology, including average price outcomes and levels of investment attracted. As one would expect, the average price coming out of SP–I4P is higher than the prices coming out of REI4P due to the smaller size of the projects (1–5 MW). However, small projects have also seen a reduction (of 20%) in price between stage 1S2 and stage 2S2, despite these rounds being run less than a year apart. Wind, solar PV, and biomass have been the only tech-nologies utilized by SP–I4P bidders, with 100% of projects under 2S2 utilizing solar PV.

Table 7.12 presents average local content outcomes from each REI4P bid window per technology type, against targets and thresholds (minimum obligation requirements for bidders).

It is evident from Table 7.13 that the average local content commitments increased over time as local industry developed around the programme. In bid window 1, local content commitments were closer to the minimum pre-scribed levels than to the targets. In bid window 2, targets were increased, and the programme saw significantly higher levels of local content commitment, although, in several cases, the average was still closer to the minimum than to the target (IRENA, 2018). In bid window 3, minimum thresholds were also

Table 7.10 Capacity and investment outcomes from REI4P bid windows 1–4

Bid windows (BW)	Wind	Solar PV	CSP	Biomass	Biogas	Landfill gas	Hydro	Total
BW 1 (2011)								
Capacity tendered (MW)	1,850	1,450	200	13	13	25	75	3,626
Capacity awarded (MW)	649	627	150	0	0	0	0	1,425
Number of projects awarded	8	18	2	0	0	0	0	28
Average tariff (US$/kWh)	0.14	0.35	0.34	–	–	–	–	–
Total investment (US$ million)	1,734	2,945	1,486	0	0	0	0	6,166
BW 2 (2012)								
Capacity tendered (MW)	650	450	50	13	13	25	75	1,276
Capacity awarded (MW)	559	417	50	0	0	0	14	1,040
Number of projects awarded	7	9	1	0	0	0	2	19
Average tariff (US$/kWh)	0.11	0.21	0.32	–	–	–	0.13	–
Total investment (US$ million)	1,736	1,743	642	0	0	0	91	4,212
BW 3 (2013)								
Capacity tendered (MW)	645	401	200	60	12	25	121	1,473
Capacity awarded (MW)	787	435	200	17	0	18	0	1,457
Number of projects awarded	7	6	2	1	0	1	0	17
Average tariff (US$/kWh)	0.08	0.10	0.17	0.014	–	0.01	–	–
Total investment (US$ million)	1,721	826	1,820	108	0	29	0	4,504

Continued

Table 7.10 *Continued*

Bid windows (BW)	Wind	Solar PV	CSP	Biomass	Biogas	Landfill gas	Hydro	Total
BW 3.5 (2014)								
Capacity tendered (MW)	–	–	200	–	–	–	–	200
Capacity awarded (MW)	–	–	200	–	–	–	–	200
Number of projects awarded	–	–	2	–	–	–	–	2
Average tariff (US$/kWh)	–	–	0.15	–	–	–	–	0.15
Total investment (US$ million)	–	–	1,741	–	–	–	–	1,741
BW 4(a) (2014)								
Capacity tendered (MW)	590	400	0	40	0	15	60	1,105
Capacity awarded (MW)	676	415	0	25	0	0	5	1,121
Number of projects awarded	5	6	0	0	0	0	0	13
Average tariff (US$/kWh)	0.05	0.07	–	0.12	–	–	0.09	–
Total investment (US$ million)	1,122	709	0	100	0	0	20	1,951
BW 4(b) (2015)								
Capacity tendered (MW)	–	–	–	–	–	–	–	–
Capacity awarded (MW)	686	398	0	0	0	0	0	1,084
Number of projects awarded	7	6	0	0	0	0	0	13
Average tariff (US$/kWh)	0.06	0.07	–	–	–	–	–	–
Total investment (US$ million)	1,226	669	0	0	0	0	0	1,895
Totals								
Capacity tendered (MW)	3,735	2,701	650	126	38	90	331	7,680
Capacity awarded (MW)	3,357	2,292	600	42	0	18	19	6,328
Number of projects awarded	34	45	7	2	0	1	3	92
Total investment (US$ million)	7,540	6,892	5,690	207	0	29	111	20,470

Source: IRENA (2018).

Table 7.11 Capacity and investment outcomes from SP–I4P, 1S2, and 2S2

Bid windows	Wind	Solar PV	Biomass	Total
Bid window 1S2 (2013)				
Capacity tendered (MW)				50
Capacity awarded (MW)	9	30	10	49
Number of projects awarded				10
Average tariff (US$/kWh)				0.11
Total investment (US$ million)				90.8
Bid window 2S2 (2014)				
Capacity tendered (MW)				51
Capacity awarded (MW)	–	50	–	50
Number of projects awarded				10
Average tariff (US$/kWh)				0.08
Total investment (US$ million)				87.9

Source: DoE (2015a, 2017e); IPP Office (2019).

increased in line with an additional 5% increase in targets across all technology types. This did not result in notable changes in the average local content outcomes, which were already quite high at this stage (IRENA, 2018). In bid window 4, the targets and thresholds remained at the same levels as in bid window 3, and local content commitment outcomes were closer to thresholds than targets.

Local content outcomes for solar PV projects saw the most significant increase, almost reaching the targets set for bid window 4. The real impact of local content requirements for economic development have been challenged, especially in the solar PV sector, where some bidders utilized transfer pricing (selling goods from one division of the company to another division of the same company) in order to meet local content requirements (Baker and Sovacool, 2017). Still, REI4P did result in the establishment of several local RE manufacturing facilities and significant local capacity to support this market (Matsuo and Schmidt, 2019).

REI4P has also created numerous employment opportunities. As of the end of December 2021, a total of 63,291 job years have been created for South African citizens (a job year is the equivalent of a full-time employment opportunity for one person for one year). Of these, 48,110 were in construction and 15,182 in operations. The construction phase offers a job opportunity over a shorter duration, while the operations phase requires fewer people but over an extended operating period. For the construction phase of projects,

Table 7.12 Average (Avg.) local content against REI4P thresholds and targets

Bid window (BW) Technology	BW 1			BW 2			BW 3			BW 3.5		BW 4	
	Min.	Target	Avg.	Min.	Target	Avg.	Min.	Target	Avg.	Avg.	Min.	Target	Avg.
						Share of local content in total project expenditure (%)							
Onshore wind	25	45	27.4	25	60	48.1	40	65	46.9	–	40	65	44.4
Solar PV	35	50	38.4	35	60	53.4	45	65	53.8	–	45	65	62.3
CSP	35	50	38.4	35	60	43.8	45	65	44.3	43	40	65	–
Biomass	25	45	–	25	60	–	40	65	40	–	40	65	47.8
Biogas	25	45	–	25	60	–	40	65	–	–	40	65	–
Landfill gas	25	45	–	25	60	–	40	65	41.9	–	40	65	–
Small hydro	25	45	–	25	60	76.3	40	65	–	–	40	65	40

Source: IRENA (2018).

Table 7.13 Number of bids per REI4P bid window

Bid window	Number of bids received	Number of bids awarded
1	53	28
2	79	19
3	93	17
3.5	3	2
4	77	26
Expedited	106	19

Source: Authors' compilation.

achieved employment opportunities across all the bid windows are 143% of the planned numbers, that is, 33,707 job years.

The share of black citizens employed during construction (79%) and the early stages of operations (83%) significantly exceeded the 50% target and the 30% minimum threshold. Additionally, the share of skilled black citizens (as a percentage of skilled employees) for both construction (68%) and operations (79%) exceeded the 30% target and the minimum threshold of 18%. The share of local community members as a share of South Africa-based employees was 49% and 67% for construction and operations, respectively—exceeding the minimum threshold of 12% and the target of 20% (DoE, 2019c).

Initially, REI4P had preponderant foreign involvement in how projects were set up and designed. Over time, many of these skills have been transferred to South Africans (Matsuo and Schmidt, 2019). Given the stringent RfP and lender requirements, local developers have often needed to partner with international companies or on-sell projects to them (Eberhard and Naude, 2017). Local–foreign partnerships have become an increasingly popular and successful option for project developers (Eberhard and Naude, 2017). Many internationally backed IPPs have established local offices in South Africa as a result of REI4P, including Biotherm, Scatec Solar, Globeleq, Gestamp, Acciona, Abengoa, Windlab, Engie, ENEL Green Power, and Building Energy (now Red Rocket). Scatec Solar is a good example of an integrated project developer, owner, and operator, covering the entire value chain (with the exception of PV panel manufacturing). The Cape Town office has more than 90 employees, 90% plus of which are South African, and houses their engineering hub and global control and monitoring centre as well as being the base for the development of their new projects in Africa and beyond.

This international–local partnering and skills transfer was not limited to project development. Under REI4P bid requirements, EPC companies had to have a minimum of 8% black shareholders and a target of 20% (Baker and Wlokas, 2015). EPCs tended to be international companies that formed joint ventures or consortiums with one or more South African firms. Local large engineering firms such as Group Five, Murray and Roberts, and Aveng, were therefore appealing to these international companies not only for their extensive experience in the construction industry in the country but also for their levels of black ownership. Partnering with one of these large, local companies removed the need to form complicated joint ventures and consortiums (Baker and Wlokas, 2015).

7.4.1 Securing equity providers

IPPs were financed through debt, or equity, or—most often—a combination of the two. Although the larger portion of financing was generally secured through debt finance, stringent rules around equity and ownership had to be met. Equity providers for REI4P needed to comply with defined ownership structures that ensured B-BBEE, local, and community ownership (Figure 7.9). The nature of these ownership structures allowed a secondary equity market to develop in which equity on-selling occurs.

Ownership requirements of IPP projects resulted in multiple complex ownership structures involving a diversity of stakeholders, including the developer and other international, national, private, and public stakeholders. These included developers of IPP projects entering into a 50/50 joint venture with a South African and foreign company, international companies setting up a South African subsidiary company, and the formation of a consortium comprising predominantly international firms (Baker and Wlokas, 2015).

On average, South Africans owned 48% of the equity of all projects approved under REI4P (DoE, 2018b). Under bid windows 3, 5, and 4 alone, this was 57.8% on average, with 64.2% of this owned by black shareholders. In contrast, only 25% of the equity was foreign. Foreign investment in renewable energy projects provided opportunities for skills transfer and the establishment of a local industry (DoE, 2018b). Local community structures owned 7.1% of the equity share under bid window 4, entitling local communities to US$ 400 million net dividends over the 20-year lifetime of the projects. The DMRE, through the IPP Office, committed to ensuring that community participation and impact were monitored (DoE, 2018b).

Equity investment was provided by a range of entities, which included South African companies such as Old Mutual, South Africa's development

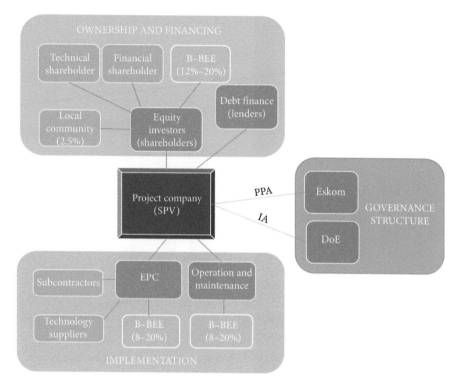

Figure 7.9 Project structure and ownership requirements for REI4P project development

Source: Adapted from Baker and Wlokas (2015).

finance institutions (DFIs), international infrastructure and investment funds, B-BBEE investors and partners, and community trusts, which were often funded by the DBSA, Industrial Development Corporation (IDC), and the Public Investment Corporation (PIC) (Baker and Wlokas, 2015).

There was also sustained interest from international companies. Firms were attracted to the potential for investor diversification and higher returns on capital in comparison to developed countries (Eberhard and Naude, 2017). Generally, the dominant equity shareholders tended to be international developers (Baker and Wlokas, 2015).

Analysing awarded REI4P bids based on the projects' majority shareholders (Figure 7.10) shows that each round of bidding generally saw more capacity being awarded to a smaller pool of mostly large international bidders (e.g. ENEL Green Power, Old Mutual, and Mainstream). In this context, there was a perceived risk that local industry could be stifled as local firms were discouraged from competing (Kruger et al., forthcoming).

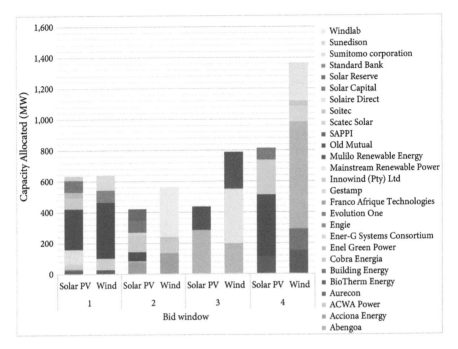

Figure 7.10 REI4P capacity awarded to project majority shareholders by technology: Bid windows 1–4

Source: Authors' compilation.

Additionally, BBEEE shareholding tended to be concentrated in no more than 10 firms.

However, it would be incorrect to conclude that market concentration took place to a significant degree. The major successful bidders tended to differ from round to round. Figure 7.10 shows that in bid window 3, only two bidders—ENEL Green Power and Mulilo Renewable Energy—secured any solar PV capacity, while these same firms, along with Mainstream Renewable Power, secured all onshore wind capacity. None of these firms secured any projects in bid window 2. Bid window 4 saw more bidders awarded, and while ENEL and Mulilo were awarded most of the onshore wind capacity, Old Mutual[6] and Scatec were awarded the lion's share of the solar PV projects.

The apparent dominance of certain international firms in REI4P's later rounds ultimately came down to cost, determined by five elements that were unique to these types of bidders:

---

[6] Old Mutual bought SunEdison's projects after the latter declared bankruptcy in 2016.

- their ability to access cheaper capital, often in the form of corporate financing;
- economies of scale;
- the ability to develop and bid a portfolio of projects, thereby aggregating and reducing costs across the portfolio;
- the negotiating power that came with being a major international player driving down supplier and service provider costs; and
- the ability to integrate the project development and operations functions, thereby squeezing margins across the value chain and opening up additional sources of revenue for a project.

What was the impact of this level of market concentration? Auction efficiency was not affected, with prices continuing their steep decline over the bidding rounds, even as larger volumes were awarded to fewer bidders. Neither was there a significant decrease in competition levels. In fact, there was a general trend of more bids being submitted during each round (Table 7.14). It is also important to note that the prominence of large, international firms in the awarded pool of bidders did not necessarily imply a crowding out of other players. They represented only one part of the value chain (in this case, majority shareholding), which was still coupled in the South African programme with community, B-BBEE, and local shareholding. More generally, the South African renewable energy industry expanded significantly over time, with many more project developers, investors, lenders, advisers, and service providers active than before (Matsuo and Schmidt, 2019). While there has been some consolidation and loss of skills in the industry in recent years, this has been driven by the uncertainty caused by the delays in the signing of the bid window 4 PPAs and government's seeming inability (or unwillingness) to launch new procurement rounds.

Equity providers for SP–I4P included corporate companies, which financed 50% of all the projects awarded (Figure 7.11) (Eberhard and Naude, 2017). Since these projects were smaller, it could have been difficult to access debt financing as the costs involved in a project financed deal remained substantial, while representing a much smaller return. Consequently, financing from corporate entities was a general expectation.

While REI4P projects' debt could be on-sold almost immediately after commercial operation began, with approval from the DoE or the IPP Office, equity could only be sold three years after COD, subject to the approval of the DoE and the initial lenders. B-BEEE ownership could, however, not be on-sold. This created a problem for many B-BEEE shareholders, whose shareholding was financed on relatively expensive terms by South African

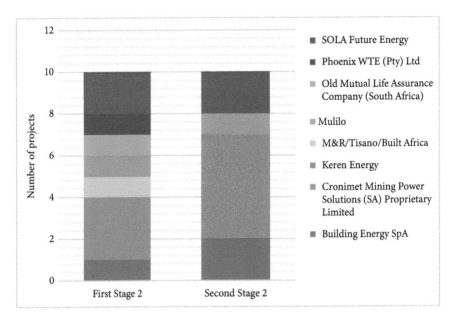

Figure 7.11 SP–I4P capacity awarded to project majority shareholders

Source: Authors' compilation.

DFIs and who consequently did not see substantial economic benefits in the short-to-medium -term (Makamure, 2016).

Equity shareholding in these projects could quickly become assets that were purchased, sold, and repackaged in financial markets (Baker and Wlokas, 2015). This could defeat the purpose of conducting due diligence of a project and posed a problem in assigning responsibility to ownership structures. Given that project owners held responsibility for implementing a project, changes in ownership structures caused by the sale of equity shares could have prevented responsibilities from being upheld (Baker and Wlokas, 2015). Thus far, this has not proved to be the case, with most equity transactions involving entities already invested in REI4P in one form or another. In addition, the significant funding provided by South African lenders and their long-term exposure on these projects ensured that they carefully monitor compliance with responsibilities, even with a chance in ownership.

7.4.2 Securing debt providers

7.4.2.1 Debt financing

A higher gearing ratio, or ratio of equity to debt, is generally an indication of lower levels of risk in an infrastructure investment project. In the case of

South Africa's REI4P, this gearing ratio was often as high as 80:20. Essentially, more debt translates into a lower average cost of funding since debt finance returns are generally lower than those required by equity, which leads to a lower tariff and, consequently, decreases the price of the project (Baker and Wlokas, 2015). Since lenders provide debt on fixed loan terms, a key priority is the minimization of risk (Baker and Wlokas, 2015). Lenders are the first in line to receive revenue generated by a project. Project sponsors (equity investors) carry more risk since their revenue returns are dependent on the success of the project.

Project finance loans are non- or limited-recourse loans, meaning that lenders have almost no access to the company's balance sheet. In the event of a default, the lender would be able to seize only the SPV's assets. Corporate finance loans are lent against a company's balance sheet, and therefore companies are more vulnerable in the event of a default. Due to the limited recourse offered by project finance loans, a significant amount of due diligence is required by commercial banks to ensure the bankability of the project, regardless of its size. It is a costly and lengthy process and so, for smaller projects like those in SP–I4P, the marginal returns of the banks were often too low (Eberhard and Naude, 2017).

Of the 92 preferred bidders to date (excluding SP–I4P), 79 projects used a combination of project finance and equity, and the remaining 13 bids used corporate finance only. As a result, external debt (project financing) accounted for a significant R 125.6 billion (65%) of the R 193 billion total funding raised in bid windows 1–4, while equity and corporate finance accounted for the remaining 23% and 12%, respectively (Eberhard and Naude, 2017). The large bidders that could afford to bid on a corporate finance basis did not necessarily end up financing projects on these terms. Rather, after using this cheaper form of debt to bid low tariffs and secure a large number of projects, these entities approached South African commercial banks to provide debt to these projects on a project finance basis.

Debt was mainly provided by local entities (Figure 7.12). South Africa's five largest banks, Amalgamated Banks of South Africa (ABSA), Nedbank, Rand Merchant Bank (RMB), Standard Bank, and Investec, contributed 68% of the debt pool (Eberhard and Naude, 2017). DBSA and IDC provided 13% of the debt, with the remainder provided by other DFIs and local insurance/asset management companies. The significant involvement of institutional investors is an important development since it represents the deepest but most risk-averse pool of funding for renewable energy projects (Wuester et al., 2016). The fact that institutional investors, such as pension funds, were willing to commit debt prior to commercial operation shows that

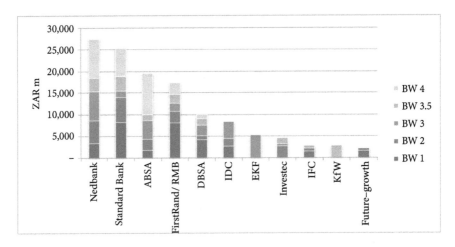

Figure 7.12 Largest nominal debt investors in REI4P at bidding stage
Source: Eberhard and Naude (2017).

the financial markets had grown very comfortable with the risks associated with renewable energy projects (Eberhard and Naude, 2017).

On average, debt financing on renewable energy projects under REI4P was based on an annual interest rate of 12% for a 20-year period. Compared to the United States and other European countries, this interest rate was significantly higher than their relatively fixed annual interest rate of 7% over a 10–15-year period (Nelson and Shrimali, 2014). Therefore, higher interest rates in South Africa for debt financing under REI4P created strong incentives for investment into renewable energy project investments in the country.

Under SP–I4P, the first 10 project financed projects would receive senior debt from the IDC and specialist black-owned fund manager, Mergence Investment Managers. However, as mentioned above, project finance, typically supplied by commercial banks, was difficult to access for smaller projects. Corporate finance and DFIs therefore became an important source of funding (Eberhard and Naude, 2017).

The difficulty small projects faced in accessing project finance was partially mitigated by KfW's Facility for Investment in Renewable Small Transactions (FIRST) Fund. This fund was a partnership between KfW and South African commercial banks where banks contribute senior debt to the fund while KfW sets up a first-loss debt facility as well as grant-type funding to fill the development finance role in the fund (Hawarden, n.d.; van Zyl, 2018). FIRST tried to overcome the challenges involved in financing smaller IPPs by having the development funding included in the debt mix as well as having a fund manager to conduct the detailed project assessment and build up a portfolio of projects that could share the burden of closing the financing. The fund was structured and closed to make US\$ 88.4 million[7] of funding available for preferred SP–I4P bidders (Hawarden, n.d.). The FIRST fund is yet to finance any SP–I4P projects, as none have had their PPAs signed, and so has diverted its funding to commercial and industrial projects.

7.4.3 Strategic management of project implementation

Strategic management, in terms of how the private sector and investors manage relationships with the public and broader society was one of the weaker areas of REI4P. The sector includes a diverse group of people and entities, making it difficult to develop a coherent message. Entities involved include, for example, the South African Photovoltaic Industry Association (SAPVIA), the South African Wind Energy Association (SAWEA), and the South African Independent Power Producers Association (SAIPPA), all with different backgrounds and interests.

REI4P aimed to contribute to B-BBEE and the creation of black industrialists, a key strategic priority for the sustainability of the industry. Black South Africans own, on average, 33% of projects that have reached financial close, that is, projects which are 3% higher than the 30% target. This includes black people in local communities that have ownership in the IPP projects that operate in their vicinities or nearby (DoE, 2019b). Previously, projects were able to use community trusts as a contributor to the black ownership target but, as trusts are not a partner in project delivery, limited skills or expertise were transferred from the foreign companies leading the projects. This has reportedly inhibited the growth of a 'genuine local energy industry' (Mthembi, 2016). Bid window 4 placed more emphasis on active ownership and participation in the project company through changing the economic development thresholds.

The communities who are most affected by, and have the most opportunity to benefit from, IPP projects have generally also not been part of the broader dialogue. The procurement documents did not clearly define a framework associated with socio-economic development (SED), ED, and local ownership (WWF, 2016). Despite the specific attention paid to local communities in REI4P, there is also no guidance, or even a mandatory process, for the

---

[7] At an exchange rate of 14.7, equivalent to ZAR 1,3 billion.

actual engagement with the local communities around projects (besides the EIAR).

The degree to which communities participate in decision-making around the project's local economic development investments was therefore at the sole discretion of the company in question (WWF, 2016). Companies were concerned about project compliance, meeting investor and shareholder expectations, and negotiating associated risks. Community involvement in projects was associated with high levels of risk, which led companies to favour the funding of established non-governmental organizations (NGOs) and pre-established projects to fulfil their obligations (WWF, 2016).

Additionally, there has been limited cooperation amongst IPPs to date regarding their ED work—although there are some examples of new governance and coordination models being tested. The uncoordinated nature of efforts by individual IPPs, community trusts, and other development partners limited the potential for meaningful development impact at the municipal and community levels. This is especially important in areas which have multiple renewable energy projects (Mabilu, 2018).

7.5 Risks and opportunities for the future of South Africa's renewable energy auction programmes

This section discusses risks and opportunities which have the potential to define the future of renewable energy procurement in South Africa.

7.5.1 Restructuring Eskom: Ensuring sustainability

Eskom's refusal to sign IPP contracts from bid window 4 has introduced significant uncertainty about the future of the programme. Normally, the need for sovereign guarantees for IPPs steadily decreases with the successful progress of the procurement programme. However, due to the bid window 4 delays, prolonged policy uncertainty (including a lack of new ministerial determinations), and Eskom's financial and operational crises there is an increased need for risk mitigation for any new REI4P projects.

The implementation of the Eskom Restructuring Roadmap will be critical in determining the future sustainability of Eskom, the electricity supply industry as a whole, and REI4P and SP–I4P programmes. One of the key objectives of the restructuring process is to ensure non-discriminatory and open access to the transmission grid, particularly for newcomers such as

IPPs, generally achieved by establishing an independent transmission system and market operator (Filipova and Boulle, 2019). Bidders and their funders are increasingly taking the view that an energy market will be established in the medium-to-long term that will enable them to sell power to alternative entities if Eskom fails to pay for power.

At the same time, Eskom's transition from being one entity to three separate subsidiaries poses challenges for REI4P. A key decision concerns whether the IPP Office will be moved into the system operator's structure, which would be the natural home for procurement—including for additional products and services such as capacity, flexibility, and ancillary services.

7.5.2 Implementing the just transition

REI4P and SP–I4P were intended to stimulate socio-economic development through local industrialization, manufacturing, and job creation, in addition to providing clean, affordable electricity. The DMRE has continued to increase economic development and local content thresholds and targets in each bid window. However, it has done this without addressing the underlying socio-economic problems or embedding these in broader strategic government policy initiatives. At the same time, local renewable energy component manufacturers and investors were held hostage by Eskom's refusal to sign contracts. Despite significant efforts of industry associations, the stalemate took years to resolve and most manufacturers who had established facilities in South Africa were forced to close down (Ntuli and Winand, 2019).

Renewable energy projects also have the capacity to empower and improve the well-being of local communities, as the outcomes in terms of socio-economic development from REI4P indicate. However, under REI4P, in some instances, the expectation that bidders need to make provisions for community development initiatives has introduced additional uncertainty and has had unintended consequences. With governance structures lacking at the local level and monitoring and evaluation systems lacking at the national level, there have been cases of increased marginalization and conflict within already vulnerable communities (Montmasson-Clair and das Nair, 2017).

There exists a perception that a transition from coal will result in a loss of tens of thousands of jobs. The country's trade unions strongly support this view, and many of them consequently refused to participate in the National Planning Commission's Just Transition dialogue process during 2018/2019. This process was aimed at ensuring that a low carbon transition protects livelihoods through providing alternatives and managing trade-offs, while ensuring reliable and affordable electricity to support social and economic development (OneWorld, 2019). This perception aligns with the IRP 2019, which highlighted the need for such a transition to be socially just and sensitive to the potential impacts on jobs and local economies (DoE, 2019d).

Currently, there appears to be a coalition of vested interests against introducing competition in electricity generation. In March 2017, coal transporters brought Pretoria to a standstill with protest action against renewable energy IPPs, who they claim are threatening their jobs as Eskom is producing less coal-generated electricity. In June 2017, the Coal Transporters Forum filed a court application against Eskom, NERSA, the Energy Minister of South Africa, and renewable energy IPPs, seeking to obstruct the signing of new PPAs. In the same month, the Congress of South African Trade Unions (COSATU) filed a notice with the National Economic Development and Labour Council (Nedlac) about possible protest action aiming to 'stop government from buying renewable energy at the expense of jobs and as an excuse to privatise Eskom' (COSATU, 2017). COSATU reinforced its position against the energy sector reform, stating that energy is a public good and, as such, it should be in the control of government and public entities as its privatization may result in an unjust transition (COSATU, 2017). In March 2019, the High Court in Pretoria dismissed the application of the Coal Transporters Forum, based on overwhelming evidence by the defendants. These, including NERSA, provided evidence that each successful IPP bidder was only issued with an electricity generation licence after following a due public participation process for their particular project (Smith, 2019). Despite the successful rebuttal of this case, the future of South Africa's electricity system is highly contentious and any change in the status quo (including the introduction of more renewable energy) will be subject to considerable pushback.

Careful planning and management of the transition are critical to ensuring that it is socially just. Policy frameworks for a just transition need to be proactive, flexible, and clear and adapt to the changes in the global energy space. Policy frameworks also need to take full advantage of opportunities afforded by the growth of emerging sectors, such as renewable energy. Government sees REI4P as a key tool for implementing the just transition process through the programme's economic development requirements and criteria. Auction design has the potential to play a key role in managing the transition and ensuring that it is economically and socially just. However, while auction design can contribute to this objective, it simply cannot be the sole, or even prime, tool for managing the transition. In fact, South

Africa's auction experience has demonstrated the complexity involved in using a procurement method to deliver a range of benefits beyond electricity price reduction and energy security. Burdening REI4P (and, by implication, private investors) with mitigating the transition impacts is problematic as neither the IPP Office nor the project developers have the resources or the mandate to fulfil this purpose.

7.5.3 New electricity business models: Opportunities for IPPs

South Africa's electricity sector is facing technological disruptions, largely driven by the reducing costs of renewable energy technologies, which make decentralized options for electricity generation ever more competitive and attractive. These changes add impetus to the need to rethink the sector's structure and business model across the value chain and at all levels of governance, including, for example, municipal electricity service delivery models. Enabling local and provincial governments to purchase electricity from IPPs will reduce the country's dependence on coal as a primary source of energy, help to reduce carbon emissions, and help cities to increase their energy security.

7.5.4 Urgent need for certainty: Launching a new bid window

Energy security concerns and the Eskom crisis have highlighted the need to urgently secure new generation capacity. The lengthy delay between IRP 2011 and IRP 2019 significantly damaged the emerging renewable energy industry in South Africa. The approval of IRP 2019 does, however, send positive signals to investors since it includes plans for an additional 20 GW of renewable energy generation to be procured and come online by 2030. However, it also acknowledges that the risk of prolonged supply shortages in the immediate term is significant in Eskom's current state (DoE, 2019d). New generation capacity takes time to procure and implement, even if it is modular and decentralized, as in the case of renewable-energy-based projects. The IRP indicates a capacity gap of 2–3 GW of short-term generation, highlighting the need for urgent procurement of new plants, coupled with the implementation of supply and demand-side measures in the short term to avoid power supply shortages and power cuts (DoE, 2019d).

The IRP 2019 makes a specific policy recommendation for the immediate initiation of a medium-term power purchase programme similar to that adopted following the IRP 2010–2030 (DoE, 2019d). In addition, the plan encourages government support for the development of generation for own use through 'the enactment of policies and regulations that eliminate red tape without compromising security of supply' (DoE, 2019d: 40).

In addition, the certainty which surrounded REI4P in the past has been eroded due to government's attempts at renegotiating PPAs. Bid window 4 projects were first asked to reduce the prices from the levels at which they were contracted. This request was later retracted as it was deemed to be unconstitutional. Later, the IPPs were asked to increase their B-BBEE shareholding shares, which they were allowed to do under the value-for-money criteria (aimed at preventing excessive success payments to awarded bidders). This introduced additional uncertainty for IPPs as another attempt to change the conditions under which they had bid. The projects awarded under SP-I4P have also been asked by the IPP Office to propose various ways of reducing their prices, from extending their PPAs to reducing enterprise development and socio-economic development commitments, among others. This has contributed to their inability to reach financial close and has, once again, undermined certainty in the programme's commitment.

The lack of decisions, changes in top leadership positions, reneging on government commitments, threats to renegotiate prices, moving of goalposts, and failure to stick to the rules of the procurement process are all contributing to a much more risky investment environment for the country. In the end, South African citizens end up carrying these costs through limited energy security, depressed economic growth levels, higher costs of borrowing, and higher electricity costs.

7.6 Lessons learned from South Africa's renewable energy auction programme

Several design features of REI4P have been instrumental in reducing barriers to entry and allowing new electricity generation actors to enter South Africa's vertically integrated power sector. It is important to note that the REI4P design was benchmarked against international best practice and in wide consultation with the private sector and lenders, thus incorporating their specific needs and requirements.

7.6.1 Enabling policy environment

In South Africa, the REI4P procurement framework could only be successfully implemented once there was policy certainty about the role of renewable energy and an associated investment strategy—clearly defining the role of the private sector (Eberhard and Naude, 2017). The importance of a coherent underlying policy framework for the success of REI4P cannot be overstated (Eberhard and Naude, 2017). National energy policies, and renewable energy policies more specifically, are key for setting up and communicating a roadmap to guide investments in renewable energy generation. Policy objectives and targets on their own are not enough to drive progress as the private sector will remain reluctant to invest on this basis alone. As noted earlier, in South Africa, renewable energy targets were in place for almost a decade prior to the introduction of REI4P but did not lead to any increase in renewable energy investments (Eberhard and Naude, 2017). A country's energy policy framework needs to include a clear implementation strategy that is linked to electricity planning and timely procurement. In addition, specific actors must be identified and mandated to drive this process.

7.6.2 Political support and coordinated governance

South Africa's commitments to increasing the share of renewable energy in the generation mix, as per the country's nationally determined contributions (NDCs), have had a significant impact on electricity planning, including the launch of REI4P. However, power shortages and power cuts between 2008 and 2011 also played a key role in both influencing electricity planning and driving political support for urgent additions of new generation capacity, which was most easily achieved by renewable energy projects (Morris and Martin, 2015; Eberhard and Naude, 2017).

Political support played a crucial role in launching REI4P and continued support has helped to sustain it. This political support has been created as a result of the REI4P procurement process, which has been underpinned by transparency and a lack of corruption. The programme's actual impact in terms of broader social and economic benefits has also contributed to strengthening the political support behind it, despite the fact that challenges remain, as seen by recent delays and the lack of progress under the long-awaited bid window 5 (Eberhard and Naude, 2017).

The independence of the implementing unit and transparency of the process helped to build and sustain trust in the programme. Bid evaluations were conducted by independent professional firms according to transparent and consistent evaluation criteria, in a secure environment, with CCTV cameras. The use of high-quality, standardized, and bankable documentation, including the PPAs and IAs, as part of the RfP, guaranteed security in terms of non-discriminatory access to the grid and removed any barriers to entry for IPPs competing with the national utility in terms of electricity generation (Eberhard and Naude, 2017).

Clearly mandated and coordinated leadership has been a key success factor behind the programme (Morris and Martin 2015; Montmasson-Clair and das Nair, 2017). The appointment of a programme champion to head up the IPP Office was key in ensuring the programme's success. Karen Breytenbach's competency and experience in managing transaction advisers and challenging them to find tailored solutions for the country was a main contributing success factor.

7.6.3 Risk allocation

Another critical factor for success was the perception of potential investors regarding the level of risk compared to the rate of return associated with participating in REI4P and SP–I4P. The design of REI4P and SP–I4P incorporates various mechanisms for mitigating risk for the bidders, government, and the off-taker (Eskom). The way in which these instruments were designed and implemented has contributed significantly to appropriate risk allocation between all stakeholders (section 7.5). In addition, international standards were applied in designing the PPA that governs the revenue streams of investors and funders alike (Montmasson-Clair and das Nair, 2017).

7.6.4 Implementation structure and process

There are several key implementation structure features of REI4P and SP–I4P which contributed to their past success. These included the *single-stage model* for REI4P, which proved to be less costly and time-consuming for the government. However, while this reduced costs for the government, it shifted the burden in terms of transaction costs to bidders as many had to incur these costs despite losing the tender.

REI4P is structured as a multiple-bid round programme, which has had several positive effects.

- It enabled a learning-by-doing model and has generated important learnings for both the DoE (now DMRE) and the bidders. Between the various bid windows, both bidders and the IPP Office had the opportunity to test different approaches. This allowed the IPP Office to improve on the overall process, and the outcomes, as seen from increased competition and low prices.

- The ongoing process and consecutive bid rounds were key in increasing competition by ensuring continued interest in the programme.
- Reduced prices from consecutive bid windows, in turn, enhanced political support for REI4P.
- The staggered procurement process has the potential to contribute to the development of a local renewable energy industry (conditional upon policy and planning certainty).

7.6.5 Lessons from the failures: The need for policy certainty

Ensuring policy certainty is absolutely critical to sustaining investor confidence in the renewable energy programme since the entire IPP auction model depends on continuous and sustained investment. The start–stop–start, delayed procurement process has leeched investor confidence, with negative impacts along the value chain. Large industrial manufacturers of critical first-tier components have either halted production, exited the market, or shelved future investment decisions. Smaller local firms, who were dependent on contracts within the value chain and unable to deal with structural breaks in supplier contracts, felt the impact the most, and many disappeared. As a consequence, the local content programme, instead of taking off, has rather limped along.

There is a clear and simple lesson to be learnt from these failures. Trust is hard won and easily lost. Building and sustaining trust should be the top priority for any auction programme as it underpins the success of the entire endeavour.

7.7 References

African News Agency (2018). 'Eskom Expresses Pride on Improved Access to Electricity'. *IOL News*, 28 September, https://www.iol.co.za/news/south-africa/eskom-expresses-pride-on-improved-access-to-electricity–17259230 (accessed 21 April 2023).

Amra, R. (2013). 'Back to the Drawing Board?: A Critical Evaluation of South Africa's Electricity Tariff-Setting Methodology'. *Biennial Conference of the Economic Society of South Africa*, Bloemfontein, 25–27.

Baker, L. (2015). Renewable energy in South Africa's minerals-energy complex: A "low carbon" transition?. *Review of African Political Economy*. Vol 42 Issue 144. https://www.tandfonline.com/doi/abs/10.1080/03056244.2014.953471

Baker, L & Sovacool, B. (2017). The political economy of technological capabilities and global production networks in South Africa's wind and solar photovoltaic (PV) industries. *Political Geographies*. Vol 60, Sep 2017. Pp 1–12. https://www.sciencedirect.com/science/article/pii/S096262981630186X

Baker, L., and Wlokas, H. L. (2015). 'South Africa's Renewable Energy Procurement: A New Frontier?' Energy Research Centre, University of Cape Town, http://www.erc.uct.ac.za/sites/default/files/image_tool/images/119/Papers-2015/15-Baker-Wlokas-RE_frontier.pdf (accessed 21 April 2023).

Baker, Lucy (2016) Post-apartheid electricity policy and the emergence of South Africa's renewable energy sector. Working Paper. UNU-Wider, Helsinki.

Bellini. (2019). 'South Africa Proposes Voluntary Reduction of Tariffs Awarded in First Three REIPPPP Rounds', 1 October, https://www.pv-magazine.com/2019/10/01/south-africa-proposes-voluntary-reduction-of-tariffs-awarded-in-first-three-reipppp-round (accessed 21 April 2023).

Bungane, B. (2018). 'NERSA Withdraws Its Draft for Small-Scale Embedded Generation Rules'. 22 May, ESI Africa, https://www.esi-africa.com/industry-sectors/business-and-markets/nersa-withdraws-its-draft-small-scale-embedded-generation-rules (accessed 21 April 2023).

Burkhardt, P., and Cohen, M. (2019). 'Two Mammoth Power Plants Are Sinking Eskom and South Africa'. *Bloomberg Business*, 9 October, https://www.bloomberg.com/news/articles/2019-10-09/two-mammoth-power-plants-are-sinking-eskom-and-south-africa (accessed 21 April 2023).

Carbon Brief. (2018). 'The Carbon Brief Profile: South Africa'. 15 October, https://www.carbonbrief.org/the-carbon-brief-profile-south-africa (accessed 21 April 2023).

Creamer, T. (2017). 'IPP Office to Be Incorporates into Overhauled Central Energy Fund'. *Engineering News*, 19 May, http://m.engineeringnews.co.za/article/ipp-office-to-be-incorporated-into-overhauled-central-energy-fund-2017-05–19 (accessed 21 April 2023).

Creamer, T. (2019). 'Gordhan's IPP Renegotiation Proposal Triggers "Breach of Contract" Warnings', https://www.engineeringnews.co.za/article/gordhans-ipp-renegotiation-proposal-triggers-breach-of-contract-warnings-2019-02–15 (accessed 21 April 2023).

Cruywagen, M., Davies, M. & Swilling, M. (2019). Estimating the cost of a just transition in South Africa's coal sector. Protecting workers, stimulating regional development and accelerating a low-carbon transition. https://tips.org.za/images/

report_Estimating_the_cost_of_a_just_transition_in_South_Africas_coal_
sector.pdf

CSIR (Council for Scientific and Industrial Research) (2019). 'Additional Renewable Energy Development Zones Proposed for Wind and Solar PV'. 4 November, https://www.csir.co.za/renewable-energy-development-zones (accessed 21 April 2023).

Deloitte Touche Tohmatsu Limited, (2017). Africa in 2017: Shaping the continent's future. Summary report of the conference held on 25 January 2017 in Johannesburg.

DME (Department of Minerals and Energy) (2003a). 'Electricity Basic Services Support Tariff (Free Basic Electricity) Policy'. *Government Gazette* No. 25088.

DME (2003b). 'White Paper on Renewable Energy, South Africa'. DME.

DoE (2012). 'IPP Procurement Programme 2012. Section 34(1) of the Electricity Regulation Act 2006'.

DoE (2015a). 'Small Projects IPP Procurement Programme First Stage 2 Bid Submission Phase Preferred Bidders' Announcement'. Presentation, https://www.ipp-projects.co.za/PressCentre (accessed 21 April 2023).

DoE (2015b). 'South Africa's Intended Nationally Determined Contribution (INDC)', https://www.environment.gov.za/sites/default/files/docs/sanational_determinedcontribution.pdf (accessed 21 April 2023).

DoE (2016b). 'Integrated Energy Plan (IEP)'. Department of Energy, South Africa.

DoE (2017b). 'Energy Budget Vote for 2017/18 Financial Year'. Parliament of South Africa, 19 May.

DoE (2017e). 'Small Projects IPP Procurement Programme: Second Stage 2 Bid Submission Phase Preferred Bidders'. Presentation, https://ipp-projects.co.za/PressCentre/GetAllPressReleases (accessed 21 April 2023).

DoE (2018b). 'Media Statement by Minister Jeff Radebe, Minister of Energy on the Independent Power Producer Programmes 8 March 2018', http://www.energy.gov.za/files/media/pr/2018/MediaStatement-on-the-Independent-Power-Producer-Programmes-08032018.pdf (accessed 21 April 2023).

DoE (2019b). 'Independent Power Producers Procurement Programme (IPPPP): An Overview'. 31 March, https://file:///Users/OWG/Downloads/20190522_IPP%20Office%20Q4_2018-19%20Overview.pdf%20(2).pdf (accessed 21 April 2023).

DoE (2019c). 'Independent Power Producers Procurement Programme (IPPPP): An Overview'. 30 June,: https://file:///Users/OWG/Downloads/20190522_IPP%20Office%20Q4_2018-19%20Overview.pdf%20(2).pdf (accessed 21 April 2023).

DoE (2019d). 'Integrated Resource Plan (IRP2019)', https://t.co/PCXvWbKPaV (accessed 21 April 2023).

DPE (Department of Public Enterprises) (2019). 'Roadmap for Eskom in a Reformed Electricity Supply Industry'.

Eberhard, A., and Naude, R. (2017). *The South African Renewable Energy IPP Procurement Programme. Review, Lessons Learned & Proposals to Reduce Transaction Costs* (Cape Town: University of Cape Town, Graduate School of Business).

Eberhard, A., (2019). The power cuts will continue unless SA's new electricity plan translates into urgent new procurements. *Daily Maverick, 17 Oct 2019.* https://www.dailymaverick.co.za/article/2019-10-17-the-power-cuts-will-continue-unless-sas-new-electricity-plan-translates-into-urgent-new-power-procurements/

Eberhard, A., Kolker, J., and Leigland, J. (2014). 'South Africa's Renewable Energy IPP Procurement Program: Success Factors and Lessons'. May, https://www.gsb.uct.ac.za/files/ppiafreport.pdf (accessed 21 April 2023).

Eskom (2019a). 'Integrated Report', http://www.eskom.co.za/IR2019/Documents/Eskom_2019_integrated_report.pdf (accessed 21 April 2023).

Eskom (2019b). 'Tariff History: Historical Average Price Increase', http://www.eskom.co.za/CustomerCare/TariffsAndCharges/Pages/Tariff_History.aspx (accessed 21 April 2023).

Filipova, A., and Boulle, M. (2019). 'Key Lessons on Institutional Arrangements for Managing the Restructuring of Power Utilities'. Policy Note. Power Futures Lab, Graduate School of Business. University of Cape Town.

Filipova, A., Wewege, S., Unite, E., Kruger, W. & Kuse, S. (2019). South Africa country report. Report 6: Energy & Economic Growth Research Programme. Power Futures Lab, University of Cape Town. Cape Town. https://www.gsb.uct.ac.za/files/South_Africa_Country_Report_EEG_1.pdf

Godinho, C., and Hermanus, L. (2018). '(Re)conceptualising State Capture—With a Case Study of South African Power Company Eskom', http://www.gsb.uct.ac.za/files/Godinho_Hermanus_2018_ReconceptualisingStateCapture_Eskom.pdf (accessed 21 April 2023).

GreenCape (2019). 'Energy Services 2019 Market Intelligence Report', https://www.greencape.co.za/assets/Uploads/ENERGY-SERVICES-MARKET-INTELLIGENCE-REPORT-WEB.pdf (accessed 21 April 2023).

Hartley, R & Mills, G. (2019). Fixing Eskom: Home trust and unavoidable action. Daily Maverick, 11 Oct 2019. https://www.dailymaverick.co.za/article/2019-10-11-fixing-eskom-home-truths-and-unavoidable-actions/

Hawarden (n.d.). 'SA's Small Renewable Energy Projects Receive Investment Boost from First Fund', https://www.rmb.co.za/news/sas-small-renewable-energy-projects-receive-investment-boost-from-first-fund (accessed 21 April 2023).

IEA (International Energy Agency) (2018). 'Market Report Series: Coal 2018'.

IPP Office (2019). 'Independent Power Producers Procurement Programme (IPPPP): An Overview. Quarterly Report', https://www.ipp-projects.co.za/Publications (accessed 21 April 2023).

IRENA (International Renewable Energy Agency) (2018). *Renewable Energy Auctions: Cases from Sub-Saharan Africa* (Abu Dhabi: International Renewable Energy Agency).

Kruger, W. (2012). 'An African Donor: Towards understanding South African aid allocation'. Masters Dissertation. University of Antwerp.

Kruger, W., Nygaard, I. & Kitzing, L. (2021). Counteracting market concentration in renewable energy auctions: Lessons learned from South Africa. Energy Policy 148 Part B, Jan 2021. Pp. 1-13. https://www.sciencedirect.com/science/article/abs/pii/S0301421520307060

Kruger, W., Stritzke, S. & Trotter, P. (2019). De-risking solar auctions in sub-Saharan Africa – A comparison of site selection strategies in South Africa and Zambia. Renewable and sustainable energy reviews. 104. https://www.gsb.uct.ac.za/files/DeriskingSolarAuctionsInSubSaharanAfrica.pdf

Mabilu, M. (2018). 'Strategic Community Development under REI4P: Current Approaches and Challenges', http://awsassets.wwf.org.za/downloads/strategic_community_development_under_rei4p.pdf (accessed 21 April 2023).

Maroga, J. (2009). 'Chief Executive Strategy Document'. *Politicsweb*, 6 November, https://www.politicsweb.co.za/documents/jacob-marogas-racial-tirade (accessed 21 April 2023).

Martin, B. & Winkler, H. (2014). Procurement models applied to independent power producer programmes in South Africa. Cape Town, Energy Research Centre. Energy Research Centre, University of Cape Town, Cape Town, South Africa. https://open.uct.ac.za/handle/11427/16896

Matsuo, T. & Schmidt. T. (2019). Managing tradeoffs in green industrial policies: The role of renewable energy policy design. World Development, Vol 122, Oct 2019, pp. 11-26. https://www.sciencedirect.com/science/article/abs/pii/S0305750X19301196

Mayer, H. (2018). 'Political Risk Insurance and Its Effectiveness in Supporting Private Sector Investment in Fragile States'. The LSE–Oxford Commission on State Fragility, Growth and Development, https://www.theigc.org/wp-content/uploads/2018/05/Political-risk-insurance.pdf (accessed 21 April 2023).

McCann, J. (2019). 'Medupi and Kusile: Costly and Faulty'. *Mail&Guardian*, 15 February, https://mg.co.za/article/2019-02-15-00-medupi-and-kusile-costly-and-faulty (accessed 21 April 2023).

Montmasson-Claire, G., and das Nair, R. (2017). 'South Africa's Renewable Energy Experience: Inclusive Growth Lessons', in Jonathan Klaaren, Simon Roberts, Imraan Valodia (eds) *Competition Law and Economic Regulation in Southern*

Africa: Addressing Market Power in Southern Africa (Johannesburg: Wits University Press), 189–214.

Morris, M., and Martin, L. (2015). 'Political Economy of Climate-Relevant Policies: The Case of Renewable Energy in South Africa'. Institute of Development Studies Evidence Report No.128, IDS/University of Cape Town.

Mthembi, F. (2016). 'Power and Local Trusts'. *Business Day*, http://www.bdlive.co.za/opinion/2016/08/24/power-and-local-trusts (accessed 21 April 2023).

National Economic Development and Labour Council (NEDLAC). 2017. NEDLAC certificate in respect of the Congress of South African Trade Unions Section 77 1(B) Notice on renewable energy and closure of coal mines. https://nedlac.org.za/wp-content/uploads/2022/08/Certificate-for-Cosatu-Renewable-Energy-and-Closure-of-Coal-Mines-Certificate-issued-on-5-September-2017.pdf

Nelson, D. & Shrimali, G. Finance mechanisms for lowering the cost of renewable energy in rapidly developing countries. Climate Policy Initiative. CPI series. https://www.climatepolicyinitiative.org/publication/finance-mechanisms-for-lowering-the-cost-of-renewable-energy-in-rapidly-developing-countries/

NERSA (National Energy Regulator of South Africa) (2012). 'Electricity Supply Statistics for South Africa 2012',

NPC (National Planning Commission) (2011). 'National Development Plan 2030. Our Future—Make It Work'. Executive Summary, Pretoria, https://www.gov.za/sites/default/files/Executive%20Summary-NDP%202030%20-%20Our%20future%20-%20make%20it%20work.pdf (accessed 21 April 2023).

Makamure, K. B. (2016). Refinancing options for the broad-based black economic empowerment (BBBEE) equity investments in the renewable energy independent power producer procurement program (REI4P) in South Africa. (Master in Business Administration), Graduate School of Business, University of Cape Town, South Africa.

Ntuli, N., and Winand, J. (2019). 'SAWEA Position Paper on RSA Manufacturing and Local Content Requirements in the REI4P'. South African Wind Energy Association, Manufacturers and Local Content Working Group, March, https://sawea.org.za/wp-content/uploads/2019/03/20190321-SAWEA-Position-Paper-on-Manufacturing-and-Local-Content-NN_VFINAL.pdf (accessed 21 April 2023).

Omarjee, L. (2019a). 'Gordhan: Govt Won't Scrap Costly Renewables Contracts, But Will Renegotiate Them'

Paton, C. (2019). 'Eskom Drags Nersa to Court'. *BusinessDay*, 11 October, https://www.businesslive.co.za/bd/national/2019-10-11-eskom-drags-nersa-to-court/?utm_source=&utm_medium=email&utm_campaign=Judges±dismiss±Zuma%E2%80%99s±claims±that±prosecution±was±too±tainted±to±go±ahead±%7C±Eskom±drags±Nersa±to±court±%7C±Peregrine±warns±of±

big±drop±in±earnings&utm_term=http%3A%2F%2Fwww.businesslive.co.
za%2Fbd%2Fnational%2F2019-10-11-eskom-drags-nersa-to-court%2F (accessed
21 October 2023).

PMG (Parliamentary Monitoring Group) 2018. 'Minister's Update on Energy Matters; With Deputy Minister Present'. Meeting Report, 8 May, https://pmg.org.za/
committee-meeting/26286 (accessed 21 April 20230.

Pombo-van Zyl, N. (2014). 'Grid Connection Delays Financial Close of South Africa's
Renewable Energy IPPs', https://www.esi-africa.com/top-stories/grid-connection-
delays-financial-close-of-south-africas-renewable-energy-ipps (accessed 21 April
2023).

SAWEA, (2019). Wind industry can release additional power into the grid now.
South Africa Wind Energy Association. https://sawea.org.za/wind-industry-can-
release-additional-power-into-the-grid-now/https://sawea.org.za/wind-energy-
sector-serves-the-countrys-development-agenda-but-requires-the-2019-irp/

Smith, C. (2019). 'Coal Transporters Forum Case against Eskom, Nersa Dismissed'.
Fin24,

StatsSA (2016). 'The State of Basic Service Delivery in South Africa: In-Depth
Analysis of the Community Survey 2016 Data'. Report No. 03-01-22.

StatsSA (2017). 'Poverty Trends in South Africa: An Examination of Absolute Poverty
between 2006 and 2015'. Report No. 03-10-06.

StatsSA (2018a). 'Electricity: Coal Use Inches Lower as Solar, Wind and Diesel Rise',
http://www.statssa.gov.za/?p=11292 (accessed 21 April 2023).

StatsSA (2019b). 'Quarterly Labour Force Survey Quarter 2: 2019', http://www.
statssa.gov.za/publications/P0211/P02112ndQuarter2019.pdf (accessed 21 April
2023).

Trading Economics (2019). 'South Africa GDP Growth Rate', https://
tradingeconomics.com/south-africa/gdp-growth (accessed 21 April 2023).

Trollip, H & Boulle, M. 2017. *'Challenges associated with implementing climate
change mitigation policy in South Africa'*. Energy Research Centre, University of
Cape Town. Research report series. https://www.africaportal.org/publications/
challenges-associated-with-implementing-climate-change-mitigation-policy-in-
south-africa/

van Zyl, N. (2018). 'Hope Springs: German Development Bank Signs Up

Wlokas, H. (2015). A review of the local community development requirements
in South Africa's renewable energy procurement programme. (WWF Technical
Report ZA 2015), World Wide Fund for Nature, South Africa. http://awsassets.
wwf.org.za/downloads/local_community_development_report_20150618.
pdf

Wright, J., and Calitz, J. (2019a). 'Brief Analysis of Variable Renewable
Energy Contribution during Loadshedding (Q1–2019)'. 15 April, https://

researchspace.csir.co.za/dspace/bitstream/handle/10204/10959/20190415-
Brief%20analysis%20of%20variable.pdf?sequence=3&isAllowed=y (accessed 21
April 2023).

Wuester, H., Lee, J. J., Lumijarvi, A., Flannery, S., Veilleux, N., & Joubert, A.
(2016). Unlocking renewable energy investment: The role of risk mitigation and
structured finance. International Renewable Energy Agency (IRENA). https://
www.irena.org/publications/2016/Jun/UnlockingRenewable-Energy-Investment-
The-role-of-risk-mitigation-and-structured-finance

Table 8.1 List of power plants in Zambia

Power plants	Location	Technology	Installed capacity (MW)	Category	COD
Chishimba Falls Hydro	Luombe River	Hydro, small (<50 MW)	6	Utility	1971
Kariba North Bank Hydro	Zambezi River	Hydro, large	720	Utility	1977 (600), 2012 (720)
Kariba North Bank Hydro Extension	Zambezi River	Hydro, large	360	Utility	2014
Lunzua Hydro	Mbala district	Hydro, small (<50 MW)	14.8	Utility	1960 (0.75), 2015 (14.8)
Lusiwasi Hydro	Lusiwasi River	Hydro, small (<50 MW)	12	Utility	1967 (to be decommissioned soon)
Musonda Falls Hydro	Luongo River	Hydro, small (<50 MW)	10	Utility	(5), 2018 (10)
Upper Kafue Gorge Hydro	Kafue Gorge	Hydro, large	990	Utility	1972, 1978, 1989 (900), 1994 (990)
Victoria Falls Hydro	Livingstone	Hydro, large	108	Utility	1938 (8), 1969 (68) and 1972 (108)
CEC Riverside Solar PV	Kitwe	Solar, PV	1	Utility	2018
Bangweulu Solar Power Plant	Lusaka South Multi-Facility Economic Zone	Solar, PV	47,5	IPP (Scaling solar)	2019
Ngonye Solar Power Plant	Lusaka South Multi-Facility Economic Zone	Solar, PV	34	IPP (Scaling solar)	2019

Continued

Table 8.1 *Continued*

Power plants	Location	Technology	Installed capacity (MW)	Category	COD
Ndola Energy	Indeni Petroleum Refinery Ltd	Diesel	105	IPP	2013 (50), 2017 (105)
TATA Itezhi-Tezhi HPP	Kafue River	Hydro, large	120	PPP	2016
Maamba mining-and-power project	Sinazongwe district	Coal	300	IPP	2016
Lunsemfwa Hydro	Lunsemfwa River	Hydro, large	24	IPP	1945 (12), 1961 (18), 2012 (24)
Mulungushi Hydro	Mulungushi River	Hydro, small (<50 MW)	32	IPP	1925 (2), 1927 (14), 1941 (20), 2009 (32)
Bulemu East Solar	Bulemu East	Solar, PV	20	IPP (GETFiT)	Awarded
Bulemu West Solar	Bulemu West	Solar, PV	20	IPP (GETFiT)	Awarded
Aurora Sola I	–	Solar, PV	20	IPP (GETFiT)	Awarded
Aurora Sola II	–	Solar, PV	20	IPP (GETFiT)	Awarded
Garneton North Solar	Garneton North	Solar, PV	20	IPP (GETFiT)	Awarded
Garneton South Solar	Garneton South	Solar, PV	20	IPP (GETFiT)	Awarded
Bancroft Diesel	Chililabombwe	OCGT	20	Embedded generation	1972
Konkola Deep Mining Project Diesel	Chililabombwe	ICE	24	Embedded generation	2012
Luano Diesel	Luano	OCGT	40	Embedded generation	1969
Luanshya Diesel	Luanshya	OCGT	10	Embedded generation	1978
Mufulira Diesel	Mufulira	OCGT	10	Embedded generation	1978

Source: Authors' compilation.

Table 8.2 Key institutions in Zambia's electricity sector

Ministry of Energy (MoE)	The Ministry of Energy was established in 2016 following a presidential directive to separate it from the defunct Ministry of Energy and Water Development (MEWD). The MoE is responsible for the formulation, development, and implementation of the national energy policy, strategy, and plan.
Energy Regulation Board (ERB)	The Energy Regulatory Board was established under the Energy Regulation Act of 1995 Chapter 436 of the Laws of Zambia. The main role of the ERB is to ensure equity across all players in the electricity value chain by ensuring that utilities are able to earn a reasonable return on investment whilst prices are affordable for customers and quality of service is not compromised. The ERB issues licences to prospective players, sets petrol and electricity prices, develops technical standards, and promotes new grid connections. It is also charged with fostering competition in the market and resolving conflicts amongst players.
ZESCO	ZESCO was established in 1970 as a state-owned (public) power utility company responsible for power generation, transmission, and distribution. ZESCO remains the largest electricity company in Zambia and is the single buyer of electricity from independent power producers (IPPs). Despite the formal liberalization of the sector, ZESCO operates as a monopoly and is fully owned by the Industrial Development Corporation (IDC). Due to a highly subsidized tariff, ZESCO has been limited in its capability to maintain existing assets, reinforce and expand the national grid, and increase generation capacity.
Copperbelt Energy Company (CEC)	The CEC owns and operates the transmission and distribution network in the Copperbelt area of the country, purchasing power from ZESCO and supplying it to the mines in the area. The CEC also operates 6 gas turbines (80 MW installed) for emergency power.
Office for Promoting Private Power Investment (OPPPI)	The OPPPI was created in 1999 as part of the then Ministry of Mines, Energy and Water. It is responsible for fostering private-sector participation in power projects in Zambia. The office is mandated to improve efficiency in the sector and ensure the use of sustainable and least-cost technologies by identifying projects, carrying out feasibility studies, developing and implementing competitive procurement programmes, and managing coordination with other government agencies.
Rural Electrification Agency (REA)	The Rural Electrification Authority (REA) is a statutory body established by an Act of Parliament No. 20 of 2003. The main role of the REA is to improve rural electrification using appropriate generation technologies. Functions include: management of the rural electrification fund; formulation, development, and implementation of the Rural Electrification Master Plan (REMP); promotion of appropriate energy

Continued

Table 8.2 *Continued*

	sources; and encouragement of private-sector players through competitive tenders, amongst others. The medium-term objective of the REA is to increase electricity access to 51% by 2030.
Zambia Development Agency	The Zambia Development Agency was created in 2006 by an Act of Parliament, and is responsible for boosting economic growth and development through the promotion of trade and investment. The agency serves as a platform for linking investors with information and services that eases market entry.
Industrial Development Corporation (IDC)	The Industrial Development Corporation (IDC) of Zambia was incorporated in 2014, pursuant to the Minister of Finance (Incorporation) Act Cap 349. It is a state-owned enterprise (SOE) that acts as an active investor and shareholder of state-owned enterprises (including ZESCO). The objective of the IDC is to position itself as the government's prime special-purpose vehicle (SPV) for facilitating investment and industrialization. IDC plays a vital role in Zambia's electricity sector by facilitating the provision of long-term finance for electricity projects.

Source: Authors' compilation.

for the Promotion of Private Power Investment (OPPPI), a specialized unit in the energy ministry tasked with increasing private investment in power generation and transmission. Despite the stated importance of increasing private participation in the power sector (World Bank, 2015; Batidzirai et al., 2018), OPPPI does not have a clear legal mandate to procure new power and is known to lack the capacity and resources needed to drive these processes (Kapika and Eberhard, 2013).

Zambia is in the top 10 of sub-Saharan Africa's power systems, with more than 2,850 MW installed capacity. Most of this capacity (2,396 MW) comes from hydropower, with two stations in particular generating most of the country's electricity: Upper Kafue Gorge hydro (990 MW) and the Kariba North Bank hydro (1,080 MW) (Figure 8.1 and Table 8.1). This makes Zambia's power system and economy particularly vulnerable to drought. The Zambian economy is mainly built around copper mining, which requires a reliable electricity supply to maintain production. In 2015, a severe drought caused daily blackouts of up to eight hours, and mines—which consume 60% of the country's electricity—were asked to cut their electricity use by 30%. This plunged the Zambian economy into crisis, with gross domestic product (GDP) growth rates falling to below 3% from levels above 10% only five years previously and the Zambian currency depreciating dramatically.

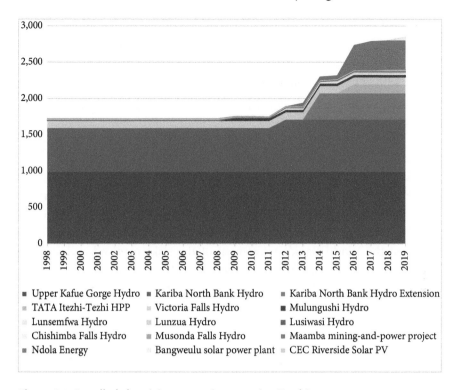

Figure 8.1 Installed electricity generation capacity, Zambia
Note: Blue = hydropower; red = thermal power; yellow = solar photovoltaic (PV) power.
Source: Authors' compilation.

The 2015 shock precipitated a financial crisis at ZESCO. Emergency power purchases from the Southern African Power Pool (SAPP)[6] (including emergency power barges anchored on the Mozambican coast) caused ZESCO to run up hundreds of millions of dollars in debt,[7] which it has not been repaying. It also had to buy expensive power from thermal-based IPPs (US$c 10/kWh), while electricity retail tariffs (US$c 6/kWh) have remained at below cost-reflective levels. Most worrying for investors is ZESCO's failure to pay these IPPs—including some of its newest suppliers, most notably the Maamba coal power station—on a timely basis or at all.

Zambia's electricity sector remains in dire straits, despite the government's attempts to address the crisis. Electricity tariffs were increased by

[6] Imports from Aggreko were pegged at USDc 18.8/kWh, while Karpower cost USDc 16.7/kWh. Imports from Mozambique cost USDc 7.6/kWh and the average SAPP tariff on imports from the day ahead market was USDc 6.7/kWh in October 2015 (Batidzirai et al., 2018).
[7] This debt burden rapidly increased through the dramatic depreciation of the kwacha in 2015.

75% in 2017,[8] and the regulatory act was amended to include the mines and their electricity supply contracts in the regulator's ambit. Historically, the mines were supplied through bilateral contracts (bulk supply agreements) with ZESCO, though the legitimacy of these contracts has been challenged in recent years through ad hoc tariff increases outside of the contracts.

It is therefore all the more surprising that IPP investors have flocked to Zambia. As already mentioned, both Scaling Solar and the GETFiT solar PV auctions attracted significant international and local interest. In fact, the GETFiT solar PV auction took place around the same time that the World Bank decided to cancel the second round of Scaling Solar procurement due to concerns about ZESCO's financial health. Investors had to take a view on the World Bank's assessment of the risks involved and seem to have based their bidding and pricing decisions largely on the quality of the procurement programmes and supporting international institutions rather than the fundamentals of the Zambian electricity sector investment climate. It is vital to unpack and understand the design of both auction programmes before completing an analysis of the management and governance structures used.

8.3 Renewable energy auction programmes in Zambia

8.3.1 Scaling Solar

Scaling Solar was the first competitive tendering programme for renewable IPPs in Zambia and followed closely on the heels of the successful renewable energy (RE) auction programmes in South Africa and Uganda. It was developed in response to the IFC's analysis of 20 promising solar markets in Africa, which found that large project developers were avoiding the region due to limited market sizes and a host of risks, costs, and uncertainties. The IFC sought to emulate the success of South Africa's Renewable Energy Independent Power Producer (REIPP) procurement programme and identified scale, transparent competition, a bankable contractual framework, and repetition as key success factors. But it also recognized that not all sub-Saharan African governments could, or wanted to, dedicate vast resources

---

[8] The ERB approved increases in tariffs that were reversed by the government in 2016, due to presidential elections, but which have since been reinstated.

to renewable energy programmes. Many sub-Saharan African countries did not have sufficiently deep financial markets, and there were various constraints caused by the small power markets in most of these countries. The off-taker credit quality and political uncertainties were also significant risk factors for investors in the area (Fergusson et al., 2015). Scaling Solar sought to mitigate the risks and costs for host governments and investors alike by combining the abovementioned success factors in a comprehensive, multi-country programme conducted under the World Bank Group umbrella.

Zambia was the first country in which the Scaling Solar programme was implemented. Agreements to implement the Scaling Solar model have since been signed with Ethiopia, Madagascar, Senegal,[9] Angola, Togo, and—significantly—Uzbekistan. The IDC of Zambia officially engaged the IFC as the lead transaction advisor. The approach taken in Zambia, and standard practice for the Scaling Solar programme, was focused on bringing solar PV projects of 50+ MW onto the grid within 24 months. It consisted of the following elements:

- conducting initial feasibility studies, site selection, and legal due diligence;[10]
- initiating a competitive bidding process with IFC acting as transaction advisor;
- developing a bankable, standardized contractual set of documents;
- offering stapled finance;
- offering additional risk-mitigation instruments, for example, Partial Risk Guarantees (PRG)s, Multilateral Investment Guarantee Agency (MIGA) political risk insurance, etc.)

Together, 'best practice' elements were meant to offer governments a standardized, straightforward solar PV procurement model with significant multilateral backing that translated into low tariffs and rapid project implementation. Thus far, the results seem to bear this out, with some notable but not unexpected hurdles along the way. Our analysis looks at exactly how this was done in the Zambian context and what it might mean for the Scaling Solar programme going forward.

---

[9] Awarded projects in Senegal reached financial close in July 2019.
[10] This was supported by a US$ 2 million grant from the United States Agency for International Development's (USAID's) Power Africa programme in Zambia.

8.3.2 GETFiT Zambia

Deutsche Bank's climate change advisors designed the GETFiT programme in response to the UN Secretary-General's Advisory Group on Energy and Climate Change request for new concepts to drive renewable energy investment in low-to-middle-income countries in 2010. The programme aimed to improve the enabling environment for private renewable energy projects by combining technical assistance (including developing standardized, bankable documentation), viability gap funding (in the form of premium payments on top of the existing feed-in tariffs), and project de-risking (through the provision of liquidity and termination support). Uganda was the first country that responded positively to this model. Donors, (including the Department for International Development (DfID) and the DECC, both in the United Kingdom, the governments of Norway and Germany, and the European Commission's Africa Infrastructure Trust Fund) committed about US$ 90 million to finance top-up payments. Launched in May 2013 and implemented by Germany's development bank, KfW, and Uganda's regulatory agency, ERA, Uganda's GETFiT programme procured 15 projects in three rounds. These were mostly small hydro, but also bagasse and biomass,[11] with project tariffs predetermined in a feed-in-tariff-like regime. In 2014, an additional procurement round was launched for solar PV, with projects competing for the award based on price. The two awarded solar PV projects reached financial close and commercial operation in record time and, at the time of commissioning, were the two largest solar PV installations in East Africa.

During the time that the Ugandan programme was being implemented, the possibility of exporting the GETFiT model was explored in countries such as Mozambique and Zambia. The Zambian Ministry of energy, which had been working on a feed-in-tariff programme that was all but destroyed by the Scaling Solar results, agreed to use the GETFiT model to contract and implement smaller-scale renewable energy IPPs. Support provided by GETFiT (and funded by a €31 million grant from the German government) included the provision of standardized procurement and legal documentation, support for the project permitting and licensing process, and support to ZESCO on renewable energy grid integration and running the procurement process. GETFiT Zambia would also provide top-up payments to eligible

---

[11] Some of the biomass projects were later removed from the programme due to commercial challenges.

projects but not for solar PV based on the technology's rapidly falling costs. It would also see a separate 5 MW micro-generation tender being launched with the explicit aim of promoting investment by Zambian firms.

The following sections focus on how the auction volume was decided (the auction demand), where the projects would be built, who was allowed to bid and how this was determined (qualification and compliance criteria), how the projects were evaluated and ranked, and which tools and mechanisms were used to ensure the commitment of bidders as well as fair risk allocation between the host government and the off-taker (seller and buyer liabilities).

8.3.3 Auction design

8.3.3.1 Auction demand

Planning remains a weak area of the Zambian electricity sector. In 2009, an electricity system development master plan was developed by the Energy Ministry, which, up to that point, had been working off a 1998 ZESCO plan. This 2009 plan has not been updated in the decade since its publication and appears to have had little impact in terms of determining actual investment decisions. While Zambia's REFiT strategy mentions that a least-cost integrated resource plan (IRP) will be developed in 2020, the practical reality is that the procurement volumes for both the Scaling Solar and GETFiT programmes were determined in a relatively ad hoc manner.

The Scaling Solar programme was meant to prop up the struggling national electricity system. As a consequence, the 600 MW Scaling Solar allocation was also the capacity shortfall caused by the 2014/2015 drought. This volume was divided into separate auction rounds: 100 MW in round 1 and 200 MW (later increased to 250 MW) in round 2. The initial 100 MW was further divided into two 50 MW projects, although the bid documentation allowed for some flexibility here: bidders could size their projects anywhere between 34 and 55 MW. Bidders were allowed to bid for both projects but would only be awarded one.

The approach to setting the auction volume for the GETFiT programme was at first more cautious. The initial allocation for the entire programme was 50 MW. This was later increased to 200 MW over three years (2017–2020) covering multiple technologies (solar PV, hydro, geothermal, wind, biomass) after grid integration studies convinced ZESCO that the system would be able to handle that much renewable energy. Of this 200 MW, 100 MW was allocated to the solar PV auction—to be met by 5 × 20 MW projects.[12] The auctioning authority maintained the right to adjust this volume post bidding, which they did by increasing the solar PV allocation to 120 MW after bids had been submitted, based on the strong price results.

8.3.3.2 Site selection

The selection and preparation of project sites has been one of the more controversial features of the Zambian auctions. Zambia has a dual land tenure system, with both privately held and communally held land owner- ship models. The two programmes decided to deal with this fact in different ways.

In the Scaling Solar programme, sites were provided to bidders as part of a strategy to reduce programme costs and risks as well as to ensure the rapid implementation of the projects. By doing this, the procurer sought to ensure that the required transmission infrastructure was available and in place and that required data (e.g. solar resource data), permits, and other requirements could be handled and coordinated by the government. In addition, given the small size of the Zambian grid and the relatively large scale of the solar projects, it was important to ensure that projects were optimally sized and located.

The selection of the project sites, the provision of the grid connection, and the collection of site data was handled by Zambian authorities. Site selec- tion was carried out by the Zambian Development Authority (ZDA), with the Lusaka South Multi-Facility Economic Zone (LSMFEZ) chosen as the location for the two projects.[13] Due to being located in this zone, projects would pay 0% tax on profits in the first five years of operation. Zambia's IDC leased the land for the two solar plants and on-leased it to the projects for the duration of the power purchase agreement (PPA). This action theoretically reduced the project development and capital expenditure costs for develop- ers. The IDC provided site climatic studies, grid interconnection information, grid stability and integration studies, site surveys, environmental and social scoping reports, legal due diligence reports, and tax and accounting due dili- gence reports. Many of these assessments were paid for by a grant from the United States Agency for International Development (USAID) Power Africa programme. Projects were responsible for building and paying for shallow grid connection works up to the sites' substation. No additional 'deep connection works' were required, and the necessary data, as well as

---

[12] Bidders could elect to submit smaller projects, since the 20 MW allocation was only a maximum. All bidders submitted projects at this size ceiling.

[13] The project sites took up about 5% of the LSMFEZ.

detailed specifications about the required purchaser interconnection facilities, was included in the PPA that was provided to bidders as part of the RfP documentation as well as in the programme's 'virtual data room'.

The environmental and social impact permitting processes, led by the IDC, needed to comply with the IFC's performance standards and are illustrative of the complexities involved in RE project development in many African countries. The project sites had a protracted history of resettlement preceding the programme. As an example, one of the project sites was provided to the project company 'clear and unencumbered' of human use and habitation. There were, however, two previous phases of government-managed resettlement for the whole economic zone that affected 35 households living on one of the project sites (established using satellite imagery). In total, 247 households were originally settled in the economic zone. A further 715 people depended on the site for farming purposes. As the area was a designated forest reserve, people were occupying and using the land illegally and could have been evicted. The government considered the 247 households living in the zone eligible for compensation and offered physical resettlement (including new land plots of 5–25 ha, temporary housing, relief food packages for three months, cash compensation, and farming inputs) to a site more than 700 km away. While 32 households opted for this relocation, the remaining 215 households opted for cash compensation. A further 20 households claimed that they had been mistakenly left out and were physically resettled. In 2015, shortly before the Scaling Solar programme, there appears to have been opportunistic settlement by 295 persons, who were moved to a village about 30 km away.[14]

The site selection and preparation processes caused serious implementation delays for both projects. Significant sinkholes were found on both sites, although the geotechnical assessments provided by the IDC were not detailed enough to allow bidders to fully cost the implications of this. The problem was severe enough to cause at least one major engineering, procurement, and construction (EPC) company to pull out of the programme. One of the project sites also bordered on a conservation area which, upon closer investigation, turned out to actually extend onto the site. This required a change in law to allow the site to be used for its intended purpose, pushing out the project's commercial operation date (COD) by at least a year. The fact that the IDC expressly stated, during the pre-qualification Q&A process, that further site due diligence was not needed only exacerbates these oversights and makes them all the more glaring. It seems that instead of reducing costs and

[14] In November 2016, these people were still staying in temporary housing, wating for land.

project development timelines, the government-led site selection process had the opposite effect (Kruger et al., 2019).

Learning from the site-related challenges of the Scaling Solar process, and based on the approach taken in Uganda, the GETFiT programme required bidders to find and prepare their own project sites. This included the provision of a draft environmental brief compliant with IFC social and environmental performance standards as a key bidding requirement. In general, the programme went to great lengths to ensure that the upfront transaction costs for bidders and Zambian authorities were kept as low as possible without compromising project quality.

The GETFiT programme used various measures to mitigate the risk of projects being located too far from the grid or causing significant additional costs to the grid operator. Projects could be located no more than 10 km away from the nearest grid connection and would be responsible for shallow grid connection costs, including land rights and construction, which were to be handed over to ZESCO at COD. Bids would also be screened after the pre-qualification stage for their impact on the grid. An interim rapid grid impact assessment (IRGA) based on power flow analyses aimed to confirm grid availability at the proposed connection points for shortlisted projects. Bidders had to ensure that their project was connecting to a substation able to handle its capacity.[15] A grid stability study, funded by KfW, divided ZESCO substations into four categories (see Appendix A: Classification: ZESCO substations—grid connection of PV plant):

- A—able to handle 20 MW PV;
- B—able to handle 10 MW PV;
- B+—able to handle 10 MW if IPP provides a 5 megavolt amp (MVar) reactor;
- C—unable to handle 10 MW PV.

A project site rejected at the IRGA stage was not automatically rejected, neither was one accepted during the request for quotation (RfQ) stages automatically approved. If a bidder was convinced that the reasons for rejection could be addressed through additional investment in the shallow grid connection, it could present appropriate solution as part of its proposal. Bidders could also change their sites after this assessment. If this was done within two weeks, then a second analysis could be done. If not, bidders would have to

---

[15] Substations dedicated to Scaling Solar rounds 1 and 2 projects would also not be eligible. During the pre-qualification process, ZESCO also informed KfW that it would be building a 100 MW PV project with the Moroccan Agency for Solar Energy (MASEN) and that four substations would not be eligible anymore.

proceed with the alternative site without this assessment. The IRGA did not consider cumulative impacts (congestion) of projects on the grid. ZESCO and GETFiT also needed to make a final determination on the compatibility of proposed connection points at the time of final award. If two or more projects caused congestion at a point, the available capacities would be awarded competitively and higher ranked projects would be prioritized. The risk for congestion would lie entirely with the bidder. No projects that required additional investments beyond shallow grid connection would be supported.

Bidders that wanted to use traditional or customary land for their projects furthermore needed to show that they had unwavering support from the traditional authorities for the conversion of the land. Land title deeds were not required at the bidding stage but for the interim grid assessment, shortlisted bidders planning to use traditional or customary land needed to provide an undertaking from the relevant chief. This was submitted in a form provided by the government of Zambia that, should the proposed site be selected, the chief would promptly execute 'Form 2 of the Lands (Customary Tenure) (Conversion) Regulations' and support the bidders' application. Customary or traditional land would need to be converted into statutory or leasehold tenure land in line with the Lands Act (1995) and subsidiary legislation, including the Lands Regulation and IFC performance standards. Uncertainty around the conversion process for traditional land could count against projects in terms of bid scoring on the implementation timeline, which seemed to disincentivize bidders from using traditional land. Bidders could also provide a (conditional) lease contract/land title or memorandum of understanding (MoU) for a lease contract on freehold land that was valid for the length of the PPA plus an additional 18 months.

8.3.3.3 Qualification and compliance requirements

Both Scaling Solar and GETFiT made use of a two-step bidding process, with a pre-qualification phase followed by the request for proposal documentation being released to shortlisted bidders (Table 8.3). Both programmes also had a relatively short period between the launch of the RfQ documentation and the RfQ submission deadline (five to six weeks), although the GETFIT RfQ process was preceded by a lengthy pre-bid clarification phase, including three clarification notices and a compulsory pre-bid meeting. This is not surprising given that GETFiT projects needed to submit project specific details as part of the RfQ process, which was not included for Scaling Solar. Scaling Solar projects had about two months to prepare their final bids as opposed to three months for GETFiT.

Table 8.3 Timelines for Scaling Solar Round 1 and GETFiT solar PV

Phase	Scaling Solar Round 1 Date	GETFiT Date
Bid announcement	–	11 December 2017
Clarification of announcement no. 1	–	21 December 2017
Clarification of announcement no. 2	–	5 February 2018
General Guidance Note on Environmental & Social Standards	–	5 February 2018
Pre-bid meeting	–	7 February 2018[a]
Clarification of announcement no. 3	–	14 February 2018
RFQ launched	5 October 2015	9 April 2018
RFQ clarification meeting	23 October 2015	–
RFQ clarification requests deadline	30 October 2015	27 April 2018[b]
RFQ clarification notice	1 November 2015 161 questions	–
RFQ submission deadline	13 November 2015 48 submissions	18 May 2018 41 submissions
Interim rapid grid assessment	–	4 June–13 July
Pre-qualified bidders announced	16 February 2016 (11 shortlisted)	20 June 2018[d] (10 shortlisted)
RFP released	16 February 2016	31 August 2018[e]
RFP comments deadline	–	–
RFP submission deadline	8 April 2016 14 proposals from 7 bidders	29 November 2018[f] 15 proposals from 8 bidders
Winner Announcement	27 May 2016 2 winners, 2 projects	5 April 2019[g] 3 winners, representing 6 projects
Financial close	21 December 2017 (Neoen/First Solar) July 2018 (ENEL)[h]	–
Project COD	11 March 2019 (Neoen/First Solar) 29 April 2019 (ENEL)	–

Notes: [a] not compulsory;
[b] originally 25 April 2018;
[d] originally planned for 1 June 2018;
[e] originally planned for 15 July 2018;
[f] originally planned for 1 October 2018;
[g] originally planned for 15 December 2018;
[h] while financial documents were signed in July 2018, the drawdown has not happened yet since a number of conditions precedent have not yet been met. Construction on the plant, however, started in August 2018.
Source: Authors' compilation.

Both programmes attracted substantial interest, with 48 submissions for Scaling Solar and 41 for GETFiT. The qualification process for both programmes was quite stringent, with 11 firms pre-qualifying for Scaling Solar round 1 and 10 for GETFiT. For Scaling Solar round 2, which has not pro-ceeded past the pre-qualification phase, only eight firms were shortlisted. Interestingly, about half of the bidders that pre-qualified for Scaling Solar also pre-qualified for GETFiT (Table 8.4). GETFiT also set an upper limit on the number of projects (20) that could pre-qualify to control transaction costs, based on a ranking that would take into account a bidder's global solar PV IPP record (for projects operational for more than one year with minimum performance standards), African renewable energy IPP record, and Zambian shareholding.

Table 8.4 Shortlisted bidders, Scaling Solar Rounds 1 & 2 and GETFiT solar PV

Scaling Solar Round 1	Bid submitted	Scaling Solar Round 2	GETFiT solar	Bid submitted
Scatec Solar	No	Scatec Solar	Scatec Solar	Yes
Access Eren Zambia	Yes	Nareva Holdings	Building Energy	Yes
Mulilo Zambia PV consortium	Yes	Acciona Energy, Swicorp, Enara Bahrain	Mulilo Group	No
Neoen/First Solar	Yes	Mitsui & Company	Innovent SAS and Copperbelt Energy Corporation (CEC)	Yes
International Power SA/Engie	No	Engie Global Develop-ments	Engie Afrique	Yes
Enel Green Power	Yes	Enel Green Power	Enel Green Power	Yes
Globeleq	Yes	Globeleq, FRV	Globeleq and Aurora Power Solutions	Yes
Shangai Electric/Avic	Yes	Tata Power Company Limited	Phanes Group	Yes
EDF Energies Nouvelles	Yes	–	EDF Energies Nouvelles	Yes
Africa Infrastructure Fund2/Old Mutual/Cobra/CDE	No	–	SolarReserve Development Co.	No
Grupo-T Solar	No	–	–	–

Source: Authors' compilation.

Neither programme saw all pre-qualified bidders submitting proposals: for Scaling Solar, only 7 of the 11 pre-qualified firms submitted a bid, while only 8 of the 10 pre-qualified GETFiT bidders submitted full proposals. One pre-qualified bidder explained their decision for not proceeding with a full proposal by pointing out that the pool of pre-qualified bidders included large international utilities, who would almost inevitably end up outpricing competitors based on their economies of scale and the ability to corporate finance projects. This proved to be more or less correct, with one of the Scaling Solar projects being awarded to ENEL Green Power, a subsidiary of Italy's utility ENEL. However, the other project was awarded to a much smaller developer (Neoen). This dynamic played out differently in the GETFiT programme, with none of the three winning bidders being linked to an international utility, despite three utility-linked consortia having qualified.

8.3.3.4 Qualification criteria

8.3.3.4.1 Legal and technical compliance

Both the Scaling Solar and GETFiT programmes made use of stringent qualification criteria to screen potential bidders. During the pre-qualification stages, firms had to prove that they had the ability to build, finance, and operate the proposed projects based on their track record. Bidders wanting to qualify for Scaling Solar needed to prove that they had financed, built, and operated at least one of the following:

- one or more grid-connected PV plant in Africa of at least 25 MW;
- one or more grid-connected power plant in Africa of 75 MW;
- three grid-connected PV plants, each in different countries in any region of the world, with a minimum aggregate installed capacity of 100 MW;
- one or more grid-connected power plant of any technology anywhere with a minimum aggregate capacity of 1,500 MW.

These requirements were viewed as particularly stringent by the market, motivated by the IFC's desire to specifically attract large, international developers to the African market.

The GETFiT reputation-based qualification requirements were both more specific and slightly less restrictive, allowing smaller players to qualify while also restricting qualifying projects to renewable energy based installations. Specifically, interested bidders[16] needed to prove that they had

---

[16] In case of a consortium, a consortium member's reference project would only be accounted for if the member had a minimum shareholding of 30% in the special-purpose vehicle (SPV).

at least 30% shareholding in projects[17] meeting one of the following requirements:

- two on-grid PV[18] projects developed, constructed, and commissioned[19] on an IPP basis with minimum installed capacity of 5 MW each in Africa after 2012; or
- a minimum of 100 MW cumulative installed capacity of solar PV projects developed, constructed, and commissioned on an IPP basis in Africa after 2012; or
- a minimum of 500 MW solar PV IPP projects having reached Financial close(FC)[20] globally; or
- a minimum 750 MW Renewable Energy Technology(RET)-based IPP projected having reached FC globally.

In addition, at least one of these projects needed to be a solar PV project not based in a developed country.[21]

GETFiT also ranked projects (due to the restriction on the number of bidders that could pre-qualify) based on the following formula:

Aggregate sums for bidder members with at least 30% shareholding =
Total MW of globally installed solar PV in IPP basis (global solar score)
+ Total MW of IPP capacity having reached FC in Africa in last 5 years
X by number of RE IPP projects having reached FC in Africa in last 5 years
(Africa RE IPP score)
+ Percentage points of (envisioned) Zambian ownership/shareholding
through Zambian companies (Zambian content score).

(Copyright Multiconsult)

Legal and technical qualification requirements were largely similar across the programmes, with bidders needing to provide letters of confirmation, registration documents, ownership declarations, organization charts, and

---

[17] This shareholding needed to be in place prior to the project reaching COD (or financial close, in the case of projects not yet at COD) and still applies even if the project has since been sold.

[18] Qualifying PV projects need to have been operational for at least one year, with a minimum average performance ration of 78% in year 1.

[19] Projects needed to have been commissioned in the past 10 years to qualify.

[20] When all project and financing agreements have been signed and all Conditions Precedent(CP)s to drawdown have been reached. Financial close must have been achieved in the past five years.

[21] Australia, Austria, Belgium, Canada, Chile, China, Czech Republic, Denmark, Estonia, Finland, France, Germany, Greece, Hungary, Iceland, India, Ireland, Israel, Italy, Japan, Korea, Luxembourg, Mexico, Netherlands, New Zealand, Norway, Poland, Portugal, Slovak Republic, Slovenia, Sweden, Switzerland, Turkey, the United Kingdom, the United States.

evidence that they were not being investigated and had not been con-
victed of fraudulent or similar misconduct. For Scaling Solar, bidders were
not required to register a special-purpose vehicle (SPV) in Zambia prior
to bidding as this would be done (together with the IDC) post award.
While bidders in the GETFiT programme did not need to have an SPV
incorporated as part of their full proposal, it was considered as part of
the evaluation process. The SPV shareholding could not be changed up to
COD, except for shareholders owning less than 20% of the project to allow
local investors to be incorporated, and then only up until the RfP submission deadline. If Zambian company shareholding changed, it needed to be
replaced by Zambian shareholding or might otherwise lead to disqualifi-
cation. GETFiT projects were also required to be at a pre-feasibility stage
at the point of bidding, although no minimum requirements on licensing
and approvals were imposed. However, having obtained these permits would
count in the bidders' favour and was taken into account in the bidder ranking
process.

   Technical requirements were harmonized across both programmes, largely
to enable the GETFiT projects to benefit from the path-clearing work done by
the Scaling Solar projects in the licensing process. Bidders were provided with
indicative equipment specifications as part of the pre-qualification round,
with various technical standards and certifications in place for modules,
inverters, power transformers, and mounting. The technical specifications
were less stringent than in Uganda's GETFiT programme and specifically
allowed for tracking equipment and bifacial modules to be used. During the
Scaling Solar RfP phase, bidders were additionally required to provide project
reference details of EPC and operations and maintenance (O&M) contractors
and needed to provide evidence of equipment manufacturers' capacity. This
could be either through having installed more than 10,000 MW or having a
manufacturing capacity of 500 MW per year (minimum).

8.3.3.4.2 Financial and commercial capability
Both programmes assessed bidders' financial ability as part of the qualification process. In the Scaling Solar programme, this was done by assessing the
net worth of bidders (minimum US$ 75 million if a single bidder). The same
process was followed with a bidding consortium but with the lead sponsor
making up at least half and the net worth to total assets ratio (15% minimum
if single bidder, 20% if a consortium). To encourage local participation, a
special multiplier of 1.5 was applied to the net worth of Zambian companies
to help them pass this test. GETFiT made use of lower thresholds, with bidders' assets needing to total at least US$ 25 million, the equity to total assets

ratio needing to be at least 10% and the current ratio to be above 0.75%. All consortium partners—in both programmes—also needed to submit audited financial statements.

Bidders were also required by both programmes to submit signed term sheets from lenders; in the case of Scaling Solar, part of these could be replaced by a signed letter indicating that bidders would be using the stapled finance offered by the IFC. This requirement served to bring projects closer to financial close by requiring a first level of due diligence from lenders prior to bid submission. Finally, bidders needed to submit full financial models based on templates provided by the procurers.

8.3.3.4.3 Environmental and social sustainability
Both bidding programmes required bidder compliance with the IFC's Environment and Social Performance Standards—the globally recognized gold standard for infrastructure impact mitigation and management. The Scaling Solar programme only considered these requirements as part of the qualification process, while, in the GETFiT programme, these formed part of both the qualification and evaluation criteria. GETFiT Zambia bidders needed to submit environmental and social (E&S) management plans, as well as appropriate permits,[22] as part of their bid package. It is vital to note that while bidders were evaluated on the degree of E&S analysis and management in the Ugandan GETFiT programme, the Zambian programme only considered whether projects had completed a draft environmental project brief[23]—a key requirement for moving towards financial close—in its evaluation matrix. Therefore, the concern in the Zambian programme appears to have shifted more explicitly to the impact of E&S management issues on the project realization timeline.

It is worth observing how the IFC performance standards translated into actual commitments. As an example, one of the Scaling Solar projects offered a range of benefits, such as improved social services, access to credit, and/or livelihood improvement measures funded by 0.5% of the annual project revenue to the local community. The project also committed to appointing a full-time community liaison officer. This was based on stakeholder engagements with nearby villages (5–9 km from the site) that had started in 2015 and included several rounds of public consultation, each time attended by

[22] Full Zambia Environmental Management Agency (ZEMA) approval was not required at the point of bidding.
[23] The bidding authorities admitted that the timelines were probably too tight to allow for a full environmental project brief to be developed and would therefore accept a draft version as part of the bid evaluation process.

about 200 people. It is interesting that legacy issues from the government resettlement programme were brought up during these meetings but then referred back to Zambian government agencies. This possibly points to some residual community-based project risks from the government site selection process.

The treatment of local content also differed between the two programmes. During the clarification process of the first round of bidding for Scaling Solar, the IDC explicitly stated that imposing local content requirements would result in higher project costs, resulting in Zambian electricity consumers subsidizing 'a few fortunate Zambian firms'. While not an explicit qualification or evaluation criterion in the GETFiT programme, the implementation agreement still requires that a percentage of project management and general staff are appropriately trained Zambian staff and that this percentage increases over time. GETFiT bidders were also required to use local content where it was comparable in terms of costs and quality to international goods.

Effectively dealing with environmental and social issues has been challenging for both programmes. As discussed, the Scaling Solar sites came with their own risks and uncertainties—some technical or bureaucratic but others of a softer (social) kind that requires ongoing management throughout the project's lifetime. It is still undecided as to whether the government's deep involvement in the Scaling Solar site selection and preparation processes resulted in fewer, or less severe, or more or less high-impact risks for the projects. The GETFiT programme in Uganda has also experienced difficulties in helping projects to effectively deal with these risks, with one project having its award revoked after a prolonged period of failing to comply with the IFC's standards. Bidders in the Ugandan programmes also complained about the lack of detailed, harmonized guidance on compliance with the standards and reporting requirements, especially since the GETFiT secretariat, project lenders, and Ugandan authorities all used different interpretations. While the Zambian GETFiT projects are yet to reach financial close and commercial operation, the E&S requirements (and perhaps the lack of guidance that was detailed enough) have already caused two projects to be disqualified during the evaluation process—a decision that is now being officially challenged by one of the affected bidders.

8.3.3.5 Bidder ranking and winner selection

The bid evaluation and ranking processes for the Scaling Solar and GETFiT programmes were relatively similar, although there were notable differences in the ranking criteria used. Both programmes used a pay-as-bid-type auction so that bidders submitted the price that they knew they would be paid in case they won the bid. Both programmes also made use of a sealed bid process that would see technical (and commercial) bids first needing to pass a compliance test before financial bids could be opened.

For Scaling Solar, the bidders were required to submit three sealed parts of their proposal:

- a technical proposal, covering all technical aspects of the proposed plant;
- a commercial proposal, which contained an offer letter, 'Project Agreement Information Schedule',[24] debt financing term sheets, details on any guarantees or insurance products to be used, and a bid bond; and
- a financial proposal, providing the proposed energy charge in US$c/kWh.

Bidders were allowed to bid on both sites (and all did) but would only be awarded one of the projects—which ensured some hedging of non-delivery risk for the IDC.

In the GETFiT programme, bidders submitted only a technical (Table 8.5) and financial (Table 8.6) proposal. Projects were expected to at least be at a pre-feasibility stage by the time they were submitted, and technical proposals were checked for completeness and compliance before being evaluated (Figure 8.2). Because bidders were providing their own project sites, the GETFiT technical evaluation process also included a site visit.

The GETFiT evaluation process included two additional innovative clauses. Bidders had to submit unconditional financial bids for each project and could submit a conditional financial bid in case an award was received for both submitted projects (for those bidders that chose to bid for two projects). This approach allowed the auctioneers to potentially benefit from economies of scale by allowing bidders to combine projects in order to achieve better pricing results. The financial bids were also beholden to a procurement clause which determined that if the project did not reach commercial operation in 18 months from its award, the financial bid could be adjusted proportionally to the degree by which the costs for PV modules have fallen (or increased) against an international benchmark price.

The Scaling Solar programme is the only programme in the sub-Saharan region (to date) to base bidder ranking on financial criteria alone. Every other sub-Saharan Africa (SSA) RE auction (including GETFiT Zambia) has based project evaluation on some combination of financial and technical/social and environmental scores, despite the theoretical and practical problems noted

---

[24] Bidders completed schedules 1 and 2 of the RFP, which would be directly inserted into the PPA and signed on bid award.

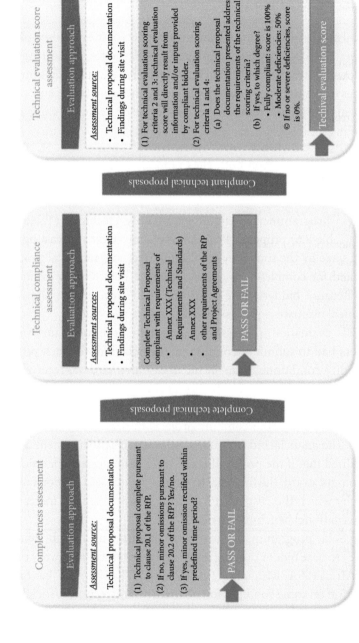

Figure 8.2 Technical evaluation process stages: GET FiT Zambia
(Copyright: Multiconsult)

Table 8.5 Technical proposal documentation: GETFiT Zambia

Document	Required content
Technical	
Detailed description of site and boundary areas	Site coordinates, scale drawing, description of topography, topsoil conditions, obstacles, description of access conditions and restrictions
Detailed description of the conceptual design of the PV plant	Modules, mounting structure, inverters, power transformers, shallow grid connection, balance of plant, O&M procedures
Site-specific yield report	Data sources, incorporation of design concepts, losses due to shading, soiling, cabling; annual and monthly production estimates, yield for year 1, P50 and P90 estimates for year 1, 10, and 20
Electrical single diagram	Ownership and operational boundaries, delivery point, substation, shallow grid connection
PQ capability diagram	–
Environmental and social sustainability	
Draft environmental project brief	E&S minimum requirements
Corporate environmental and social management system	As above
Legal	
Consortium agreement	Division of tasks, internal organization and management, liability, indemnification, confidentiality
If above not yet executed: MoU for consortium agreement	
Draft consortium agreement	

Source: Authors' compilation.

with this approach in the literature (Manelli and Vincent, 1995; Burguet and Che, 2007; Estache et al., 2009). Scaling Solar's exclusive use of price as evaluation criterion was meant to signal to the market how important a good price outcome was for the programme as well as to allow for transparent, simple evaluation. Uganda's GETFiT programme used a range of technical criteria to score and rank projects, which has not been without its share of criticism (Kruger and Eberhard, 2018). One would perhaps have expected the Zambian GETFiT auction to follow in the footsteps of the Scaling Solar scoring approach, yet this was made impossible by KfW's procurement policies, which required technical scoring alongside price.

Table 8.6 Financial proposal documentation: GETFiT Zambia

Document	Required content
Financial	
Financial model	For each project, plus separate financial models for conditional bids
Initialled term sheet from each envisioned lender and/or guarantee provider	Max./intended amount of loan/coverage; applicable interest rates/pricing; fees; tenor; E&S standards; conditions for final approval; term sheet shall also include statement by each lender/provider to provide the loan/coverage, conditional upon final due diligence
Site-specific yield report	Data sources, incorporation of design concepts, losses due to shading, soiling, cabling; annual and monthly production estimates, yield for year 1, P50 and P90 estimates for year 1, 10, and 20
Signed letter of support from equity providers	Availability of required amount (liquid assets); commitment to invest; commitment to make available equity to develop project and bring it to FC in 12–18 months

Source: Authors' compilation.

The GETFiT programme therefore made use of a combined scoring approach that was weighted on a 80:20 basis in favour of price. The scoring methodology (Tables 8.7 and 8.8) that determined the remaining 20 points aimed to incentivize increased project preparation and rapid realization commitments. This approach has previously been criticized for failing to translate into actual results, with minimal impact on the Zambian grid (in terms of system losses) and the local capacity building and training. As the winning bidders were only announced in March 2019, it remains to be seen what impact these criteria had in terms of project implementation. The GETFiT secretariat also offered detailed guidance to bidders in terms of the technical evaluation scoring criteria (summarized in Table 8.8), which was further elaborated on and explained during the clarification rounds of the bidding process.

To decide on winning bidders, the GETFiT investment committee first met to review the technical proposals as evaluated by the tender agent, in this case, also the GETFiT secretariat. Financial bids were only opened for bidders passing the investment committee technical evaluation stage. After projects were evaluated and ranked, a cumulative grid impact assessment was conducted that could still lead to the rejection of any project if it was found to lead to significant grid congestion. The final award decision also required a no-objection from KfW.

Table 8.7   Scoring methodology for technical evaluation score: GETFiT Zambia

Technical evaluation score criterion	Assessment
1. Project maturity	To what degree does the quality and substance of project documentation represented reflect a mature project?
2. Scheduled commercial operation date (COD) as per PPA	The sooner a project can reach COD after its effective PPA date, the more points it will be awarded, ranging from 7 to 11 months.
3. Contribution to total system losses	This is the degree to which the PV plant will contribute to system losses.
4. Local capacity building and training	To what degree does the quality and substance of project documentation represented reflect a strong local capacity-building and training programme?

Source: Copyright: Multiconsult.

Table 8.8   Technical evaluation score criteria: GETFiT Zambia

1. Project readiness	
A. Technical: details of the project site, resources, and contracts	20
B. Additional environmental and social risk mitigation	10
C. Land acquisition: level of execution of land agreement	5
D. Any other documented project preparation activities tangibly benefiting project maturity and expected project preparation timelines	5
Scheduled commercial operation date as per PPA	20
Contribution to total system losses	25
Local capacity building and training	15
Total	100

Source: Copyright: Multiconsult.

8.3.3.6 Seller and buyer liabilities

8.3.3.6.1 Financial pre-qualifications and penalties

The Scaling Solar and GETFiT programmes made use of a number of financial pre-qualification and penalty instruments to ensure compliance and commitment from bidders. Financial pre-qualification instruments, such as bid bonds, generally serve two purposes: they signal that bidders have the financial capacity to realize the project, and they serve as a possible penalty in the case of a bidder failing to stand behind their bid. Scaling Solar bidders were required to post a bid bond of US$ 1.3 million per project—or US$ 26,000 per MW (assuming that the proposed project is 50 MW), making it the most expensive bid bond yet in the SSA region. The GETFiT Zambian bid bond was set at US$ 15,000 per MW. While cheaper than the Scaling Solar bond, it was still US$ 5,000 per MW more than in the Ugandan version of the programme and US$ 7,000 more than in the South African RE auction. Setting a bid bond level too high may decrease the number of bidders able or willing to submit a bid, which leads to reduced competition and potentially higher prices (Kreiss et al., 2017). Both programmes had strong market responses in the pre-qualification stages and, while the eventual number of proposals submitted were not that many (in large part also due to very stringent pre-qualification criteria), they were from strong bidders. Also in evidence were the record-breaking prices and the fact that successful bidders signed the contract agreements, which together seem to show that these bond levels were effective in achieving their intended purpose.

Winning Scaling Solar bidders were also required to post a performance bond of US$ 15 million—which, in reality, seems to have acted more as a construction bond as it was set to expire after the project reached its COD (similar to GETFiT Uganda). According to the bidding contracts, failure by projects to complete commissioning by the longstop COD would not only result in the bond being called but also in the PPA being terminated. A similar termination clause is contained in the GETFiT Zambia documentation. In reality, neither the bond nor the termination clause were called upon, despite the Scaling Solar projects being more than a year late on delivery. This has mainly been attributed to the fact that many of the factors causing the delays were within the control of the Zambian government or ZESCO. But it also forms part of a bigger global trend where auctioneers are increasingly reluctant to penalize or terminate projects (which is, in effect, what calling on the performance bond would also do) once a project is awarded. This reluctance to use penalty mechanisms undermines their raison d'être and has, in some cases, ultimately led bidders to disregard them. It also points to the fact that penalty regimes—especially of the 'binary' kind—are perhaps not well suited to ensuring timely project realization outcomes.

The GETFiT Zambia programme chose to incentivize timely project realization through introducing liquidated damages clauses (US$ 500/MW per day delay up to a capped amount) in the project contracts instead of performance bonds. This is a departure from the programme's approach in Uganda, where a series of increasingly expensive performance bonds (in addition to liquidated damages provisions) were used to cover the project periods up to and including financial close and COD.

Both Scaling Solar and GETFiT also used liquidated damages to incentivize project performance: winning Scaling Solar projects were expected to pass a PV plant performance ratio test (85% threshold, based on the estimated

PV plant performance ratio) as part of the test signalling the COD. The PV plant performance ratio would also be calculated at the end of each contract year. If the project failed to achieve an annual PV plant performance ratio of at least 75% of the estimated PV plant performance ratio, the project would have to pay ZESCO liquidated damages at the rate of US$ 7,500 for every 0.1% below 75%. The total liquidated damages payable was limited to US$ 750,000 per year. The GETFiT programme required bidders to pay only US$ 150 for each 0.1% if a project's annual performance ratio fell below 90% of the estimated annual performance ratio for that year, capped at US$ 15,000 per MW.

The type of penalty regime employed can impact a project's price level. The incentive created by the penalty regime also needs to align with the goal it wants to achieve to be effective. Performance bonds are generally seen as binary penalty regimes where either the full amount gets called or none of it is used. While liquidated damages clauses act in a more gradual, progressive fashion, using binary penalty regimes have been shown to increase project risks, leading to a higher cost of capital for projects (AURES Consortium, 2019). Nonetheless, both progressive and binary penalty regimes have a negative impact on a project's realization probability since using them would mean causing even more pain to a project that is already in distress. Late project delivery or poor technical performance already have a financial impact on the project. Imposing financial penalties is unlikely to help the project overcome whatever problems are keeping it from performing. Where penalties are warranted is where the financial impacts might not be immediate or direct for the project, such as controlling environmental and social performance. Scaling Solar's use of a decommissioning bond of US$ 100,000 per MW (US$ 5 million for a 50 MW plant) seems to conform to this idea. Likewise, GETFiT Zambia's approach of requiring a performance bond (US$ 100,000) to cover projects' IFC and E&S performance standards commitments makes sense, although it could be argued that a liquidated damages clause might have been as effective without necessarily increasing the projects' risk-based cost of capital.[25]

8.3.3.6.2 Buyer liabilities

Both investors and the Zambian government face significant inflation and currency-related financial risks over the lifetime of the projects. ZESCO provided winning bidders in both programmes with 25-year PPAs. For Scaling Solar, tariffs were non-indexed over that period, while, for GETFiT, only the

---

[25] It still needs to be established whether the performance bond increased the cost of capital in the end.

O&M component of the tariff (up to a maximum of 10%) was indexed to the United States Consumer Price Index (US CPI). Winning bid tariffs were thus significantly lower in real terms than what was initially announced as the winning bid prices, further underscoring the ground-breaking nature of these tariffs. For both programmes, tariffs were denominated in US dollars in deference to the lending requirements of international financiers (including development finance institutions (DFIs)). This potentially exposed the Zambian government to significant foreign exchange risks, especially given the significant depreciation of the local currency in recent years. This exposure is slightly offset by an unusual characteristic of the Zambian power market: the mines, which consume 40–60% of the country's electricity, pay their electricity tariffs in US dollars and can therefore help to cover this gap.

The risks for transmission infrastructure provision to the projects, as well as power dispatch, was fully allocated to ZESCO as the most appropriate institution able to manage these risks. The PPA contained a take-or-pay clause that required ZESCO to pay for all power produced by the projects, regardless of whether it needed it at that point in time. If ZESCO was, for some reason, unable to take delivery of any power produced, it would provide projects with deemed energy payments. This is a standard requirement in most renewable energy PPAs since these sources are non-dispatchable. Because ZESCO was providing the grid connection for the Scaling Solar projects, it was also liable for providing deemed energy payments in the case of delays with the provision of this infrastructure. The GETFiT programme had the further provision of early operating energy, which would see projects being paid 75% of their tariff for any electricity produced pre-COD, thereby incentivizing early project delivery.

8.3.3.7 Securing the revenue stream and addressing off-taker risk

It is impossible to make sense of the price and investment outcomes of the Zambian auctions without understanding how the programmes sought to protect projects' revenue and mitigate investor risks. As ZESCO was in such poor financial shape, lenders required termination and payment or liquidity guarantees to be willing to provide debt. Both programmes made use of a range of guarantees and credit-enhancement mechanisms—Scaling Solar arguably more so than GETFiT. Off-taker default and some *force majeure*[26] risks were covered in both programmes by a government support agreement,[27] initially developed for Scaling Solar. In the case of payment default

---

[26] If the bidder does everything right but is not granted a permit, this becomes a 'lapse of consent' and, in turn, a local political *force majeure* event. If other *force majeure* events occur, 80% of the tariff would be payable while debt is outstanding. If all debt was paid off, only the O&M component of the tariff would be covered.

[27] This agreement included provisions for the possible unbundling of ZESCO that would ensure that the guarantee agreements would not be affected.

by ZESCO, the government does not step into the shoes of the off-taker to assume responsibility for all PPA payments, as would be the case in a standard sovereign guarantee. Instead, the government buys the asset or shares in the project company at a pre-determined price meant to cover outstanding equity (plus returns) and debt and associated transaction costs (Table 8.9). Provisions for a prolonged local political *force majeure* event are more or less similar, though the purchase price will be reduced by any insurance proceeds.

The Scaling Solar auction also had relatively standard liquidity support mechanisms in place, including letters of credit, as well as World Bank partial risk guarantees for payments and (if required by commercial lenders) loans. The letters of credit (from Standard Chartered) covered six months' worth of PPA payments. The presence of the World Bank PRGs meant that ZESCO did not have to cash-collateralize the letters of credit since the banks were essentially providing credit to the World Bank. The market opted for the payment

Table 8.9 Termination clauses and provisions: GETFiT Zambia

Event	Who can terminate	Put/call	Buyout price
Seller/company default	ZESCO/GRZ	Call	Outstanding debt Termination costs Transfer costs
ZESCO/GRZ default	Seller	Put	Outstanding debt Outstanding equity Equity return Termination costs Transfer costs
Prolonged local political *force majeure* event	Seller—180 days ZESCO—365 days	Put	Outstanding debt Outstanding equity Equity return Termination costs Transfer costs Minus insurance proceeds (if any)
Prolonged foreign political *force majeure* event	Seller—180 days ZESCO—365 days	Call	Outstanding debt Termination costs Transfer costs Minus insurance proceeds (if any)
Prolonged other *force majeure* event	Seller—180 days ZESCO—365 days	Call	Outstanding debt Termination costs Transfer costs Minus insurance proceeds (if any)

Source: Authors' compilation.

guarantees but not the loan guarantees. This is not surprising considering that loans were being provided by DFIs. Figure 8.3 provides a visual representation of the various agreements in place around the Bangweulu Power Company, including the guarantees and credit-enhancement mechanisms.

Payment guarantee support was provided by the RLSF with GETFiT (Figure 8.4). This facility was initiated by KfW with grant funding from the German government. Many African utilities are typically not able, or willing, to provide the cash collateral needed to backstop commercial letters of credit. Through a mixture of grant funding (€31.6 million through KfW from the German government) and a matching guarantee from Africa Trade Insurance (ATI), a letter of credit was provided by ABSA. ABSA was selected on a competitive basis, based on the bank's willingness to take on risks and its fee/cost structure. This letter covered 9 months of PPA payments and was valid for a maximum of 10 years. The cost of the letter was determined by the quality of risk, the formal comfort provided by the host government and off-taker, and the issuing bank handling charges.

The RLSF is managed by ATI, which is an A-rated multilateral credit and political risk insurer based in Nairobi. Its function is to facilitate investments and trade in the African region, especially for its 14 member states.[28] ATI has preferred creditor status in its member countries and has signed MoUs with ZESCO as well as Zambia's Ministries of Energy and Finance. RLSF cover is only provided once ATI's investment committee has assessed projects as well. The RLSF is set to be rolled out to more countries in the region, including Burundi, Benin, and Uganda (all of which have signed MoUs) and possibly also Ethiopia, Malawi, and Madagascar.

ATI also developed a transparency tool that is aimed at increasing trust in, and creditworthiness of, off-takers in the African region. The tool is an online, public platform where IPPs report utility payment behaviour. This is to provide a transparent, accessible, baseline platform that might mitigate lender bias when it comes to lending to African utilities. At the time of completing the report, the tool was still to be implemented.

8.3.4 Auction implementation

The institutional setting is a basic but often neglected element of an auction programme that plays a crucial role in determining outcomes. For an

---

[28] Benin, Burundi, Cote d'Ivoire, Democratic Republic of Congo, Ethiopia, Kenya, Madagascar, Malawi, Rwanda, South Sudan, Tanzania, Uganda, Zambia, Zimbabwe.

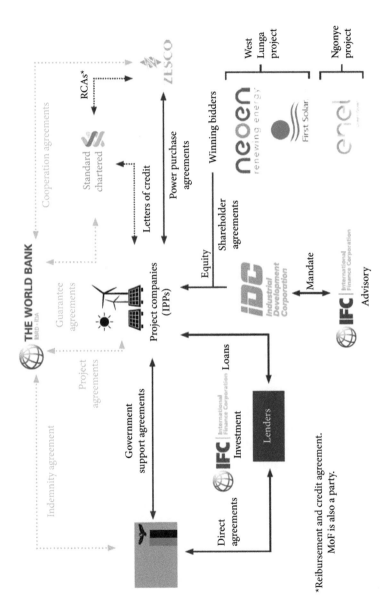

Figure 8.3 Scaling Solar Zambia: Structure and contractual agreements, including guarantee structure

Source: https://thedocs.worldbank.org/en/doc/208821518200595153-0100022018/original/BriefsGuaranteesZambiaScalingSolar.pdf.

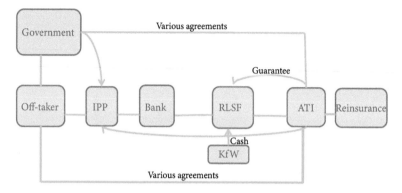

Figure 8.4 Regional liquidity support facility (RLSF) guarantee mechanism
Source: Authors' compilation.

auction to deliver projects at low prices, it needs to be implemented by a credible, capable, and well-resourced authorized agency in a way that is seen as fair, transparent, and consistent. Potential bidders need to trust both the auctioneer and the auction process to be willing to incur the costs of bidding. Furthermore, the implementing organization plays a crucial role in bringing awarded projects to commercial operation. To be effective at both establishing and maintaining bidder trust, as well as supporting project implementation, a careful matching of existing institutional resources with the needs of bidders is required. If the institutional resource pool is found to be lacking, it is to be augmented in such a way that it does not disrupt or diminish existing resource flows.

The two auction programmes employed different strategies to deal with the Zambian institutional setting—both building on and supplementing existing institutional resources. These strategies resulted in very different working arrangements with the Zambian institutions. The Scaling Solar model required the host country to hire IFC as the transaction advisor. In Zambia, the Ministry of Energy—the obvious choice for running such a programme—did not have the funds and capacity to conclude such a contract. Zambia's IDC, which is an investment holding company for the Zambian state-owned enterprises, was chosen as the best alternative. It was seen as a small (20 personnel[29]), nimble, and politically supported procurement focal point with sufficient institutional capacity and resources to drive the programme.

Scaling Solar was led and implemented by the IDC, with the IFC playing an intensive but fundamentally supporting role as transaction advisor. While the World Bank Group, and the IFC in particular, featured prominently as

---

[29] The IDC has since grown to about 75 people in 2019.

the institutional partner behind the Scaling Solar programme, their involvement with the day-to-day procurement and project implementation activities was conducted at arm's length. It was the IDC that convened a procurement committee that conducted the bid evaluations, with the IFC available to the committee for support and clarification. The IDC also played a role in the design of the procurement process, leading to the inclusion of the special 1.5 financial pre-qualification multiplier that was applied to local Zambian companies.

The Zambian government's (including the IDC's) lack of experience with project-financed RE projects has been highlighted as one reason for the delay in project implementation. The IFC's advisory role did not officially extend beyond the procurement process, although the involvement of the IFC finance maintained a link to the projects. The IFC's reduced role post procurement meant that there was no dedicated advisory support to the Zambian government during the crucial stages leading up to financial close. While the IFC had six staff members working on Scaling Solar's first procurement round (plus technical, E&S, legal, tax, and accounting consultants), none of them were permanently based in Zambia. This lack of a neutral third party that could act as an honest broker between the Zambian government and the projects made it more difficult for both parties to navigate the complicated project implementation processes.

GETFiT followed a different approach, opting to embed its role to such a degree that the distinction between it and the Zambian government was essentially erased. GETFiT first secured €31 million grant funding from the German government to cover transaction advisory services. This opened up the possibility for establishing a partnership between KfW and the Ministry of Energy. The Ministry of Energy, as the project executing agency, subsequently authorized KfW by way of an agency contract with delegated authority. This meant that KfW was legally authorized to make binding statements and commitments on behalf of the Zambian government, to represent the Ministry of Energy, and to implement procurement rounds. The Ministry, however, remained deeply involved in the strategic decisions and daily operations of the programme.

The GETFiT secretariat (staffed by KfW-funded consultants and Multiconsult Norge ASA) fulfilled the equivalent roles of both the IDC and IFC, not only designing, leading, and implementing the procurement programme but also providing and contracting the necessary advisory services. This included KPMG as tax advisors to provide a detailed schedule of baseline taxes to bidders—a solution to the lesson carried over from GETFiT Uganda's experience with tax-based project implementation delays. The secretariat's mandate also extended beyond the procurement process to include the day-to-day management of the programme, supervision of the GET-FiT projects (including support to achieve financial close and construction supervision to ensure compliance), management of the grid integration programme, capacity development of the Ministry of Energy, and coordination with ATI and the RLSF.

The GETFiT institutional governance (Figure 8.5) set-up also included a steering committee tasked with advising on the overall programme's strategy and an investment committee responsible for reviewing tender submissions and making ultimate investment decisions. The GETFiT steering committee comprised two categories of participants: voting participants (including representatives from the Ministry of Energy (chair), Ministry of Finance, ERB and cooperating partners (German government)) and non-voting participants, including the GETFiT secretariat and KfW. The investment committee was made up of independent experts that were mostly from Zambia and served in their individual capacity. While this governance set-up is broadly similar to that used in the Ugandan GETFiT programme, the Zambian version also included a task force including representatives from ZESCO, the Zambian Environmental Management Agency (ZEMA), the Water Resources Management Authority (WARMA), the ERB, the Ministry of Finance (MoF), the Ministry of Energy (MoE) (OPPPI, Department of the Environment (DOE)), the Zambia Public Procurement Authority (ZPPA), the Ministry of Justice, and the National Health Research Authority (NHHC). This broad Zambian government stakeholder consultation group provided inputs and guidance on the programme generally and the procurement programme design and set-up specifically.

GETFiT projects also benefited from the pioneering work done by the Scaling Solar projects. For example, the Zambian grid code is not compatible with solar PV. As a result, each project needed to present and defend each required exemption to the Grid Code to the ERB's technical committee.[30] This was a time-consuming process, which introduced an additional element of risk to the Scaling Solar programme and was also responsible for much of the project implementation delays. The GETFiT projects would now be able to benefit from an expedited process based on the technical committee's previous decisions for the Scaling Solar projects.[31] Similar path-clearing work

---

[30] GETFiT sought to secure eight grid code exemptions prior to the bidding window opening. The ERB rejected two exemptions, which were appealed to the MoE. There was no final decision at date of bidding. Bidders were to assume that all exemptions were granted. One of the rejected exemptions was the redundant line (n – 1) requirement. The motivation from the programme was that this required upgrading of substations too, and that the plants are too small. This was also rejected in Scaling Solar round 1.

[31] The decisions by the technical committee are project-specific so no blanket exemption can be given from Grid Code requirements.

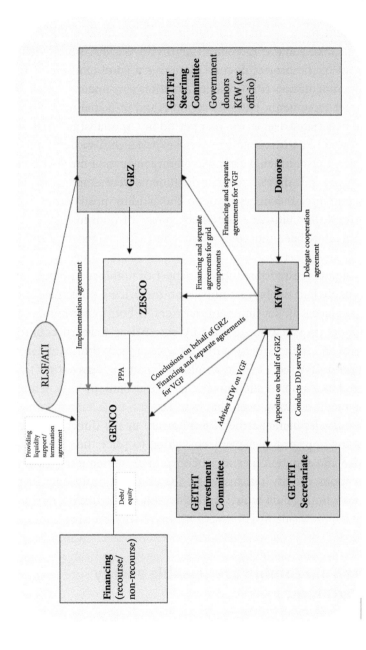

Figure 8.5 GETFiT Zambia institutional set-up
Source: Authors' compilation.

has been done by Scaling Solar in numerous other areas, including risk allocation decisions on solar PV with ZESCO, and should ultimately benefit the GETFiT projects and the market in general.

While the Scaling Solar programme was initiated in the throes of daily load shedding and therefore marked by the need for rapid results, GETFiT was able to take a more measured approach. GETFiT's approach to the development of the project documentation is a good example of this. The project documentation (PPA, implementation agreement, connection agreement, direct agreements, liquidity support, and principal permits) was developed and negotiated over a two-year period by a specialist international legal firm (Trinity LLP) with notable regional experience. Two development finance institutions also initiated early bankability reviews of the documents through their own legal advisors, and the documents were subsequently also tested with (commercial) lenders prior to the bidding programme being launched. By the time that these documents were introduced to the market, they had therefore been thoroughly tested and adjusted for the Zambian context.

A key and often discussed institutional aspect of both programmes, and one which arguably had the biggest impact on the pricing outcomes, is the prominent role played by development partners in both programmes. We have seen support provided to auctions by external agencies in countries like South Africa and Malawi, but the prominence of the World Bank Group (Scaling Solar) and KfW (GETFiT) in Zambia led many bidders to treat these programmes not as Zambian auctions but as World Bank or KfW tenders. While bidders might not have been that familiar with the Zambian context, they knew the development partners, were aware of the direct roles they were playing, and appeared to have been willing to price their risk based on the presence and reputation (and, of course, risk-mitigation measures) of these institutions. Equity returns were, for example, reportedly in the 9–10% range for winning bids, which is considerably lower than the normally expected 15%.

8.4 Results from Zambia's renewable energy auction programmes

8.4.1 Securing equity providers

The Scaling Solar projects were awarded to two (or three) of the largest global renewable energy companies at highly competitive prices (Table 8.10). The West Lunga site project went to the Neoen/First Solar consortium at a non-indexed price of US$c 6,015/kWh while the Mosi-oa Tunya site was awarded to ENEL Green Power (US$c 7.83/kWh). Neoen is one of the biggest French renewable energy developers with more than 2.8 GW of capacity (including a 300 MW PV plant in France), in operation or under construction in 13 countries (most of this—1 gigawatt (GW) plus in Australia). First Solar was founded in 1990 and is the second largest manufacturer of solar PV modules globally. The US company forms part of the US State Department's Power Africa programme and is a dominant global industry player. ENEL Green Power is a subsidiary of Italy's power utility ENEL and the most successful renewable energy project developer in global auctions, with 1,200 plants in operation and more than 43 GW under management. The company entered the African market through its participation in South Africa's REIPPP programme, where it came to dominate the market during the later rounds of procurement. Apart from the abovementioned shareholders, the IDC also retained a minority (20%) stake in each project at full cost (Table 8.11).

The project implementation phase of the Scaling Solar programme had not been marked by the same speed and efficiency as the procurement stages. Neoen/First Solar's Bangweulu Power Company Limited (US$ 60 million) was incorporated on 6 November 2016 when the shareholders' agreement

Table 8.10 Scaling Solar bid prices (USD)

	West Lunga site	Mosi-oa Tunya site
Neoen/First Solar	6.0150	6.1350
ENEL Green Power	7.7989	7.8390
Access/EREN Zambia 1	8.2879	8.9509
MULILO Zambia PV1 Consortium	8.4000	8.4000
EDF Energies Nouvelles	10.0400	9.9850
SEP/AVIC Intl	10.6000	10.6000

Source: Authors' compilation.

Table 8.11 Shareholding of Scaling Solar projects

Bangweulu Power Company Limited	Ngonye Power Company Limited
Neoen—67%	ENEL Green Power—80%
First Solar—13%	IDC—20%
IDC—20%	

Source: Authors' compilation.

was signed between the three parties, about five months after the award was announced. Financial close was originally foreseen for March 2017 but with a presidential election in November 2016 and, this being Zambia's first project financed deal, it was only achieved in December 2017. This was very different from Scaling Solar's original timeline, which included an eight-month construction period that would have seen the project reach commercial operation in November 2017. Commercial operation commenced in March 2019. ENEL's Ngonye project (US$ 45 million) PPA was signed only in April 2017 and financial documents in June 2018 (although there had been no drawdown of funds prior to COD, some conditions precedent were still outstanding). It reached commercial operation in April 2019.

The shareholder profiles of the awarded GETFiT solar PV projects look somewhat different from the Scaling Solar programme (Table 8.12), even though several of the same firms pre-qualified (Table 8.4). Some of the winning firms could be described as second-tier developers, many only recently expanding beyond their domestic markets. Building Energy is an Italian developer that first entered the African market through South Africa's REIPPP programme. It was also awarded one of the GETFiT Uganda solar PV projects in 2014 (10 MW). While a global player, it is not a company with the same presence or track record as ENEL or Neoen, with about 160 MW in operation—most of this (91 MW) in Africa. Pele Energy—a minority shareholder in the projects—is a South African project developer involved in eight of the country's REIPPP projects. This is the company's first successful venture outside of South Africa's market. Globeleq is Africa's biggest IPP developer, with more than 1,340 MW in operation, most of which is gas-based (846 MW). The company's two shareholders are the Commonwealth Development Corporation (CDC) and Norfund, with an explicit development mandate exclusively focused on sub-Saharan Africa. While active in

Table 8.12 GETFiT Zambia solar project details

Projects	Bidders	Size	Price
Bulemu East and West	Building Energy and Pele Green Energy	2 × 20 MWac	US$c 3,999/kWh
Aurora Sola One and Two	Globeleq and Aurora Power Solutions	2 × 20 MWac	US$c 4,52/kWh
Garneton North and South	Innovent and CEC	2 × 20 MWac	US$c 4,80/kWh

Source: Authors' compilation.

South Africa's REIPPPP (seven projects), the company also has operations in the Ivory Coast, Cameroon, Tanzania, and Kenya. Aurora Power Solutions is a South African developer and EPC company that has mainly been active in developing solar PV for the commercial and industrial sector in South Africa, Namibia, and Mozambique (37.5 MW). It has also been one of the most successful bidders in South Africa's small IPP procurement programme, although none of these project have received a signed PPA. Innovent is a French developer with about 514 MW in operation, 140 MW of which is in Africa: Senegal, Benin, South Africa, and Namibia. The inclusion of the CEC in the list of winners is a notable result for the programme, being the only Zambian shareholder in both Scaling Solar and GETFiT (apart from the IDC's mandated minority shares). The CEC's presence shows that the GETFiT qualification and evaluation criteria were effective in securing at least some degree of local participation and creates the foundation for further domestic market development.

Much has been said about the tariff levels already, but it is again worth noting that at the time of their announcement, these were the lowest solar PV tariffs in Africa. The programme had originally proposed to the Zambian government that if tariffs were above US$c 10/kWh, GETFiT would cover the residual; between US$c 7 and 10, GETFiT would provide a maximum top-up of US$c 1/kWh and below US$c 7/kWh would see no top-up being provided. What makes the submitted tariffs even more notable is that, unlike Scaling Solar, these were smaller projects (assuming pricing on a 2×20 MW basis and not 1×40 MW) that had to find and secure their own sites, without stapled IFC financing and facing an increasingly risky investment environment and off-taker. It is also notable that apart from one bid, all submitted bid tariffs were below US$c 5/kWh.

8.4.2 Securing debt providers

In both programmes, the debt pool has been dominated by DFIs and other sources of concessionary finance (Table 8.13). In Scaling Solar, the IFC offered one tranche of debt financing on what it considered commercial terms and another tranche on concessional terms (London interbank offered rate (LIBOR) + 0 at 20-year tenor) based on available grant funding from the Canada Climate Change programme. A third tranche of financing needed to be sourced by bidders from other financiers, whether commercial banks or export credit agencies. The reasoning behind offering stapled finance was, in large part, an attempt to strengthen the non-negotiable, bankable nature

Table 8.13 Scaling Solar project debt providers

	Bangweulu Power Company Limited	Ngonye Power Company Limited
IFC A loan	US$ 12 million	US$ 22 million
IFC–Canada Climate Change Programme concessional senior loan	–	–
Parallel senior loan	OPIC—19.9 million	EIB—11.75 million

Source: Authors' compilation.

of the contracts offered.[32] The Neoen/First Solar project secured its third tranche of debt (US$ 19.9 million) from the Overseas Private Investment Corporation (OPIC), a US export credit agency, which matched the blended average of the IFC and climate change loan interest rates. The ENEL project secured financing from the European Investment Bank (EIB) at a very high (75/25) gearing ratio. One thing to note is that ENEL was not able to use this debt funding prior to COD due to some outstanding conditions precedent. Nonetheless, the project reached commercial operation in April 2019, suggesting that the company corporate-financed the development of the plant in an effort to avoid further delays.

For the Scaling Solar projects to eventually have reached commercial operation in early 2019 required extensive and sustained effort from the winning bidders, not only in terms of managing the technical building process but also from a strategic management point of view. This was partly why Neoen established a Zambian country office, arguing that having a permanent local presence helped them to develop the strategic relationships and know-how in-country to bring their West Lunga project (52 hectares, 460,000 thin film modules, 12 transformers) to commercial operation. Despite there having been substantial site-related issues, ENEL managed their Ngonye project (50.2 hectares, 105,000 tracker modules, 28 inverters) from the company's South African regional office and brought it online only a month after the Neoen project. Managing issues related to the project sites, licensing frameworks, and connection agreements in particular required day-to-day involvement from the winning bidders.

Although the project prices played an important part in securing strategic support from the Zambian government, projects also needed to ensure

[32] Internal IFC sensitivity analyses seem to indicate a price impact of less than US$ 10/MWh due to concessional elements in the financing, indicating a limited impact on the market.

that the local communities around their projects granted them (and continued to grant them) a social licence to operate. Despite using international EPC contractors (Sterling & Wilson for West Lunga, TerniEnergua for Ngonye), projects also made use of as much local labour as possible during the construction and operations phases. For example, The West Lunga project employed more than 200 workers during construction, mostly from neighbouring communities. In addition, it employed seven full-time technical operations staff as well as 37 unskilled personnel for security, cleaning, and groundskeeping. The aforementioned local community investment programmes played a further important role in securing and maintaining support for the projects' ongoing operation.

There has been a lot of criticism of the IFC's approach, with some critics claiming that it is crowding out commercial financiers, while others have noted that the concessional debt created unrealistic market expectations (Elston, 2016; Dunlop, 2017). The IFC estimates that the combination of concessional elements in the programme (low equity return expectations, concessional debt, full PRG cover, no interconnection costs, low development costs, Zambian tax incentives) probably shaved about US$c 2/kWh off the bid tariffs. This is a significant amount and seems to support the critics' assertions.

The GETFiT results are a powerful counterpoint to many of these critical arguments. These bidders were able to achieve much lower prices, on smaller projects, without most of the concessional elements mentioned. Nonetheless, the debt for all of the winning projects is being provided by development finance institutions, possibly on quite concessionary terms. This means that the entire utility-scale solar PV sector in Zambia's debt is coming from DFIs, leaving no scope for local or regional commercial finance providers.

These developments seemed to indicate that the momentum that had been created by Scaling Solar would sustain a deeper transformation of the ailing Zambian power sector. At a project level, the extremely competitive GET-FiT results were announced within weeks of the pioneering Scaling Solar projects reaching financial close. At the same time, the Zambian government was developing a new energy policy, electricity act, and electricity regulatory act—approved by cabinet and parliament in November and December 2019—to pave the way for fundamental sector reforms and further accelerated investments. It thus appeared that these well-structured, competitive procurement programmes were resulting in transformative momentum at both the project and country levels.

The accelerating decline in ZESCO's (and also Zambia's) fortunes quickly brought much of this positive movement to a halt. It soon became clear that ZESCO was effectively bankrupt, reportedly being more than USD 1 billion in arrears, largely as a consequence of government-negotiated expensive, hard-currency deals for emergency power, and unsolicited IPPs (African Energy, 2019; Chakwe, 2019; Garcia et al., 2020). Zambia's GDP growth rate had furthermore fallen to 3% in 2019 from levels above 10% in the early 2000s, driven by low commodity (especially copper) prices, production and profitability difficulties in the copper mining industry, and stagnating agricultural output. In addition, aggressive borrowing (88% plus debt-to-GDP ratio), a growing fiscal deficit (9% of GDP), coupled with continuing currency depreciation meant that the Zambian state was in a precarious financial position, leading to successive credit rating downgrades in 2019 and 2020 and Africa's first post-COVID bond default (African Energy, 2019; Moody's Investor Service, 2019; Cotterill, 2020; Fitch, 2020).

Despite the severity of the problems, there appears to be little appetite to deal with the underlying issues. There has, for example, been no real movement on much-needed reforms at ZESCO—officially blamed on the long-outstanding cost of a service study initiated in 2017[33] but in large part due to a combination of political economy factors at both the national and sectoral level. Zambia has a long history of repeatedly short-circuiting power-sector reform efforts to maintain the hidden cross-subsidies (rents) in the system and to secure high-level access to the discretionary resources—cash, tenders, and jobs—that make its highly centralized, patronage-based system of governance possible (Fritz et al., 2014).

As economic and financial pressure increased on Zambia and the sector in recent years, there have been several examples of overt, high-level political interference that undermined both the governance and overall financial health of the sector. ZESCO's expensive emergency PPAs and unsolicited IPP deals—directly responsible for the utility's financial distress—were, for example, all negotiated by the Zambian government (in the case of the emergency power deals, shortly before a presidential election). A surprising announcement in May 2020 also revealed that PowerChina had been awarded 600 MW (the original Scaling Solar allocation) of solar PV projects on an EPC basis through a directly negotiated deal—a move that caught many key energy sector decision-makers off guard and which appears likely to continue the unfortunate trend of expensive, non-transparent procurement (Largue, 2020; Mavrokefalidis, 2020; Mfula, 2020; Sinynagwe and Marks, 2020). Given the record-breaking solar PV project prices secured through

---

[33] The consultants originally hired to complete the study cancelled their contract in 2018, citing political interference and a lack of support and access to information. New consultants were only hired in December 2019.

the Scaling Solar and GETFiT programmes, it is difficult to make sense of this decision without seeing it as a cynical attempt at further delaying reforms at ZESCO while also appeasing Zambia's biggest creditor—China. President Lungu also decided to scrap ZESCO's (ERB-approved) tariff increase in May 2019 (Sinynagwe and Marks, 2020), exacerbating not only the utility's but also Zambia's financial problems while, at the same time, further undermining the sector's governance structures. The Zambian government's extraordinary step of declaring the CEC's transmission and distribution lines a 'common carrier' in June 2020, effectively nationalizing the private utility's assets in a bid to keep it from suspending power supply to the non-paying, government-controlled Konkola Copper Mines (KCM), certainly did not improve investor sentiment either (African Energy, 2019; Sinynagwe and Marks, 2020). This decision meant that ZESCO now had to maintain power supply to a major, non-paying customer, further intensifying its financial problems.

This 'governance-by-centralized-discretion' system is propped up by powerful narratives about the country's colonial history and resentment about the controversial privatization programme of the 1990s, which many saw as stripping Zambia of its crown jewels—the copper mines—along with several state-owned enterprises (Fritz et al., 2014; Larmer, 2005; Mususa, 2014). This resentment is compounded in the energy sector by the fact that the best customers—the mines, which contribute 80% of ZESCO's revenues and pay their tariffs in hard currency—belong to the CEC, which was also privatized in 1997. There is thus a great deal of sensitivity about the role that seemingly Western-backed, foreign, private-sector interests play, especially in the infrastructure sector (Fritz et al., 2014). Long-standing battles about mining royalties, as well as a controversial electricity bulk supply agreement to the mines (which consume about 50% of the country's power) are ongoing manifestations of this tension (Mills, 2016, 2019a, 2019b; African Energy, 2019; Sinynagwe and Marks, 2020).

As a result, none of the GETFiT projects have been able to advance to financial close, with lenders insisting on faster and more drastic measures to clean up ZESCO's balance sheet as well as additional risk-mitigation cover. No such movement appears to be forthcoming. A faint light at the end of the tunnel is the possibility of changing the off-taker to Africa GreenCo—a new, as yet untested, independent intermediary off-taker styled on India's Solar Energy Corporation of India (SECI) model. Africa GreenCo's proposed approach is to act as an investment-grade off-taker for IPPs in the Southern African region that will be able to sell power to multiple entities—including large industrial and commercial consumers as well as other national utilities through the Southern African Power Pool—in an attempt to offset some of the risks involved in these deals. Africa GreenCo has received a US$ 45 million guarantee from the Agence Française de Développement (AFD), backed by the European Fund for Sustainable Development, to provide capital protection to commercial lenders (Africa GreenCo, 2017). By diversifying the pool of possible off-takers, it is hoped that the model will increase the bankability of projects that would normally require a suite of risk-mitigation and credit-enhancement products. In the case of Zambia, Africa GreenCo will, for example, sign back-to-back PPAs with ZESCO but will also be able to sell directly to the CEC, the mines, or other large consumers, thanks to the recently passed electricity law and electricity regulatory act. This could dampen the impact of a possible ZESCO payment default and offers some comfort to project investors. At this stage, it is unclear whether the already procured GETFiT solar projects will be able to make use of this proposed model as it would potentially open up the procurement process to a legal challenge. It does, however, remain an interesting and potentially transformative model that could unlock much more power-sector investment in the region.

8.5 Lessons learned from Zambia's renewable energy auction programmes

What contributes to the success of IPPs in Africa and other developing regions? Previous literature and case studies have shown that a combination of country- and project-level factors explain project outcomes in a variety of settings (Eberhard and Gratwick, 2005, 2011, 2013a, b; Woodhouse, 2005a, b; Malgas et al., 2007; Eberhard et al., 2017; Meyer et al., 2018). Zambia is no different. At a country level, Zambia represents a difficult investment climate, compounded by a utility that is not creditworthy and has been in default on payments to IPPs. Still, there is a broad policy, legislative and regulatory framework for private investment, and an independent regulator. Historically, this has not led to a flood of investment, in part also due to the ineffectiveness of the OPPI, poor planning, and little experience in running competitive procurements. Here, the Scaling Solar and GETFiT programmes have broken new ground. At a project level, these programmes have attracted experienced debt and equity providers; created bankable project documents—including implementation agreements and PPAs with reasonable risk allocation; and been backed by strong credit-enhancement, security, and risk-mitigation measures. But key to these programmes' achievements have been programme design innovations and support for running effective auctions, which have resulted in surprisingly good outcomes. Zambian bids have broken African solar PV price records twice, and despite setbacks and delays, the Scaling Solar projects reached COD within a reasonable amount of time. GETFiT projects are, however, stuck in limbo, with little prospect of them reaching financial close soon.

The involvement of international institutions and their advisors—World Bank/IFC advisory, in the case of Scaling Solar, and KfW/Multiconsult, in the case of GETFiT—was crucial to earning and sustaining the market's trust in the bidding programmes, especially in the face of implementation challenges. Both programmes also went to great lengths to embed the auction programmes in local institutions—arguably more so in the case of GETFiT, which set-up steering and investment committees as well as a programme secretariat.

In terms of auction design, the Scaling Solar and GETFiT programmes were run along broadly similar lines. Both programmes were set up as two-stage, sealed-bid, pay-as-bid tenders that prioritized project price (exclusively so in the case of Scaling Solar) in the bid-scoring process. Financial and physical qualification criteria were substantial, project documents were non-negotiable, and penalty regimes robust. The GETFiT programme additionally allowed bidders to submit conditional bids to combine both project sites, explicitly screened bids based on grid impacts, and included a clause that would see project prices reduced commensurate with PV cost trends if financial close was significantly delayed.

Both programmes have also attracted their share of criticism. The selection and preparation of the project sites was a key (but eventually resolved) challenge for the Scaling Solar projects, and lessons appear to have been learned. Local and international commercial lenders have also complained about being crowded out by DFIs and export credit agencies. There are, likewise, questions being asked about the sufficiency of the risk-mitigation package offered to GETFiT projects in light of the deepening financial troubles of ZESCO and the Zambian state.

Still, the Zambian auction programmes offer powerful lessons on auction design and implementation for the region. It foregrounds the importance of trust, underpinned by institutional capacity, communication, and transparency. It shows that simple, yet innovative auction design, coupled with effective risk-mitigation measures, can deliver incredible results. Finally, Scaling Solar and GETFiT are learning iterative lessons across countries which have the potential to benefit further countries in the future.

8.6 Appendix A

Table 8.14 Classification: ZESCO substations—grid connection of PV plant

Region	Substation	Category	Maximum PV size	Ttf Voltage (kl/)	Ttf size (MVA)
	Msoro	A	20MW	330/66	2 × 45
Eastern	Azele	B	10MW	66/33	2 × 25
	Mfuwe	B	10MW	66/11	2.5
	Chipata	A	20MW	132/33	2 × 45
	Sesheke	A	20MW	66/11	10
	Senanga	B+	10MW	66/11	1 × 5; 1 × 2.5
Western	Mongu	C	N/A	66/11	2 × 10
	Kalabo	C	N/A	11/0.4	1
	Kaoma	C	N/A	66/33;66/11	1 × 5; 1 × 2.5
	Kasa.ma	A	20MW	330/66	2 × 65
	Mbala	A	20MW	66/33	10
	Ltlwingu	B	10MW	66/11	5
	Mporokoso	C	N/A	66/11	25
Nonhem	Mpika	A	20MW	330/66	2 × 90
	Chinsali	B+	10MW	66/11	5
	Isoka	B+	10W	66/11	5
	Nakonde	B+	10MW	66/11	10
	Mansa	B	10MW	66/33	10
	Kawambwa	B	10MW	66/11	5
	Lumwana	A	20MW	330/132	2 × 90
	MfumbWe	A	20MW	132/33/11	1 × 10
NorthWestern	Kabompo	B	10MW	132/33/11	2 × 25
	Mumbezhf	B+	10MW	132/33	1 × 5
	Mwitlllunga	B	10MW	132/33/11	1 × 25

Note: PV maximum size connection categories—A = 20 MW; B = 10 MW; B+ = 10 MW with 5 MVar reactor; C = not available.

8.7 References

Africa GreenCo, (2017). An overview, https://africagreenco.com/wp-content/uploads/2017/11/GreenCo-BP-Overview_October-2017.pdf.

African Energy (2019). Zambia's Zesco seeks to renegotiate power tariffs with IPPs, African Energy News. https://www.africa-energy.com/article/zambia-government-takes-zesco-debt.

AURES (Auctions for Renewable Energy Support) Consortium (2019). 'Effect of Auctions on Financing Conditions for Renewable Energy. https://backend.orbit.

dtu.dk/ws/portalfiles/portal/197901914/AURES_II_D5_1_final_uploaded_web_version.pdf

Batidzirai, B., Moyo, A., and Kapembwa, M. (2018). 'Willingness to Pay for Improved Electricity Supply Reliability in Zambia—a Survey of Urban Enterprises in Lusaka and Kitwe'. May, 57, https://www.theigc.org/sites/default/files/2019/01/Batidzirai-2018-Final-report.pdf.

Burguet, R., and Che, Y.-K. (2007). 'Competitive Procurement with Corruption'. *RAND Journal of Economics*, 35(1), 50. https://doi.org/10.2307/1593729.

Chakwe, M. (2019). Zesco a large inefficient and bankrupt parastatal – Mwaanga, Mast. https://www.themastonline.com/2019/10/19/zesco-a-large-inefficient-and-bankrupt-parastatal-mwaanga/.

Cotterill, J. Stubbington, T. (2020) Zambia headed for Africa's first Covid-related debt default, Financ. *Times*. 46–48. https://www.ft.com/content/0b744d46-46b1-48c3-81cd-be0d78d99262.

Dunlop, S. (2017). 'Doubts Whether the IFC's Scaling Solar Programme Is "Good Thing for Africa"'. *PV-Tech*, 1–2, http://www.pv-tech.org/news/to-be-determined-whether-the-ifcs-scaling-solar-programme-is-good-thing-for1/2 (accessed 23 April 2023).

Eberhard, A., and Gratwick, K. N. (2005). 'The Kenyan IPP Experience'. *Journal of Energy in Southern Africa*, 16(4), 152–165.

Eberhard, A., and Gratwick, K. N. (2011). 'IPPs in Sub-Saharan Africa: Determinants of Success'. *Energy Policy*, 39(9), 5541–5549. https://doi.org/10.1016/j.enpol.2011.05.004.

Eberhard, A., and Gratwick, K. N. (2013a). 'Contributing Elements to Success of IPPs in Sub-Saharan Africa', pp. 2–5. https://blog.private-sector-and-development.com/2013/12/02/contributing-elements-to-success-of-ipps-in-sub-saharan-africa/?output=pdf

Eberhard, A., and Gratwick, K. (2013b). 'Investment Power in Africa: Where From and Where To?'. *Georgetown Journal of International Affairs* (Winter/Spring), 39–46.

Eberhard, A., Gratwick, K. Morella, E. & Antmann, P. (2017). 'Independent Power Projects in Sub-Saharan Africa: Investment Trends and Policy Lessons'. *Energy Policy*, 108, 390–424. https://doi.org/10.1016/j.enpol.2017.05.023.

Elston, L. (2016). 'IPPs Get Their Claws Out for Scaling Solar'. *Natural Gas Daily*, July, http://interfaxenergy.com/gasdaily/article/21242/ipps-get-their-claws-out-for-scaling-solar (accessed 23 April 2023).

Estache, A, Iimi, A, and Ruzzier, C. (2009). 'Procurement in Infrastructure: What Does Theory Tell Us?'. Policy Research Working Paper, July, pp. 1–40. https://doi.org/10.1596/1813-9450-4994.

Fergusson, J., Croft, D., and Charafi, Y. (2015). 'Scaling Solar: Making the Sun Work for Africa'. *Africa Energy Yearbook*, 113–117.

Fritz, V., Levy, B., Ort, R. (2014). Problem-driven political economy analysis: The World Bank's experience. *World Bank*. https://doi.org/10.1596/9781464801211.

Garcia, R. (2018). ZESCO in "load-shed" by Mozambique over US$70 million debt, Zambian Obs. https://www.zambianobserver.com/zesco-in-load-shed-by-mozambique-over-us70-million-debt/.

Gratwick, K. N., and Eberhard, A. (2008). 'An Analysis of Independent Power Projects in Africa: Understanding Development and Investment Outcomes'. *Development Policy Review*, 26(3), 309–338. https://doi.org/10.1111/j.1467-7679.2008.00412.x.

Industrial Development Corporation (2016). 'IDC Zambia Issues Request for Proposals for Round 1 of Scaling Solar Program for 100MW and Starts Work on Round 2 for 200MW'. Lusaka.

Kapika, J., and Eberhard, A. (2013). 'Power-Sector Reform and Regulation in Africa: Lessons from Kenya, Tanzania, Uganda, Zambia, Namibia and Ghana', http://www.gsb.uct.ac.za/files/Powersector.pdf (accessed 23 April 2023).

Kreiss, J., Ehrhart, K. M., and Haufe, M. C. (2017). 'Appropriate Design of Auctions for Renewable Energy Support—Prequalifications and Penalties'. *Energy Policy*, 101(October), 512–520. https://doi.org/10.1016/j.enpol.2016.11.007.

Kruger, W., and Eberhard, A. (2018). 'Renewable Energy Auctions in Sub-Saharan Africa: Comparing the South African, Ugandan, and Zambian Programs'. *Wiley Interdisciplinary Reviews: Energy and Environment*, February, 1–13. https://doi.org/10.1002/wene.295.

Kruger, W., Stritzke, S., and Trotter, P. A. (2019). 'De-risking Solar Auctions in Sub-Saharan Africa—A Comparison of Site Selection Strategies in South Africa and Zambia'. *Renewable and Sustainable Energy Reviews*, 104, 429–438. https://doi.org/10.1016/j.rser.2019.01.041.

Mavrokefalidis, D. (2020). Zesco and Power China sign $548m deal for three solar projects in Zambia, *Energy Live News*. https://www.energylivenews.com/2020/05/26/zesco-and-power-china-sign-548m-deal-for-three-solar-projects-in-zambia/.

Largue, P. (2020). Power China awarded $548 million, 600MW ZESCO solar contract, ESI Africa. https://www.esi-africa.com/industry-sectors/generation/solar/power-china-awarded-548-million-600mw-zesco-solar-contract/.

Larmer, M. (2005). Reaction & resistance to neo-liberalism in Zambia, *Review of African Political Economy*. 32, 29–45. https://www.jstor.org/stable/4006908.

Malgas, I., Nawaal Gratwick, K., and Eberhard, A. (2007). 'Two of a Kind: Lessons from Tunisian Independent Power Projects'. *Journal of North African Studies*, 12(4), 395–415. https://doi.org/10.1080/13629380701307126.

Manelli, A. M., and Vincent, D. R. (1995). 'Optimal Procurement Mechanisms'. *Econometrica*, 63(3), 591–620.

Marcel, D., and House, S. (2016). 'Effects of Multilateral Support on Infrastructure PPP Contract Cancellation'. 7751, Working paper: https://ppi.worldbank.org/content/dam/PPI/documents/WPS7751.pdf.

Meyer, R., Eberhard, A., and Gratwick, K. (2018). 'Uganda's Power Sector Reform: There and Back Again?'. *Energy for Sustainable Development*, 43, 75–89. https://doi.org/10.1016/j.esd.2017.11.001.

Mfula, C. (2020). Zambia's state-owned utility contracts with Power China to develop 600MW of solar generation. *Reuters*. https://ieefa.org/zambias-state-owned-utility-contracts-with-power-china-to-develop-600mw-of-solar-generation.

Mills, G. (2016).The deficits behind Zambia's power problems, Dly. Maverick. Moody's Investor Service, Rating Action: Moody's downgrades Zambia's ratings to Caa2, outlook changed to negative, Moody's investor service, 2019. https://www.moodys.com/research/Moodys-downgrades-Zambias-ratings-to-Caa2-outlook-changed-to-negative--PR_400332.

Mususa, P. N. (2014). There used to be order: Life on the Copperbelt after the privatisation of the Zambia Consolidated Copper Mines, Doctoral dissertation, University of Cape Town, https://open.uct.ac.za/handle/11427/9291

Fitch Ratings, Zambia's (2019). debt rise highlights fiscal challenges, Fitch Ratings Agency, 2020. https://www.fitchratings.com/research/sovereigns/zambia-2019-debt-

Sinynagwe, C. Marks, D. (2020). Zambia government's power grab signals further trouble ahead, African Energy Newsl. https://www.africa-energy.com/article/zambia-governments-power-grab-signals-further-trouble-ahead.

Woodhouse, E. J. (2005a). 'A Political Economy of International Infrastructure Contracting: Lessons from the IPP Experience', 52. https://fsi9-prod.s3.us-west-1.amazonaws.com/s3fs-public/PESD_IPP_Study%2C_Global_Report.pdf

Woodhouse, E. J. (2005b). 'The Obsolescing Bargain Redux? Foreign Investment in the Electric Power Sector in Developing Countries'. *Journal of International Law and Politics*, 38(1&2), 121.

World Bank (2015). *6th Zambia Economic Brief: Powering the Zambian Economy* (Washington DC: World Bank).

World Bank Group (2016). 'Scaling Solar Delivers 6 Cents Solar in Zambia', World Bank Group.

9
Namibia

Bidding on the Sun

Wikus Kruger and Anton Eberhard

9.1 Introduction: A rapid turn towards the sun

In the space of five years, Namibia's power sector has quietly undergone a rapid and fundamental transformation. In 2015, the country had no utility-scale renewable energy installations and no private power-sector investment. NamPower—the state owned power utility—owned and operated 424 mega watts (MW) of installed power generation assets—mostly hydro, coal, and heavy fuel oil- (HFO)-based—and covered the shortfall in demand (around 60%) with imports from South Africa and the Southern African Power Pool. Fast-forward to 2020 and Namibia had the fourth largest number of independent power producers (IPPs) in sub-Saharan Africa—all renewable energy-based—representing more than 25% of the country's installed generation capacity (Alao and Kruger, 2020). This does not include the rapid growth in renewable energy-based embedded generation installations, which increased the contribution to at least 31%. The transformation has been accompanied by some of the lowest solar prices in the region—US$c 6.3/kilo-watt hour (kWh) in 2016, and US$c 2.9/kWh in 2020—achieved without any risk-mitigation or credit-enhancement measures provided by the state.

   In one sense, the Namibian case is probably the best regional example of the cumulative impact of a well-designed procurement programme implemented in a conducive, enabling environment. At a country level, Namibia is generally viewed as a stable democracy with moderate economic growth under-pinned by solid macroeconomic fundamentals and strong institutions—especially the judiciary and the electricity sector regulator, the Electricity Control Board (ECB) (Fauconnier et al., 2017; Kruger et al., 2019; UNPAF, 2017; United Nations Namibia, 2019; African Development Bank, 2020; Dalrymple, 2020). Although energy sector policies and regulations in the past have commonly made provision for private power investment, recent years

Wikus Kruger and Anton Eberhard, *Namibia*. In: *Renewable Energy Auctions: Lessons from the Global South.*
Edited by: Anton Eberhard and Wikus Kruger, Oxford University Press. © Oxford University Press (2023).
DOI: 10.1093/oso/9780192871701.003.0009

have seen the promulgation of increasingly supportive policies for IPPs, renewable energy, and distributed generation (Kapika and Eberhard, 2013; MME, 2017b; Kruger et al., 2019; *The Namibian*, 2019). The ECB has, furthermore, presided over a market reform process that has opened up the sector to accelerated investment through publishing new market rules (The Modified Single-Buyer Market Market Rules (Draft), 2019; *The Namibian*, 2019).

Until 2018, NamPower had the curious distinction of being the only utility in sub-Saharan Africa with an investment-grade credit rating,[1] thanks, in large part, to cost-reflective end-user tariffs and good management (Kaze, 2014; Reuters, 2017b; Eberhard et al., 2019; African Development Bank, 2020). In the past, these positive, country-level factors resulted in less than a handful of private power projects being developed, mostly through directly negotiated processes at relatively expensive tariffs. The implementation of a feed-in tariff programme accelerated the pace of investment but did not drive down the cost of power. It was only when Namibia implemented a competitive procurement programme—after an early false start—that the country was truly able to take full advantage of its abundant renewable energy and land resources.

This chapter seeks to understand how the country-, programme-, and project-level factors worked together to achieve these remarkable outcomes, tracing the development of the sector and, in particular, the renewable energy auction programme, through various iterations over a five-year period. In doing so, the chapter also seeks to uncover what it is about Namibia that allowed the country to embrace the transformative impact of these renewable energy investments—something which seems to have been much more difficult to sustain in many other African countries despite similar investment outcomes.

9.2 Overview of Namibia's economy

The Republic of Namibia is situated in the south-western region of Africa, sharing borders with Angola, South Africa, and Botswana. It is one of the least densely populated countries in the world, with about 2.5 million people spread out across more than 850,000 square kilometres. Namibia gained independence from South African 'administrative rule' in 1990 and has since

---

[1] NamPower's credit rating was revised from BBB– to BB+ (2019) and BB (2020) based on downward revisions of the sovereign's credit ratings and its high reliance on power imports from Eskom, which itself has faced multiple downgrades in recent years. NamPower nevertheless remains the strongest performer among its peers, including Eskom, the Saudi Electricity Company, and Poland's PGE (Fitch Ratings, 2019, 2020).

held multiparty elections in 1994, 1999, 2004, 2009, and 2014—all won by the South-West African People's Organization (SWAPO) (UNPAF, 2017; BBC, 2018).

Namibia is one of the few upper-middle-income countries in sub-Saharan Africa, with nominal gross domestic product (GDP) per capita at US$ 5,227. It is highly ranked in most governance and investment attractiveness indices, in large part due to its political stability, macroprudential policies, and effective legal system that ensures enforcement of contracts. Namibia has developed a strong financial market and a world-class banking system, and the Namibian Stock Exchange is the second largest by market capitalization in Africa. Nonetheless, the country's small market size has resulted in below average foreign direct investment (FDI) and an overall investment attractiveness ranking outside the top 10 in sub-Saharan Africa (Fauconnier et al., 2017; UNPAF, 2017).

The Namibian economy remains closely linked to that of South Africa. The Namibian dollar (N$) is pegged to the South African Rand (ZAR) and South African-linked companies represent a large portion of the firms listed on the Namibian Stock Exchange. The Namibian financial industry also maintains strong links with South African banks and financial services companies. Payments made to Namibia through the Southern African Customs Union[2] (SACU) make up more than 35% of government revenue and largely come from South Africa. This effectively means that any changes in South Africa's economic fortunes have a significant and, at times, disproportionate impact on Namibia's economy (Fauconnier et al., 2017; Southern African Customs Union, 2017; UNPAF, 2017; BBC, 2018).

While Namibia has experienced GDP growth rates above 5% for most of the 2000s, global ratings agencies revised its economic outlook from stable to negative in 2016. It has since experienced several quarters of economic contraction, and public debt levels increased to more than 40% of GDP in 2017. The economic stagnation is, in large part, due to South Africa's own economic slow-down as well as the impact of lower oil prices on Namibia's other major regional trading partner, Angola. While Namibia's poverty rate has declined from 28% in 2010/2011 to 18% in 2016, the recent economic woes are threatening to undo many of the country's socio-economic gains (Fauconnier et al., 2017; UNPAF, 2017; BBC, 2018).

---

[2] The Southern African Customs Union is the world's oldest customs union and effectively means that a single tariff is applied to goods entering the union (South Africa, Botswana, Lesotho, Swaziland, and Namibia) and that no customs duties are charged between the members. All revenues are paid into a central revenue pool, which is distributed according to a formula that is heavily weighted in favour of the smaller customs union members (effectively, all member countries except South Africa).

9.3 Namibia's power sector: First steps towards reform and security of supply

Namibia has a relatively small power sector that is dependent on power trade with regional partners. The country has 594 megawatts (MW) of installed generation capacity (as of 2019), the majority of which derives from the Ruacana hydropower plant[3] (347 MW) on the Angolan border (Figure 9.1). The national electricity access rate increased to 51% in 2016 from just above 25% in 1990. Peak electricity demand surpassed installed capacity in 2006 and the gap has been widening ever since, although there has been a slight recent decrease in demand—from 677 MW in 2017 to 639 MW in 2018. This slowing of demand growth is set to continue as economic growth falters and embedded generation (especially rooftop solar photovoltaic (PV)) increases. Given the country's excellent solar resources and its relatively high electricity tariffs, Namibia already has one of the fastest growing rooftop solar PV markets in sub-Saharan Africa (ECB, 2016; MME, 2016).

The majority of Namibia's electricity demand (60% plus) is met through imports from the Southern African Power Pool (SAPP)—primarily governed by bilateral contracts with South Africa, Zambia, and Mozambique. South Africa's Eskom is the main contributor to the power pool and has been supplying around 2,000 gigawatts (GWh) of the 4,800 GWh consumed annually.[4] Namibia has also been increasing its purchases on SAPP's short-term energy market (STEM) from 55 GWh in 2016 to 828 GWh in 2018. With almost all SAPP members facing electricity supply shortfalls of their own in recent years, Namibia is actively seeking to decrease its reliance on power trading (ECB, 2016; MME, 2016, 2017a).

Most of the country's generation capacity and all of its transmission infrastructure is owned and operated by NamPower—the vertically integrated, state-owned utility company. In 1990, following Namibia's independence from South Africa, South West Africa Water and Electricity Corporation (SWAWEK) was transferred to the Namibian government and was later

---

[3] Ruacana is a run-of-the-river hydropower plant on the Kunene River that was commissioned in 1978. The plant's electricity output is very seasonal, with average monthly output ranging from 200 gigawatts (GWh) in wet months to less than 60 GWh in dry months. The plant originally had 332 MW of installed capacity (3 × 80 MW plus 1 × 92 MW), but a recent major refurbishment increased this to 347 MW. Ruacana also has black-start capability from on-site diesel generators.

[4] Namibia has two types of contracts with Eskom. An off-peak bilateral contract (renewed annually) stipulates that electricity can be used only during off-peak periods and is priced based on season and time period (peak, standard, off-peak). The supplemental contract of 200 MW is a special-assistance agreement that is conditional on Eskom being able to meet demand and functions as a supply of last-resort option. Namibia also has a 10-year 50 MW contract with the Zambia Electricity Supply Corporation (ZESCO) that will expire in 2020 and a 80 MW supply agreement with the Zimbabwe Electricity Supply Authority (ZESA) that expires in 2025.

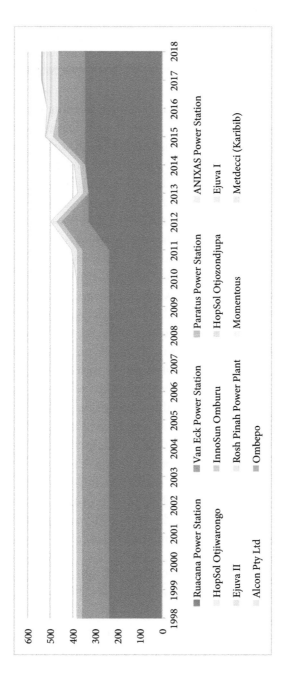

Figure 9.1 Installed electricity generation capacity, Namibia, 1998–2017

Note: Blue = hydropower; red = thermal power; yellow = solar photovoltaic (PV) power; green = wind.
Source: Authors' calculation, NamPower (2018).

renamed NamPower. Although owned by the state, NamPower enjoys relative autonomy from the government in comparison with other state-owned utilities in sub-Saharan Africa, although a high turnover in recent years at chief executive officer (CEO) level[5] and questionable government appointments to its board and management have somewhat tainted its status as a 'well-governed utility' (Kapika and Eberhard, 2013; *The Namibian*, 2015, 2018).

Nonetheless, NamPower is generally still regarded as being well managed, with full cost recovery, high bill collection rates, and efficient employee levels. The utility's financial and technical performance is highly ranked in comparison to its regional peers, and it is also the only utility in sub-Saharan Africa with an investment-grade credit rating. In stark contrast with other utilities in the region, NamPower paid dividends of more than US$ 5.7 million in 2019 and US$ 4.6 million in 2018 to its shareholder. NamPower finances most of its large projects—for example, transmission networks—by raising bonds on capital markets (Kapika and Eberhard, 2013; Fitch Ratings Agency, 2014; Kaze, 2014; Reuters, 2017a; Eberhard and Dyson, 2019).

The Namibian distribution sector has several players, including regional electricity distributors (REDs) and local and regional authorities as well as NamPower distribution. To address the lack of capacity and resources at local distributor level, in the early 2000s it was recommended that there be a gradual unbundling of the distribution sector into REDs (SAD-ELEC, 2000). In 2002, the distribution sub-sector was unbundled into five REDs, commencing with the establishment of the Northern Region Electricity Distributor (NORED), covering the northern region of Namibia; the Central North Regional Electricity Distributor (CENORED), covering the central-northern region of Namibia; and the Erongo Regional Electricity Distributor Company (Erongo RED), covering the central coastal part of the western region of Namibia (Kapika and Eberhard, 2013). The proposed Central RED was fiercely opposed by the City of Windhoek and will most probably not be established any time soon, while the Southern RED is currently in the initial phases of being set up.

The Energy Policy White Paper of 1998 was Namibia's earliest effort to develop a harmonized policy for the energy sector (MME, 1998). A study on the operationalization of the policy recognized the role of IPPs in achieving electricity supply security and proposed a power-sector structure that would enable IPPs to supply power to the REDs and other local and regional

---

[5] NamPower has had three CEOs in the past seven years: two managing directors (MDs) and one acting MD.

authorities through a single buyer as well as entering into export contracts directly with third parties. It also proposed the monitoring of bulk-sale agreements by an independent regulator so that the utility (as single buyer) would not ultimately support its own generation over that of IPPs (SAD-ELEC, 2000).

The Electricity Act of 2000 established an independent regulator called the Electricity Control Board (ECB). The regulator is responsible for approving tariffs over the entire power sector (generation, transmission, and distribution). The approved bulk electricity tariff charged by NamPower for the 2018/2019 financial period is NA$ 1.72/kWh (US$ 0.12/kWh). The Ruacana hydropower plant is the cheapest source of power on the system and produces electricity at NADc 20–40/kWh (US$ 0.014–0.029/kWh). End-user tariffs in the capital city of Windhoek range from NA$ 1.44/kWh (US$ 0.10/kWh) for low-income residential consumers to NA$ 3.06/kWh (US$ 0.22/kWh) during peak hours (in the high season) for commercial customers (ECB, 2016; City of Windhoek, 2018; NamPower, 2018).[6]

Not long after the Act was passed, various loopholes were identified. Most importantly, the Act made no provision for the promulgation of mechanisms that would enable private-sector investment, it did not stipulate the asset transfer arrangement from municipalities to the REDs, and did not explicitly furnish the ECB with exclusive regulatory authority over the distribution sub-sector (Kapika and Eberhard, 2013). The Act was thus revoked, and a new Electricity Act was passed in 2007 (MME, 2007).

More recently, the National Energy Policy (MME, 2017a), the National IPP Policy (MME, 2017b), and the National Renewable Energy Policy (MME, 2017c) have been adopted to spell out the government's intent, direction, and undertakings for the energy sector. The main goals of the policies are to ensure electricity supply security, affordability, and reliability, primarily by increasing private-sector renewable energy investment (both on-grid and off-grid). The IPP policy also stipulates that small IPPs (<5 MW) are to be procured through a renewable energy feed-in tariff (REFiT) scheme, whereas medium (5–100 MW) and large (100 MW plus) IPPs are to be procured through a competitive tender process (MME, 2017b). Through the policy amendments, the country further formally implemented the modified single-buyer market model. This allowed IPPs to sell to NamPower and

---

[6] This refers only to the energy charge and excludes an additional capacity charge, ECB levy, and National Energy Fund (NEF) levy. As a rule of thumb, the cost components of the average end-user tariff typically comprise 50% generation cost, 20% transmission cost, 5% levies, and 5% distribution costs. The average retail tariff in Namibia is estimated at NA$ 2,45/kWh.

transmission customers such as distributors or large consumers[7] and endow the national integrated resource plan (NIRP) with legislative power. This is discussed further in section 9.3.

The pronounced policy focus on increasing private power investment was in part motivated by the public sector's struggle to increase generation capacity.[8] NamPower has, for many years, unsuccessfully tried to develop two large generation projects—Baynes (600 MW hydro—to be shared with Angola) and Kudu (800 MW combined-cycle gas turbine (CCGT) fuelled by off-shore gas resources) (Boxes 9.1 and 9.2). These projects have experienced slow development, with NamPower unwilling to allow full private-sector involvement.[9] By contrast, the country has recently embarked on one of sub-Saharan Africa's most rapidly successful private power investment programmes, with more than 20 IPP projects reaching financial close in the past three years (Table 9.1). This is a significant development considering that Namibia had no private power generation capacity prior to 2016. The majority of this new capacity is made up of relatively small (5 MW) renewable energy projects (primarily solar PV) procured through a feed-in tariff programme. There is also a handful of directly negotiated projects that reached financial close, some of them selling directly to REDs. Both the REFiT and directly negotiated deals are considered to be quite expensive, for the most part selling power at prices above the average cost of NamPower generation. The competitively procured 37 MW Hardap solar PV project at Mariental is an important exception and will be the focus of this report.

Private power investment has also spread beyond the government procurement programmes and is presenting potential competition to the national power utility. Three utility-scale embedded generation/corporate power purchase agreement (PPA) power projects have been built in recent years (Table 9.2), with several more being developed. The story of most significance for the Namibian power sector is, however, the rapid development of the commercial and industrial rooftop solar market, with PV systems now covering a significant percentage of all commercial and industrial roof space in the country. The country's cost-reflective electricity tariffs have driven much of this development: the relatively high price of electricity, coupled

---

[7] Transmission customers are allowed, under the modified single-buyer model, to buy up to 30% of their electricity consumption from private generators (IPPs), under the first phase of the model, until 2021. The regulators will come up with new rules and allocations for the second phase, which will last until 2026. Part of the modified single-buyer framework includes the promulgation of a wheeling framework and unbundled tariff framework.

[8] The Ministry of Finance also wants to loosen fiscal constraints through increased use of public–private partnerships (PPPs).

[9] NamPower committed to a maximum of 51% equity stake in the Kudu Power Station to allow participation of the private sector in the project. The upstream development included the National Petroleum Corporation of Namibia (NAMCOR) and a privately owned company.

Table 9.1 Key institutions in Namibia's electricity sector

Ministry of Mines and Energy (MME)	The MME is responsible for developing energy policy; approving licences (as recommended by the ECB); rural electrification planning, funding, and implementation; and the regulation of the petroleum industry.
Electricity Control Board (ECB)	The ECB is the statutory regulator for the Namibian electricity sector. It was established in 2000. ECB activities are funded by the ECB levy on electricity sales. Under the updated Electricity Act of 2007, the ECB is responsible for the regulation of techno-economic aspects of the electricity sector. ECB also manages licences and sets tariffs as well as promoting private sector investment.
NamPower	NamPower is a private company which is 100% owned by the state, responsible for power generation, transmission, and energy trading.
National Planning Commission (NPC)	The NPC was established in 2013 to 'plan and spearhead the course of national development'. Amongst other functions, the NPC is responsible for identifying Namibia's socio-economic development priorities and formulating, evaluating, and implementing national development plans.
National Energy Council (NEC)	The NEC was established in 1990 and advises the Minister of Mines and Energy on issues regarding energy coordination, development, exploitation, and utilization in Namibia.
Regional electricity distributors (REDs) and other distributors	REDs are autonomous companies tasked with the distribution of power to electricity consumers in a specified region of the country. In return for contributing their distribution network assets to the REDs, the local authorities received shares in their respective RED.

Source: Authors' compilation.

with the high solar irradiation levels, allows payback periods of only two to three years for most of these systems. As solar PV prices continue to fall, Namibia is bound to see rapid expansion of this market into the high-end residential sector. This means that, in the medium term, the grid operator is facing a significant 'duck curve'[10] drop in demand during the day, with high power ramp rates in the evenings. Rapid rooftop PV expansion also means that electricity revenues from high-income, high-consumption customers, who have traditionally cross-subsidized tariffs for lower-income customers, are on the decline. The development of battery storage represents a further,

[10] The duck curve (so named by the California Independent System Operator based on the daily residual electricity demand curve's resembling the outline of a duck) refers to the phenomenon where increased solar-PV penetration on the grid significantly depresses demand during daytime hours. This means that the required ramp rate during the hours when solar PV decreases output (usually coinciding with the early evening peak) becomes ever steeper. The duck curve presents significant challenges for conventional power-generation technologies, which have to balance out the system, since many of them are not able to ramp up quickly enough. For more information, see NREL (2018).

Table 9.2 List of power plants in Namibia

Power plants	Location	Technology	Capacity[a]	Category	COD
Van Eck[b]	Windhoek	Coal	30	Utility	1972
Paratus[c]	Walvis Bay	HFO	24	Utility	1976/Decomm.
Ruacana[d]	Omusati	Hydro	347	Utility	1978
ANIXAS[e]	Walvis Bay	Diesel	22.5	Utility	2011
Ejuva 1	Gobabis	Solar PV	5	IPP (REFiT)	2017
Ejuva 2	Gobabis	Solar PV	5	IPP (REFiT)	2017
Camelthorn	Outapi	Solar PV	5	IPP (REFiT)	2018
Momentous	Keetmanshoop	Solar PV	5	IPP (REFiT)	2017
Hopsol	Grootfontein	Solar PV	5	IPP (REFiT)	2016
Sertum	Trekkopje, Erongo	Solar PV	5	IPP (REFiT)	2018
Aloe Investment	Rosh Pinah	Solar PV	5	IPP (REFiT)	2017
ALCON	Aussekher	Solar PV	5	IPP (REFiT)	2017
UNISUN	Okatope	Solar PV	5	IPP (REFiT)	Construction
Tandii	Okatope	Solar PV	5	IPP (REFiT)	Construction
NCF	Okatope	Solar PV	5	IPP (REFiT)	Construction
Ombepo	Luderitz	Wind	5	IPP (REFiT)	2017
Osona	Okahandja	Solar PV	5	IPP (REFiT)	2016
Metdecci	Karibib	Solar PV	5	IPP (REFiT)	2017
GreeNam	Keetmanshoop	Solar PV	10	IPP (DN)	2018
GreeNam	Mariental	Solar PV	10	IPP (DN)	2018
Diaz	Spergebiet	Wind	44	IPP (DN)	Construction
Omburu	Omaruru	Solar PV	4.5	IPP (DN)	2016
Hopsol	Otjiwarongo	Solar PV	5	IPP (DN)	2016
Hardap (Alten)	Mariental	Solar PV	37	IPP (ICB)	2018
OLC Arandis	Arandis	Solar PV	3.8	IPP (ICB)—Erongo RED	2018

Sun EQ Four	Otavi	Solar PV	5	Embedded generation—Ohorongo Cement	2018
B2Gold	Otjikoto Mine	HFO/Solar PV	31	Embedded generation	2018
Ohorongo Cement	Otavi	Diesel	7.5	Embedded generation	2018
Hopsol	CENORED	Solar PV	5	IPP (DN)—CENORED	2018
Xaris	Walvis	LNG	250	IPP (ICB)	On hold[f]
Unspecified	Arandis	CSP	150	IPP (ICB)	Anticipated[g]
Unspecified	Otjiwarongo	Biomass	40	IPP (ICB)	Anticipated[h]
Unspecified	Otavi	Unspecified	20	IPP (ICB)	Anticipated[i]

Source: Authors' compilation; NamPower (2017a).

Note: COD = commercial operation date; DN = directly negotiated; ICB = internationally competitive bid; HFO = heavy fuel oil; CSP = concentrated solar power.

[a] The capacity mentioned in this column refers to export capacity. The installed capacity of most of the IPPs is slightly above the export capacity and is included as such in the calculation of Namibia's overall installed capacity.

[b] The Van Eck power station was commissioned in 1972 (NamPower, 2015) and was built as an interim measure as Angola's grapple for independence from Portugal (1961–1975) further delayed the development of the Ruacana hydropower project (Kapika and Eberhard, 2013). Between 2012 and 2014, the power station was out of service for rehabilitation work and was recommissioned in 2015 (NamPower, 2015). Due to various constraints, the plant can only operate three of its four units at a time, and the ageing equipment, as well as the poor emissions profile, limits output to between 60 and 80 MW at a time. Coal for the plant is imported from South Africa through the Walvis Bay harbour terminal, making this an expensive plant, used mainly for peaking and back-up.

[c] The Paratus power station was commissioned in 1976 (NamPower, 2017a). Like Van Eck, the Paratus power station was built as an interim power plant because of the ongoing delay of the Ruacana project (Kapika and Eberhard, 2013). The power station was decommissioned in 2016 (NamPower, 2017a).

[d] The Ruacana power station was commissioned in 1978, with an installed capacity of 240 MW. In 2012, NamPower increased the power output to 332 MW by installing a fourth generator. In 2014, NamPower further increased the power output to 347 MW by replacing the runners of the initial three existing generators (*Namib Times*, 2016; NamPower, 2017a).

[e] The ANIXAS power station was commissioned in 2011 to serve as a peaking power plant.

[f] See https://allafrica.com/stories/201706080689.html and http://www.energy100fm.com/?q=content/government-halt-xaris-gas-power-plant-walvis (both accessed 167 April 2023).

[g] See Reuters (2017b).
[h] See Reuters (2017b).
[i] See Reuters (2017b).

potentially more severe challenge to the structure and sustainability of the country's power utilities.

Box 9.1 The Kudu Gas Power Project

The Kudu Gas Power Project was, for a long time, considered to be Namibia's flagship PPP. It is an 800-MW, combined-cycle natural gas-fired power station, to be situated 25 km north of Oranjemund. The power station was set to be developed by Nam-Power through KuduPower, a special-purpose vehicle (SPV) established in 2005. A consortium led by Chevron oil company discovered the Kudu gas field at Oranjemund in 1974 (CSIR, 1999). In 1988, NAMCOR (formerly SWAKOR) drilled two wells and estimated that the well contained a reserve of about five trillion cubic feet of gas (CSIR, 1999).

In 1997, a joint venture (JV) comprising NamPower, Eskom, and Shell planned to build a 750 MW combined-cycle gas turbine plant with an estimated cost of NA$ 4 billion. Following further feasibility studies in 1998, Eskom realized that the electricity produced by the project would be too expensive and consequently withdrew from the JV in early 1999 (*Namibian*, 1998). This jeopardized the project's overall feasibility since a significant regional off-taker was a key requirement for the plant's commercial viability (Kapika and Eberhard, 2013).

In 2002, Shell transferred its rights to its partners, ChevronTexaco and Energy Africa, when it was discovered that the actual gas reserves amounted to only 1.3 trillion cubic feet. In late 2003, ChevronTexaco withdrew from the concession and relinquished its rights to Energy Africa (Kapika and Eberhard, 2013). Subsequently, NAMCOR acquired a 10% stake in the concession (*Namibian*, 2003).

In 2004, Eskom revived interest in the project and signed a memorandum of understanding (MoU) with NamPower pledging to negotiate a PPA and other associated agreements relating to the operation and maintenance of the project. Energy Africa, NAMCOR, and NamPower entered into a JV with the expectation that the project would come online in 2009 (Kapika and Eberhard, 2013). By 2007, while PPA negotiations between NamPower and Eskom were in progress, the gas-supply agreement between NamPower and Energy Africa stalled due to NamPower insisting that the gas-supply agreement be in Namibian dollars (*New Era*, 2008). Thereafter, Energy Africa sold its 20% stake to a Japanese firm Itochu (Kapika and Eberhard, 2013).

By 2009, currency risk still presented a stumbling block to negotiations (Kapika and Eberhard, 2013). Gazprom—a Russian energy giant—expressed interest in the project and, in 2010, acquired a 54% stake in the concession—but withdrew within a year (Kapika and Eberhard, 2013). As a result, the Namibian government agreed to provide government guarantees to NamPower and NAMCOR to minimize the associated risk that these state entities posed to prospective upstream investors (*New Era*, 2012).

NamPower's latest plans have focused on reducing the scale of the planned Kudu Power Project (from 800 MW to 442.5 MW), because the off-take agreements with Eskom and Zambia's Copperbelt Energy Corporation (CEC) failed to materialize. The latest cost estimate for the power station is approximately NA$ 9.4 billion (US$ 760 million). At the time of writing, the Kudu Power Project is far from reaching financial close.

Box 9.2 The Baynes Hydropower Project

The planned Baynes hydropower plant is located along the Kunene River (200 km downstream of Ruacana) and is envisaged as a 600-MW, mid-merit/peaking power station to be evenly shared between Namibia and Angola (NamPower, 2018).

In 1969, the South African government (the colonial authority in Namibia at that time) and the Portuguese government (the colonial authority in Angola at that time) entered into a bilateral agreement to develop the first phase of the Kunene River water resources. The bilateral agreement included a plan to develop a hydropower plant at Ruacana (currently operational), to be followed by a sequence of hydropower plants along the length and breadth of the Kunene River. This agreement gave rise to the construction of three schemes in the 1970s—Gove Dam in Angola, Ruacana Hydropower plant in Namibia, and the Calueque Water Scheme—that would facilitate water supply to Namibia and Angola (ERM, 2009).

In the late 1980s, NamPower (then SWAWEK) began negotiations for constructing a hydropower plant in the Epupa district. The Namibian and Angolan governments decided to carry out technical and environmental feasibility studies in 1991—which were finalized only in 1998. The Baynes and Epupa sites were selected as the most technically viable for potential hydropower. This decision was preceded by a rigorous investigation of all probable hydropower development sites along the Kunene downstream of Ruacana (ERM, 2009; NamPower, 2018).

Further studies focusing on the technical, social, and ecological features of these two sites continued. The final report concluded that only the Baynes Hydropower Project would undergo further development and eventual construction since the proposed site would be the least disruptive to the local Himba people (ERM, 2009; NamPower, 2018).

The plans to further develop the Baynes hydropower plant was reinvigorated by the expiration of NamPower's firm power contract (FPC) with South Africa's Eskom in 2005. Moves to renew the FPC proved futile, coinciding with the period during which South Africa was suffering severe power shortages. This resulted in more expensive imports, particularly during peak hours (NamPower, 2018). While the procurement process was expected to be finalized by 2017, at the time of writing, there has still not been any noteworthy development of the project.

9.4 Private power investment and REFiT progress in Namibia

Until recently, Namibia had limited experience with private-sector participation in its power sector. In 1996, the Namibian government signed a six-year, competitively tendered deal with a newly established private company—Northern Electricity—for the operation of distribution networks in a rural, underserved district in the northern region of the country. Although the company was responsible for all operating expenses and revenue of the distribution system, the government maintained ownership of the assets, that is, a concession agreement. The government declined to renew the contract in 2002, despite the private company's notable success in operating and managing the distribution infrastructure. In early 2002, the concession was transferred to the newly established NORED (Kapika and Eberhard, 2013).

2014 marked a true turning point for private power investment in Namibia. The directly negotiated Omburu solar PV project reached financial close and began construction in 2014, showing that it was possible to finance and build this type of smaller renewable energy project without any form of sovereign guarantee (Kaira, 2017). Motivated by this 'proof of concept', the interim REFiT scheme was designed as a pilot programme to increase generation from non-hydro sources. REFiT tariffs were initially set at quite generous levels but were revised prior to projects being awarded, based, in part, on price levels achieved in neighbouring South Africa's second bid window of the Renewable Energy Independent Power Producer Procurement Programme (REI4P). Final feed-in tariffs ranged from US$ 0.078/kWh for onshore wind to US$ 0.099/kWh for solar PV and were indexed to inflation (Table 9.3).

Initially, 27 projects had been granted provisional licences by the ECB in the period leading up to the launch of the feed-in tariff programme but had failed to advance to financial close in the absence of a structured procurement programme. These projects were all invited to participate in the REFiT programme and were given six months to submit all required documents.[11] Fourteen projects (totalling 70 MW) were selected on a 'first-come, first-meeting-the-requirements' basis.[12] They then had 6 months to achieve the PPA effective date with NamPower[13] and a further 12 months to reach the commercial operation date (COD).[14] The remaining IPPs were placed on a waiting list. The REFiT process therefore effectively became a race to the finish line, which helps to explain the rapid development of these projects.

In 2016, 14 REFiT projects (5 MW each), totalling 70 MW and more than US$ 123 million worth of private investment, reached financial close (NamPower, 2017b). All 14 REFiT projects reached their PPA milestones (ECB, 2017) and 13 reached COD by the required date[15] (Table 9.3). One is still

Table 9.3 Namibian feed-in tariff rates

RE technology	Capacity	FIT levels in NA\$/kWh[a]	FIT levels in US cents/kWh[b]
Biomass	5 MW	1.28	9.3
Solar PV	5 MW	1.37	9.9
Onshore wind	5 MW	1.08	7.8

Source: ECB (2017).
Notes: [a] The initially announced tariffs were higher for solar PV (NA\$2,46/kWh) and wind (NA\$1,16/kWh). For biomass, it was lower (NA\$1,23/kWh).
[b] Based on a NA\$:US\$ exchange rate of 0.072.

[11] Credit-approved term sheet from a reputable lender/funder: IPPs that are funding the project through their balance sheet and/or equity investment must render a reputable commercial bank's guarantee confirming funds availability; a letter from the same reputable lender confirming its willingness to provide financing on the terms and conditions of the contract agreements—PPA and transmission connection agreement (TCA). Otherwise, IPPs that are funding the project through their balance sheet and/or equity investment must render a letter, in tandem with the contract agreements—PPA and TCA, a shareholding certificate indicating a minimum share of 30% for previously disadvantaged Namibians (PDNs) (NamPower 2016b).
[12] Twenty-seven interested parties (already licensed) were invited. NamPower facilitated the submission and procurement process, with each party being provided a token based on the time the proposal was submitted.
[13] An IPP would have reached effective PPA date when the following documents were submitted: copy of a signed PPA, copy a signed TCA with NamPower, site permit, environmental impact assessment (EIA) certificate of the site, financial close document/s, generation licence, and a copy of the PPA regulatory oversight letter from the ECB.
[14] IPPs had to find their own land less than 5 km from the grid.
[15] Projects that have not reached their projected PPA dates have been granted more time by the ECB, primarily due to *force majeure* risks materializing in the construction phase. For example, landmines were discovered on three of the project sites, requiring a lengthy clearing process and official police confirmation prior to development.

under construction. This signalled a significant departure for the country's power sector, with the private sector quickly coming to represent a significant portion of installed generation capacity. The rapid increase in investment also stands in stark contrast with the prolonged, and as yet unsuccessful, efforts at getting the Kudu and Baynes generation projects off the ground (Table 9.4).

An important condition for all IPP generation licences in Namibia is that there needs to be a minimum 30% previously disadvantaged Namibian (PDN)[16] shareholding in the project company. It is a condition set by the Ministry of Mines and Energy (MME) and enforced by the ECB through the licensing process. In the REFiT programme, much of the PDN shareholders' equity was financed by a shareholder loan from the lead developer. Several PDN shareholders have subsequently approached financial institutions such as the Government Institutions Pension Fund (GIPF) to refinance their shareholding, which would allow them to make decisions as equal partners on issues such as dividend declarations as well as free up cash flows for earlier dividend flows. According to the ECB, there are also changes afoot to ensure that there is more meaningful PDN shareholding in future power projects, based in part on what has been learned through the REFiT process.

Apart from the REFiT programme, there have also been a number of private power projects procured directly by REDs. REDs are allowed to procure up to 12% of their total electricity consumption from IPPs under current regulations and are, in part, motivated to secure these projects as a way of attracting investment to their region. CENORED was the first RED to start purchasing power directly from IPPs, competitively procuring the 5 MW Hopsol solar PV project in 2015 at a price level close to that of the REFiT programme.[17] It was followed by Erongo RED's 3.8 MW procurement of the OLC Arandis project in 2016 at NA$ 1.18/kWh (US$ 0.085/kWh).[18] CENORED awarded a further 6.4 MW to OLC Arandis in 2017—although this project has not yet reached financial close. Windhoek municipality has also indicated their intention of procuring 5 × 5 MW solar PV plants in the near future[19] (CENORED, 2013; Confidente, 2015; De Klerk, 2016; Kaira, 2017).

Namibia's experience with directly negotiated (DN) projects has been less successful. While the 4.5 MW Omburu solar PV project (NA$ 1.50/kWh, US$ 0.11/kWh) paved the way for other IPPs by showing that it was possible to finance and quickly build an IPP without sovereign support, other directly

[16] This includes racially disadvantaged persons, women, and persons with a disability.
[17] The Otjiwarongo municipality is a shareholder in the project company based on the land that is being leased to the project.
[18] This project is apparently facing transmission congestion, which is likely to result in Erongo RED needing to make significant deemed energy payments.
[19] This procurement is currently on hold to align with the new PPP legislation.

Table 9.4 List of Namibia's REFiT projects

Company name	Capacity	Location	PPA signed	TCA signed	COD
Benzel & Partner Investment Pty Ltd	5 MW	Gobabis (Ejuva 1)	28 October 2015	25 April 2016	19 September 2017
OKA Investment Pty Ltd	5 MW	Gobabis (Ejuva 2)	27 October 2015	25 April 2016	19 September 2017
Camelthorn Business Venture Pty Ltd	5 MW	Outapi	27 October 2015	25 April 2016	
Momentous Energy Pty Ltd	5 MW	Keetmanshoop	30 October 2015	18 March 2016	24 October 2017
Hopsol Pty Ltd	5 MW	Grootfontein	22 October 2015	27 January 2016	30 June 2016
Sertum Energy Pty Ltd	5 MW	Trekkopje, Erongo	21 October 2015	20 April 2016	
Aloe Investment Number 27 Pty Ltd	5 MW	Rosh Pinah	29 October 2015	22 April 2016	23 July 2017
ALCON Pty Ltd	5 MW	Aussenkehr	29 October 2015	22 April 2016	29 September 2017
UNISUN Energy Pty Ltd	5 MW	Okatope	29 October 2015	27 April 2016	
Tandii Investment Pty Ltd	5 MW	Okatope	29 October 2015	25 April 2016	
NCF Energy Pty Ltd	5 MW	Okatope	29 October 2015	25 April 2016	
Ombepo Energy Pty Ltd	5 MW	Luderitz	13 January 2016	23 March 2016	8 September 2017
Osona Sun Energy Pty Ltd	5 MW	Okahandja	21/10/2015	05/01/2016	01/09/2016
Metdecci Energy Investment Pty Ltd	5 MW	Karibib	23 October 2015	24 February 2016	7 March 2017

Source: Authors' compilation; NamPower (2017b).

negotiated IPPs have been slower off the mark. The Diaz wind project was, for example, the first IPP in the country to be awarded a licence by the ECB in 2007 but has still not reached commercial operation more than 12 years later. The project was initially unable to secure financing without sovereign support, after which the technical partners withdrew. The project eventually signed a PPA (without a sovereign guarantee) in 2017 with strict conditions precedent (CP) deadlines. It is unclear at this stage whether the project will be able to meet these deadlines, largely due to difficulties in securing permits for the environmentally sensitive site. The project tariff was also adjusted from NA\$ 1.27/kWh (US\$ 0.09/kWh) to NA\$ 1.07/kWh (US\$ 0.077/kWh) by the ECB.[20] Greenam also signed a PPA with NamPower in 2016 after long nego-tiations for 2 × 10 MW solar PV projects close to Mariental (Hardap) and Keetmanshoop at NA\$ 1.16/kWh (*The Villager*, 2016).[21] The initial develop-ers (F. K. Group, Israel) exited the project as soon as the PPA was signed. Both projects, however, started construction in 2018 and reached COD in 2019.

Namibia's experience with private power investment thus represents the entire procurement spectrum, offering a useful test case for comparing out-comes. The competitively procured Hardap solar PV project has delivered the lowest price (Figure 9.2) and is being hailed as evidence of the superiority of competitive IPP procurement by the Namibian government and regulatory officials. In the following sections, we focus on the project and analyse the design, implementation, and outcomes of this solar PV auction.

9.5 The design of Namibia's renewable energy auctions

9.5.1 Auction design

Although the Hardap PV project obtained its legacy from the original 3 × 10 MW project, the Hardap solar PV project procurement was conceptualized and managed as a completely new tender. It was designed as a single-stage, two-envelope, sealed-bid, pay-as-bid tender process. Successful tenderers were offered a bankable and standardized, 25-year PPA with NamPower. In the final tender process, which was advertised on 13 May 2016, project devel-opers were given 3 months to prepare their bids, which was extended to 22 September 2016 providing for a 19-week tender period. Although the tender

---

[20] This was based on the ECB's internal due diligence and benchmarking analyses. The developers apparently threatened to take the ECB to the minister due to the tariff revision; the ECB countered with the credible threat of putting the project out to tender, which is all but guaranteed to deliver a lower tariff.
[21] Negotiations started at NA\$ 2,40/kWh. The final tariff for the projects is NA\$ 1.16/kWh. The Karas project will feed into the same Mariental substation as the Hardap PV project.

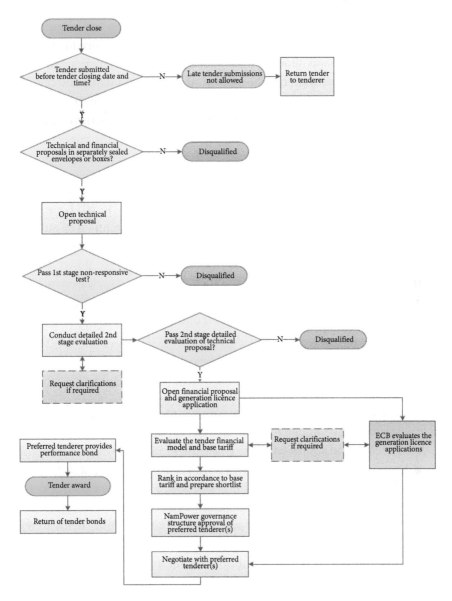

Figure 9.2 Overview of the tender evaluation process

Source: NamPower (2016a: 13).

validity period was six months, the evaluation process was completed by the end of November and the tender was awarded early in December 2016. The post-award project development process took longer than anticipated, with financial close and commercial operation deadlines being extended multiple times.

In this section, we analyse the tender set-up, focusing on how the auction volume was determined (auction demand), where the projects would be built (site selection), who was allowed to bid and how this was determined (qualification and compliance criteria), how the projects were evaluated and ranked, and which tools and mechanisms were used to ensure the commitment of bidders as well as fair risk allocation between the host government, the off-taker, and bidders (seller and buyer liabilities).

9.5.1.1 Auction demand

Namibia's use of least-cost electricity expansion planning is a recent phenomenon that initially struggled to gain formal traction. In 2011, the ECB contracted Canadian consultants to develop a NIRP, with financial support from the World Bank. The NIRP was the most comprehensive overview of the Namibian electricity sector, outlining future options for power system expansion based on scenario analysis. When the NIRP was released in 2013, the least-cost expansion plan was built on the assumption that the Kudu gas power project would be realized by 2017. It offered no allocation for solar PV or wind in the next 20 years (apart from the projects that had already been committed to), and the only renewables allocation was limited to biomass[22] (Hatch, 2013). The 2013 NIRP was never sent to cabinet for approval and consequently never adopted by the government.

The second version of the electricity plan has proven to be more influential and somewhat less beholden to existing project commitments. The NIRP was updated in 2016 and approved by the government in 2017, with the least-cost scenario excluding the Kudu and Baynes projects. NIRP 2016 (Table 9.5) also increased the overall renewables allocation, with 229 MW of solar PV, 149 MW of onshore wind, 250 MW of concentrated solar power (CSP), and 80 MW of biomass expected to be online by 2035. The remaining demand was projected to be met by new thermal power plants (720 MW[23]) and imports (350 MW—phased out by 2017). Importantly, the annual allocations for specific technologies were relatively small (20 MW for solar PV and biomass, 50 MW for wind and CSP), meaning that Namibia would be unlikely to benefit from significant economies of scale in its procurement programmes. The biggest allocation for solar PV was in 2018 (50 MW), providing space for the anticipated competitive procurement of three 10 MW solar PV projects (that would later become the single 37 MW Hardap project) as well as the start

---

[22] Cost assumptions used for solar PV and wind were also too high, ranging from NA$ 1.73/kWh (20% capacity factor) to NA$ 0.99/kWh (35% capacity factor) for wind and NA$ 2.42/kWh (20% capacity factor) to NA$ 1.61/kWh (30% capacity factor) for solar PV.

[23] The thermal allocation is made up of a 120 MW emergency power plant as well as 2 × 300 MW thermal (coal, liquefied natural gas (LNG), or HFO) plants to be procured by NamPower.

Table 9.5 NIRP 2016 implementation plan and schedule

Column groups: **New generation addition[a]** — Renewable (MW)[b]: Hydro, Solar PV, Wind, Biomass, CSP; Thermal[c]; Import. **Retirement**: Plant, Capacity MW. **System Capacity MW**. **New generation investment cost[d] (N$ millions)**: Renewable, Thermal. **Energy production[b] (GWh)**: Renewable[b], Thermal, Import, Total. **Load forecast**: Peak MW, Energy(2) GWh.

Year	Hydro	Solar PV	Wind	Biomass	CSP	Thermal[c]	Import	Plant	Capacity MW	System Capacity MW	Inv. Renewable	Inv. Thermal	Energy Renewable[b]	Energy Thermal	Energy Import	Energy Total	Peak MW	Energy(2) GWh
Existing	346.5	9.5	—	—	0	135.8	330	—	—	821.8	—	—	—	—	—	—	—	—
2015	—	—	—	—	—	—	—	—	—	—	1,200.8	—	—	—	—	—	—	—
2016	—	70	—	—	—	—	—	—	—	821.8	2,744.4	—	1,530.0	923.4	1,788.1	4,241.5	645.7	4,241.5
2017	—	50	—	—	—	—	20	—	—	911.8	1,295.9	—	1,713.9	928.0	1,907.2	4,549.2	692.7	4,549.2
2018	—	50	49	—	—	120	—	Paratus & Imp	26.3	1,104.5	343.1	3,305.1	2,011.2	1,598.3	1,170.6	4,780.1	733.4	4,780.1
2019	—	—	—	—	—	—	—	—	—	1,104.5	228.7	4,406.8	2,011.2	1,656.0	1,263.1	4,930.3	758.4	4,930.3
2020	—	20	—	20	—	—	—	—	—	1,124.5	1,108.4	3,305.1	2,063.8	1,697.8	1,338.6	5,100.2	785.9	5,100.2
2021	—	—	—	—	—	300	—	ICRE & Imp	370	1,054.5	1,048.1	—	2,063.8	2,701.2	522.7	5,287.7	815.9	5,287.7
2022	—	—	50	—	—	—	—	—	—	1,104.5	755.3	3,305.1	2,217.1	2,694.8	531.3	5,443.2	841.7	5,443.2
2023	—	—	—	—	—	—	—	—	—	1,104.5	537.9	4,406.8	2,217.1	2,797.4	591.7	5,606.1	868.5	5,606.1
2024	—	20	—	20	—	—	—	—	—	1,144.5	1,869.5	3,305.1	2,436.0	2,775.7	581.2	5,792.9	898.5	5,792.9
2025	—	—	—	—	—	300	—	Van Eck & Imp	188	1,256.5	2,573.5	—	2,423.3	3,442.6	145.0	5,990.9	930.7	5,990.9
2026	—	20	—	—	—	—	—	—	—	1,276.5	4,573.5	—	2,475.9	3,635.8	85.1	6,196.9	963.8	6,196.9
2027	—	—	—	—	50	—	—	—	—	1,326.5	3,083.3	—	2,826.3	3,532.9	65.5	6,424.8	1,001.0	6,424.8
2028	—	—	50	—	—	—	—	—	—	1,396.5	2,178.7	—	3,146.0	3,454.1	55.1	6,655.2	1,038.7	6,655.2
2029	—	—	—	—	50	—	—	—	—	1,446.5	2,167.4	—	3,483.6	3,369.1	42.6	6,895.3	1,077.6	6,895.3
2030	—	—	—	20	—	—	—	—	—	1,466.5	2,996.7	—	3,536.2	3,545.6	65.1	7,146.9	1,118.5	7,146.9
2031	—	—	—	20	—	—	—	—	—	1,486.5	3,693.8	—	3,702.7	3,623.0	79.4	7,405.1	1,158.4	7,405.1
2032	—	—	—	—	50	—	—	—	—	1,556.5	3,870.9	—	4,092.8	3,487.6	55.1	7,635.6	1,195.4	7,635.6
2033	—	—	—	20	—	—	—	—	—	1,576.5	3,561.7	—	4,259.3	3,586.4	72.2	7,917.9	1,239.3	7,917.9
2034	—	—	—	—	50	—	—	—	—	1,626.5	1,526.4	—	4,596.9	3,523.8	60.2	8,180.9	1,280.4	8,180.9
2035	—	—	—	—	50	—	—	—	—	1,676.5	—	—	4,947.3	3,488.0	54.2	8,489.5	1,328.5	8,489.5
Total	346.5	189.5	149	80	250	855.8	350		584.3		41,358	22,034						
			1055			1205.8			584.3		63,391.7							
			1,677															

Note: [a] For Scenario 6 of Option 2.
[b] The values shown do not include the contribution od Solar PV installations implemented under the Net Metering Program.
[c] Assumes the short-term emergency diesel generators would be rented and there would be no investment cost.
[d] Annual capital investment flow as per the typical capital disbursement schedule for each type of new plant. The capital investment required for solar PV installations under the Net Metering Program is not included.
Source: MME (2016: 23).

of commercial operations of the 2 × 10 MW Greenam PV projects (MME, 2016).

The NIRP planning process has not been without flaws, and steps are underway to increase the accuracy, status, and influence of the resulting plans. Both the 2013 and 2016 versions of the NIRP have proven to be outdated before they were published, with prices achieved in South Africa's, Zambia's, and Namibia's own auctions for solar PV (and wind) being notably lower than those assumed in the NIRP 2016 model.[24] The slow economic growth and an increase in distributed solar PV has resulted in the overall electricity demand being lower than projected. A revision of the plan and its underlying assumptions is therefore underway. While the NIRP provides some certainty to the market in terms of government's intentions, the plan has no official legislative status. Accordingly, the state and its entities are not bound by the plan in their procurement decisions. Amendments to the Electricity Act currently being processed will change this, also giving the Minister of Mines and Energy the power to make determinations as to who should build new power projects. The minister has already made a determination—in 2018—on 220 MW of new capacity, allocating 150 MW to NamPower and 70 MW (20 MW solar, 50 MW wind—in line with the NIRP) to the private sector (Kaira, 2018).

What seems to emerge from this analysis is that the Hardap PV project, as well as its preceding 3 ×10 MW projects, were conceived in line with the Energy White Paper, but without a NIRP in place. This has been confirmed by the MME and NamPower, who indicated that the inability to close the Kudu and Baynes projects and concerns about electricity supply security from SAPP prompted the government to rather focus on smaller projects that could be financed without a sovereign guarantee. The sizing of the initial 3 × 10 MW solar PV projects was therefore mainly determined by fiscal concerns, and the resulting auction was consequently set to be run as a test case.

The programme has been plagued by a sense of uncertainty as a consequence. The auction programme was initially developed in 2015/2016 for 3 × 10 MW solar PV power plants at Okahandja, Omaruru, and Mariental. At a late stage in the procurement process, NamPower realized that they were unable to secure the two sites at Okahandja and Omaruru. As the preferred tenderer for all the 3 × 10 MW projects was the same, the Alten Renewable

---

[24] Unit cost assumptions in NIRP 2016: NA$ 1.54/kWh for onshore wind, NA$ 1.61 for solar PV. By the time the NIRP was published, the latest rounds of procurement in South Africa had seen prices drop to below 50% of the assumed costs in the NIRP. These prices were also higher than the Namibian REFiT tariffs in place at the time.

Energy Development consortium, it was decided to relocate the two projects to the Hardap site, which was big enough to accommodate the 3 × 10 MW developments. ENEL Green Power, one of the bidders and also one of the largest global renewable energy IPP developers, launched a legal challenge to the tender award based on this perceived material change. In early 2016, the 3 × 10 MW solar PV tender was set aside and referred back to NamPower by the High Court of Namibia. NamPower therefore tendered a new solar PV project (the Hardap project) with a maximum export capacity of 37 MW in 2016. The increased size of the project (37 MW) was now based on what the site could accommodate and offered benefits in terms of economies of scale (and therefore a lower tariff). The new Hardap Solar PV project capacity was based on a new original and conservative estimation to allow potential tenderers enough flexibility to design a suitable direct current (DC)/alternating current (AC) ratio which can accommodate the newly required capacity factor guarantee. It is hoped that the strengthening of the planning framework, combined with the outcomes and lessons from the Hardap PV procurement round, will lead to greater certainty through predictable auction rounds in the near future.

9.5.1.2 Site selection

Kruger et al. (2019) have analysed renewable energy project site selection as a salient determinant of auction outcomes in sub-Saharan Africa. The research finds that while a government-led site selection and preparation process is the most popular option, often chosen based on a belief that it will hasten the development process and reduce project risks (and costs), it can lead to higher costs and risks, as well as longer lead times, when the process is poorly executed. This is mainly because the process can violate one of the fundamental rules of project finance: that risks are allocated to those parties most able to bear or control them (Shen-fa and Xiao-ping, 2009). With a government-led site selection process, the private sector is often allocated a set of site-related risks that they have little to no control over. Namibia's experience seems to support both sides of this argument, with problems with the initial project sites leading to a dismissal of the auction results.

NamPower opted to undertake the site selection and development processes for the original 3 × 10 MW sites in the belief that, had this been left to the private sector, a pricing war on land would result in higher electricity tariffs from the projects. Sites were thus selected based on the ability of the local substation to evacuate the generated capacity as well as alignment with the potential solar resource. After the bids had been submitted, NamPower realized that it would not be able to secure the sites at Okahandja and Omaruru in time.[25]

In Namibia, there are various types of land classifications, each which their own set of procurement difficulties and different procurement processes. In the case of the 3 × 10 MW project, the Mariental and Okahandja sites formed part of an existing commercial farm. As such, the land procurement process was governed under the Agricultural (Commercial) Land Act of Namibia. For the Okahandja site, the land owner rescinded on the offer to purchase, and consequently, NamPower failed to execute a sale agreement and the offer to purchase was terminated by mutual consent. The project site situated near Omaruru was classified as town lands, and the prolonged procurement process was not finalized before tender award. NamPower, who is a proponent of the approach where government procures the project site as part of the project development, argues that this approach vastly reduces development timelines and de-risks the project. This is due to the fact that the EIA and geotechnical studies can commence and the risk of any fatal flaws be eliminated early in the project development phase.

When the Mariental site was put out to tender again (this time with a maximum export capacity of 37 MW), NamPower wanted to avoid a similar situation. The project site was leased by NamPower since Namibia does not allow foreign ownership of agricultural, commercial, or communal land. Typically, leases on agricultural land are granted for a maximum of 10 years; NamPower therefore had to apply for exemption from local legislation (the Agricultural Land Reform Act of 1995) to allow for a lease length corresponding to that of the PPA (25 years).

Apart from securing the lease for the site (Figure 3), NamPower also undertook all preparatory studies and provided the transmission connection (including upgrading of the Hardap substation, Figure 9.2). The preparatory studies included EIAs (with NamPower providing the Environmental Clearance Certificate[26]), topographical studies, geotechnical assessments,[27] hydrological studies, and meteorological analyses. Interviewed bidders commented

---

[25] For one of the sites, the town council appeared to be unable, or unwilling, to proceed with the lease without securing some kind of 'rent' from the process, while, for the other site, the owner wanted shareholding in the project.

[26] The Hardap site's EIA clearance certificate was obtained following an EIA study for the initial development of the three potential sites in 2016. The certificate was still valid at the time of the 37 MW bid. However, NamPower filed for an amendment to the certificate so as to be exclusive to the site. The original EIA certificates for all three sites were also originally awarded for a maximum of 30 MW projects. When the project size was increased to 37 MW, this necessitated a revision of the certificate.

[27] The geotechnical assessments were carried out by GEOINTEC for the original 3 × 10 MW project at Mariental. This study was subsequently bought and provided to all interested bidders during the procurement of the 37 MW project.

favourably on the quality of the preparatory work. NamPower also provided detailed information on the grid capacity and proposed connection. In return for providing the site, the connection infrastructure, and the related development activities, NamPower expected to be given between 10% and 19% equity (it was eventually provided with 19%) in the project company, depending on the overall equity contributions related to the value of the project and compared with NamPower's investment.

Despite providing the site, the geotechnical study, the environmental clearance certificate, and the transmission infrastructure, the responsibility for adequately preparing and the final development of the site[28] ultimately fell to the bidders. The tender documents were clear about the fact that bidders would bear all site-associated risks—including subsurface and environmental risks (weather inclusive). Bidders also had to construct a road for site access and needed to secure any other permits required. NamPower strictly enforced its mandatory site-visit policy, with no one allowed to submit a bid who had not attended the formal site visit (that formed part of the pre-bid conference). Bidders were allowed further site visits and additional investigations—if deemed necessary and approved by NamPower.

This approach ultimately worked the second time around in the sense that the project was awarded and eventually built. Nonetheless, the successful implementation of the 14 REFiT projects—all of whom had to find, secure, and prepare their own sites—asks whether the NamPower site selection and preparation process truly resulted in superior investment outcomes. Given that NamPower's provision of the land and grid infrastructure came at a shareholding cost to bidders, it is also not clear whether project prices were positively impacted by this approach. Far from supporting a position that sees the government as better placed to select and prepare sites for renewable energy projects, Namibia's experience merely shows that the public sector can be almost as good as the private sector in executing this function.

9.5.1.3 Qualification and compliance requirements

The original 3 × 10 MW auction was guided in its approach to bidder qualification by the 'pilot' conceptualization of the programme: NamPower used the auction to test the market and extract valuable lessons through a 'learning-by-doing' approach that filtered through into many of the auction design and implementation decisions. The mandatory pre-bidding conference, for example, made use of an unusual informal 'market testing' exercise: bidders were asked whether they would be able to submit a bankable bid without

---

[28] The technical specification documents provided detailed specifications regarding the site development requirements.

any sovereign guarantee. They were also asked to provide an indication of potential project price level by ticking one of three boxes: NA$ 1.20–NA$ 1.50/kWh, NA$ 1.00–1.20/kWh, and less than NA$ 1.00/kWh. This exercise not only provided an indicative price ceiling (NA$ 1.50, US$ 0.11/kWh) to the market but also gave the procurer the chance to test its assumptions. The results were generally positive,[29] with most bidders indicating a willingness to bid without a sovereign guarantee at levels below NA$ 1.00/kWh (US$ 0.072/kWh). The 3 × 10 MW auction also made use of a more conventional pre-qualification round, with bidders provided with draft technical specifications and project agreements, which they were asked to comment on as part of their pre-qualification submission.

When the 37 MW project was taken to market, there was already an established sense of who would be interested and what they would be willing to commit to—in large part, based on the bids received for the 3 × 10 MW project(s). The approach taken emphasized speed and technical quality to make up for the time lost during the first attempt at procurement and to ensure NamPower's comfort with the technology. For several aspects of the bidding process, this emphasis translated as a preference for standardization and simplicity. The emphasis on speed also meant that there was no pre-qualification round, with all interested bidders needing to submit a full technical and financial proposal. No bidder that had not attended the pre-bid conference and project site visit, which attracted more than 250 interested parties, would be allowed to bid.[30]

Submission timelines turned out to be optimistic, with the request for proposal (RfP) released in May 2016 and the submission deadline set for 4 August that same year. In response to bidder requests, the submission deadline was extended by more than a month, to 22 September 2016. This was mainly to allow for the adjustment of the financial model after certainty was gained on the exact costs for the upgrading of the transmission infrastructure (deep and shallow connection works).

NamPower spent a great deal of time and resources on establishing clear communication channels with the market before and during the bidding process. During the period between the publication of the RfP and the bid submission deadline, there were 11 clarification rounds (Table 9.6), with all questions and answers posted on the NamPower website. The quick turn-around on clarification requests, as well as the willingness to incorporate

---

[29] Some bidders found this exercise most unusual, opting not to proceed with the bidding process because of concerns about its legitimacy.

[30] Everyone participating in the pre-bid conference and site visit was automatically considered a participating bidder.

bidder comments in the project documents, are emblematic of NamPower's overall approach to the procurement programme: maintaining effective communication, in part also to learn throughout the process. Both NamPower and bidders commented on the value of this communication throughout the bid preparation phase, with NamPower in particular finding the comments helpful in ensuring that the bidding documents were bankable by the submission deadline. While it generally discouraged negotiations on and mark-ups to the project documents, several amendments were made through the clarification process.[31] Bidders were also allowed to make comments on the documents as part of their submission and were provided with templates on which to do so. NamPower had the discretion to disregard the comments and/or dismiss the tender as non-compliant if these comments were considered material or would unfairly advantage a bidder. NamPower could also ask

Table 9.6 Timelines for the Hardap solar PV bidding process

Phase	Date	Bidders	Description
RfP released	13 May 2016	200	No. of requests for EOI documents
Clarification No. 1	7 June 2016	–	–
Mandatory clarification meeting	8 June 2016	200	No. of private attendees (companies/consortia)
Mandatory site visit	8 June 2016	200	Held with interested developers to allow for issues to be raised
Clarification No. 2	13 June 2016	–	–
Clarification No. 3	15 June 2016	–	–
Clarification No. 4	28 June 2016	–	–
Clarification No. 5	12 July 2016	–	–
Clarification No. 6	18 July 2016	–	–
Clarification No. 7	1 August 2016	–	–
Clarification No. 8	15 August 2016	–	–
Clarification No. 9	23 August 2016	–	–
Clarification No. 10	5 September 2016	–	–
Clarification No. 11	5 September 2016	–	–
Deadline for clarification requests	5 September	–	–
RfP submission deadline	22 September 2016	13	No. of complete tender submissions

Note: EOI = expression of interest.
Source: Authors' compilation.

---

[31] Some of these related specifically to baseload-related clauses that were part of the PPA.

Table 9.7 Submitted bids

The Power Company
Phanes Africa Pty (Ltd)
Aussenyen Energy Investments Pty (Ltd)
JV: Jordaan Oosthuysen & Nangolo QS
BioTherm Energy (Pty) Ltd
Alten Energy
JV: China Jiangxi International (Namibia) (Pty) Ltd and Profile Technologies (Pty) Ltd
Mulilo Sunpower Total Consortium
Green Energy Technology Holdings
Building Energy S.P.A.
Montenya Energy
JV: Afres & Deutche Eco.
MBHE African Power

Source: Authors' compilation.

for clarifications on bids during the evaluation process.[32] Generally speaking, bidders interviewed indicated that they were happy with the quality of the documents and the preparation work done.

Thirteen complete bids were submitted on 22 September 2016 (Table 9.6).

9.5.1.4 Qualification criteria

While there was no pre-qualification round, bid evaluation for the 37 MW project was set up as a two-stage process: a technical evaluation process, followed by a financial evaluation process. Only bids passing the technical evaluation process would proceed to financial evaluation. The bidding procedure therefore made use of a two-envelope, sealed-bid process: envelope 1 would contain the technical bid details, while envelope 2 would contain only the financial proposal. If any aspect of the financial proposal was included in the technical proposal (envelope 1), the entire bid would be disqualified.

Bidders needed to meet a number of minimum criteria for their technical proposal (envelope 1) to be considered 'responsive', although these were largely concerned with securing bidder commitments to the core bidding requirements. Any bid that failed the minimum acceptable standard of completeness, consistency, and detail could also be rejected as non-responsive. Once a bid met the 'minimum responsiveness' threshold, it would proceed to a more detailed, technical bid analysis process. This process investigated

---

[32] For written submissions, bidders had two days to respond. NamPower could also call bidders to a clarification meeting during the evaluation process.

the legal, technical, commercial, financial, environmental, and social components of the bid.

The technical proposal consisted of more than 45 highly standardized and prescriptive documents that established a tenderer's capacity and eligibility for carrying out the project, compliance with the tender specifications, and acceptance of the project documents. NamPower set out a range of minimum requirements—technical and otherwise—that bidders would need to meet in order to reach the technical scoring stage. Technical scoring of proposals was based on only three components.

9.5.1.4.1 Legal and technical compliance
Each submitted bid was first subjected to a legal review to verify its completeness, the bona fide credentials of the bidders (including a background check), and the legal nature of any submitted deviations to the project documents. The bid would then proceed to a detailed technical evaluation phase, which focused on three aspects:

- confirmation of the technical and delivery capability of the project sponsor(s); engineering, procurement, and construction (EPC) contractor; and operations and maintenance (O&M) contractor,
- the completeness and comprehensiveness of the technical solution; contracted performance guarantees; and compliance with, and/or deviations from, the technical specifications;
- confirmation that the bid met all the minimum tender requirements.

Bidders were required to provide evidence of their and the subcontractors' capability to successfully implement the project. The lead tenderer needed to prove that they had sufficient project and human resource experience in the power sector. Bidders also needed to submit at least two 10 MW reference projects that had been completed in the past eight years and which the tender evaluation committee could visit if necessary. This is a departure from standard practice in the region, where bidders are normally required to provide evidence of projects of a size at least similar to that being proposed, usually having been completed within a more recent timeframe (three to five years). It is not entirely clear what motivated the 10 MW reference projects determination and the longer timeframe. It could be argued that NamPower wanted to expand the pool of prospective bidders, perhaps wishing to include Namibian developers as well. If that were the case, though, the 10 MW requirement would be too high a threshold for any of the REFiT project developers to meet, based solely on their REFiT experience. It is more probable that the 10 MW project reference requirement was taken from the original 3 × 10 MW procurement process. If this reference project size had been increased to something closer to the actual project MW, the originally awarded party (Alten) would not have been eligible.

The bidding requirements were also geared towards ensuring that all technical equipment (down to the wiring used) and service providers were of sufficient quality. NamPower therefore required copies of all prospective contracts with EPC and O&M service providers, and any other major contracts, as part of the technical proposal. EPC and O&M service providers specifically needed to submit proof (reference projects) of work done on projects similar in nature and size to the Hardap PV project. Bidders, furthermore, had to specify all equipment suppliers and service providers—including datasheets for all equipment used. All equipment needed to be of a proven design and quality, meeting, at the very minimum, South African National Standards (SANS).[33]

The technical specifications for the plant also set out a number of additional key minimum technical requirements:

- the degradation factor of the plant could not be more than 20% in year 25;
- the capacity factor for the plant needed to be 30% at COD—reducing to no more than 20% in year 25;
- the lifetime of the plant needed to be guaranteed at 25 years;
- an availability guarantee of 98% was required during daytime hours;
- the minimum performance ratio of the plant was specified at 0.75.

While these specifications served as minimum requirements, bidders were also required to make specific commitments on each of these—projected annually for the duration of the plant's lifetime. These projected annual values became part of the performance guarantee (discussed in more detail under section 9.5.1.6).

9.5.1.4.2 Financial and commercial capability

The evaluation of the technical proposal aimed to establish the commercial and financial ability and commitment of the bidder(s). NamPower therefore assessed the financing arrangements (equity and debt) of the project,

---

[33] Equipment needed to be designed, manufactured, tested, and installed according to the most recent South African National Standards, International Organization for Standardization (ISO), International Electrotechnical Commission (IEC) or Institute of Electrical and Electronics Engineers (IEEE) and National Electrical Code (NEC) codes and standards. Where there was a conflict between national and international codes/standards, the more onerous specification or standard would take precedence.

specifically requiring signed term sheets from lenders. This went beyond an in-principle agreement to finance the project, effectively requiring lenders to have conducted due diligence on the project. Signed term sheets were also required for any financing of PDN shareholders. The project implementation schedule, furthermore, needed to be signed by all equity and debt providers to the project as well as the EPC contractor.

The financial ability of the bidder was assessed by analysing the audited financial statements (for the past three years) of the lead bidder.[34] The bidding instructions made provision for bidding by entities younger than three years and did not specify minimum turnover or other financial health indicators. It is therefore unclear how the financial ability of bidders was evaluated.

Bidder compliance with the commercial tender requirements required a number of submissions. Bidders needed to provide letters of good standing from the Receiver of Revenue, the Social Security Commission, and the Employment Equity Commission (or their local equivalents in the bidding companies' countries of origin). They also needed to submit an organizational chart, company shareholders chart, and shareholders table clearly indicating the commercial relationships and specifically making clear the PDN shareholding arrangements. This stage also evaluated whether bidders had submitted the correct security guarantees and performance guarantees.

9.5.1.4.3 Environmental and social sustainability

The tender requirements featured a number of local content, ownership, and employment requirements. Apart from the 30% PDN shareholding in the project company already discussed, the technical specifications also required that all unskilled labour used on the project were Namibian citizens. Although further minimum levels of local content or employment were not specified, bidders needed to list all local contracting, professional services, and equipment suppliers as part of their technical proposal (along with proof of Namibian citizenship of the contractors/suppliers). Bidders were similarly required to specify the origin and value of all items (equipment, materials) to be used in the project. These local content and employment commitments were captured in the performance guarantees and formed part of the licensing conditions for the plant. A key clause in the performance guarantee document also stated that local content requirements would be further negotiated as part of the licensing process but provided little clarity on the process or requirements.

---

[34] All participating parties/shareholders still needed to submit their audited financial statements, even though they might not be analysed.

NamPower ensured that the environmental clearance certificate[35] for the project site was secured by the time the Hardap PV project went to tender, having provided an environmental scoping report and environmental management plan to the satisfaction of the Ministry of Environment and Tourism. The involvement of a development finance institution (DFI) in the financing of the project introduced an additional layer of social and environmental due diligence in line with the International Finance Corporation (IFC) performance standards.

Once the technical evaluation (and scoring) was completed, compliant bidders' financial proposals were opened and checked for completeness and compliance (including the information needed by the ECB to apply for the generation licence). If a bidder failed to comply with the requirements, their bid could not proceed to the financial scoring stage.

9.5.1.4.4 Financial proposal

The financial proposal (envelope 2) consisted of only four components aimed at establishing the project price (tariff) and securing a generation licence. It was assumed that once a bid had reached this stage of evaluation, it would have been sufficiently vetted from a technical and commercial point of view. The financial model provided to bidders, and which they were obliged to use in their submission, was intentionally quite basic as it was the same model used by the ECB in its generation licence approval process.[36] The intention with providing this model was to ensure that there was no discrepancy between the tariff submitted and that which the ECB would approve. Only tenders which were found to be technically responsive were fully evaluated and scored. All sealed financial proposals were returned to the tenderers which were found to be non-responsive. During the financial evaluation process, NamPower validated all the assumptions used in the model. The evaluation process also allowed for an adjustment of the listed base tariffs for evaluation purposes only to compensate for any inputs used in the tender financial models which were considered erroneous, inaccurate, or non-representative of the technical tender submission.

The financial model was one of the more controversial aspects of the programme. One bidder that had been very successful in South Africa's stringent

---

[35] The original certificate was replaced by an amended one during the course of the clarification procedures. The original certificate referred to the original 3 × 10 MW sites, while the amended certificate was valid only for the Mariental site.

[36] During the clarification process, bidders pointed out a number of problems with the model. These were consequently fixed by NamPower, but the amendments needed to be officially approved by the ECB. This was one of the reasons for the submission deadline extension.

REI4P programme chose to change the model to allow for a debt reserve facility. NamPower saw this as a material change that rendered the model invalid and provided different results and therefore disqualified the bid. The bidder argued that the financial model provided was not sophisticated enough to handle a variety of financing arrangements. A second bidder—similarly experienced in South Africa's renewable energy programme—was also disqualified at this stage. Both bidders indicated that they had submitted tariffs lower than that which was eventually awarded and were distrustful of the financial evaluation process and the final result. NamPower maintains that it had stuck to the rules set out in the RfP documentation, which did not allow for any deviation from the financial model. It would be worth considering improving the sophistication of the financial model used in new procurement rounds to allow for a wider variety of financing options.

9.5.1.5 Bidder ranking and winner selection

Once a bid had passed the legal and technical compliance and evaluation stage, as well as the financial proposal compliance evaluation stage, it was assigned a score and ranked. Bid scoring and ranking were based on a combination of financial and technical criteria, weighted on a 70:30 basis. The project tariff therefore played the most important part in the scoring of the bid—in line with practice in the region, for example, South Africa or Uganda. The bidder that offered the project at the lowest price would be awarded the full 70 points, and all other bids would be scored relative to this benchmark.

The technical scoring criteria used again illustrates the tender programme's emphasis on simplicity, speed, and technical rigour. Bids were scored based on the plant's total degradation factor in year 25, the guaranteed capacity factor in year 2,[37] and the project schedule from bid award to COD. These values would become contracted values in the project documents between NamPower and the successful bidder. This seems to present a much simpler scoring template than that used in Uganda, for example, where more than 300 technical criteria in 27 sub-categories were assessed. It also departs from standard practice in the region by assigning no score to environmental and socio-economic criteria.[38] The scoring criteria also seem to support a

---

[37] In the original 3 × 10 MW procurement programme, bids were evaluated on the performance ratio of the plant. NamPower determined, through that exercise, that it was, in fact, too difficult to accurately estimate the plant's performance ratio and therefore opted for the simpler 'capacity factor' and 'degradation factor' metrics in the 37 MW procurement programme. The capacity factor of the winning Alten project was 34.56%.

[38] In South Africa, for example, bidder commitments on a range of socio-economic issues were the only factors apart from the project tariff to determine bid ranking.

Table 9.8 Bid scoring criteria

Criteria	Points
Technical score	30
Total degradation factor on year 25	10
Guaranteed capacity factor for year 2 (as will be estimated)	10
Project schedule from bid award until target COD	10
Base tariff—normalized (financial score)	70
Total score	100

Source: NamPower (2016b).

transparent ranking process, with the all criteria lending themselves to simple quantification (Table 9.8).

It is therefore quite surprising that the proposal scoring and ranking process and outcomes were somewhat controversial—as was previously mentioned. From the clarification documents, it is clear that NamPower was asked on two occasions (Clarification Cl1 and at the pre-bid conference) to provide more details on the formulas to be used to determine the scoring of both the technical and the financial criteria. NamPower, however, viewed the information provided in the RfP documentation as sufficient for the tenderers to prepare and submit a responsive tender submission.

Finally, the significant weight assigned to the project schedule in the award decision appears to have had little impact on the actual project development process, with the project having achieved commercial operation more than a year after the original target COD. This is despite the use of performance guarantees and bonds that contractually committed the bidder to this proposed schedule. The 12-month window required for reaching COD after the project award was already considered to be very tight. Ensuring bidder commitment to this timeline through the performance guarantee and bonds should have been sufficient. Why bidders were asked to commit themselves to an even speedier—and ultimately unrealistic—project implementation schedule as part of the ranking criteria is not clear. Alten's bid commitment was 11 months—not much less than the 12-month maximum and proven to be ultimately irrelevant.

Running throughout the tender process has also been a NamPower concern regarding the technical quality of the projects—perhaps reflecting its limited experience with private investment, and solar PV projects in particular. This has been one of the main motivations behind NamPower's shareholding in the project company. It also explains the inclusion of the capacity factor and degradation factor scoring criteria. But perhaps it also reveals a limited appreciation on the part of NamPower of the incentives at work in the project development and financing processes. Given that the project owners' revenue maximization is entirely dependent on the plant's performance, it is arguably not necessary to include these two technical factors as scoring criteria—especially since the project documents already require compliance with international equipment and performance standards. It can therefore be argued that the inclusion of these technical scoring criteria actually had no additional impact on the technical design of the project.

9.5.1.6 Seller and buyer liabilities

Bidders were effectively competing for a 25-year take-or-pay PPA with Nam-Power, denominated in local currency[39] (NA$ or ZAR) and fully indexed to the local inflation rate. Failure by NamPower to meet its obligations in terms of the site, the grid connection, and/or its shareholding commitments, would result in relief from contracted responsibilities for and/or deemed energy payments to the project company. This would depend on the project development stage. As has already been mentioned, the country offered no further sovereign support to the programme, neither was there any liquidity support on the table. In combination, the local currency tariff, along with the sovereign's refusal to underwrite the off-taker, limited the participation of international financiers in the programme.[40] NamPower's investment-grade credit rating and its overall good performance provided some comfort to interested local and regional lenders, but DFI involvement was ultimately required to get the project financed on reasonable terms. The PPA also indicated that the site of arbitration would be Namibia. While investors typically prefer a neutral arbitration location, Namibia's effective courts system and independent judiciary appears to have allayed most concerns on this point.[41]

NamPower used a range of contractual financial instruments to commit bidders to realizing the project within the desired parameters and deadlines.

---

[39] Some developers had an expectation that there would be some form of forex risk exposure mitigation at financial close similar to South Africa's set-up. NamPower, however, indicated that this would not be the case, and bidders would subsequently be fully exposed to forex movements on their equipment costs.

[40] Nevertheless, at least one bidder had secured a financing commitment from the African Development Bank.

[41] This was, for example, a particularly sticky point in Egypt's renewable energy procurement programmes, leading to the delay and eventual cancellation of many large projects.

This included a bid bond of NA$ 400,000 (US$ 800/MW)—10 times cheaper than the bid bond requirement in the South African REI4P programme, a first performance bond to the value of 2% of total EPC costs (valid up to financial close), and a second performance bond to the value of 15% of the total EPC costs (valid from financial close up to successful completion of the Final Acceptance Test or payment in full of the performance liquidated damages).[42] Bidders needed to submit not only the bid bond but also the signed performance bonds as part of their bid submission. These bonds all had to be provided by local Namibian banks and were unconditional, irrevocable, and had to be available on demand. The second performance bond specifically covered the plant's licensability, its compliance with the Namibian Grid Code (including frequency and power factor), the plant's capacity, the committed capacity factor (annually projected), the degradation factor (annual), the plant's performance ratio, the lifetime of the plant, the availability guarantee, the use of Namibian content, and the health-and-safety requirements on site (specifically, lost time to injury frequency rate). Many of the values used for these parameters were taken directly from the project bidding documents. Nevertheless, the limited lifespan of the performance bond seemed not to correspond with some of the commitments it sought to guarantee, for example, the annual capacity and degradation factor projections. The PPA also contained a performance liquidated damages clause, payable[43] if the project failed to meet the contracted capacity, performance ratio, or degradation factors and failed to meet the target COD.[44] If the project failed to meet the minimum performance guarantees as stipulated in the PPA, it would count as a default event.

Despite the seemingly comprehensive and rigorous penalty regime that was set up, it has not been used in practice. NamPower's shareholding in the project company (and therefore exposure to the penalties and performance guarantees) plays into this dynamic and possibly exposes the utility to a conflict of interest.

9.5.1.7   Securing the revenue stream and addressing off-taker risk

As has been mentioned before, NamPower is one of a handful of utilities in sub-Saharan Africa considered to be in a healthy financial position. Nevertheless, the Namibian power sector—and NamPower in particular—is facing a set of challenges that could undermine this strong financial position

---

[42] From the technical and up to the final acceptance test.
[43] 1% of EPC cost for every 0.1 of the measured performance ratio being below the contracted performance ratio.
[44] 0.25% of EPC cost for every week expended from the target COD to eventual COD.

in the medium-to-long term. The first set of challenges relate—somewhat ironically—to Namibia's cost-reflective tariff regime, the consequence of which has been the proliferation of rooftop solar PV in the commercial, industrial, and (increasingly) residential sectors. This is an unsurprising development given the country's excellent solar resources, the dramatic cost reductions in solar panels, and the relatively high electricity costs paid by larger electricity consumers. The pace at which this has developed has, however, taken most stakeholders by surprise, with at least the commercial and industrial market having apparently reached a saturation point.[45] The effect of this on the power sector is only starting to dawn on decision-makers, with planning scenarios needing to constantly adjust electricity demand projections downwards to accommodate these dramatic changes. With battery-based storage becoming increasingly cheaper as well, Namibia might well be one of the first countries in the world to experience mass grid defection by commercial and high-income residential users in the near future. This will fundamentally undermine the financial health of NamPower, possibly triggering an early 'utility death spiral' that could lead to it defaulting on its payment obligations.

At the same time, Namibia is embarking on a large-scale restructuring of its electricity industry, with reforms being pushed by the regulator (the ECB) and the MME. The scale and pace of the reforms are, however, not a foregone conclusion: while the modified single-buyer model has been promulgated, powerful incumbents in the industry such as NamPower, but also the City of Windhoek, are resisting wholescale changes. Nevertheless, private power generation is growing rapidly, and regional and local government distributors are increasingly starting to procure power directly from IPPs. This situation represents less of a direct threat to the Hardap project's revenue stream but introduces some degree of uncertainty for the medium-to-long term.

The abovementioned developments, along with some hesitance about the fact that the PPA contained no provisions for political risk protection or off-taker default, necessitated the involvement of a DFI in the financing arrangement for the project. Nevertheless, the programme's high-quality documentation (including draft direct agreements), along with NamPower's willingness to engage with the market prior to and during the bidding process, provided a great deal of comfort to investors. The allocation of risks and responsibilities in the project documentation (including robust deemed energy payment clauses in the PPA) and the indexation of the tariff to the

---

[45] The full extent of Namibia's embedded/distributed generation/rooftop solar PV market is difficult to assess as the ECB does not track this information (despite its strategic importance).

Namibian Consumer price index (CPI) further mitigated many of the perceived long-term project risks. Moreover, one of the main, and possibly underappreciated, risk-mitigation strategies employed was the shareholding by NamPower—the off-taker—in the project company. While NamPower's shareholding was predicated on its desire to be involved in the day-to-day business of the project company, it also meant that there is now a strong alignment between the interests of the project and the off-taker.

9.5.2 Auction implementation

The pilot nature of the procurement programme also appears to have played a determining role in how the auction was designed and rolled out. NamPower, the ECB, and the MME openly admit that the procurement programme was largely conceived as a 'test case' for Namibia: the aim was to test the market and learn along the way. While the emphasis on learning is admirable, it also exposed the programme to accusations of poor preparation and a lack of transparency.

The institutional set-up[46] for the 3 × 10 MW procurement process ended up being its Achilles heel. Namibia had set up a Renewable Energy (RE) Project Steering Committee to design and implement the procurement programme, influenced by the institutional set-up of South Africa's IPP office. The RE Steering Committee was chaired by the Minister of Mines and Energy, and committee members included officials from the ECB, NamPower, and the Namibia Energy Institute. It was established to facilitate the rapid development of RE in the absence of the requisite policies. The Auditor-General's decision to set aside the 3 × 10 MW project award was not based on the changes introduced during the bidding process but on the fact that the RE Steering Committee had no legal standing. It subsequently played only an advisory role.

The procurement of the resurrected 37 MW project was therefore handled entirely by NamPower, the only institution in the energy sector able to handle a process of this magnitude—through its procurement structures and policies—in close consultation with the MME and with support from other government departments (notably Environment and Tourism). The ECB's role was limited to evaluating the generation licence application (as part of the financial proposal) and granting the licence as soon as possible after the

---

[46] The original intention had been for the ECB to run the procurement process. However, they realized that this would present them with a conflict of interest and therefore declined.

tender award.[47] Being one of the best-performing state-owned enterprises (SOEs) in Namibia and the highest rated utility in sub-Saharan Africa, Nam-Power had a well-established reputation in the market that helped secure bidder interest. Remarkably, NamPower was also able to develop (internally) a set of project documents that several bidders remarked on as being 'as good as those used in [South Africa's] REI4P programme'. The ECB had initially engaged an international consulting firm to develop the key project documents, which were almost entirely based on a US template and therefore proved to be ultimately unsuitable for use in Namibia. When NamPower therefore took over the procurement process, it relied on a set of mostly standardized documents that had been developed in-house. Interviewed bidders also remarked on the clear, simple tender rules and regulations (including the shareholding agreement) and the quick turnaround on clarification requests. The entire procurement process was designed and implemented by a small, capable team of no more than 10 people[48] representative of all business units, including finance, energy trading, electricity pricing, legal, power system development, transmission, and Nampower Equity Economic Empowerment Policy (NEEEP) Compliance office. The MME and the ECB also seconded personnel to the evaluation process for the 3 x 10 MW projects but not the 37 MW tender and only for capacity-building purposes and to check compliance with the generation licence application requirements. Unlike the REI4P evaluation process, no external experts were used to audit or validate the results.

The bid evaluation process was conducted in accordance with the Nam-Power tender and procurement policy. Security was strict and of the utmost importance. After the technical proposals had been opened (in the presence of participating bidders), the evaluation team conducted the detailed evaluations in a secured room with CCTV surveillance. Evaluation committee members had to sign a strict code of conduct that covered confidentiality, were not allowed to leave the secure facility during the evaluation process, and could not even take in their own pens or pencils.

Despite NamPower's reputation and the emphasis on protecting the integrity of the evaluation process, certain decisions on the design of the auction and communication with the market still managed to taint the

---

[47] The generation licence for the Hardap PV plant was provided in May 2017.
[48] This is remarkable when one considers that South Africa's REI4P programme had more than 150 consultants/advisors working on the programme at once during its set-up. However, it might also be one of the reasons for some of the controversies surrounding the outcomes of the programme.

final award decision and played into a troubling narrative around the eventual award. The award decision—or at least the resulting generation licence application—was therefore challenged again, although, this time, the complaint went to the ECB and not the courts. The ECB conducted a review of the award process and decision, concluding that it was merited and fair. This is, nevertheless, a troubling outcome for the process, and one would hope that NamPower will, in future, not only maintain the level of security and confidentiality but also be more transparent about its evaluation process to avoid further controversy.

Namibia has since established a number of key policies, including an RE policy and an IPP policy. The country has also determined that any procurement will now have to be run by a central procurement board. How this new policy environment and institutional set-up will interact with the processes and policies of established SOEs such as NamPower is not yet clear. NamPower has received exemptions under the provisions of the Public Procurement Act to run bids in 2020 for a 20 MW solar PV IPP and a 50 MW wind IPP internally; all future IPP and PPP tenders are bound to be subject to the PPP act and institutional provisions.

9.6 Results from Namibia's renewable energy auctions

The Hardap PV auction attracted a great deal of interest. More than 250 parties registered their interest in the project. The response was so overwhelming that it necessitated an urgent venue change for the pre-bid conference. In the end, 'only' 13 bids were submitted (Table 9.6).[49] While a much smaller number than the initial 250 interested entities, it is still one of the best responses to a competitive call for power project procurement in sub-Saharan Africa (excluding the REI4P in South Africa). While at least three of the bidding entities (Building Energy, Biotherm, and Mulilo) had secured projects in South Africa's REI4P programme, the likes of ENEL Green Power and other large utilities are conspicuous in their absence from this list.

The tender award process seemed particularly rigorous (if not entirely transparent) up to the point of announcing the highest ranked bidder—after which the process seemed to take on a less structured format. For example, the highest ranked bidder was invited to start negotiations with NamPower after the announcement was made, with the stated understanding that if parties failed to reach a negotiated conclusion, the next ranked bidder would

---

[49] Interestingly, whereas ENEL Green Power attended the conference, it declined to submit a bid.

be contacted to proceed with negotiations. It was not made clear up front which issues would need to be negotiated after the ranking process—apart from stating that consensus would need to be reached on all project agreements. While this maintained some level of flexibility in the procurement programme for NamPower, it also came at a cost to the integrity of the process. Nonetheless, the standardized nature of the project documents and the clarification process appear to have helped the negotiations process along. Negotiations between NamPower and the highest ranked bidder (Alten) concluded in November 2016—only about six weeks after the tender submission deadline (22 September 2016).

The Hardap PV plant has been developed as a 45 megawatt peak (MWp) facility with a maximum export capacity of 37 megawatts of alternating current (MWac). It covers approximately 100 hectares, consisting of more than 140,000 solar panels. The plant is planned to operate at a very high capacity factor of 34.5% (based on the AC export figure for year 1)—which is 4.5% higher than the already high minimum capacity factor required in the bidding documents.[50] As has been mentioned, the procurement process placed a great deal of emphasis on the technical performance of the plant. This is not only contained in the bidder qualification and evaluation criteria but also in the performance guarantees. The project implementation process experienced two delays: one from Alten on reaching financial close, which saw the FC date shifting out by a month from 31 January to 28 February 2017; and a delay in reaching COD due to *force majeure* (strikes in the transport sector) from 7 September 2018 to 15 November 2018. None of these delays can be directly attributed to NamPower, either in its capacity as off-taker, transmission grid operator, or shareholder. COD was eventually achieved on 15 November 2018.

NamPower, together with the ECB, recently included an energy payment for reactive power support as an ancillary service, which the plant is able to provide. While it is encouraging to see these kinds of services being valued and compensated, it also feeds into the troubling narrative around the lack of transparency in the bidding process since these payments did not form part of the original bidding requirements or evaluation criteria.

---

[50] Some bidders indicated that they saw this as an unreasonably high expectation for the site during the bidding clarification process. For reference, the average capacity factor for utility-scale solar PV plants in South Africa is 24%.

9.6.1 Securing equity providers

The project was awarded to Alten Energias Renovables (Alten Renewable Energy), a Spanish IPP developer, who had submitted a bid tariff of NA$ 80.,7/kWh. Alten has six IPPs in operation in Spain, ranging between 1.98 and 9.06 MWp, which were not large enough to pass the qualification thresholds. However, Alten had also developed two projects (16.51 MW Grupo Solar Alcorena and 11.13 MW Grupo Solar Hinojosa del Valle) as a 50% member of a consortium with Group Ortis, which allowed it to qualify. The NamPower tender was the company's first venture outside of Spain; it has subsequently developed a significant emerging market focus, securing 350 MW of solar PV capacity in Mexico's 2016 auction and developing a substantial pipeline of projects in Kenya and Nigeria. The Hardap project company has five shareholders: Alten Africa (51%), NamPower (19%), and three PDN entities: Mangrove (12%), Talyeni Investments (6%), and First Place Investments (12%).[51] The EPC contract was awarded to Sterling & Wilson, an Indian EPC contractor, who subsequently subcontracted the majority of works to Namibian companies.

Alten Renewable Energy established Alten Africa with Inspired Evolution (through the Evolution II fund) as a subsidiary platform for project development and investment in Africa—including for the Hardap project. Inspired Evolution, an investment management business specializing in clean energy investments in Africa and emerging markets, is headquartered in Cape Town and was a prominent equity investor in South Africa's REI4P programme, through its Evolution I fund. The Evolution II fund is mainly focused on sustainable infrastructure in Africa. Inspired Evolution's approach is to help projects to reach normalized operations—usually 16–18 months after COD for solar PV projects—after which they will normally exit. Investors in the fund are mainly DFIs: the Dutch Development Bank (FMO); the Global Energy Efficiency and Renewable Energy Fund (GEEREF); the Swiss Investment Fund for Emerging Markets (SIFEM), managed by Obviam; Quantum Power; the African Development Bank; Swedfund; and the Finnish Fund for Industrial Cooperation (FinnFund). It is therefore remarkable that even for this seemingly low-risk, bankable solar PV project in Namibia, considerable DFI equity funding was still involved.

---

[51] No change in majority shareholding is allowed within three years of the project reaching COD without ECB/NamPower consent.

Prior to setting up the Alten Africa platform, Inspired Evolution subjected Alten to a rigorous independent due diligence process. With the significant exposure of DFI funding in the Evolution II fund, investors needed to ensure that there were no ethical question marks around the project or the company.[52] While there seems to have been a lot of 'noise' around the Hardap project (much of which has already been discussed), the due diligence process found the company and the project to be sufficiently clean. The due diligence process also extended to the PDN shareholders in the project company.[53]

The financing of the PDN loan has been one of the more contentious issues in the project. The PDN shareholders are all Namibian women between the ages of 35 and 55. Their shareholding in the project company was established through a longstanding professional relationship with Alten's Namibian country manager. The three PDN shareholders approached a number of local entities—most notably the Development Bank of Namibia (DBN)—to finance their shareholding. The DBN declined to provide them with financing, citing concerns about the low margins (given the low tariff) and the fact that the shareholders were not committing any of their own resources. Alten therefore extended a shareholders' loan to the PDN companies, but the exact terms and conditions of this loan agreement is one of the areas that has caused project implementation delays. The financing arrangement was initially challenged,[54] not only due to what was seen as unfavourable financing terms (e.g. the spread on the loan) but also due to the fact that it apparently failed to give the PDN shareholders a significant 'voice' in the project company. After lengthy negotiations, a compromise was reached that saw shareholding being provided to the PDN entities on better financing terms.

NamPower's shareholding in the project company also came to influence the project in a number of other ways. NamPower's internal calculations valued its contribution to the project company (through the provision of land, transmission infrastructure) at around NA$ 58.25 million (US$ 4.12 million). According to the terms of the shareholders' agreement, their contribution would determine their shareholding in the project company, based on the overall value of the project—but would be no less than 10% and no more than

---

[52] Any corruption is an immediate event of default for these investors.

[53] There were accusations that the project award was due to the politically connected nature of the PDN shareholders in the Hardap project. The due diligence process did not find this to be true.

[54] Conflicting information regarding NamPower's role in this negotiation has been provided to the researchers.

19%.[55] The utility was adamant that it wanted to 'see what is going on inside the SPV [special-purpose vehicle]', especially from a technical reliability point of view. According to NamPower, the level of comfort that it required went beyond the legal and commercial due diligence traditionally performed by lenders to the project. It has subsequently used its 'seat at the table' to influence the project's technical scope and implementation, even after its award. It also wanted to ensure that it had substantial veto rights—again, especially when it came to the technical quality of the project.

NamPower's roles as procurer, off-taker, and shareholder have exposed the utility to multiple potential conflicts of interest. At the same time, the utility's shareholding has meant that some of the shareholder risks associated with these delays—such as calling on the performance guarantees—have been mitigated by NamPower's self-interest. Whether this is a sustainable model of project governance going forward remains to be seen. Given the obstructive behaviour of Eskom in South Africa's REI4P programme and the dominant role played by state-owned utilities throughout the continent, it perhaps make sense to ensure that the off-taker is committed to the success of the project(s) through some sharing of benefits.

9.6.2 Securing debt providers

Convincing lenders to finance this project was always going to be tricky. While Namibia is one of the more stable sub-Saharan African democracies, and NamPower is regularly held up as a star performer SOE in the region, most banks would still like to have seen some sort of sovereign support for the project. This was not forthcoming due to Namibia's fiscal constraints—a not unfamiliar situation on the continent. When NamPower therefore approached potential lenders to test their willingness to finance the project and the bankability of the documents, the issue of a sovereign guarantee was raised repeatedly. Without some form of sovereign support, most commercial banks would be unable to provide loan tenors that were sufficiently long. In addition, the local currency denomination of the PPA meant that most international lenders—including international development finance institutions—would be unable to lend directly to the project.[56]

---

[55] The 19% limit was set to accommodate the lead developer's 51% and the 30% PDN shareholding. Were NamPower to have received shareholding proportionate to its estimated contribution to the project, this would have been closer to 31%.

[56] Nonetheless, at least one bidder had secured African Development Bank (AfDB) financing for its bid.

The innovative financing structure developed for this project is therefore a notable achievement.[57] Due to the NA\$–ZAR currency link, the PPA could be denominated in South African Rands—which enabled Standard Bank to provide a ZAR 760 million (US\$ 56.4 million)[58] loan to the project.[59] Due to the abovementioned constraints, Standard Bank could initially offer only an eight-year tenor on the loan.[60] A guarantee offered by Proparco—the French development finance institution—enabled Standard Bank to stretch the loan term to 15 years. The guarantee was structured in such a way that it covered 30% of the debt (principal and interest) in year 1, increasing to 100% in year 8 of operations. This arrangement enabled Standard Bank to provide a loan tenor that would normally only be available from DFIs. It also enabled Proparco to help finance this project without being exposed[61] to long-term currency fluctuations on the actual loan amount.

Given the relative novelty of the financing arrangement, it should come as no surprise that it took longer than expected for the project to reach financial close.[62] It helped that both Standard Bank and Alten had been in regular contact with Proparco prior to the project being put out to tender. Nevertheless, DFI involvement meant that financial close was delayed by a month, with Proparco's due diligence process alone taking about six months to complete. The project eventually managed to reach the critical financing deadline on 28 February 2018.

As the renewable energy IPP market matures and the Hardap project enters the low-risk operations phase, it is possible that the project owners might consider refinancing the project on better terms. The PPA allows for such a change in financing terms, or even financing providers, but with the proviso that the project tariff be amended by the ECB to ensure that the benefits are shared between the company and the off-taker on a 50:50 basis. Given the off-taker's shareholding in the company, NamPower might be strongly incentivized to push for better financing terms.

---

[57] Alten originally wanted to finance the project on its balance sheet but opted for project finance after the project was awarded.

[58] At an exchange rate of US\$ 10,2 to the ZAR.

[59] The project was financed on an 80:20 debt:equity basis.

[60] Standard Bank also provided long-dated interest rate and currency hedges. Facilities provided included the loan, VAT facility, and debt service reserve facility.

[61] Proparco is exposed on the guarantee fee that it is taking but not on the actual loan principal.

[62] Alten's decision to switch from a corporate-financing to a project-financing model after the project was awarded has also contributed to this delay.

9.7 Lessons learned from Namibia's renewable energy auctions

Until recently, any survey of private power investment in sub-Saharan Africa would not have considered Namibia. The country simply had no private-sector involvement in electricity generation. This situation has since changed dramatically, powerfully illustrating the importance of the contributing elements to successful IPP investments at both the country and project levels. Namibia is a stable democracy with good governance indicators, prudent macroeconomic policies, and a well-developed financial industry. Its electricity sector is effectively governed and run and has, as a result, an efficient and creditworthy utility company. These country-level factors have allowed Namibia to secure substantial and rapid private power investment without the need for sovereign guarantees, credit enhancements, or hard-currency denominated payments.

At the project level, the Namibian case also offers lessons in innovative risk management that address some of the key barriers and long-term risks for private power investment on the continent. The Standard Bank–Proparco lending guarantee structure not only enabled a long-tenored loan to be provided to the project but also addressed the other key concern in many of these types of projects: currency depreciation risks. By combining Standard Bank's ability to lend in local currency with Proparco's risk cover, the Hardap PV project showed that it is possible to finance a utility-scale power project in Africa without exposing the sovereign to additional contingent liabilities or the electricity consumers to currency-linked price fluctuations.

Furthermore, Namibia's experience shows that structured procurement programmes such as the feed-in tariff programme are able to unlock private power investment at scale and within relatively short time frames. The competitive procurement of the Hardap PV facility goes further, demonstrating that this can be done at an even larger scale and, more importantly, at a much lower cost. The strengthening of the rational, dynamic, least-cost power system expansion planning framework will do much to cement and leverage the gains from these procurement frameworks for future investments.

In a sense, the story of the eventual success of the Hardap PV project is built on a strong foundation of getting the fundamentals right: ensuring that the project documentation is of a high quality and bankable, ensuring that project site preparation and data gathering is done properly, and committing to clear and ongoing communication with the market. It is also a story of pragmatism and cautious learning, with NamPower's approach throughout the process emphasizing technical rigour and project quality, on the one hand, while, on the other hand, focusing on keeping the procurement process (and especially the commercial and financial aspects) as simple as possible. The intention of 'learning from' this exercise has been clear from the start, and one can observe progress in the way that the programme was designed and implemented over time.

The future looks bright for Namibia's power sector: the Hardap project provided a powerful signal to decision-makers that competitive procurement offers superior price and investment outcomes for private power projects. The ECB has accordingly indicated that it will not be offering a feed-in tariff for utility-scale projects anymore. For a country that struggled for years to do mega power projects, the success of these smaller, RE-based projects shows that an incremental approach can deliver rapid, cost-effective results. NamPower has recently launched competitive procurement programmes for two 20 MW solar PV projects—one to be established on an IPP basis and the other an EPC contract with NamPower as the owner and operator. A 50 MW wind IPP tender was also launched.

The results from both the IPP and EPC procurement processes appear to have bolstered Namibia's RE ambitions. For example, a bold 5 GW cross-border solar PV plan was announced with Botswana in late 2020 with the aim of exporting cost-competitive power to the rest of the SAPP (Mguni and Nhongo, 2020). NamPower—aware of the fact that its customers are buying the region's most expensive power—sees these projects as a way of decreasing its overall cost base and thus reducing its end-user tariffs. The utility is thus already gearing up for the procurement of wind and biomass projects in the coming year in the hope that these will support the current downward price trajectory. ECB, for its part, views the results as ringing in a new structure for the sector, with NamPower set to increasingly become a transmission-only company that creates the necessary infrastructure for accelerated private investment. Cumulatively, these developments seem to be setting Namibia on a new path that is likely to accelerate the country's energy transition.

9.8 References

African Development Bank Group, 2020. *Electricity regulatory index for Africa: 2020.* Abidjan: AFDB.

Alao, O., Kruger, W., 2020. Prospects for private power investment in sub-Saharan Africa in the new decade. Power Futures Lab, Graduate School of Business, University of Cape Town, South Africa.

BBC (2018). 'Namibia Country Profile', https://www.bbc.com/news/world-africa–13890726 (accessed 11 January 2019).

CENORED (Central North Regional Electricity Distributor) (2013). 'CENORED Signs the First Non-NamPower IPP in Namibia'. News release, Otjiwarongo, https://www.cenored.com.na/news/191 (accessed 24 April 2023).

City of Windhoek (2018). 'Schedule of Approved Tariffs 2018/2019'. Windhoek.

Confidente (2015). 'CENORED Enters Solar Power Plant Deal', Confidente, 9 July.

CSIR (Council for Scientific and Industrial Research) (1999). 'Integrated Overview of the Offshore Oil and Gas Industry in the Benguela Current Region'. Benguela Current Large Marine Ecosystem Thematic Report No. 4 (Stellenbosch: CSIR).

Dalrymple, K., (2020). Moody's - Namibia's credit profile balances stable business environment and wealth levels against fiscal imbalances. Moody's Res. Announc.

De Klerk, E. (2016). 'Namibia: Arandis to Benefit from New Solar Plant'. *New Era*, 12 October.

Eberhard, A., and Dyson, G. (2019). *Revisiting Power Sector Reforms in Africa* (Abidjan: African Development Bank).

Eberhard, A., Dyson, G., Alao, O., Godinho, C., (2019). Revisiting reforms in the power sector in Africa. Final Report prepared for the African Development Bank and Association of Power Utilities of Africa

ECB (Electricity Control Board) (2016). *ESI Statistical Bulletin* (Windhoek: ECB), https://www.ecb.org.na/images/docs/Statistical_Bulletin/ESI_Stats_Bulletin_ 2016.pdf (accessed 24 April 2023).

ECB (2017) *REFIT Projects in Namibia* (Windhoek: ECB).

Electricity Control Board, (2019). The Modified Single Buyer Market: Market rules (Draft). (Version 1.1) Nambia.

ERM (Environmental Resources Management) (2009). 'Baynes Hydropower ESHIA: Final Scoping Report',

Fauconnier, C., Ramkhelawan-Bhana, N., and Mandimika, N. (2017). 'Where to Invest in Africa 2017/2018',

Fitch Ratings Agency (2014). 'Fitch Affirms NamPower at "BBB–"; Stable Outlook'. *Reuters Africa*, 21 April, https://af.reuters.com/article/commoditiesNews/ idAFFit92009320150421 (accessed 10 January 2019).

Hatch (2013). *National Integrated Resource Plan: Task 5 Final Report—Conclusion and Documentation of the Outcome and Results of the Project* (Windhoek: ECB).

Kaira, C. (2018) 'Energy Ministry Plans 220 MW of Additional Power'. *Windhoek Observer*, 19 October.

Kapika, J., and Eberhard, A. (2013) *Power-Sector Reform and Regulation in Africa: Lessons from Kenya, Tanzania, Uganda, Zambia, Namibia and Ghana* (Cape Town: HSRC Press) https://repository.hsrc.ac.za/handle/20.500.11910/2926.

Kaze, H. (2014) 'NamPower to Raise N$2.5b on Bond Market'. *The Villager*, May.

Kruger, W., Strizke, S., and Trotter, P. A. (2019). 'De-risking Solar Auctions in Sub-Saharan Africa: A Comparison of Site Selection Strategies in South Africa and Zambia'. *Renewable and Sustainable Energy Reviews*, 104, 429–438. https://doi.org/10.1016/j.rser.2019.01.041.

Mguni, M. & Nhongo, K. (2020). Botswana, Namibia set to sign 5 GW solar energy plan. Bloomberg. 21 Aug 2020. https://www.bloomberg.com/news/articles/2020-08-21/botswana-namibia-set-to-sign-5-gigawatt-solar-energy-plan#xj4y7vzkg

MME (Ministry of Mines and Energy) (1998). *White Paper on Energy Policy* (Windhoek: MME).

MME (2007). *Electricity Act of 2007* (Windhoek: MME).

MME (2016). *National Integrated Resource Plan—2016 for the Electricity Supply Industry in Namibia* (Windhoek: MME).

MME (2017a). *National Energy Policy* July (Windhoek: MME).

MME (2017b). *National Policy for Independent Power Producers (IPPs) in Namibia* (Windhoek: MME).

MME (2017c). *National Renewable Energy Policy* (Windhoek: MME).

Namib Times (2016). 'Paratus Power Station to Be Upgraded to 40mw'. *Namib Times*, 21 October.

The Namibian (2015). 'Audit Confirms NamPower Blew Millions'. *The Namibian*, 22 July.

The Namibian (2018). 'Geingos-Xaris Article Clarification'. *The Namibian*, 6 March.

The Namibian, (2019). Namibia revises electricity buying market model. The Namibian.

NamPower (2015). 'Update on the Current Power Supply Situation and Progress Made on NamPower Projects and Initiatives to Ensure Security of Supply in Namibia'. 13 April, https://www.nampower.com.na/public/docs/communications/Media%20Release/Media%20Briefing%2013%20April%202015.pdf (accessed 11 January 2019).

NamPower (2016a). 'Tender for the Development of a Solar Photovoltaic Power Plant on a Build–Own–Operate (BOO) Basis Near Mariental, in Namibia. Volume A1: Instruction to Tenderers'. Tender No: NPWR/2016/22, Windhoek. https://doi.org/10.1016/j.resmic.2013.03.016.

NamPower (2016b). 'Tender for the Development of a Solar Photovoltaic Power Plant on a Build–Own–Operate (BOO) Basis Near Mariental, in Namibia. Volume B1: Technical Specification'. Tender No: NPWR/2016/22, Windhoek, http://www.nampower.com.na/Tenders.aspx?id=668&v=TlBXUi8yMDE2LzIy (accessed 24 April 2023).

NamPower (2017a). 'NamPower Annual Report 2017', https://www.nampower. com.na/public/docs/annual-reports/Nampower%20Annual%20Report%202017 %20FA%20LR.pdf (accessed 24 April 2023).

NamPower (2017b). 'REFiT Progress Report', Nampower, September.

NamPower (2018). '2018 Annual Report'. Windhoek, https://www.nampower. com.na/public/docs/annual-reports/Nampower%202018%20AR_web%203.pdf (accessed 11 January 2019).

NREL (National Renewable Energy Laboratory) (2018). 'Ten Years of Analyzing the Duck Chart'. 26 February, https://www.nrel.gov.news/program/2018/10-years-duck-curve.html (accessed 24 April 2023).

Fitch Ratings, (2019a). Fitch Ratings Report: Namibia Power Corporation (Propri-etary) Limited. Fitch Ratings Agency.

Fitch Ratings, (2019b). Namibia Power Corporation (Proprietary) Limited, Corpo-rates. Fitch Ratings Agency.

Reuters (2017a). 'Fitch Affirms Namibia at "BBB–"; Outlook Negative'. *Reuters Africa*, 19 October.

Reuters (2017b). 'Namibia to Build Three Power Plants to Boost Electricity Security'. *Reuters Africa*, 2 May.

SAD-ELEC (2000). 'Study of the Restructuring of the Namibian Electricity Supply Industry, Phase 3: Public Presentation Document'. Windhoek, MME.

Shen-fa, W., and Xiao-ping, W. (2009). 'The Rule and Method of Risk Allocation in Project Finance'. *Procedia Earth and Planetary Science* 1, 1757–1763. https://doi. org/10.1016/j.proeps.2009.09.269.

Southern African Customs Union (2017). '2017 Annual Report'. Southern African Customs Union, Windhoek.

United Nations Namibia, 2018. United Nations Partnership Framework (UNPAF) 2019-2023 - A Partnership for the Eradication of Poverty and Inequality. United Nations, Windhoek.

UNPAF (United Nations Partnership Framework) (2017). 'Namibia Annual United Nations Country Results Report 2016'. June, https://namibia.unfpa.org/sites/ default/files/pub-pdf/Namibia%20Annual%20United%20Nations%20Country %20Results%20Report%202016.pdf (accessed 11 April 2019).

The Villager (2016). 'NamPower Signs Deal with IPP'. *The Villager*, 18 July.

10

Contributions from the Global South and Future Directions

Wikus Kruger and Anton Eberhard

The world needs to urgently transition to a low-carbon energy future to avoid catastrophic climate change. Renewable energy auctions—pioneered and refined in the Global South—have emerged as an important tool for accelerating this transition. Auctions have driven down the cost of renewable energy-based electricity and delivered significant new investment in generation capacity—often in very challenging investment contexts. Auctions have also been able to incorporate a wide range of objectives, including socio-economic development, integration cost optimization, and energy security. There are important lessons to be learned—both between countries in the Global South and for more developed countries in the North—regarding the design and implementation of these procurement programmes to ensure a sustained accelerated energy transition.

This final chapter summarizes and extracts key lessons on the design and implementation of these procurement programmes in the Global South. The chapter is divided into three parts, covering the impact of renewable energy auctions in the Global South, lessons learned from the use of renewable energy auctions in the Global South, and the potential role of auctions in the rapidly unfolding energy transition.

10.1 The impact of renewable energy auctions in the Global South

Countries in the Global South have not only pioneered the use of renewable energy auctions but also introduced several important innovations in the design of these programmes. Latin America, in particular, has a long history of inventive energy auctions, starting with Brazil's competitive awarding of long-term offtake contracts in the early 2000s. Auctions have since

Wikus Kruger and Anton Eberhard, *Contributions from the Global South and Future Directions*. In: *Renewable Energy Auctions: Lessons from the Global South*. Edited by: Anton Eberhard and Wikus Kruger, Oxford University Press.
© Oxford University Press (2023). DOI: 10.1093/oso/9780192871701.003.0010

become a cornerstone of Brazilian energy markets and policy, with almost all new contracts for energy and capacity, as well as transmission lines, being competitively awarded. Throughout this process, there has been an unwavering commitment to learning and innovation, with each new round of procurement informed by careful analysis from Brazil's Energy Research Office (Empresa de Pesquisa Energética—EPE). On the other side of the continent, Chile's use of time and seasonal 'blocks' in its technology-neutral auctions has allowed for the cost-competitive penetration of renewables into a market traditionally dominated by natural gas and coal, while Mexico's auctions have used location incentives to optimize the grid integration of renewables. In India, auctions are the cornerstone of the country's massively ambitious Solar Mission programme. And in South Africa, auctions have been used not only to reduce renewable energy costs but also to achieve a range of socio-economic development objectives.

Not only has the Global South been an important site of pioneering auction innovations, but the region has also arguably benefited the most. At the most basic level, auctions have resulted in improved energy security. They have proven effective at attracting investment for new generation assets by providing long-term investment signals and contracts, both in contexts with fully unbundled power sectors and those dominated by vertically integrated state-owned utilities. Brazil is probably the most obvious example of this, introducing the competitive awarding of long-term off-take contracts to mitigate merchant price risks in a system dominated by hydro. A similar dynamic is especially apparent in sub-Saharan Africa, where auctions have introduced a step-change in the volume of power investment. Increasing the amount of private power investment is crucial to addressing the continent's long-standing energy security and energy access deficits, and auctions have proved especially adept at doing this, even in countries with no history of private participation in the power sector.

Auctions have improved energy security not only through increasing investment but also through improving sector resilience. In all countries studied, auctions resulted in an increasingly diversified power sector, with more players (especially from the private sector), more technologies (mostly renewables), and more sources of funding—including development finance institutions, commercial banks, and institutional investors. This increased diversity of actors, technologies, and funding sources improves a system's ability to withstand shocks and optimize outcomes.

In particular, auctions have been successful in increasing investment in, and penetration of, renewable energy technologies in the Global South. While mechanisms such as feed-in tariffs proved to be instrumental in increasing renewable energy investments in the Global North, they failed to have a similar impact in the South. It was only through the introduction of auctions that we started to see significant volumes of renewables coming online in the Global South. This impact can primarily be attributed to auctions' ability to reduce the price of renewable electricity through the power of competition, which reveals and reduces costs. In addition, auctions provide long-term investment signals in often challenging investment contexts, resulting in reduced risks and a lower cost of capital. As a result, renewable energy is now the least-cost option for new power generation in almost all markets analysed in this book, a crucial shift in the global transition.

One final important impact is that auctions have either bolstered power-sector reforms in largely unreformed sectors or introduced the need for further reforms in unbundled contexts. In Latin America, auctions have generally been an important pillar of a comprehensive power-sector reform programme, either as a second wave of reform (as in Brazil or Chile) or as part of an initial reform package (Mexico). This is due to the fact that auctions are recognized as being not only aligned with but also, in fact, essential for the achievement of the reform goals in these countries, such as electricity cost reductions and increased energy security. By successfully delivering new power at competitive prices, the auctions support the underlying economic rationale for the sector reform programmes.

In sub-Saharan Africa, and perhaps also to some degree in India, the transparency, cost reductions, higher level of renewable energy penetration and increasing private-sector participation facilitated by auctions are forcing markets that until recently were comminated by state-owned monopoly utilities to introduce reforms. New auctions are forcing a reckoning with the status quo in many of these markets by clearly showing that the private sector, and renewables in particular, are able to outcompete the market incumbents. This has been proven in South Africa, Namibia, and Zambia, where privately developed, owned, and operated renewable energy projects are now the cheapest source of power on the grid. For financially constrained African countries, many of which are still locked into unattractive deals with expensive, directly negotiated independent power producers (IPPs), the possibility of securing privately funded, cost-competitive power through auctions is gradually opening up the space for greater private involvement in the sector. In addition, the increasing penetration of variable renewables on these grids necessitates the procurement of flexibility and balancing products and services—most efficiently delivered through shorter-term markets. The system operators in these countries are therefore increasingly looking at both short-term markets and special auctions for these products—representing a further opening for the private sector. Cumulatively, these impacts are creating the momentum needed to accelerate reforms and improve outcomes in these hitherto unreformed markets.

10.2 Lessons from the Global South

The experiences of countries in the Global South offer a number of lessons on auction design and implementation to other developing regions and Organisation for Economic Co-operation and Development (OECD) nations.

Good auction design is an iterative process. Each round of procurement offers new lessons that need to be purposely extracted and implemented. This requires a flexible, learning-orientated approach to the auction design process. In the absence of such an approach, the auction programme is doomed to repeat past mistakes and fail to adjust to changing conditions and needs, ultimately undermining the programme's aims. Practically, this means that a good auction programme needs to dedicate adequate time and resources (including human resources) to analysing each round and making the necessary adjustments. The role of Brazil's EPE in analysing and advising on each auction round is a good example of such an approach, but there are numerous other permutations available. The principle, however, remains important: good auction design is firstly about being open to learning and making adjustments based on evidence. This is essential since auction design is inherently an exercise in managing trade-offs.

In terms of specific auction design choices, there are broadly two categories of lessons that can be extracted from the studied country cases: those concerned with project prices and those impacting project realization. The prices of projects awarded through auctions are generally determined by the level of competition in the auction and the cost of capital. Competition is, in turn, a product of both the number of bidders and the quality of these bidders. Stronger bidders—meaning larger, experienced companies that often have international linkages—are able to submit more competitively priced bids through their stronger negotiation positions with suppliers and service providers, their ability to integrate more parts of the project value chain (thereby reducing margins and creating multiple revenue streams), their access to multiple sources of funding (including corporate finance), and economies of scale. This means that auction design choices need to maximize both quantitative and qualitative aspects of competition.

Strong competition is the result of various design choices that act as signals, barriers, and incentives in the auction process. Stronger bidders need to know that the auction process is credible and that they will not be competing against inexperienced bidders submitting unrealistic offers. As such, it is crucial that the auction uses qualification requirements that only allow experienced, capable bidders to participate and penalty regimes that ensure their commitment to their bids. To further stimulate competition, it is also important that auction volumes are informed by a rigorous planning framework and set at low enough levels to ensure competitive pressure between bidders. Project sizes, in turn, need to be large enough to attract experienced international bidders and allow for economies of scale.

Clear lessons on how bids should be scored and awarded are perhaps less obvious. What seems clear is that there is a relationship between the level of power market sophistication and the complexity of the bidding formats and rules employed. In general, the less reformed a power sector, the more likely it is to stick to tried-and-tested, sealed-bid, pay-as-bid formats. This is the case in all of the African cases studied, most of which are still dominated by vertically integrated monopoly utilities and generally inexperienced with private-sector involvement in electricity. On the other side of the spectrum, countries such as Chile, Brazil, Mexico, and to some degree, India, are more likely to employ descending clock/Dutch-style auctions (or a hybrid version), and—in the case of Chile—a uniform style of pricing format. Nevertheless, many countries in the Global South seem quite willing to experiment and adjust their designs based on outcomes. So, for example, India recently announced a shift away from a real-time descending clock-type auction to sealed bid due to low project realization rates, blamed largely on unrealistic bids being submitted. Chile has also moved away from seasonal bidding blocks, while South Africa is exploring the introduction of real-time descending clock-style auctions. These decisions support a flexible approach to auction design which acknowledges that these kinds of decisions are perhaps of secondary importance compared to factors that more directly affect competition levels and costs.

The auction design area where the Global South has a number of important lessons to offer is bid scoring. Several countries have employed a number of factors beyond price in their bid-scoring criteria, meant to incentivize improved performance in socio-economic development (in the case of South Africa) or project location and system integration costs (Mexico and Chile). The deliberate incorporation of these price-plus factors shows that auctions are flexible enough to address a wide range of priorities beyond price. As auctions spread across the globe, we are bound to see new and interesting designs meant to address a wide range of technical and societal needs—built on the foundations of what has been learned in these Global South test cases.

As already mentioned, the case study countries indicated that project realization rates are impacted by qualification requirements and, to some degree, penalty regimes. This is largely in line with what one would expect based on the existing auction design literature. However, what is notable from the case study countries is the prominent role played by lenders in determining project realization. The requirement for lender commitment as a qualification requirement in South Africa is a key reason behind the country's high project realization rates. Lenders provide the majority of project funding and are often exposed to the longest period of risk. As such, they are often the ultimate decision-makers when it comes to bid feasibility. By asking for commitment letters from lenders as a qualification requirement, auction designers are effectively outsourcing project due diligence to these financial institutions, ensuring a high level of project quality. This, however, means that lenders need to have visibility on, and be able to provide inputs to, the bidding documents before the auction, including all contracts, to ensure that they are 'bankable'. The lack of lender commitment was one of the main reasons for Argentina's low project realization rates as projects were unable to find funders for their bids when financial conditions changed. Incorporating lender requirements in auction design, and explicitly asking for lender commitment as part of the qualification requirements, is therefore a key measure to increase project realization.

A further important set of lessons revolve around the provision of project land or sites. Access to, and the preparation of, project sites is often a complex and risky exercise in both developed and developing countries. In developed countries, projects often face opposition from local residents and businesses. In many developing countries, private land ownership might not be allowed, land titles might be unclear, grid infrastructure limited, and the surrounding communities often impoverished. In addition, renewable energy resource data might not be readily available. As a response, several governments chose to provide and prepare the sites for the auctioned projects. While this seems to be a reasonable measure to reduce investor risks, the reality is that this intervention often increased project risks and costs. Geotechnical and land ownership problems in Zambia led to more than a year's delay in the Scaling Solar projects' commissioning, while the inability to secure land led to the cancellation of Namibia's first solar auction. India seems to have had more success with its provision of solar parks—a concept that has since been widely adopted in the Middle East to drive down project costs. The lesson thus seems to be that while the provision of land by the government is a viable and potentially impactful measure, it needs to be carefully planned and executed—preferably with input from the private sector—who ultimately still carry the land risk—to ensure success.

Grid access is a further significant design consideration—one that is growing in importance as the share of renewables on the grid increases. The cases studied offer two broad alternatives to dealing with this issue: in many cases, grid access risk is allocated to the IPP. The extent of this risk allocation differs somewhat depending on how liberalized the market is, with more market-based electricity systems generally allocating more risk to the private sector. In the case of South Africa, for example, where the state-owned electricity utility owns almost all generation, transmission, and distribution assets, IPPs need to ensure that there is sufficient capacity at the substation they intend to connect to (and include the costs for shallow connection works)—but will receive deemed energy payments if the grid is late in arriving or upgrades are not completed. In Brazil, this entire set of risks falls onto the private-sector bidders. Both cases also introduce a competitive sub-process in the auction for allocating grid capacity. In general, though, the more information is available on grid expansion and upgrade planning, the easier it is for these risks to be optimally allocated and priced. The alternative is, of course, to merely provide the project site(s), with the requisite grid connections, as has been done in Zambia, Namibia, and India. While feasible, this approach can run into problems as programmes need to start scaling up—perhaps beyond the capacity of the government or auctioneer's site preparation and provision capacity—and might also lead to suboptimal outcomes as developers are generally more capable of finding the best renewable resources.

Apart from the specific auction design lessons, there are further, perhaps more important, lessons regarding the broader necessary conditions surrounding the auction. What is especially important in emerging markets is the explicit incorporation of the broader investment environment conditions in the design of the auction programme. This requires a thoroughgoing understanding of project finance—both its internal logic and approach to risk allocation—as this is the funding structure that is most likely to be used by projects. Brazil's introduction of auctions for long-term contracts was based on this understanding, and the auction explicitly sought to ensure that the programme met these requirements. This same logic is apparent in all of the successful cases studied. In addition, and based on project-financed deals' ultimate dependence on long-term revenue certainty, it is often necessary to include sovereign guarantees and/or other risk-mitigation and credit-enhancement measures in auction design, especially where there are concerns about the financial health of the off-takers of power. This has been shown to be key to auctions' ultimate success (or failure) in Zambia, South Africa, India, and Argentina.

What is also clear from all the cases studied is that long-term predictability and certainty are needed to fully unlock the value of auctions. The true value of auctions only becomes clear when there are repeated rounds of procurement, resulting in a strong project pipeline, growing competition, and resulting price reductions over time. The iterative nature of auction design discussed above further reinforces this point since it is often the case that the earliest rounds of procurement deliver suboptimal outcomes due to design flaws that are only addressed in subsequent rounds. This reinforces the importance of the planning–procurement nexus: procurement rounds need to be based on transparent long-term, dynamic energy expansion planning that matches supply and demand on a least-cost basis. This planning framework provides the long-term certainty that investors are looking for when deciding whether to enter a market and incur the costs of bid development and helps to ensure that the procured technologies, products, and volumes are in line with system requirements. Transparency in terms of auction schedules and plans further strengthens this long-term certainty, increasing competition and lowering costs. Underpinning this certainty is the auctioneers' level of commitment to the announced schedules, including the timelines to financial close and commercial operation dates (CODs). When these dates start to slip, it undermines the industry's trust in the auction process and can lead to reduced competition and higher prices.

The experience of the Global South furthermore shows that good auction implementation, not just design, is crucial for success. How, and by whom, the auction is implemented plays an important role in determining bidder trust, influencing the bidding decision and subsequent competition levels. Potential bidders need to know that the auction is being implemented by a capable team that is politically supported and that the auction process will be fair and clear. In contexts where institutions are weak and transparency limited, building the capacity and governance mechanisms to earn and retain the market's trust is even more important. This requires high levels of capacity, support, and resources for the auctioneer.

Finally, the case study chapters show that there are limits to what auctions can do. Auction programmes' effectiveness is often constrained by political economy factors beyond the control of those designing and implementing the programmes. In South Africa, this became apparent when the auction programme was stalled in 2015 by those who saw the programme as threatening the interests of industry incumbents. In Mexico, the incoming new administration reversed several important power-sector reform measures—including the cancellation of the auction programme—to protect the utility company. And in Zambia, the quickly deteriorating financial position of the state-owned utility, the Zamibia Electricity Supply Corporation (ZESCO), as well as the Zambian state in the face of unsustainable debt levels and limited sector transparency ultimately derailed the Global Energy Transfer Feed-In Tariff (GETFiT) solar projects.

There are also legitimate questions being asked about how effectively auctions can deliver on mandates beyond low-cost electricity provision. In South Africa, for example, the numerous socio-economic development requirements included in the programme's qualification and evaluation criteria constitute a substantial financial and technical burden for the projects and potentially open them up to additional social risks. It is not always clear that decision-makers appreciate the fact that these requirements, and their explicit inclusion as evaluation criteria, necessarily imply a trade-off in outcomes—and that this trade-off becomes all the more severe as competition levels increase. In addition, in the absence of clear supportive policies and programmes, it is not clear that these kinds of requirements are leading to meaningful long-term development. And, ultimately, it has to be asked whether private project developers and their shareholders can and should be providing services and benefits that are effectively the responsibility of the state.

Despite these important caveats, it is still clear that auctions are one of the most effective tools available to governments in their pursuit of future-proof power systems and the energy transition.

10.3 The role of auctions in the global energy transition

Finally, it is worth reflecting on the role of auctions in the global energy transition that is underway. What is clear from the preceding analysis is that auctions are an essential tool for kick-starting and, at times, accelerating the transition to renewables, especially in emerging markets with limited or no experience with renewable energy technologies and private investment. Auctions can also play an important role in counteracting much of the volatility experienced and expected in electricity markets as fossil fuel supplies are disrupted and renewable energy penetration increases. The auctioning of long-term contracts can offset much of this uncertainty for investors and consumers, resulting in more investment and potentially locking in low prices.

While auctions have, thus far, mainly been used to procure energy from renewables in the Global South, they can also be used to procure new technologies and services needed for the transition. This includes auctions for storage, demand response and flexibility, and ancillary services. Several countries are already embarking on procurement processes for large-scale battery storage programmes, and we are also seeing dispatchability and flexibility requirements increasingly being incorporated in auction programmes in the Global South. Auctions have also been successfully used to build transmission lines—especially in Latin America. Transmission infrastructure is the new frontier in the transition as many countries in the Global South and beyond are needing to fundamentally reconfigure their power systems to include renewable energy generation and increase interconnections to improve stability. The use of auctions to secure new investments in transmission infrastructure, perhaps bundled with generation assets, will be crucial to accelerating and sustaining the transition. Auctions have also been used to award contracts for green hydrogen production as well as coal retirement compensation schemes—important areas for the transition. Nevertheless, it is important to realize that auctions are but one tool—albeit an important one—of many tools needed for a successful energy transition. An 'all-of-the-above' approach is needed for an accelerated and just energy transition, and decision-makers need to be aware of the full suite of growing options at their disposal.

10.4 Concluding thoughts

The world is facing a fundamental shift in how the global energy system is structured, operated, and governed—ushered in by a new era of cheap, distributed renewable energy technologies and innovative business models. The current innovation and disruption in the energy sector is unmatched in recent history. Renewable energy auctions have been instrumental in ushering in this new era, nowhere more so than in the Global South. Auctions have increased investment volumes, reduced costs, and shortened project realization timelines, often in challenging investment contexts with little or no experience with private-sector power investment. As more countries—106 at the last count—adopt auctions as the main method of allocating support for renewable energy technologies, it is essential that we learn from the frontier adopters and innovators in this space, most of which are located in the global South. This volume aimed to extract the key lessons on auction design and implementation from frontier markets in Latin America, sub-Saharan Africa, and South Asia. It is our hope that by taking heed of and applying these lessons, the global energy transition may be both accelerated and strengthened to ensure a more sustainable future for all.

Index

For the benefit of digital users, indexed terms that span two pages (e.g., 52–53) may, on occasion, appear on only one of those pages.

Tables, figures and boxes are indicated by an italic *t*, *f* and *b*, following the paragraph number; 'n.' after a paragraph number indicates the footnote number.